POLITICAL ELITES IN THE MIDDLE EAST

Presented by the American Enterprise Institute for Public Policy Research
as the ninth study within the framework of its Middle East Research Project,
George Lenczowski, director.

POLITICAL ELITES IN THE MIDDLE EAST

EDITED BY
GEORGE LENCZOWSKI

American Enterprise Institute for Public Policy Research
Washington, D.C.

ISBN 0-8447-3163-3 (Paper)
ISBN 0-8447-3164-1 (Cloth)
Foreign Affairs Study 19, June 1975

© 1975 by American Enterprise Institute for Public Policy Research, Washington, D.C.
Permission to quote from or to reproduce materials in this publication is granted when due acknowledgment is made.

Library of Congress Catalog Card No. L.C. 75-10898

EDITOR'S NOTE

Publication of this collective volume pertaining to the Middle East calls for two elucidations. The first refers to the substance of the chapters written by individual contributors. Opinions and judgments are the authors' own, and neither the American Enterprise Institute nor the editor assumes responsibility for the views and conclusions expressed.

The second refers to the form. Writing about Middle Eastern subjects poses the problem of transliteration from Arabic, Iranian, Turkish, and Hebrew scripts. We have followed the principle of simplified rendering of foreign names and expressions, consonant with the practice widely adopted by nonspecialized Western journals and publications.

G.L.

CONTRIBUTORS

JAMES A. BILL is associate director, Center for Middle Eastern Studies, and associate professor, Department of Government, University of Texas at Austin.

FREDERICK W. FREY is professor, Department of Political Science, University of Pennsylvania.

EMANUEL GUTMANN is professor and chairman, Department of Political Science, Hebrew University, Jerusalem.

ILIYA F. HARIK is professor, Department of Political Science, Indiana University.

JACOB M. LANDAU is professor, Department of Political Science, Hebrew University, Jerusalem.

GEORGE LENCZOWSKI is professor, Department of Political Science, University of California at Berkeley.

PHEBE A. MARR is associate professor, Department of History, University of Tennessee.

ROBERT SPRINGBORG is assistant professor, School of Historical, Philosophical, and Political Studies, Macquarie University, Australia.

GORDON H. TORREY is visiting professor, Johns Hopkins University School of Advanced International Studies, Washington, D.C.

CONTENTS

I. SOME REFLECTIONS ON THE STUDY OF ELITES 1
George Lenczowski
Early Exponents of Elite Theory 1
The Two Aims of Elite Theory 3
A Special Case: The "Organizational" Elite 5
The Methodology of Elite Studies 6
Varying Approaches and Emphases in This Volume 8

II. THE PATTERNS OF ELITE POLITICS IN IRAN 17
James A. Bill
The Iranian Patrimonial System 17
Profile of the Political Elite 21
Elite Cohesion and the Challenge of Modernization 28
Elite Recruitment and Circulation 32

III. PATTERNS OF ELITE POLITICS IN TURKEY 41
Frederick W. Frey
Introduction 41
Political Elites in the Turkish Republics 43
The Social Backgrounds of the Parliamentary Elite 54
Key Aspects of Elite Political Culture 64
Elite-Mass Linkages 72
Conclusion 82

IV. PATTERNS OF ASSOCIATION IN THE EGYPTIAN POLITICAL ELITE 83
Robert Springborg
Politics without Organized Groups 83
Political Clientelism 87
Clientelism on the Periphery of Contemporary Egypt 89
Units of Informal Organization in the Elite 93
Formal Organizations 104
Conclusion 106

V. THE POLITICAL ELITE IN IRAQ 109
Phebe A. Marr
Historical Perspective 110
Educational Background 113
Occupation 125
Socioeconomic Background 133
Ethnic and Religious Background 137

The Political Direction of Iraq's Revolutionary Leaders 140
The Costs of Instability 143
The Weakness of Political Institutions 145
The Importance of Leadership 148

VI. ASPECTS OF THE POLITICAL ELITE IN SYRIA 151
Gordon H. Torrey
Factors Working against Political Stability 151
The New Elite 155

VII. THE POLITICAL ELITE AND NATIONAL LEADERSHIP IN ISRAEL 163
Emanuel Gutmann and *Jacob M. Landau*
The Emerging State 163
The Founding Fathers 166
Party System and the Elite 168
Elite Consensus versus Cleavage 170
Elite Selection and Circulation 172
The Cabinet System 175
Socio-demographic Analysis of the Elite 178
Some Concluding Remarks 189
Appendix: Profiles of Some Elite Members 195

VIII. POLITICAL ELITE OF LEBANON 201
Iliya F. Harik
Background of the Elite 201
The Cabinet Member 207
Turnover and Recruitment in Parliament 209
The "Counter-Elite" 217
Conclusion 219

GENERAL INDEX 221

INDEX OF NAMES 225

I. SOME REFLECTIONS ON THE STUDY OF ELITES

George Lenczowski

The purpose of this volume is to describe and analyze the political elites in seven countries of the Middle East: Iran, Turkey, Egypt, Syria, Iraq, Lebanon, and Israel. Two criteria served as a basis for this selection: (1) the process of change characteristic of all seven countries in question, and (2) the availability of data permitting more than merely impressionistic studies. The seven selected countries represent a wide variety, culturally and politically. Two—Iran and Turkey—are major states of the non-Arab Northern Tier, and both have been subjected to substantial sociopolitical transformations in the last half-century. Three—Egypt, Syria, and Iraq—are Arab countries in which the old order was overthrown by revolutions with varying degrees of violence. One—Lebanon—is an Arabic-speaking land whose commercial civilization goes back to the Phoenicians, and whose modern political processes substantially differ from those prevailing in the surrounding Arab world. And another—Israel—is a new state reviving the national identity of an old people through the process of the "ingathering of exiles."

Early Exponents of Elite Theory

The subject of elites has been treated in a variety of ways and has given rise to theoretical, ideological, and methodological controversy. The basic concept of the political elite was introduced by Gaetano Mosca and Vilfredo Pareto in the early part of the twentieth century, the age of "empirical innocence." Both Italian scholars advanced the thesis that in any society there is always a group that rules and a group that is ruled, and that the former is numerically smaller than the latter. Mosca called the ruling group a "political class," while Pareto designated it as a "governing class," distinguishing it from a nongoverning elite.[1] Both viewed elites as minorities of talent and wealth, groups composed of superior individuals.

Karl Marx and Robert Michels agreed on the basic division of society into ruling and nonruling groups, but they defined the problem in different ways. Marx perceived society as divided into antagonistic classes whose mutual conflict was the essence of the historical process. The ruling class was invariably the one that owned the means of production. In the modern—that is, postfeudal—era, ownership of land was replaced by that of industry as the principal economic base of wealth, and hence of political power. This situation, however, was expected to

[1] Vilfredo Pareto, *The Mind and Society* (1916), 4 vols. (New York: Harcourt, Brace & Co., 1935), p. 1573: "A governing class is present everywhere, even where there is a despot, but the forms under which it appears are widely variable. . . . In so-called democratic governments it is the parliament. But behind the scenes . . . there are always people who play a very important role in actual government." See also Gaetano Mosca, *The Ruling Class* (New York: McGraw-Hill, 1939), initially published in 1896 and revised in 1923 as *Elementi di scienza politica*.

change. When the industrial proletariat, along with other exploited classes, constituted a majority, it would seize control of the means of production, inevitably by revolution, and would put an end to the rule of the minority over the masses once and for all. In fact, the elimination of minority rule would lead to the abolition of the government itself, that is, to the "withering away of the state." [2]

Michels, who also spoke of the rule of the minority, formulated his theory as the "law of oligarchy." Focusing his study on Europe's socialist parties, Michels came to the conclusion that any human organization, including a party dedicated to egalitarianism, was bound to develop a smaller inner group which in due course would arrogate political power to itself.[3]

The common denominator of all four theories was their view that the concept of democracy (that is, rule by the majority of the people) was fraudulent inasmuch as it was inconsistent with reality. But beyond this basic finding agreement ended. Marx mixed his analysis of historical determinism with a subjective condemnation of capitalist practices and, by advancing his theory of the socialist-proletarian revolution, claimed that there was a remedy for minority rule. By contrast, Michels, while he deplored the emergence of elites within a democracy, believed it to be inevitable. As for Mosca and Pareto, they unmasked the alleged hypocrisy of democracy with some relish but, in view of the superiority of governing elites, saw no moral objection to their rule. Thus, though they shared with Marx a belief in the basic division of society, they found themselves ideologically opposed to him and came to be regarded, however inaccurately, as spiritual precursors of fascism.

This is not the proper place for a detailed criticism of Marxist theory. Suffice it to say that, in the perspective of more than a century, Marxism appears as a grossly oversimplified and inaccurate view of history and society, whose fallacies have been amply exposed by subsequent democratic and revisionist writers alike.[4] Marx's monocausal view of social change, his historical determinism, his dogmatism about the necessity of class conflict, and his narrow concept of the alienation of the masses as stemming from the control of the means of production by the capitalists have been challenged—and refuted—on many occasions. What concerns us here is the fact that his concept of the ruling class is too broad to satisfy a student of elites. An elite is smaller and more select than an entire social class. Consequently, even if one were to accept the Marxist view of the political supremacy of the capitalist class, one would have to probe further to discover which capitalists constitute the governing group and on what their supremacy is based.

As for Mosca and Pareto, closer scrutiny reveals that their thesis also fails to provide a meaningful theory of society. Mosca's finding that those who rule are

[2] For a concise statement of Marxist theory, see R. N. Carew Hunt, *The Theory and Practice of Communism* (London: Geoffrey Bles, 1950), and Hans Kelsen, *The Political Theory of Bolshevism* (Berkeley: University of California Press, 1955).

[3] Robert Michels, *Political Parties* (Glencoe, Ill.: Free Press, 1949).

[4] See Sidney Hook, "Evaluation of Marx's Contributions," *Marx and the Marxists: The Ambiguous Legacy* (Princeton, N.J.: Van Nostrand, 1955), ch. 2; Max Eastman, *Marxism: Is It a Science?* (New York: W. W. Norton, 1941); K. R. Popper, *The Open Society and Its Enemies,* 2 vols. (New York: Harper & Row, 1962), esp. vol. 2, chs. 21 and 22; Joseph A. Schumpeter, *Capitalism, Socialism and Democracy,* 3d ed. (New York: Harper & Row, 1950), esp. pt. 1; Leopold Labedz, ed., *Revisionism: Essays on the History of Marxist Ideas* (New York: Praeger, 1962).

less numerous than those who are ruled is hardly more than a truism. "We are told," says one critic, "that rulers do rule their subjects; and that a ruler is unlikely to bake his own bread or be a member of his own police force." [5] Viewing the task of governing as a specialized function, another critic points out that the rulers must necessarily be less numerous than those who are ruled, just as in most societies there are "fewer bakers than eaters of bread, fewer teachers than students," and so forth.[6]

The Two Aims of Elite Theory

If we devote some space to Pareto and Mosca, it is not only to acknowledge their pioneering role in the study of elites but also to point out that such a study may have two different objectives. One—to which they obviously aspired—would be to construct a comprehensive theory of society. The other, more modest, would be to describe and analyze ruling groups as one of many approaches to understanding political reality.

When the purpose of a study of elites is to develop a comprehensive elite theory of society, it is necessary to prove (1) that behind the formal holders of power in the state there is some stable or enduring group possessing certain traits that distinguish it from other groups, (2) that this group exerts decisive political influence, and (3) that it serves as a recruiting ground for members of the government. Such a group may have an informal and loose structure. Within a democratic-capitalistic system, according to many elite theorists, it enjoys economic and social power, privilege, and status, either acquired or inherited. Because of its superior position in society the group is called "elite." Other labels used by various authors include the earlier-mentioned "oligarchy," "ruling class," "dominant stratum," and the more current and fashionable "establishment."

It is not sufficient to state that such a group exists. It is also necessary to ascertain whether it is stable in its composition and, therefore, whether it tends to be exclusive. Pareto's concept of the "circulation of elites" draws attention to this problem without resolving it. His reference to the constant decadence and renewal of elites and his statement that history is the "graveyard of aristocracies" reflect two different aspects of what he means by "circulation": (1) the replacement of individuals within the elite and (2) the replacement of one elite by another. The replacement of individuals, of course, must occur, if only because humans are not immortal and any group is subject to the natural process of attrition and replenishment. The issue is whether this process of individual replacement is exclusive, or whether it is open, giving an opportunity to individuals from less privileged strata to join the ranks of the powerful and influential group. But if the "open door" principle is operating—in other words, if there is sufficient social mobility to allow individuals of talent and merit to climb upward—can we speak of a stable and exclusive elite, that is, an elite that denies the reality of the democratic process in its social dimension? Do we not come back to the basic truism

[5] W. G. Runciman, *Social Science and Political Theory* (Cambridge: Cambridge University Press, 1963), p. 67.

[6] Dankwart Rustow, "The Study of Elites: Who's Who, When, and How," *World Politics,* vol. 18, no. 4 (July 1966), p. 711.

inherent in Mosca and Pareto, that in any system the number of rulers is smaller than the number of those who are ruled?

If, on the other hand, we understand by the circulation of elites a process of group change by peaceful means, we have to ask whether a new group is basically of the same socioeconomic nature as the outgoing group or of an altogether different background and composition. If the latter is the case, again, the element of stability and exclusivity essential to the classical concept of elite is lacking. A system capable of providing a collective change of its politically dominant group clearly does not conform to the elite model in which a self-perpetuating group enjoys a monopoly of political power. Once we admit the possibility of peaceful competition among a variety of would-be elite groups, we cease dealing with classical elite theory and, instead, enter the realm of "pluralism." The pluralist theory does not deny the existence of politically influential or even dominant groups in society: it only claims that they are multiple and capable of achieving power without having to overcome a priori obstacles.

The universal validity of the elite theory has been questioned by such writers as David Riesman, H. Stuart Hughes, and James H. Meisel. They claim that the great number of pressure and veto groups in a country like the United States invalidates the notion of an exclusive and stable "ruling class."[7] Similarly, Robert Dahl rejects the elite theory. Defining a ruling elite as "a minority of individuals whose preferences regularly prevail in cases of difference on key political issues," Dahl finds that the empirical evidence needed to sustain such a hypothesis is lacking. He urges that a distinction be drawn between the inequality of power and the existence of a ruling elite. Inequality of power among groups and individuals is, according to him, compatible with the notion of democracy with its multiparty system.[8]

In spite of the serious challenge that the pluralist theory presents to the elite theory, a good number of modern social scientists have adopted the elite approach in their study of politics. But they have done so to varying degrees; while some have adhered to the thesis that the elite theory provides the only valid method of studying political reality, others have looked upon the study of elites as a useful but not exclusive way to understand political processes. In his *Politics: Who Gets What, When, How,* Harold Lasswell seems to fall into the former category. His opening paragraph dogmatically proclaims: "The study of politics is the study of influence and the influential. . . . The influential are those who get the most of what there is to get. . . . Those who get the most are *elite;* the rest are *mass.*"[9]

The elite approach as a nonexclusive method has enjoyed considerable popu-

---

[7] David Riesman *et al., The Lonely Crowd: A Study of the Changing American Character,* abr. ed. (New Haven: Yale University Press, 1963), pp. 206, 213; H. Stuart Hughes, ed., *Teachers of History* (Ithaca, N.Y.: Cornell University Press, 1954), p. 166; and James H. Meisel, *The Myth of the Ruling Class* (Ann Arbor: University of Michigan Press, 1958), pp. 362–63.

[8] Robert A. Dahl, "A Critique of the Ruling Elite Model," *American Political Science Review,* June 1958, p. 463ff. See also his *Modern Political Analysis* (Englewood Cliffs, N.J.: Prentice-Hall, 1963), pp. 33–35.

[9] Harold Lasswell, *Politics: Who Gets What, When, How* (Cleveland and New York: Meridian Books, 1958), p. 13. Similarly, Lewis J. Edinger and Donald D. Searing in "Social Background in Elite Analysis: A Methodology Inquiry," *American Political Science Review,* vol. 61 (June 1967), pp. 428–45, say: ". . . it would seem that the central concern of political science is competition for and the exercise of leadership by various elites. . . ."

larity. Its usefulness has been hailed because, as one writer put it, "it does not carry the ideological baggage that is often attached to class approach and it permits in-depth analysis of a group of the most important individuals in society." [10] T. B. Bottomore was equally enthusiastic. By advancing the concept of "counter-elites" existing alongside elites, he implicitly established a connection between elitism and pluralism.[11] Dankwart Rustow, meanwhile, found that "today, research on the social background of political elites holds particular promise in the study of Asian, African, and Latin American politics, where the institutional approach tends to mislead and the functionalist approach to confuse." [12]

A Special Case: The "Organizational" Elite

"Classical" elite studies have tended to focus on elites in the democratic and capitalistic systems. These elites, as perceived by many writers, including Mosca and Pareto, have a connotation of socioeconomic and sometimes cultural superiority over other groups in the society. However, it is possible to envisage a new type of elite that does not conform to this standard model of qualitative superiority, but rather, secures and maintains its political influence and power as a result of other characteristics. These elites may occur in both democratic and nondemocratic systems. The predominance of such groups may be chiefly attributed to their manipulative skills and sometimes, as in the case of nondemocracies, to the use or the threat of force. But whether their predominance depends upon manipulation or the use of force, the ultimate skill is organizational. Obviously, greater organizational skill in one group denotes a certain type of superiority over rival groups. The point here is that, in some cases, this may be the only qualitative advantage that the new elite has over its competitors: on other counts—culture, education, experience, honesty, public spirit—it may be inferior to them.

This problem emerges with particular force in totalitarian and dictatorial or one-party systems. Abolition of free elections and the other freedoms necessary to the competitive interplay of groups and individuals, together with the adoption of an official ideology bolstered by coercion, may be taken as proof of the inherent inferiority complex of a dominant group that fears challenge in an open society. Perhaps this is the most useful place to introduce the concept of "natural leadership." Such leadership possesses qualities and attributes which, whether ascriptive or based on merit, inspire trust in a large part of the community. This trust, it should be pointed out, does not produce unquestioning approval of the leadership's policies under all circumstances. It merely means that the role played by the dominant group or individual is not considered contrary to the conventional patterns and expectations of the society. Thus, to give an example, if an attorney, a judge or a law professor assumes the function of minister of justice, his appointment seems "natural" because it conforms to the common-sense expectation that the head of the department of justice be a man with legal training and experience. If, by contrast, the ministry of justice is entrusted to the captain of a tank regiment whose

[10] James A. Bill, "Class Analysis and the Challenge of Change," *Comparative Political Studies,* vol. 2, no. 3 (October 1969), p. 395.

[11] T. B. Bottomore, *Elites and Society* (New York: Basic Books, 1964).

[12] Rustow, "The Study of Elites," p. 716.

only qualifications are his technical and military expertise, the appointment will appear to be "unnatural," even if that same captain is a ranking member of the political party in power, and owes his special cabinet responsibility to this connection.

The Methodology of Elite Studies

If we settle for less than an exclusive elite theory and choose instead to study elites as one of the acceptable methods of research, we still need to clarify two preliminary issues: first, how to define the concept of elites and, second, how to decide what it is about elites that we want to know. Authors employing the elite approach vary considerably in their definitions. Bottomore, for example, distinguishes three tiers: "the elite," defined as functional, mainly occupational, groups that have high status in a society; "the political class," which includes all those groups that exercise political power and influence and are directly engaged in struggles for political leadership; and "the political elite," a smaller group within the political class comprised of individuals who actually exercise political power in a society at any given time.[13]

Bottomore's formulation demonstrates that it is possible to define elites broadly or narrowly. At one extreme the elite is understood as a high status group or stratum with a *high potential* for political influence; at the other, the elite is seen as the *actual key officeholders.* If this narrow definition is adopted, it may still be necessary to specify which political offices are to be studied: the head of state and the cabinet, members of parliament, members of the central organs of the ruling political party in a single-party system, the leadership of the armed forces (especially in the states where the military has intervened in the political process), or the high echelons of bureaucracy as a "sub-elite" without whose cooperation and expertise the "top elite" could not exercise its power. Seen from a different angle, the division between the broad and narrow concepts of elite may be defined as a division between larger informal groupings, on the one hand, and *institutional* groups of the highest executive branch officials, legislators, party and military dignitaries, on the other.

A decision on which type of group to study—the broader or the narrower—is an individual author's privilege. He may want to justify his choice on various grounds, substantive or procedural. Thus he may argue that in a given system certain groups count while others do not; or he may find that such factors as the availability of data make it feasible to study certain groups while precluding the study of others. It is, of course, notoriously difficult to decide which individuals to include in a study of broader informal groupings. A "reputational" approach necessarily based on advice from a selected group of informants has been criticized as impressionistic and imprecise. It is perhaps this procedural difficulty that has led many contemporary students of elites to adopt the narrower institutional concept of elite as the focus for their research.

Once a governing elite has been defined for the purposes of research, an author must decide which of its characteristics should be studied. Ultimately, it would be

[13] Bottomore, *Elites and Society,* pp. 8–9.

futile to try to understand a given political reality without inquiring into the behavior of the ruling group—its short-range decision making and its long-range policy formulation. The behavior of this group may derive from its basic attitudes, and these attitudes, in turn, may be traced to the elite's background characteristics. However, "background" is another stretchable concept. It may include anything from social origins through personality, education, and career, to political socialization. Again, a broader or a narrower approach will have to be chosen and justified, implicitly or explicitly, by any author.

Although there appears to be a logical progression from background characteristics to attitudes and to behavior, a number of scholars are very reluctant to admit the existence of foolproof causal links between them. A contributor to this volume, Professor Frey, typifies this caution in one of his earlier writings by saying: "To leap from the knowledge of social background of national politicians to inferences about the power structure of society is quite dangerous. Even to proceed from such knowledge to judgments about the political behavior . . . can be treacherous." [14] Yet, the description of an elite's background must be followed by some conclusions, however tentative, to justify the labor invested in collecting the data. The impulse to establish a link between background and attitudes is understandable. "What we would like to know," say two contemporary students of elites, ". . . is whether we can predict with a high degree of probability that particular background characteristics are associated with particular attitudes. . . . That is, can we expect that a given elite background will also yield certain orientations and to what extent?" [15] On the basis of a comparative study of the German and French elites, these two authors give an affirmative though qualified answer to this question. Similarly, one of the contributors to this volume, Robert Springborg, has earlier advanced the thesis that "in societies with deep cleavages, be they vertical, horizontal, or both, the knowledge of social background characteristics may be tantamount to knowing the entire array of an elite's political attitudes." [16]

This view appears eminently justified. Dedication to "scientism" in political science has prevented many scholars from drawing conclusions from the empirical data that have been gathered concerning the social background of elites. While their hesitation may be understandable in purely scholarly terms, it is disappointing in some practical situations. A parallel may be suggested between the study of an elite and personnel recruitment in a corporation. Recruitment procedures invariably call for an inquiry into the personal background of candidates, often accompanied by an interview. What would be the purpose of such activities unless to permit personnel managers to draw inferences as to the character, ability, reliability, and work ethic of the candidates? Surely, a personnel manager must make some sort of prediction about a prospective employee without having scientifically established a causal link between his background and his attitudes or behavior. Similarly, the foreign office of country A, upon learning of the formation of a new government in country B, tries to secure (through its embassy and other

[14] Frederick W. Frey, *The Turkish Political Elite* (Cambridge, Mass.: M.I.T. Press, 1965), p. 157.

[15] Edinger and Searing, "Social Background in Elite Analysis," p. 431.

[16] Robert Springborg, "Social Background Analysis of Political Elites," unpublished ms. (1972), p. 16.

means) information about the background of the new cabinet members because it wants to know what to expect from them. In either case—of a corporation or of a government—inferences, even intuitive ones, must be drawn on the basis of whatever imperfect data are available.

Of course, the scholar must proceed with caution in drawing inferences about an elite's attitudes from its social background. The dangers inherent in this sort of analysis are illustrated by the thesis that the military background of members of revolutionary juntas in Arab countries has been the determining factor in the progressive and radical-reformist policies they have pursued. The military, so the argument runs, are patriotic, disciplined, uncorrupted, and familiar with modern technology; as such they are the most logical group to espouse and implement the ideas of progress and development. "Little wonder, therefore, that many of the most enterprising members of the new middle class have been attracted to it. The special caliber of the army leadership has been evident."[17] Because the army is often presented as a modern organized force that draws its personnel from the middle and lower classes and is contrasted with a traditional power elite, the thesis that the army is progressive appears attractive and convincing. Yet such a thesis could be challenged if the scale of comparison were to include not only military dictatorship and the traditional ruling group, but also the competitive system in which achievement criteria play a substantial role in the political process. Should such a comparative scale be allowed, one might refute the military-progressive model by making a number of observations: (1) It is the lower achievement students in Arab secondary schools that tend to embrace the army as a career. (2) Young men become officers out of a desire for economic security and social status more often than out of patriotism or a commitment to public service. (3) It is difficult to prove that the military are less corrupt than other groups. If this claim is true among lower and middle officer ranks, it may result from a combination of virtue with incomes and fringe benefits higher than those of ordinary civil servants; among higher officers cases of corruption in connection with arms supplies and contracts are a matter of record. (4) The common assumption that the military is highly unified and disciplined is based on a simplistic view of the drill and obedience patterns, and has often been belied by rampant factionalism, especially when armies have been drawn into the political arena. (5) Army officers are not necessarily more familiar with modern technology than certain civilian groups. (6) As a consuming, nonproductive organization, the army is not likely to develop among its members an appreciation or a practical grasp of the intricate economic process, whether in a socialist or free enterprise situation.

Varying Approaches and Emphases in This Volume

In this collective volume the reader will find almost as many approaches to the study of elites as there are authors. We have felt that it would have been erroneous to impose a rigid methodological pattern upon the contributors. None of them

[17] Manfred Halpern, *The Politics of Social Change in the Middle East and North Africa* (Princeton, N.J.: Princeton University Press, 1963), p. 259.

appears to subscribe to an exclusive elite theory of society, but all view the study of elites as instrumental to the understanding of political conditions in the countries on which they focus. Their definitions and the scope of their research differ, depending on the authors' judgments as to the relevance of institutional or informal elite groupings and on their selection of particular aspects of elite study.

The volume opens with a chapter on Iran, a state that in a number of ways is unique among the countries discussed here. Iran is the only monarchy studied here; the other countries having (at least ostensibly) a republican form of government. Furthermore, Iran's kingship is a very special institution. Two thousand five hundred years old—as the world was reminded during the much publicized celebrations at Persepolis in 1971—Iran's monarchy has behind it an impressive tradition that combines a semi-deification of the rulers with a vivid symbolism based on elaborate ceremonial. Historically, the kings of Iran did not merely reign, they also and emphatically ruled, and, moreover, the peoples of this vast empire accepted this situation as natural. The ineptness of the declining Qajar dynasty brought about in 1906 a revolution which, while maintaining the monarchy, limited its powers through a constitution. With the advent to power of the reformer-king, Reza Shah the Great, in the 1920s, Iran's monarchy resumed its authoritarian features but did not abolish its official constitutional forms.

Under Reza's successor, Mohammed Reza Shah Pahlavi (1941 to the present), the regime underwent an evolution from ascendancy of parliament (accompanied by disruptive interference of foreign powers) to a resumption of strong royal power in the 1960s. To legitimize this revived concept of Achaemenian kingship, Iran's regime invoked three points of justification: (1) time-honored tradition, (2) need for a centrally directed reform and development, and (3) imperatives of national security. The first was expressed in a continuous apotheosis of kingship, symbolized by the suggestive title of Shahanshah (King of Kings) Aryamehr (the Light of the Aryans); the second took the form of the so-called White Revolution, which generated in Iran not only profound social changes but also an unprecedented rate of economic growth; and the third was translated into firmer authoritarian measures taken against often violent dissenters, whom the regime viewed as Marxist subversives and, ipso facto, foreign agents. Bounded in the north by Russia whose threats to the survival of Iran are a matter of historical record, in the west by a revolutionary Baath regime in Iraq, in the east by the uncertainties of the fluid situation in Pakistan and Afghanistan, and in the south by the Persian Gulf where the withdrawal of British power in 1971 left a disturbing power vacuum, the ruling group in Iran has felt justified in endowing the monarchy with the strength which would safeguard the country's sovereignty and assure it an internal stability needed for rapid modernization. With reference to the basic framework of this book, the question discussed in the first chapter is: who are the members of this ruling group and what are their characteristics?

Professor James Bill defines the Iranian political elite as "the individuals in the upper class who exercise most power in the system." These are "the national decision-makers, and in Iran they are those who cluster most closely about the person of the Shah." Professor Bill views the Iranian system as essentially patrimonial; its dominant characteristics are informality, personalism, rivalry, and tension. Using "a combined positional [that is, institutional], reputational, and decisional approach" to identify elite membership, he finds that the members of the Iranian political elite are drawn from seven major "categoric" groups and distinguishes three concentric circles composed of the inner circle, linkage figures, and major elite groups. Within this framework, the author asks a number of searching questions about the elite's socioeducational background, its patterns of circulation and continuity, and its attitudes and policies concerning reform and revolution.

In his chapter on Turkey, Frederick Frey justifies the study of elites by advancing the thesis that elite politics has been, until recently, the essence of the Turkish political process. Elite actors, elite institutions, and elite urban settings have preempted the political arena, not unlike in most other less developed societies. He is, therefore, of the opinion that mass elements were not in the past conspicuous on the political scene and that, more recently, their appearance in Turkey's political life could be mainly seen through interactions within the elite itself. For this reason, to understand Turkish politics, it is practical and advisable to focus on the political elite. The author warns, however, that with the passage of time such a focus might prove increasingly inadequate. According to Professor Frey, the methodological problems of such a study center around the question of how to locate and measure power relations with an eye to determining whether the putative political elite is really the one that wields disproportionate real power in the system. His study opens with the history of elite politics from 1920 to the present and covers such subjects as key aspects of the elite political culture, main elite institutions, elite-mass linkages, and socioeducational background of elite members. His approach tends to be institutional in terms of defining elite membership.

Professor Frey believes that an analysis of the social backgrounds of members of the parliament is bound to provide an important perspective in the understanding of the Turkish political dynamics. This is so, according to him, because over the past half-century the Grand National Assembly has served as the main forum for Turkish politics. In fact, the leading politicians almost invariably found their way into the assembly. Thus while Turkey's republican system with its center located in the assembly would seem to differ substantially from Iran's patrimonial monarchy, there appear to be certain similarities revealed in Professor Frey's description of "elites within the elite" and of patron-client clusters that are expressive of the ingroup-outgroup complex characteristic of the Iranian political culture. According to Professor Frey, the Turkish political elite underwent a metamorphosis: the structural change of the political system from tutelary control to openness and competition entailed a change in the composition of its elite. This was expressed in the decrease within the ranks of political leadership of the military and the bureaucrats (specialists in force and administration) and the corresponding increase of lawyers and members of other professions (specialists in advocacy and technology). In other words, the absorption by the polity of Western institutional characteristics found its reflection in the composition of its personnel, which likewise acquired resemblance to that of the Western systems.

The chapters on Iran and Turkey are followed by that on Egypt, the leading Arab country in terms of population, numbers of formally educated intelligentsia, agricultural resources, size of the military establishment, and a pioneering role in the pan-Arab revolutionary movement.

Nasser's revolution of 1952 brought about substantial transformations in the Egyptian polity. The pre-Nasser era could be given the designation of a constitutional monarchy with a competitive (however imperfect) parliamentary mechanism noted for its corruption and socioeconomic injustices. In this pseudo-democracy more emphasis was put on procedures than on socially desirable goals. By contrast, Nasser's regime—not unlike other dictatorships that later emerged in the Arab world—was goal-oriented, the goals being broadly defined as assertion of national independence, social justice, and development. This "activist" attitude of the new regime entailed two consequences. On the one hand, it precluded major concern for procedural niceties, to the point of neglecting to erect a firm institutional framework which would be stronger than personalities and which would survive the departure of the charismatic leader. On the other, it called for a major expansion of the bureaucratic-managerial apparatus of the state, which had taken upon itself the major task of industrialization. Thus the goal of meaningful mass participation in the political process that might logically be expected after the overthrow of the privileged social structure under the monarchy was definitely neglected in favor of organizing a strong, centrally directed government bent upon rapid modernization.

To be sure, a regime of this sort usually resorts to the slogan of "mobilizing the masses" and for this purpose attempts to form a single political party to serve as a communication device between the bureaucracy and the people. But active, intelligent, and critical participation in the political decision making by the people is not the real purpose of such an organization, because if it were, the regime would have to allow the possibility of being removed from power by popular will, should its performance not be up to expectations. Thus the word "mobilization" must be understood primarily as the process of generating an attitude of obedience to the authority and acceptance (with somewhat faked enthusiasm) of the measures enacted by it.

It is against the background of such a situation prevailing since 1952 that Robert Springborg describes and analyzes the recruitment, character, and behavior of Egypt's political elite. He begins by advancing the thesis that while Nasser's revolution did accomplish some notable transformations, it was not radical enough to discard certain deeply embedded traditions, some having their roots in the economic conditions of Egypt and some in the religion of Islam. Quoting C. H. Moore, he states, "Egyptians do not act politically primarily through organized groups," and he partly attributes this to the fact that "Islam, unlike Christianity, was never effectively institutionalized. Islam has never provided a counterbalance to arbitrary rulers nor checked their ambitions by imposing a clearly delineated, theoretical guideline to circumscribe the exercise of secular power."

The result has been that, in the absence of cohesive, vertical or horizontal categorical ties, formal organizations based on professional, class, ethnic or religious solidarity have never become powerful. Instead, the political process, including elite recruitment, has been carried out through informal devices and groupings:

> Egypt's rulers continue to exercise the prerogatives of leadership unfettered by the constraints of organized constituencies. . . . Egyptian rulers can be authoritarian but, in the absence of any means of organizing mass behavior . . . , they are incapable of establishing either totalitarian government or government based on a system of checks and balances between institutions.

Informal groupings that are characteristic of the Egyptian elite formation and behavior may best be described as "clientelism." Clientelism is a traditional phenomenon that adapted itself to the current process of modernization. "Modern political and administrative organizations . . . ," finds Dr. Springborg, "do in fact provide fertile breeding grounds for patron-client relationships." Reforms instituted by Nasser did not diminish the scope of clientelism; they merely caused it to appear under new forms. While the old clientelism was based on land ownership and wealth, the new one is rooted in strategic contacts with other people who may be useful to an individual's career. Moreover, the new clientelism is more volatile as compared with the stability and longevity of the old patterns.

The political elite in contemporary Egypt is thus both large and poorly integrated. "It is honeycombed with constantly shifting cliques and factions." Among the latter, Dr. Springborg singles out three for special analysis: the family (still important under Nasserism), the *dufaa* (the graduating class in any institution of higher or secondary learning), and the *shilla,* "a small group of friends who work together to obtain individual goals and particularly career advancement."

According to Dr. Springborg, "clientelism effectively integrates those on the political periphery," that is, on the secondary level of the elite. But on the upper levels of the elite it fails to "provide sufficient cohesion." By stressing loyalties which focus on persons rather than on principles, clientelism has proved to be a major obstacle to the achievement of the stated goals of the revolution.

In his chapter on Syria, Gordon Torrey draws a sharp distinction between the old elite, which ruled Syria till the early 1960s, and the new. With regard to the old elite, he favors an institutional approach, saying that it can be well analyzed by reviewing "the composition of the country's parliaments and cabinets from the end of World War I, until the Syrian union with Egypt in 1958." As for the new elite, he sees it as an emerging "lower-class group of civil servants, white-collar workers, small merchants, some small farmers, and especially the Syrian military." The military holds "the levers of power" and dominates the new elite. This elite has pressed for radical social change. Possibly as a result of its social origins, the Syrian elite appears to hold more revolutionary political attitudes than most other national elite groups reviewed in this volume.

In her treatment of Iraq, Phebe Marr views "political management" as the key element of Iraq's progress—or stagnation—and thus proposes "to discover those factors in the background of the political elite which are relevant to the contemporary political situation." To accomplish her objective, Professor Marr includes in her inquiry "the larger educated elite of which the political elite is the most important and representative segment." She defines the political elite as "the group of people who make decisions on national policy." Her approach also is institutional: She lists in her sample group cabinet members, three presidents of the Republic, and members of the Revolutionary Command Council.

Altogether, this group includes 177 people. Miss Marr not only asks the pertinent questions about the elite's education, skills, and qualifications, but also draws inferences from these data as to the political attitudes and, to a degree, policies of the elite. She finds that

> The top posts are still controlled by military men or . . . by Baath party politicians whose education has been more limited and whose exposure to outside environments has been minimal. The best-educated men in Iraq have not reached the top of the political ladder. . . . Moreover, the decline of familiarity with the West among top leaders, especially among the current Baathists, may well be contributing to the pronounced anti-Western sentiment of the regime, as well as to policies which have isolated Iraq from the outside world.

Having found an increasing polarization between the inadequately educated men at the top and the well-educated men below, Marr draws attention to an interesting phenomenon (which seems to transcend the experience of Iraq proper), namely, the disappearance from the elite of a professional politician and his eventual reappearance, though in a different category. She also stresses the relevance of the ethnic and religious factors in the process of elite recruitment—a feature that distinguishes Iraq from a number of its Arab neighbors, but is, as we shall see, active in the political process of Lebanon also.

In his study of Lebanon, Iliya Harik focuses his attention on the "top political elite," which he defines as members of parliament, cabinet ministers, and the presidents of the republic. He acknowledges that "like political leaders elsewhere, those occupying formal decision-making positions in Lebanon are influenced by other elite groups in society in a variety of ways and in varying degrees," but leaves the inquiry into these broader groups outside the scope of his study. Instead, he proposes to emphasize the "social characteristics of the elite, the recruitment process, the staying power of its members, and their ability to determine their own succession."

The Lebanese political system is, according to Professor Harik, dominated by an ever-growing bourgeoisie that clearly overshadows the much smaller group of descendants of the feudal aristocracy. An occupational survey of the deputies in seven Lebanese parliaments since 1943 shows a definite proportional increase in the number of lawyers, professionals, and businessmen at the expense of the landowners. "The competitive political game of parliamentary government," says the author, "has not enhanced the political fortunes of the declining patrician families. Instead, it has advanced the position of those distinguished in terms of their skills." Professor Harik devotes considerable attention to the high turnover rates in the Lebanese cabinet and parliament. In the case of the eight parliaments since independence it is 42 percent. "The rate of change in the Lebanese parliament is higher than it is often thought to be. The erroneous impression may be created by the fact that those few members of parliament who are often reelected are prominent and well known by the public. This gives the impression of a stable oligarchy entrenched in the chamber." The author also states, "In fact, a career in the Lebanese parliament is quite insecure, and even among the dozen prominent members all but two have lost their seats at least once."

In his discussion of elite recruitment, Professor Harik attributes only minor importance to the fact that Lebanon's political system is confessional, that is, based on proportional representation according to religious affiliation. Harik argues that

> Lebanon has been constitutionally divided into religious communities, each of which is entitled by law to a fixed number of deputies relative to the size of its population. In effect, the electoral law limits political competition to individuals from the same religious sect and precludes competition between candidates from different religious communities. As a consequence, the voter's religious attitude has been deactivated, since he is deprived of a religious option in casting his vote.

The fact that members of the Lebanese political elite "belong to the high status occupations and stand out from the rest of society in terms of wealth and skills" has not prevented Lebanon from functioning as a parliamentary democracy in which the turnover rate of its leaders is healthy and high offices are accessible to opposition candidates.

Israel is the third example of a working parliamentary system—following Turkey and Lebanon—treated in our volume. The co-authors of the chapter on Israel, Emanuel Gutmann and Jacob Landau, define the political elite as "those groups that actually exercise, or could exercise, considerable political influence . . . those having power in the system." Their definition transcends the limits of institutionalism by not being restricted to actual office-holders. This is understandable because, on the one hand, Israel has a highly developed party system and, on the other, it has such powerful and politically influential organizations as the Histadrut, its General Confederation of Labor, which controls a substantial segment of its economy. Consequently, the authors propose to encompass in their analysis "cabinet ministers, their deputies, members of the Knesset, and others who are either major policy makers or influentials."

Professors Gutmann and Landau regard the Israeli system as pluralist, yet highly suited to an elitist approach. This kind of political system, affirm the authors, "puts a particularly high premium on its elite. The elite has to overcome very considerable social heterogeneity and deep-rooted ideological cleavages in order to create a national consensus."

Because of the entrenchment of the party system in Israel, the incidence of professional politicians in the Israeli political elite tends to be high. In fact, say the authors, "The Israeli case is striking in that the political elites are entirely party based or affiliated, and most leaders have risen through the ranks of their respective parties." Israel's elite recruitment process presents some paradoxes. Generally, it is assumed that a well-functioning democracy must provide for considerable upward mobility within the political realm, hence for a reasonably swift circulation or turnover of elite members, compatible with the notion of stability and continuity. Israel's destinies, however, have been directed by a group of nearly forty "Founding Fathers" whose political careers have spanned the pre- and post-independence periods and whose role as builders of a sovereign state and signatories of its declaration of independence has endowed them with a "halo" that had a major effect on their political longevity. This top elite group was largely of east European origins and, as time went on, its composition began increasingly to differ from the post-independence demographic composition of Israel with its massive influx of Oriental Jews and the numerical upsurge of the native "sabras." Hence, the authors conclude, Israel is currently undergoing a transition from the old elite to a new one, which is expected to reflect more accurately its new composition. This transition, however, has not affected the fundamental party-based recruitment of political leadership. This being the case, according to Professors Gutmann and Landau,

> the usual selection process is even more oligarchical in Israel than is customary elsewhere. The cooptation system, or appointment-from-above, common to almost all political parties or for political office, must take wide party opinion into account, but not to the point of its actually determining the selection. At times, a genuine and vigorous competition for political office takes place; but in almost all cases, the effective decision is in the hands of restricted nomination committees (whatever their formal title). The popular or general membership vote usually grants merely the final approval of what has been decided in private council.

The above references to, and quotations from, the contributing authors of this volume have not been intended as systematic summaries. Such a treatment, if attempted, would have done less than justice to the wealth of data, subtleties of analysis, and depth of insights that the authors provide in their chapters. Our intention has rather been to show a variety of methodological approaches, differences and shadings in the definitions of elites, and some highlights of the authors' findings that justify differing foci of research geared to the polities which are being investigated. The *raison d'être* of this volume has been the belief that a study of elites, whether in democratic or nondemocratic systems, is not only a valid but also one of the most productive ways of understanding political reality. We trust that this belief has been vindicated by the substance of the chapters that follow.

II. THE PATTERNS OF ELITE POLITICS IN IRAN

James A. Bill

The Iranian Patrimonial System

The Heart of the System: The Elite. Iran is a proud and independent nation that has survived in the face of internal malaise and external invasion for well over two millenia. The people of Iran, who now number over thirty million, have managed to maintain their own culture and identity despite persistent cultural, political, and military challenges from outside, and they have developed a profoundly sophisticated and complex system of social and political processes. One way of exposing and explaining these processes is to concentrate analysis upon the group of political actors who are most powerful, those who direct and control the Iranian political system and who are its model of political activity and success.

The individuals in the upper class who exercise most power in the system constitute the political elite. They are the national decision makers, and in Iran they are those who cluster most closely about the person of the Shah. Among the questions that we will raise concerning the Iranian political elite are the following: Who are the members of this elite, and what are their dominant characteristics? What is their origin, education, and formal occupation? What basic lines of cohesion and conflict prevail within the elite? Where does the elite stand on the fundamental issues of continuity and change? What is elite policy concerning reform and revolution? What are the essential mechanics of elite maintenance and elite circulation? What are the patterns of mobility through which the elite absorbs members of the nonelite? What does the continuing vitality of the elite and its policy suggest about the future of Iranian politics?

The Iranian political elite exists and operates at the center of the network of patterns and processes that constitute Iran's political system. These patterns are woven just as tightly into the fabric of elite politics as they are into the fabric of social and political relations in general, or of specific sociopolitical institutions. In order to analyze elite formation and elite relations, therefore, it is necessary to outline the general characteristics of the system of political processes within which the political elite moves.

Characteristics of Iranian Patrimonialism. In his classic typology of political systems, the German sociologist Max Weber includes two types which he calls *patriarchal* and *patrimonial* systems.[1] In the patriarchal system, the basic power relationship is one that binds master and family. The head of the household "has no administrative staff and no machinery to enforce his will. . . . The members of

[1] For Weber's presentation of patriarchal and patrimonial political systems, see his study *The Theory of Social and Economic Organization* (New York: Oxford University Press, 1947), pp. 341–58. See also Reinhard Bendix, *Max Weber: An Intellectual Portrait* (Garden City, N.Y.: Doubleday and Co., 1962), pp. 330–60.

the household stand in an entirely personal relation to him."[2] The patrimonial system, on the other hand, is one that maintains an elaborate administrative organization that spreads throughout the society. The tasks of government are highly specialized and technocratic. As a result, the ruler's relationship with the ruled is filtered through a huge network of administrative officers and officials. Although contemporary Iran boasts rapid industrialization and impressive economic development, its important political patterns are fundamentally patrimonial in nature.[3] The political system is wrapped around the person of the Shah who is its ultimate model, guide, innovator and protector.

The Iranian manifestation of the patrimonial type is distinguished by the highly personal and informal manner in which power is exercised. Rivalry is ever present. Tension between individuals and groups is institutionalized at all levels in society, and the drive to maximize one's power and to extend one's influence is the essential political reality. Often cloaked in formal linguistic and public behavioral patterns denoting deference and altruism, this drive has been an essential force behind the survival and well-being of Iran and Iranians for centuries. Preoccupation with power and highly personal competition have promoted ascription, individualism, and insecurity in Iranian social relations.

Political processes in Iran take place largely in informal groups and cliques. Rigid associational structures and formal institutions are not the settings for political decision making and bargaining, while factions, cliques, coteries, and ad hoc gatherings of all sorts are the formations that count. Much has recently been written about the pervasive network of personal cliques that constitutes what is known in Persian as the *dawrah* system. A *dawrah* is an informal group of people who meet periodically, usually at meeting places provided by the members in turn. The basic organizing principle about which individuals cluster in a particular clique may be professional, familial, religious, recreational, intellectual, or political. The most important effect of the *dawrah* is that it builds up and reinforces patterns of personal ties. Members help one another in their political and economic endeavors, so that when political fortune smiles on one member—when he is appointed to a ministerial position, for example—the other members of the clique can also expect political advantages. The informal politics at work in this web of personal cliques underlies the activities and decisions of the formal organs of government. The informal groupings in the Majlis (the Iranian parliament) are called "fractions." One elderly veteran of five different legislative sessions has written that "most fractions tend to meet outside the Majlis in the homes of the individual members. They make their decisions concerning bills, proposals, speeches. and committees before each particular meeting."[4]

The informal style of Iranian politics has had a number of direct implications for patterns of elite formation. First, the ruling political elite is composed of individuals drawn from a small number of key cliques. The two *dawrahs* that have been most important in providing personnel for the elite over the last decade are

---

[2] Bendix, *Max Weber,* p. 330.

[3] For an analysis documenting this point, see Ahmad Ashraf, "Historical Obstacles to the Development of a Bourgeoisie in Iran," *Iranian Studies,* vol. 2 (Spring-Summer 1969), pp. 54–79.

[4] Ali Mu'ayyad-Sabeti, "The Fourteenth Legislative Period," *Donya—1342* (a 1968–64 almanac), p. 141. In Persian.

the *Goruh-e Iran-e No* (New Iran group) and the *Kanun-e Taraqqi* (Progressive club). Both of these groups were formed in the 1950s and were made up of highly trained and educated middle- and upper-class members. In 1968, half a dozen ministers in the Iranian cabinet were members of these two *dawrahs*. Second, the network of informal groups in Iran has served to narrow the explosive gap that divides elite from nonelite, for *dawrahs* often draw membership from across class lines. This is especially true of upper- and middle-class *dawrahs*. When a professional or intellectual clique is composed of members drawn from both the elite and the nonelite, lines of communication are held open between those who rule and those who are ruled. Furthermore, the *dawrah* network spans the entire class structure, working to close gaps, soften confrontation, and siphon off discontent at all levels. The informal contacts that take place in them help defuse the conflict built into all social systems and often render unnecessary the politics of violent confrontation. In short, the informal nature of the social and political process in Iran has had an important influence on both the patterns of elite formation and the actual dynamics of elite rule.

Closely related to the pattern of informality is the personalism that pervades Iranian political processes. Patrimonial politics are by definition personal politics, and Iranian society is above all "a community where everything is personal." [5] Indeed the critical network of *dawrahs* and cliques manifests the triumph of informal contacts over formal procedures. Similarly, power is concentrated in personalities rather than in institutions. In a system of this kind contacts and connections assume extraordinary significance for an individual's strategy of political preservation and advancement and are often the determining factors in his career. Personal and familial loyalty are vital to the system, while institutions in themselves are usually hollow structures marginal to the real political process. Results and rewards accrue to those who maintain the strongest personal ties with the most powerful politicos. Kinship ties, of course, are the most intimate and lasting of personal relations, which is why family configurations have always been a critical determinant in Iranian society and politics.

Personalistic politics stress the value of "proximity," that is, physical and social proximity to the personal center of power. In Iran, there is a fierce and implacable drive to be near those with power. Bureaucrats scheme to be near ministers and deputy ministers, whether socially or on the job. Ministers and deputy ministers maneuver to develop more intimate ties with the prime minister and the closest confidants of the Shah, while the prime minister and royal confidants themselves compete to spend more time in the actual presence of His Majesty. At the national level it is a basic axiom of Iranian politics that the closer an individual gets to the monarch and the longer he stays there, the greater his own opportunities to advance in the system will be.

Personalism has been crucial in determining how elites crystallize and act in Iran. It has meant that people who are born without the right personal connections strive to form them, for it is difficult to move into the political elite without strong personal ties with someone who is already a member. And it has made family relations the most easily documented means of entry into the elite. In fact, elite

[5] Sir John Malcolm, *The History of Persia from the Early Period to the Present Time,* 2d ed., vol. 2 (London: John Murray, 1829), p. 410.

politics operate almost exclusively upon a personal level. Thus the emphasis on proximity, combined with the pattern of informality, has traditionally made the personal attendants of the Shah formidable members of the political elite whether or not they held formal political positions. When asked about his sources of "proper information," the present Shah said that in addition to information services he had his valet, gardeners, and others of his household.[6] Other than members of the royal family, the most important members of the present Iranian political elite—the immediate entourage of the Shah—include a personal physican, a former military tutor, a former classmate, and a lifelong friend and companion. The Shah's "individual approach to kingship" [7] is perhaps the most important manifestation of the personalistic character of elite politics in Iran.

A final major pattern discernible in Iran's political process is that of unrelenting rivalry and tension. The competition generated by the intense drive for power and survival takes on a personal flavor best illustrated by the level of personal insult that is considered acceptable criticism in both private and public discussions. Debates over public issues and governmental programs consistently break down into exchanges of personal accusations and vilification. Another characteristic of this pattern of rivalry, which carries even deeper implications than its personal flavor, is its role as a balancing mechanism: universal competition leads to absolute political domination by no one. The Shah is the hub of the system, the ultimate balancer, and power is seldom given the opportunity to crystallize anywhere but in his hands. When power begins to concentrate within groups, the groups are splintered; when an individual becomes too influential, he is likely to be demoted, dismissed, retired, or penalized. The system is structured in such a way that this occurs automatically through the intervention of countervailing rivals. A system of this kind, of course, breeds great insecurity, attested to by the dramatic rises and falls of individuals who are formidable members of the political elite one day, only to be unemployed the next. But it also fosters stability. Threats to the ongoing system from concentrated and organized opposition forces are detected in their embryonic stages and checked before they can effectively challenge, much less destroy, the system.

The closer one gets to the center of the national power structure in Iran, the more pronounced become the patterns of rivalry and tension. Since most power is concentrated there, it is essential to the preservation of the system that there always be strong forces opposing one another at the center of the structure. Numerous threads of rivalry, then, run through the political elite itself, arraying cliques and personalities against one another in a myriad of shifting alliances and coalitions. The Shah plays a key role in protecting and stabilizing the system as he shuffles personalities in and out of positions in order to maintain the delicate balance at the center.

The characteristics of elite politics in Iran—informality, personalism, intense competition for power—have revealing parallels in an unsuspected quarter, namely, in Teheran traffic patterns. The similarities are striking enough to warrant a glance at this microcosm of the social and political system. The Teheran driver's object is

[6] For the Shah's statement, see E. A. Bayne, *Persian Kingship in Transition* (New York: American Universities Field Staff, 1968), p. 235.

[7] Ibid., p. 239.

to arrive at his destination as quickly and forcefully as possible. Established routes are abandoned whenever detours along sidewalks and grass boulevards promise faster results, and rules and regulations respected only when they happen to enhance speed. Informal and extralegal tactics, on the other hand, are highly developed, from ignoring speed limits and traffic signs to crowding smaller vehicles off the road (preferably into *jubes* or gutters), passing other vehicles on curving mountain roads,[8] and bribing police officers to tolerate any infraction. Every hour is rush hour in Teheran, so drivers develop extraordinary agility at getting ahead of other vehicles and an ability to maneuver in impossible situations. They are ready to move in any direction at any time, to cut off other cars and bluff competitors to the side and rear; they learn to let other vehicles run interference for them, and they give ground only before more powerful contenders. Finally, they take chances in order to get ahead. The closer the destination the greater the danger of accidents, for at the end of their journey drivers are tired, their reflexes slow. The traffic, always densest when success is closest, often forces to the side of the road drivers who have almost arrived.

The intense and unceasing effort to move forward, omnipresent rivalry, indifference to formal rules, insecurity, and reliance upon maneuver and agility—they are all there, in elite politics and Teheran traffic. There is, however, one fundamental difference. Social and political relations in Iran are governed by extreme courtesy, which softens the tensions that pervade the system. This cultural phenomenon is related to the peculiar resources of the Persian language, which can express various levels of politeness and is filled with pleasantries, and to the personal nature of the ties between individuals. By curbing explosive confrontations, it allows institutionalized rivalry to serve as a stabilizing force. In anonymous settings like traffic where the steel of the machine strips away all individuality, courtesy no longer mediates between rival forces, and competition flares into accidents, arguments, insults, and violence.[9]

Thus, although Iranian political processes are marked by a sharp competitive drive to maximize power and to move ahead in the system, this drive is confined within civilized channels by the culture of the Iranian peoples. Personal courtesy serves as a buffer that balances power against power, which in turn invests the Iranian political system with dynamic stability. In this sense personalism, which is the primary feature of patrimonial politics, is the fundamental reality of the Iranian polity.

Profile of the Political Elite

Identifying the Political Elite. Political leadership in Iran belongs to those individuals who wield most political power in the society—which means, as in all patrimonial systems, those who have the greatest access to and influence with the patrimonial leader. Our analysis will focus upon the *political* elite, and will bring

[8] This maneuver is monopolized by trucks and buses.

[9] In 1970, over 2,100 automobile accidents per month were reported to the police in Teheran. Statisticians in central police headquarters in Teheran estimate that three times the reported number do, in fact, occur. One could roughly estimate on this basis that there are more than 200 automobile accidents a day in Teheran. Personal interview, Teheran, September 27, 1970.

into consideration other elites—notably the economic and intellectual elites—only insofar as these groups play a significant role in the formation and policy of the political elite. There are, of course, as many elites as there are value hierarchies in a society. Indeed, the most widely agreed upon definition of the term is that the elite are those who have the most of what there is to have in a particular society, and who get the most of what there is to get.

Patrimonialism both simplifies and complicates the process of elite identification. On the one hand, the leader and his circle of advisors and officials are known to constitute the elite. On the other hand, to pinpoint the truly important and powerful personalities within this circle is often extremely difficult. The informal and personalistic nature of patrimonialism obscures the actual relationships between the central ruler and his advisors. Elite rivalry further heightens uncertainty about the real distribution of power as elite actors and their allies attempt to magnify their own importance as opposed to that of their rivals. But these difficulties can be minimized. In this paper a combined positional, reputational, and decisional approach has been used to identify elite membership. To begin with, the list of institutional leaders—members of the cabinet and the Majlis, for example—is long and accessible. Many of these office holders will be bona fide members of the political elite, while others, predictably, will turn out to have relatively little power or influence. The reputational method, meanwhile, relies on guidance from knowledgeable informants who may or may not be members of the elite themselves. It is most effective in helping pinpoint the informal political leaders, those who cannot be found in institutional positions. This researcher enjoyed close personal ties with several members of the political elite, notably three informal leaders who, although close confidants of the Shah, held no political office. Finally, the decisional approach—the study of the individuals upon whom the patrimonial leader relied for information and advice in making a number of key decisions—was especially helpful in ranking roughly the amount of power and influence exercised by various members of the elite.[10]

The Components of the Political Elite. The personalities of the Iranian political elite are drawn from and differentiated by membership in seven major groups. These categories, in decreasing order of power and influence, are the following: the inner circle, the royal family, courtiers and confidants, military-security organization leaders, ministers and deputy ministers, Majlis and senate members, and high-ranking business, professional, and quasi-governmental personalities. Figure 2–1 is a diagram of the Iranian political elite and the groups that comprise it. It depicts the relative size of the groups and shows how the inner circle is made up of members of the other six elite segments, and it emphasizes the manner in which the elite is wrapped around the person of the patrimonial leader. The Iranian political

[10] The efforts to develop complex and precise power rankings and the debates attempting to determine whether x or y is a member of the elite are sometimes interesting academic exercises. They need not impede this study, however, since we are more interested in patterns than we are in faces. We assume that it is possible to expose elite formation and explain elite processes without having to identify and document every member of the elite. This task tends to be fruitless in any case, since no two scholars will agree as to exactly who is in the elite and since elite membership is a constantly changing phenomenon. For a major effort to cope with such methodological issues in studying elite politics in Iran, see Marvin Zonis, *The Political Elite of Iran* (Princeton: Princeton University Press, 1971).

elite analyzed in this study will be confined to the 250 most powerful personalities who fill the 375 elite positions charted in Figure 2–1. Beyond these admittedly arbitrary numbers, it becomes incredibly difficult to determine who is and who is not a member of the elite. The figure 250 limits the field of analysis to manageable proportions and permits more in-depth investigation of the patterns of elite formation.

Figure 2–1

THE IRANIAN POLITICAL ELITE, 1973–1974: INTERLOCKING NETWORK OF PATRIMONIAL LEADER, INNER CIRCLE LINKAGE FIGURES, AND MAJOR ELITE GROUPS

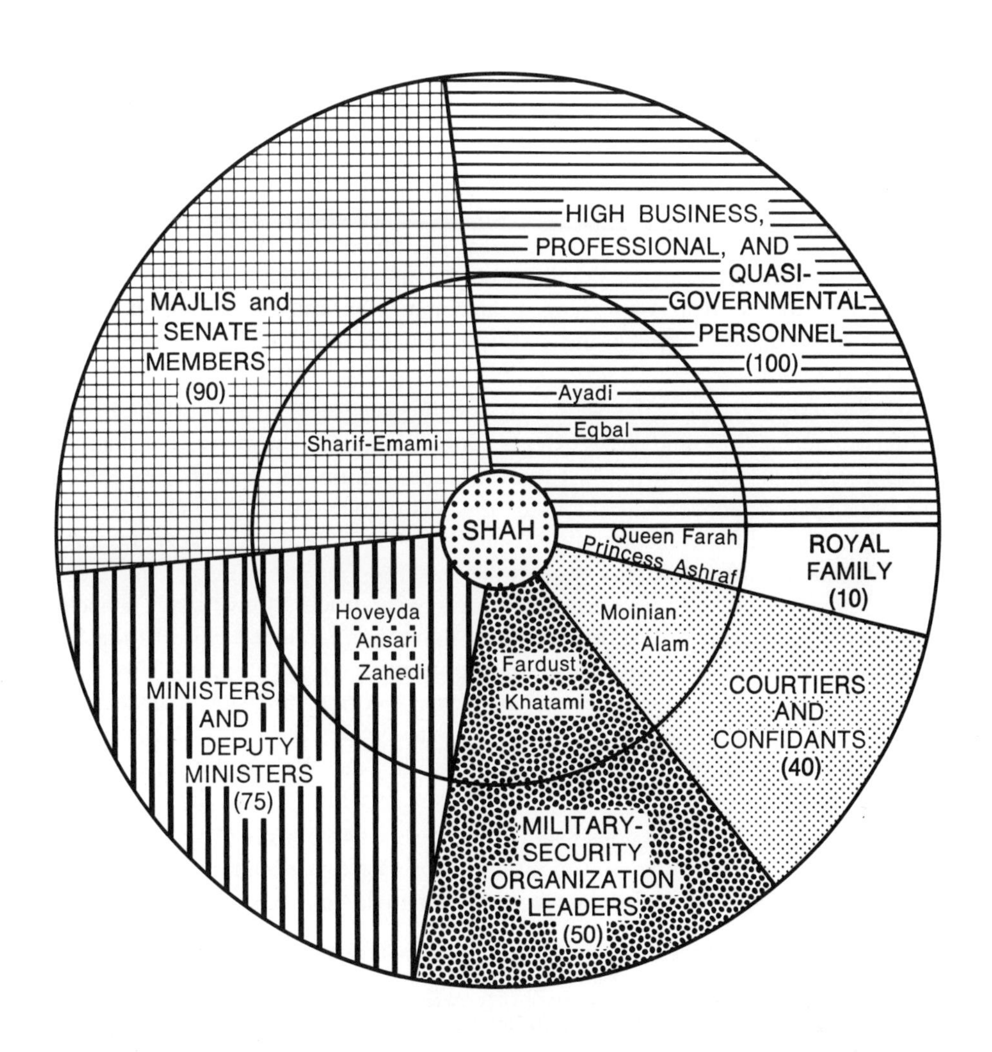

Note: Numbers in parentheses refer to total membership in each group.

The inner circle is composed of twelve individuals who are the core of the Iranian political elite. They enjoy more political influence with the patrimonial leader than anyone else in the society. The members of the inner circle at present are Her Majesty Empress Farah Diba Pahlavi, Her Highness Princess Ashraf Pahlavi, Amir Asadollah Alam, General Hossein Fardust, Nosratollah Moinian, Minister of Economy and Finance Hushang Ansari, Prime Minister Amir Abbas Hoveyda, Ambassador Ardeshir Zahedi, Jaafar Sharif-Emami, General Mohammed Khatami, General Abdol Karim Ayadi, and Dr. Manuchehr Eqbal.[11] The most important and pivotal member of this group is Empress Farah. She is a woman of deep intelligence and is genuinely concerned for her people. Her views are relied upon more and more by the Shah. After a decade of championing humanitarian causes, the empress now addresses herself increasingly to the social and political problems of Iran. In 1970 she headed 26 different groups and organizations designed to solve social problems and to alleviate human suffering. The empress also maintains a private secretariat where Iranians from all walks of life can petition for help. Over the last six months of 1970, the empress received 30,951 petitions.[12] Thirty percent of these were delivered to the empress's office by the petitioner in person, while the rest were sent by mail. Of the total number of petitions presented over this six-month period, 17,581 or nearly 60 percent explicitly involved complaints against the government. Unlike many members of the elite who are motivated solely by political opportunism and personal ambition, Empress Farah struggles to organize programs and promote policies that will benefit the Iranian people as a whole.

Princess Ashraf, who is the Shah's twin sister, has long been a power in Iran, but her influence ebbs and flows. Her strong personality, however, has kept her within the political elite for the last three decades. Alam and Fardust, meanwhile, have both been personal companions of the Shah since childhood. Their political styles, however, differ substantially. Alam has held practically every important formal position in the political system: he has been prime minister, minister of interior, minister of labor, governor general, party leader, university chancellor, and minister of court. Fardust, on the other hand, has remained close to the Shah behind the scenes where he holds an important security position. Nosratollah Moinian is the Shah's personal private secretary. A former minister of information, Moinian took charge of the royal secretariat in 1967. Like General Fardust, he wields a great amount of informal influence in Iran. And also like Fardust, Moinian possesses a degree of integrity that is sometimes unusual in these circles.

General Ayadi's influence goes back to the early 1940s, while Sharif-Emami and Eqbal have consolidated their positions over the last two decades. Hoveyda, who has been prime minister of Iran since 1965, has held that position over a greater

[11] Other prime candidates for inner circle positions are Seyyid Hassan Emami, Emam Jomeh of Teheran, and Parviz Sabeti, a key official in the Security Organization and a personal adjutant of the Shah. Sabeti boasts nearly twenty years of service in the organization. In 1974, he was exerting tremendous investigatory power in Iran.

[12] The precise six-month period referred to was March 21–September 21, 1970. These figures do not always include the numerous petitions that the empress receives through channels other than her secretariat. The director of the empress's office of petitions estimates that close to 100,000 petitions a year are now being processed by his staff. Personal interview, Teheran, December 5, 1970.

number of consecutive years than any premier in contemporary Iranian history. Ardeshir Zahedi holds the important post of Iranian Ambassador to the United States. He is the son of the late General Fazlollah Zahedi who led the forces that overthrew Musaddeq in 1953. General Khatami is the commander of the Imperial Iranian Air Force and is an unusually fine officer and pilot. Khatami established his credentials in 1953 when as a major in the Air Force he piloted the escape craft in which the Shah fled the country. Hushang Ansari is a quietly clever minister who in 1974 took control of the critically important ministry of economy and finance.

The second segment of the political elite is composed of relatives and in-laws of the Pahlavi family. This group includes three or four relatives of the queen as well as members of the Pahlavi family and a few of their spouses. Obviously not all of the princes and princesses in the Pahlavi family can be included in the political elite. Those lacking rather dramatically in talent and reputation, for example, have lost most of their influence in the national political arena. The Shah has been quite sensitive about this subject and has occasionally acted to curtail the influence of members of his own family. At the same time, a number of very powerful political actors are drawn from the royal family. The outstanding case in point is Empress Farah Diba who is the spouse and regent of the patrimonial leader.

The Shah of Iran is surrounded by a relatively large number of courtiers and personal confidants among whom Asadollah Alam is perhaps the most influential. Many of these members of the political elite are associated in some way with the ministry of the imperial court. Besides those who theoretically concern themselves with royal protocol, administration, and recreation, there are a number of civil adjutants who serve as intermediaries between the patrimonial leader and important personalities in society at large. Their power and position in the political elite derive from the institutionalized access they have to the Shah. This segment of the political elite has traditionally included royal secretaries, scribes, entertainers, physicians, valets, stablemen, fortune-tellers, and caterers. A dozen important members of the present elite are trained physicians and owe their leading political influence to the relations they formed with the Shah and royal family in their role as doctors. These physician-politicos include two members of the inner circle (Ayadi and Eqbal) as well as individuals of the stature of Professor Yahya Adl, Jahanshah Saleh, and Jamshid Aalam. Although it is true that the patrimonial retinue of old has weakened considerably, it is also important to recognize that its remnants are still very much in evidence and play an important part in Iranian politics. It is a little known fact that a small number of soothsayers and conjurer-dervishes still attach themselves to the Iranian elite and the royal court, where they are not without influence.[13]

The leaders of the military and security organizations are an especially important segment of the elite for two basic reasons. First, they are in direct control of the coercive instruments of the society and, despite the emphasis on more subtle

[13] Three such dervishes currently enjoy the company of many of the most powerful political personalities in Iran. Having been in the company of one of these conjurers several times at the home of an elite family, the writer can attest to the effective and influential role played by figures of this kind in the political process.

forms of influence in Iran, force remains the ultimate repository of power. Second, the military-security heads have an organizational structure behind them. Unlike informal leaders who must operate personally and individually, military leaders always have a base of institutional support at their service. The leaders of the following organizations must be counted as members of the political elite: the military per se (army, navy, air force), the special forces, the gendarmerie, the national police organization, the royal guard, and the various security-intelligence organizations.

The bureaucratic elite in Iran is the most obvious reservoir of members of the national political elite. In 1970, the civil bureaucracy was headed by an elite whose number fluctuated between 450 and 500 persons. At that time, there were 22 ministers, 111 deputy ministers, and 331 directors general. A scattering of other individuals who were extremely powerful in the ministries bore titles such as "high inspector" and "technical advisor." All 22 ministers and slightly fewer than half of the deputy ministers have been included here as members of the national political elite. Half a dozen directors general have also been included because of their important personal and family connections with elite members in any of the above four categories. Besides the prime minister, the most powerful members of this segment of the elite regularly include the minister of foreign affairs, the minister of economy, the minister of interior, and the minister of information.

A relatively large number of elite members are found in the senate and the Majlis. These include all the senators and approximately thirty Majlis deputies. The Iranian senate is the natural habitat of elitedom, because 50 percent of the senators are appointed directly by the Shah. Most senators are older, more or less distinguished gentlemen who have served Iran and its leader loyally for an extended period of time. As such, they have long been members of the political elite, and even in the twilight of their lives when their influence has undoubtedly waned they enjoy access to the ranks of the powerful. On the other hand, the role of the Majlis as a center of elite power has been weakened considerably over the last decade by the measures the Shah has taken to widen class representation. Turnover in Majlis membership from one legislative period to the next has increased, and some traditional elite members have been excluded. The landed provincial magnates are an example of these. While the land reform program deprived them of an economic base of influence in the countryside, elimination from the Majlis all but destroyed their political influence in Teheran.

The final category of the Iranian political elite consists of leading business, professional, and quasi-governmental personalities. It includes some of the biggest industrialists, contractors, and bankers, as well as the elites of journalism, law, engineering, and education. It also includes the heads of such extra-ministerial and quasi-governmental organizations as the Plan Organization, the Vaqf (Endowment) Organization, the municipality of Teheran, the National Iranian Oil Company, the National Steel Company, the Tourist Organization, the National Gas Company, the Iranian Carpet Company, the High Council of Guilds, the Red Lion and Sun Organization, the Imperial Organization of Social Services, the Physical Training and Recreation Organization, the Teheran Bus Company, the Pahlavi Foundation, the Central Bank, and the Insurance Company of Iran. The members of this group are in general the least powerful politically. Some of them, however, hold positions in one or more of the above groups as well. These include General Ayadi and Dr. Manuchehr Eqbal, who are inner circle members. Ayadi is one of Iran's leading business and financial magnates, while Eqbal is chairman and managing director of the National Iranian Oil Company.

The above breakdown of political elite membership in Iran reveals a number of important patterns. Perhaps the most significant of these is the pattern of simultaneous membership in two or more elite categories by what we will call "linkage figures." The Shah, of course, is the prototype of the linkage figure because of his ultimate control of and direct involvement in each of the seven elite categories. Aside from the Shah, the twelve members of the inner circle are the central linkage figures. As Figure 2–1 graphically illustrates, each of them is a leader in one of the key elite arenas as well as a member of the inner circle. They act as linchpins, holding together the individuals and groups that compose the political elite, and cementing the larger political system. A key case in point is General Abdol Karim Ayadi who, besides belonging to the inner circle, is a leading courtier and confidant of the Shah, a military advisor, and a national financial wizard. The occupants of the 375 elite positions considered here include approximately 100 linkage figures, several of whom exert direct influence in more than two elite categories—which explains our estimate that the Iranian political elite numbers nearly 250 *different* individuals.

Educational Background. The Iranian political elite is a highly sophisticated group. With the possible exceptions of Israel and Lebanon, Iran boasts the most highly educated, widely travelled, and linguistically skilled elite in the Middle East. Iranian political leaders have traditionally been intellectually talented and well educated, but they have become dramatically more so in the course of the last

Table 2–1

LEVEL OF EDUCATION OF DIRECTORS GENERAL IN IRANIAN GOVERNMENT, 1970

Educational Level	Number of Directors General	Percent of Total
Grammar school	3	.8
Beyond grammar school	5	1.2
Secondary school	28	7.0
Beyond secondary school	5	1.2
Baccalaureate degree	206	51.4
Masters degree	72	17.9
Doctorate	82	20.5
Total	401	100.0

Note: In this table the term director general refers not only to the specific rank of *Modir-e Koll* but also to the two closely related categories of office head and general bureau chief.

Source: Government of Iran, Organization of Administrative Affairs and State Employment, *A Statistical Examination of the Directors-General, Office Heads, and General Bureau Chiefs in the Official Governmental Ministries and Institutes* (Teheran, 1970). In Persian.

twenty-five years. A statistical survey of the lowest echelons of the political elite carried out in 1970 by the Iranian Organization of Administrative Affairs and State Employment reveals how pronounced this trend has been. The study included all administrators in the general classification of director general *(Modir-e Koll).* Table 2–1 is a detailed breakdown of its findings about their educational backgrounds. Only 2 percent of the directors general had failed to complete secondary school, while 90 percent held at least a college degree and 20 percent of these held doctorates.

A similar study of the educational backgrounds of Majlis deputies from the first through the twentieth legislative periods further demonstrates the high educational standard of the political elite.[14] Its findings, which are given in Table 2–2, can be summarized as follows: during the first constitutional period (the first five Majlises, 1906–1926), the average proportion of deputies holding at least college degrees was 18 percent; during the second period (the sixth through the thirteenth Majlises, 1926–1941), the percentage dropped slightly to 14 percent; but over the third constitutional period (the fourteenth through the twentieth Majlises, 1941–1963), the proportion of deputies with baccalaureate degrees or better increased to an impressive 36 percent. Clearly, the educational level attained by Majlis deputies has risen dramatically. Only deputies who received modern, as opposed to traditional, religious educations are included in this study, but in the course of the half century it covers, this group has come to predominate. In the early Majlises, an average of nearly 60 percent of the deputies had been trained in the traditional manner.[15] Today, fewer than 10 percent come from traditional backgrounds. There has also been an increase in the percentage of deputies educated abroad. One-third of the deputies in the twenty-first Majlis (1963–1967) had received their higher education outside Iran. This trend is even more marked within the political elite as a whole. Over 90 percent of the members of Prime Minister Hoveyda's cabinets (1965–1974) had been educated abroad.

All of these indicators reveal that the Iranian political elite is an increasingly well educated group. To put it in terms of the basic issues of class and change, increasing numbers of the intelligentsia are being absorbed into the elite. This important pattern will be discussed in more detail below.

Elite Cohesion and the Challenge of Modernization

The Iranian political elite has been a remarkably cohesive group, especially by Middle Eastern standards. There are a number of reasons for this. The patrimonial leader, to begin with, has served to anchor the elite and has very effectively neutralized its centrifugal tendencies. He has been supported by the linkage figures mentioned above who act as agglutinating and connecting agents. Another key

[14] For an analysis of the social and political patterns that dominate the Iranian legislative system, see James A. Bill, "The Politics of Legislative Monarchy: The Iranian Majlis," in Herbert Hirsch and M. Donald Hancock eds., *Comparative Legislative Systems: A Reader in Theory and Research* (New York: Free Press, 1971), pp. 360–69.

[15] The second and third Majlises were exceptionally well-educated groups. Fifty-eight and 51 percent of the deputies in these two legislatures had higher education (either traditional or modern). See Zuhrah Shaji'i, *The Representatives of the National Consultative Assembly during the Twenty-One Legislative Periods* (Teheran, 1965), p. 217. In Persian.

Table 2–2

LEVELS OF MODERN EDUCATION ACHIEVED BY MAJLIS DEPUTIES FROM TWENTY LEGISLATIVE PERIODS, 1906–1963

	Legislative Period																			
Educational Level	**1**	**2**	**3**	**4**	**5**	**6**	**7**	**8**	**9**	**10**	**11**	**12**	**13**	**14**	**15**	**16**	**17**	**18**	**19**	**20**
Grammar school education	23	15	12	25	17	22	26	32	30	33	34	32	36	22	24	25	10	26	20	16
Secondary school	12	10	2	6	13	4	4	9	9	6	6	6	9	13	15	15	12	13	16	25
Baccalaureate	15	17	13	10	12	9	9	9	10	5	5	6	6	17	20	15	24	22	27	28
Doctorate	4	8	4	2	4	3	3	6	6	8	8	7	8	9	11	13	14	11	20	20

Note: Figures shown are percentages. We are concerned with secular education here as opposed to the traditional, religious education that centered on the *maktabs* and *madressehs.* Many deputies, especially those who were members of the earlier Majlises, received traditional educations.

Source: Zuhrah Shaji'i, *The Representatives of the National Consultative Assembly during the Twenty-one Legislative Periods* (Teheran, 1965), p. 226. In Persian.

integrating factor has been the balancing effect of the personal rivalries that dominate intra-elite relations; competition discourages explosive division and binds together the various elite levels. The informal nature of elite politics also promotes cohesion. Serious causes of division and potential cleavages are often sensed and dealt with behind the scenes before they become hardened into public issues. Finally, clusters of cliques and family groupings increase contact and communication among members of the political elite.

The Elite and the "White Revolution." While these mechanisms have been working to unify the Iranian elite, a number of specific political issues have had profound implications for the processes of elite integration and disintegration. The most important of them has been the issue of development. Over the last decade, Iran has instituted one of the most dramatic programs of modernization in the world. This policy, however, has provoked a great deal of debate and even resistance within the elite.

In 1963, the Shah of Iran outlined a six-point reform program that became the core of what is now known as the White Revolution. The original six reforms plus six additional programs are the strategy for development advocated by the more progressive faction of the elite. The twelve-point program consists of (1) land reform, (2) nationalization of forests and pastures, (3) public sale of state-owned factories to finance land reform, (4) profit sharing in industry, (5) reform of electoral law to include women, (6) literacy corps, (7) health corps, (8) reconstruction and development corps, (9) rural courts of justice, (10) nationalization of waterways, (11) national reconstruction, and (12) educational and administrative revolution. Greatest emphasis has been placed on land redistribution and the literacy corps, which have, indeed, brought about substantial progress.[16] Most of the other points have remained largely on paper and have not had serious results. Part of the reason for this is that the reform program is designed to preserve rather than uproot the traditional patterns of patrimonialism that underlie Iranian sociopolitical relations.[17] Only the twelfth point is directly relevant to this end, and in 1973–1974 members of the inner circle of the political elite were publicly expressing their dissatisfaction with the lack of results in terms of educational and administrative change. Another important reason for the White Revolution's failure to have an appreciable impact on power relationships has been the subtle passive resistance of some members of the political elite. As long as they observe traditional patterns in their own day-to-day activities, there is no reason to expect that change can be successfully imposed from above.

The issues of social and economic change divide the political elite into two major groups. The progressive faction is headed by the Shah and includes most of the members of the intelligentsia who have joined the political elite in the last decade or two. The opposition, less visible, includes many members of the old landed aristocracy who objected above all to land reform. On the whole, however, this group has recognized the futility of any attempt to obstruct the reforms and

[16] For a good analysis of the land reform, see A. K. S. Lambton, *The Persian Land Reform, 1962–1966* (Oxford: Clarendon Press, 1969).

[17] For detailed documentation, see James A. Bill, *The Politics of Iran: Groups, Classes and Modernization* (Columbus: Charles E. Merrill, 1972).

has adjusted quickly to the changes. In fact the most significant cleavage within the elite is not that between progressives and conservatives, but rather the one dividing those who vociferously support the White Revolution. The proponents of change differ sharply over the extent and direction of reform.

Patrimonial political systems have traditionally encouraged sycophancy, opportunism, and intrigue, and the Iranian system is no exception. Highly educated members of the elite often engage in maneuvers and machinations of all sorts. Many of the most opportunistic members of the political elite are members of the intelligentsia, wearing "new masks on old faces." [18] This is not, however, universally the case. The empress herself has attacked the very essence of patrimonial politics in one of the most often discussed public statements made in Iran in recent years. She said that "sycophancy is perverting all classes of the people," and strongly criticized "sycophants who try to name every public place after a member of the royal family, imagining they would benefit by doing so." The empress argued that "If the only criterion for assigning people to various posts is merit and if those who are praised are truly worthy of such praise, we could, perhaps, hope that flattery and sycophancy will gradually be eliminated." [19] In a private audience in 1970, the empress discussed the continued prevalence of patrimonial patterns of behavior within the elite and indicated that the only way to disrupt and transform them is through formal education, beginning at the very lowest levels.[20] Despite her efforts and those of a small minority of elite members, however, the traditional style of politics continues to dominate. Most of the reform successfully initiated from above has been concentrated in other directions.

Changes in Iran's land tenure system and important attempts to broaden literacy have been accompanied by unprecedented economic prosperity. Over the last ten years, Iran has had an annual economic growth rate second only to that of Japan in Asia. Oil revenues which amounted to a billion dollars in 1970 burgeoned to more than $20 billion in 1974. Iranian officials predict that these revenues will total well over $100 billion over the next five years. Recent development in the areas of agribusiness and the copper and natural gas industries also indicates that the economic dynamism of the 1960s has carried over into the 1970s. Since the Shah and his family, like many members of the elite, are personally involved in and deeply committed to industrial development, it is clear that Iran's economic boom, upon which the success of the White Revolution is largely founded, has occurred in the context of patrimonial politics.

The contemporary Iranian political elite is an extraordinarily dynamic group. Although its members have disagreed over the depth and direction that social and economic change should take, they have made a real effort to confront the challenge of modernization. They have remained united behind the Shah, who has written a book on revolution, on that important issue. And they have inspired the policy of reform from above buttressed by impressive economic progress. This program is circumscribed by the patrimonial sociopolitical system, yet in the end it has probably contributed more to elite cohesion than to elite division. Since

[18] For this expression as it applies to the co-optation process at work within the Iranian Bar Association, see M. A. Saffari's article in *Ayandigan* (Teheran), February 6, 1968.

[19] *Kayhan International* (Teheran), July 30, 1969.

[20] Personal interview, Teheran, Niavaran Palace, November 18, 1970.

few members of the elite wish to uproot the basic patterns of power, there is, in fact, very little intra-elite dissension concerning the White Revolution. At the same time, the modernization program has further vitalized the elite by attracting to it members of the intelligentsia who are willing to work within a patrimonial system toward such goals as land reform and economic development.

Elite Recruitment and Circulation

Two extreme views have been taken of elite membership and formation in Iran. The first is that the Iranian political elite (like all other elites) is a closed aristocracy that has always adamantly refused to admit outsiders into its circle. Those who hold this view have repeatedly voiced the "thousand families" cliché to support their position. The expression "thousand families" has come to mean that Iran is a society ruled and controlled by a tightly knit group of one thousand families that has remained relatively constant over a long period. The second view is that Iran has been a society of unfettered social mobility; that it does not boast an ancient heritage of familial, dynastic politics, but rather has had a surprisingly rapid turnover of elites and dynasties. The contemporary political elite is cited by proponents of this view to illustrate the peripheral role of the aristocratic element in the political system, and the importance of the intelligentsia as a recruiting ground for the elite is emphasized. The debate between the two is relevant to any discussion of elite formation in Iran, for it raises the fundamental issues of elite recruitment and elite circulation.

Elite Continuity: The Importance of Family. Family and tribal relations have traditionally been crucial considerations in the Iranian political system. Although family has somewhat less impact on political decision making than it did in the past, it is still one of the most important factors involved. A number of families have been continuously represented in the political elite since before the middle of the nineteenth century. After 100 years, they continue to exert crucial influence and to occupy key positions.

The term "thousand families" is misleading since, in fact, only a fourth this many families have maintained positions of political power for relatively extended periods of time. In terms of relative power and influence, they fall into two groups. The more influential are the *national elite families* who have risen above their original local bases of power to positions of national importance. They all have relatives in the provinces, but their headquarters are in Teheran. Their members are active in various segments in the political elite, but, equally, hold leading positions in industry, education, law, medicine, and the arts. These families exercise power throughout society and in all the major systems by which man organizes his life. The second group are the *provincial elite families* whose influence is strong in relatively limited geographic areas. These families remain clustered in a particular town, city, or province where they occupy the apex of the social structure and have traditionally been the key landlords. Until the recent restriction of their role in national politics, some of their members sat in the Majlis in Teheran, but they have not been a steady source of new recruits for national elite positions.

There are forty national elite families in Iran today (see Table 2–3). Even when the fortunes of particular members fall, these families always manage to survive and to protect themselves. In terms of sociopolitical power, the ten families that form the core of the elite are the following: Pahlavi, Alam, Diba, Qaragozlu, Esfandiari, Ardalan, Samii, Farmanfarmaian, Mahdavi, and Busheiri.[21] Each of these families exerts tremendous influence and each has direct access to the patrimonial leader. Table 2–3 shows the number of Majlis seats that each of the forty families has held in the first through the twenty-first Majlises (1906–1967), and indicates the total number of different individuals drawn from each of these families who have served in the Majlises. With the exception of the ruling Pahlavi family, not a single national elite family has failed to enjoy parliamentary representation. Together, they have occupied over 400 Majlis positions in the last half-century, and the average is slightly more than four members per family. The first five Senates (1949–1971) were even more heavily dominated by these nationally prominent families who occupied more than a fifth of the seats.

Representation in the Iranian parliamentary bodies is only a very partial indication of the extent to which the elite is saturated with members of these particular families. Over the last two decades, twelve different men have served as prime minister of Iran. Half of them have been bona fide members of the forty first families. Three others have belonged to the second level of major families. Only two—Fazlollah Zahedi and Ali Razmara, both of them senior military officers—have had their origins well outside of the big family arena. The final individual is the incumbent, Prime Minister Hoveyda, whose father was of lowly background but who pulled himself well into the circle of leading families by marrying a woman of Vusuq and Emami descent.[22]

The influence of provincial elite families—that is, by and large, the traditional Iranian aristocracy—is especially strong in the areas of wealth and finance. The following is a representative list of Iranian cities and the important families associated with them (national elite families in italics):

KERMAN: *Ebrahimi,* Amir-Ebrahimi, Kalantari, Ameri, Arjomand;
TABRIZ: *Diba, Adl, Vakili, Panahi,* Adl-e Tabatabai, Fotuhi, Ghazi;
BIRJAND: *Alam,* Khozemeh Alam, Asadi, Monsef;
ISFAHAN: *Sadri,* Nikpay, Masud, Eshraqi, Kazeruni, Kashefi, Harati;
NAIN: *Pirnia,* Tabatabai;
QAZVIN: Yar Afshar, Amirshahi, Haj Seyyid Javadi, Shadman;
DARAB: Sarfarraz, Baharlu;
REZAIYEN: Afshar;
LAHIJAN: Saffari; and
SARI: Sang, Kasemi, Mokri.

Family continues to play a much more important role in Iranian politics and elite formation than is evident on the surface. There are a number of reasons for

[21] Others that are very nearly core families today include the Adl, Bayat, Akbar, Afkhami, Dowlatshahi, Eqbal, and Jahanbani families. The important Bakhtiyari tribal family, which has through time contributed an unusually high number of its members to the elite (see Table 2–3), is not included because its political influence has now declined sharply.

[22] It is a little-known fact that on his mother's side Prime Minister Hoveyda carries impeccable aristocratic credentials. His mother was the granddaughter of Shirkhan Eyn al-Molk and Ezzat al-Dowleh. Ezzat al-Dowleh was the elder full sister of Naser al-Din Shah Qajar.

Table 2–3
THE FORTY FAMILIES: MEMBERSHIP IN MAJLIS AND SENATE, 1906–1967

Family	Majlis Seats	Different Deputies	Senate Seats	Different Senators
Aalam	2	1	3	2
Adl	9	5	4	2
Afkhami	11	2	1	1
Akbar	15	5	4	1
Alam [a]	1	1	0	0
Amini	4	2	0	0
Ardalan	10	4	0	0
Ashtiyani	8	3	2	1
Bakhtiyari	41	20	3	2
Bayat	15	5	1	1
Busheiri	13	6	6	2
Daftari [b]	2	2	4	1
Diba	9	3	2	1
Dowlatshahi	18	5	0	0
Ebrahimi	10	7	0	0
Emami	9	4	2	2
Emami-Khoy	8	3	2	2
Eqbal	11	3	1	1
Esfandiari	19	7	3	2
Farmanfarmaian	10	5	0	0
Hakimi	3	2	2	1
Hedayat	9	5	5	2
Jahanbani	4	2	6	2
Khajeh-Nuri	15	4	2	1
Khalatbari	4	2	1	1
Mahdavi	21	6	1	1
Mansur	1	1	0	0
Pahlavi	—	—	—	—
Panahi	9	3	0	0
Pirnia	13	4	0	0
Qaragozlu	13	8	0	0
Qashqai	14	7	1	1
Qavam	6	2	0	0
Sadri	1	1	0	0
Saffari	11	3	0	0
Samii	27	9	4	1
Vakili	6	2	5	2
Vusuq	9	3	0	0
Zand	3	3	0	0
Zanganeh	4	3	0	0
Zolfaqari	12	4	1	1
Total	410	167	66	34

Note: The information in this table refers to the first twenty-one Majlises and the first five Senates through 1967.

[a] Although elected to the Majlis in 1961, Asadollah Alam later resigned his seat.

[b] The Daftari designation includes the Matin-Daftari family.

Source: Shaji'i, *Representatives of the National Consultative Assembly,* pp. 291–381; Senate of Iran, *Lists of Names and Biographic Data Concerning the Representatives to the Senate;* unpublished documents.

this. First, it is often difficult, if not impossible, to ascertain whether or not an individual is a member of an elite family. For a number of reasons, names are not sufficient indication. Since marriage is a major means of access to the elite, it often happens that key elite members bear middle-class names, while, in fact, they are married to the offspring of the leading families. At least four members of the present cabinet are linked directly with the familial aristocracy in this way. Then too, at various times social and political expediency have induced individuals to change their surnames. Three particularly relevant examples of nuclear families whose members bear different appellations are Diba-Valatabar-Shahmir, Firuz-Farmanfarmaian, and Minbashian-Pahlbod. Members of the great tribal families such as the Bakhtiar and Qashqai often bear dozens of different surnames.

A much more common difficulty is the wide variety of names that are attached to the branches of some families. The prototype of this situation in Iran is a family from the town of Ashtiyan that dates back six generations. Its members are known by the following eleven surnames: Daftari, Matin-Daftari, Mostowfi al-Mamaleki, Meykadeh, Dadvar, Vusuq, Qavam, Farhad, Shokuh, Musaddeq, and Moqtadder. The family is, nonetheless, one, and whatever loosening has occurred in the course of time has been counteracted by a complex web of marriages between cousins that continue to knit the group tightly together. Over the last half-century, five different members of this family cluster have been prime minister and these five have led twenty-nine different cabinets. The power of this kinship group, which has contributed hundreds of its member to the Iranian elite, is reflected in the fact that three of the last four prime ministers have been members of it by marriage.

The power of the national elite families has been considerably buttressed and expanded by intensive intermarriage. The branches of the family cluster referred to above, for example, have intermarried not only with each other, but also with an enormous number of other elite families. Their members are married to members of twenty-two of the thirty-seven national elite families excluding their own, and have multiple kinship ties with members of the Farmanfarmaian, Khajeh-Nuri, Emami, Bayat, Khalatbari, Amini, Qaragozlu, Dowlatshahi, and Esfandiari families.

In Iran, the bonds among families tend to be dyadic. The general pattern is for two elite families to grow closer and closer together through continual intermarriage, which produces identifiable pairs of families like the following: Afkhami/Zolfaqari, Nafisi/Khajeh-Nuri, Adl/Panahi, Shaybani/Ghaffari, and Behzadi/Kia. In this last case there has been so much intermarriage that the families are indistinguishable to everyone except genealogists.

The existence of a fluctuating network of key families in Iran has built an element of continuity into the political elite. Through patterns of intense interaction and intermarriage over long periods, the more than 300 elite families have anchored their positions. The forty national elite families are bound to one another and to the other elite families in a complex web of kinship ties, social intercourse, economic cooperation, and political expediency. Even the dynastic family has rooted itself into the system by family ties: Fath Ali Shah Qajar married an important daughter of the fallen Zand dynasty, and Reza Shah, the first of the Pahlavis, married two women of Qajar blood.

Still, however crucial the role played by elite families in Iranian political processes, it is only part of the story. It is impossible to understand elite formation and political processes in Iran by studying family relations alone. The recent land reform program, the rise of a professional middle class, the demand for technological skill, and the marked traditional patterns of mobility all indicate the limitations of the aristocratic explanation.

Elite Circulation: The Challenge of the Middle Class. The present ruling family in Iran was founded by an illiterate soldier, and some important members of the political elite are the sons of servants, mule drivers, peddlers, peasant farmers, and grocers. Relatively few influentials are of such lowly origin, but a substantial number come from the middle class. In fact, the offspring of merchants, bureaucrats, clerics, and professional people, none of whom come from elite families, increasingly move into the political elite. One of the clearest symptoms of this process is the increasing criticism from members of the first families of "the mushroom aristocracy" that has risen to power overnight, without background, roots, or ancestral experience.

In the 1960s the political elite received a sudden infusion of individuals drawn from the middle classes. With the land reform progam, the power of the traditional aristocracy came under attack, and the landlord class in particular fell victim to change. Many members of provincial elite families were slowly removed from the political elite.[23] Thus, only 35 percent of the deputies in the twenty-first Majlis (1963–1967) were landlords, while landlord representation in the twenty preceding parliaments had averaged 52 percent. The number of deputies of bureaucratic, professional, and technical backgrounds, on the other hand, has increased significantly over the last decade. Both the Iran Novin party, which was officially formed in 1963, and the newly created Iranian party (1970) have directed their efforts to recruiting the educated middle class, as have organizations such as the National Iranian Oil Company, the Central Bank, regional development organizations, and the more recently formed ministry of science and higher education.

The relatively recent emphasis upon recruitment of the intelligentsia for elite positions has strengthened Iranian society and politics in several important ways. First, there can be no doubt that the present Iranian political elite is the most highly educated and technically qualified that Iran has ever seen, or that its high standard will continue to be met in the future. One of every four Iranian college students is studying outside of Iran. Of those studying abroad, 41 percent are in the United States, 28 percent in West Germany, 12 percent in Great Britain, 8 percent in Austria, 7 percent in France, and 6 percent in Turkey, while fewer than 1 percent are studying in the Eastern-bloc countries.[24] Of the students living abroad for whom we have information, 87 percent are majoring in the natural

[23] The political and economic influence of the national elite families (the first forty), however, has not been diminished by the land reform. Many of these families had already begun transferring their resources to domestic industry and foreign investment before the land reform program took effect. Other families of national stature have been able to hold on to much of their land, although this is less and less often the case.

[24] Government of Iran, Ministry of Science and Higher Education, *Statistics Concerning Iranian College Students Within and Without the Country* (Teheran, 1969), pp. 74–75. In Persian.

sciences; engineering and medicine alone account for 67 percent of the total. Slightly more than 1 percent are studying history and the social sciences.

As Table 2–4 indicates, the pattern of study within Iran differs in one major respect from that prevailing outside. Approximately 20 percent of the students in higher education in Iran are concentrating on language and literature. The bulk of the remaining students are majoring in engineering, medicine, and the physical and biological sciences. These statistics provide an overall view of the expertise that can be expected of the future Iranian intelligentsia. In the fields of engineering and medicine especially, Iran is educating an impressive and badly needed cadre. Relatively few students, on the other hand, are pursuing the important social, administrative, and agricultural sciences. The extraordinarily high percentage of Iranians studying outside the country helps provide Iran with an intelligentsia that is cosmopolitan as well as thoroughly familiar with techniques first introduced abroad.

In 1922, there were ninety-one students enrolled in institutions of higher education in Iran; in 1953–1954, there were nearly ten thousand; today the figure is approaching 100,000.[25] Thanks to this dramatic increase in higher education, Iran will continue to produce the skilled cadre essential to the program of economic and industrial modernization upon which it is embarked. While it is true that many important members of the intelligentsia come from elite families, it is also fair to say that more and more of them are of humbler class origin. A 1966 survey of two hundred Teheran University students, for example, revealed that close to 80 percent of them were of middle- and lower-class origin.[26] In the early days of modern education in Iran, by contrast, "only the children of the nobles and aristocrats could participate." [27]

The second important way in which recruitment of middle-class members of the intelligentsia for elite positions has strengthened the Iranian system is political. It hinges on the fact that the greatest threat to the ongoing political system emanates from the intelligentsia. By absorbing many of these individuals into itself and thereby harnessing its potential opponents to the business of ruling and reforming, the elite has hoped to avert political upheaval and violent revolution. With the creation of two political parties designed to appeal to the intelligentsia in the last decade, and the sharp expansion of high bureaucratic positions, the elite has sought to raise the political absorptive capacity of the system in general.

Despite the political elite's sensitivity to the challenge of the middle-class intelligentsia, and its attempts to siphon off some of their dissatisfaction, the professional middle class remains alienated. The major source of discontent is the patrimonial basis of politics in Iran, for, while it is true that the contemporary elite supports reform in many arenas and that an increasing number of middle-class professionals continue to move into the elite, the basic social and political processes remain fundamentally unaltered. Personalism, informality, and tension imply in-

[25] The 1970 figure was 67,268. Government of Iran, Ministry of Science and Higher Education, *Statistics on Higher Education in Iran* (Teheran, 1970), p. 5. In Persian.

[26] Abd al-Hossein Nafisi and Eftikhar Tabataba'i, *An Examination of the Problems and Difficulties of Teheran Secondary and University Students* (Teheran: Plan Organization Publication, 1966), p. 3. In Persian.

[27] Government of Iran, Ministry of Labor, *Investigation of the Problems of Manpower,* vol. 3 (Teheran, 1964), p. 2032. In Persian.

Table 2–4

FIELDS STUDIED BY IRANIANS IN HIGHER EDUCATION, 1968–1969

Field of Study	Group Studying within Iran		Group Studying outside Iran		Total Iranians in Higher Education	
	Number	Percent	Number	Percent	Number	Percent
Humanities, law, and social sciences						
Language and literature	11,184	19.0	431	2.4	11,615	15.2
Economics and business	7,201	12.2	416	2.3	7,617	10.0
Social science and history	4,755	8.1	193	1.1	4,948	6.5
Law	2,274	3.8	402	2.3	2,676	3.5
Education	2,259	3.8	95	.6	2,354	3.1
Public administration and management	1,266	2.1	96	.6	1,362	1.8
Natural sciences and engineering						
Engineering and technology	9,919	16.9	4,083	22.9	14,002	18.3
Medicine	9,364	15.8	4,345	24.3	13,709	18.0
Math, chemistry, physics, biology, and geology	6,994	11.9	1,444	8.1	8,438	11.1
Agriculture	2,433	4.2	760	4.3	3,193	4.2
Arts and crafts	864	1.4	291	1.6	1,155	1.5
Miscellaneous and unspecified	48	.8	5,261	29.5	5,309	6.8
Total	58,561	100.0	20,317[a]	100.0	78,878[a]	100.0

[a] Includes 2,500 Iranians studying in Great Britain. Information concerning the fields of study of these particular students was not available and is therefore not included in the body of the chart.

Source: Adapted from Government of Iran, Ministry of Science and Higher Education, *Statistics Concerning Iranian College Students Within and Without the Country* (Teheran, 1969), pp. 11–12, 74–75. In Persian.

security, opportunism, ascription, and inefficiency. Technocrats are often accused of gaining admission to the elite by nepotism, sycophancy, and compromise.

In November 1970 an editorial in a leading Teheran daily summarized the intelligentsia's role in politics and reform:

> Our intellectuals are going through difficult times. At a time when this country is experiencing a complex, transitional period, Iran no less than any other society in a similar position needs the intellectual and mental assistance of its own intellectuals. This group, however, has not concentrated its strength and resources behind the current revolution. They will not participate and act as if they have no share in the revolution.[28]

The Shah himself has indicated concern in this regard and has stated, "I believe that the peasantry are with me but it is not so true with the younger intelligentsia. . . . They are a problem to me." [29] The continuing inability of the political elite to cope with the demands of the middle-class intelligentsia became vividly evident in 1972 when the regime began to intensify its authoritarian methods. The number of political prisoners increased dramatically between 1971 and 1975, and censorship policies became more severe than at any time in the last two decades.[30]

The future of Iran depends on the ability of the contemporary political elite to change this situation—to gain the support and commitment of the middle-class intelligentsia. Important strides have undoubtedly been made in this direction as the political elite has absorbed a good number of talented intellectuals and technocrats into its ranks and has acquired ideological appeal by initiating a reform program while making impressive progress in economic development. In terms of foreign policy and international politics, too, the current political elite has an outstanding record due largely to the high standard of statesmanship maintained by the patrimonial leader himself. Yet, for all this, the gap between the elite and the intelligentsia has continued to widen. At the root of the difficulty lies the distrust that many leading middle-class intellectuals feel for the patrimonial style of politics. More and more of them are unwilling to subordinate their modern educations and technical skills to the traditional practices of "connectioneering" and opportunistic maneuver. The Iranian political elite may well have to step up the pace of change in the fundamental power and authority relations that now prevail.

Although it is extraordinarily difficult for those who rule in a patrimonial setting to dismantle the basic patterns by which they have directed the system for years, this policy is sometimes necessary. The contemporary political elite in Iran may

---

[28] *Ayandigan,* November 15, 1970.

[29] Bayne, *Persian Kingship,* p. 52.

[30] In June 1974, the Shah of Iran made the following statements concerning the subject of torture in Iran to a *Le Monde* reporter in Paris:

> Asked whether torture exists in Iran, the Monarch replied, "Torture? . . . But you have more advanced methods in your country and in the United States. You very well know that people are psychologically tortured."
> *Le Monde:* "Newspapers reproach the use of torture and even if it happens in France we criticize it."
> *The Shahanshah:* "Very good. We in some ways torture prisoners; but what do you call torture?"

See *Le Monde,* June 25, 1974, p. 3. The above quotes are the translated comments carried in *The Tehran Journal* of June 27, 1974.

need to adopt it, not only to protect its own positions, but also to preserve the independence and strength of the Iranian nation-state. Since the elite has already sensed the challenge of change in the world, there is hope that the reform programs initiated in the 1960s will be broadened and accelerated in the 1970s and 1980s.

III. PATTERNS OF ELITE POLITICS IN TURKEY

Frederick W. Frey

Introduction

Turkey is one of the most significant of all developing nations. This is usually recognized in geopolitical terms. Turkey is seen as the "bridge between Europe and Asia—between West and East." It is respected as the protector of the southern flank of NATO and as the largest land power in the Near East, indeed, one of the largest in Europe. Defensively in particular, it is regarded as a formidable foe or potentially sturdy ally. It is valued as a site for electronic monitoring stations penetrating far into the southern Soviet Union and for its control over the crucial waterways linking the Black Sea to the Mediterranean and Atlantic.[1] It is seen as a buffer between the Soviet Union and the Arab states or, from the other side of the cold war, as a potential wedge between western Europe and the Near East. As we know all too well, it is also a key actor in the continuing dispute over one of the world's hot spots—Cyprus. Though Turkey's strategic geopolitical significance may have declined recently as the technology of global conflict has changed (for example, the missile bases there are less important), one has only to consider the previously unimaginable but now somewhat plausible prospect of a Turkey hostile to the West to be reimpressed by its pivotal position.

However, to perceive the international importance of Turkey primarily in military or geopolitical terms, as is usually done, is a mistake. For even when geopolitical considerations are ignored, Turkey still emerges as crucial for the study of developing societies. The fundamental reason is the exemplary course of its political development. For special historical reasons, political development has assumed clearer, more vivid patterns in Turkey than in most other countries. The lines of conflict, the opposing forces, and the sequences of change all have been more sharply drawn in Turkey than elsewhere. Moreover, the entire process has gone further than in most other emerging nations. Indeed, it has long seemed that if effective yet democratic political development can succeed anywhere, it should succeed in Turkey. Nevertheless, Turkey is currently in political trouble. Promise has given way to discouragement, confidence to doubt, cohesion to conflict, and stability to violence and volatility. Close inspection of the modern Turkish experience is thus valuable for discovering potentially general patterns in the process of political development.

The author, who wrote most of this essay while a fellow at the Center for Advanced Study in the Behavioral Sciences, Stanford, California, wishes to express his gratitude to the center and its gracious staff for their help and support.

[1] In 1967, for example, about 45 percent of all Soviet merchant marine traffic passed through the Turkish straits, in addition to some 240 Soviet warships. Harry N. Howard, "Turkey: A Contemporary Survey," *Current History,* vol. 56, no. 331 (March 1969), p. 145.

Until quite recently, Turkish politics have been, for all major purposes, *elite* politics. As in most other developing societies, the political drama was limited to elite actors, elite institutions, and elite urban settings. Mass elements were excluded by the nature of the culture, the distribution of resources, and the design of the rulers. Thus until two decades ago an analysis of political elites in Turkey took one a long way toward comprehending most of the meaningful political activities in the society. And even now, the main impact of the entry of mass elements into political life has been the change produced in elite interactions, as we shall see. It therefore is still possible to analyze much of the thrust of Turkish politics by focusing on the political elite—although this perspective will probably become increasingly inadequate in the future.

Most analyses of Turkish politics have been general and impressionistic. This essay cannot transcend that limitation. Where convincing empirical evidence is available we shall use it, of course; but the basic research needed for fairly definitive conclusions has not been done in most of the areas under discussion here. It should also be noted that many methodological problems still plague elite studies—especially problems of locating and measuring power relations so that one has confidence that the putative political elite actually does wield the disproportionate real power ascribed to it.[2] These problems, too, cannot be resolved in the present essay. Therefore, the analysis that follows is put forth as a tentative interpretation rather than a definitive summation, more indicative of broad outlines and basic trends than authoritative on particulars.

As a final cautionary note, I should point out that even when one discusses a political elite rather than elites in general, the topic is still enormous. The treatment must be highly selective, dealing only with certain aspects of certain elements within the political elite rather than with all aspects of all elements. It is important that this limitation also be recognized.

After a glance at the Ottoman political legacy to the republican Turks, I shall briefly sketch the history of elite politics in Turkey from about 1920 to the present in order to provide a context for the analyses and comments which follow. Then I shall examine the social backgrounds of the parliamentary elite and its important subdivisions. Next I shall describe several key aspects of elite political culture in Turkey. This much neglected topic can only be treated subjectively; nevertheless, it pervades all issues so profoundly that even a tentative analysis seems essential. And, finally, I shall look at some of the more critical elite-mass linkages in Turkish society, namely, the administrative control system, the link between the internal affairs bureaucracy and village leadership, and the link that is supposed to be most vital of all, the electoral process. These phenomena are usually neglected in elite studies, which typically describe internal elite characteristics but present no analysis of elite connections with other subelite and nonelite segments of the society. To understand any political elite even in outline, the nature of its contacts with other sectors of the society must be at least generally understood.

---

[2] See, for example, Frederick W. Frey, "The Determination and Location of Elites: A Critical Analysis" (Paper presented to the annual meeting of the American Political Science Association, Los Angeles, California, September 1970).

Political Elites in the Turkish Republics

The Political Legacy of the Ottomans. The Kemalists who forged the Republic of Turkey clinched elite modernization in their society, but they did not start it. Its roots go back at least two centuries into the Ottoman past. Awareness of the main legacies of the Ottoman system is essential for understanding the contemporary situation. For instance, many of the situations and problems confronted today developed in earlier eras. Institutions occupying the scene today were shaped in previous epochs, and the political culture of today is in many respects the product of older events and experiences. Indeed, one of the most salient questions we shall ask is whether and to what extent the new Turkish political elite really differs from the old Ottoman ruling group. Thus, a quick survey of the essential political legacies of the Ottoman Empire is required.

Structure and institutions. One of the central problems of Turkish politics is and long has been the problem of elitism. By this term I mean the tendency of a small privileged sector to dominate society and, consciously or unconsciously, to regard its domination as legitimate and desirable because of the cultural or intellectual inadequacy it attributes to nonelite elements. The elite may be primarily self-serving or may use its power for the welfare of the masses, but the critical ingredients of an elitist situation are (1) that the elite actually wields highly disproportionate power, and (2) that fundamentally it feels justified in so doing because of a durable, culturally-based disrespect for the capacities of nonelite elements. Naturally, such tendencies derive from or are strongly reinforced by a reluctance to lose keenly valued elite benefits. These benefits are often material, but sometimes the principal benefit is prestige. At the very least, however, the benefits depend on and confer power. Hence, the one value that such an elite is most loath to surrender is its power, its dominant position in the society.

Perhaps the paramount political characteristic of Ottoman society was its elitist nature. As Serif Mardin has noted, "If there is such a thing as a simple dichotomy between the elite and the mass, or between the 'great tradition' and the 'little tradition,' no social structure seems to reflect it better than that of the Ottoman Empire." [3] Virtually all other analysts concur. Roderic H. Davison, for example, observes that "there always has been an elite in one form or another [in Ottoman and Turkish society]. It has been the ruling element and the moving element throughout Turkish history. . . . Without the ruling group, Turkish history is inexplicable." [4]

In other words, despite manifest structural changes and fluctuations within Ottoman society over the years, and despite even deeper alterations under the two Turkish republics, one of the basic and most enduring patterns is a strong tendency toward elitism. Both structural and cultural factors press the Turkish political system heavily in this direction. As we shall see, perhaps Turkey's central political problem at present is how to deal with these strong residual tendencies

---

[3] Serif Mardin, "Opposition and Control in Turkey," *Government and Opposition,* vol. 1, no. 3 (May 1966), p. 382.

[4] Roderic H. Davison, *Turkey* (Englewood Cliffs, N.J.: Prentice-Hall, Spectrum Books, 1968), pp. 8–9.

toward elitism in the face of much newer but comparably strong pressures toward structural and cultural pluralism.[5]

Throughout most of the Ottoman period, the composition of the political elite ("ruling group") was remarkably consistent. Four major institutions occupied the heights of power. These were the military, the bureaucracy, the religious institution, and the court. Near the middle of the nineteenth century it was possible to represent these (in English) as "the four S's": the *sultan* (emperor), the *serasker* (leader of the military arm, or *seyfiye*), the *sadrazam* (grand vizir, head of the administration, or *kalemiye*), and the *seyülislam* (chief mufti, head of the religio-judicial institution, or *ilmiye*).[6] These institutions dominated the political system, insofar as it was centrally controlled at all. At various times one or another would rise or decline, but at all times each had to take the others profoundly into account.

At certain periods in Ottoman history these four dominant institutions were joined by more limited and specialized groups of importance. In the seventeenth, eighteenth, and early nineteenth centuries, for example, the local notables *(ayan)* and valley lords *(derebey)* constituted such a group. Sultan Mahmud II ultimately broke their most conspicuous power in the early nineteenth century, although significant vestiges remain regionally important today. In the waning days of the empire, during the latter half of the nineteenth and the first years of the twentieth century, an influential intelligentsia emerged. It has exerted conspicuous power throughout the republican era, first as a key element of the modernizing coalition and now as a political factor of uncertain unity and direction, but of indubitable influence.

The third echelon of the Ottoman power structure consisted of nonelite elements that gained sporadic or limited power either through their formal position in society or through strategic informal location. Examples of the former were the leaders of the main religious nationalities *(millet),* the tribes *(asiret),* and the guilds *(esnaf),* who played sometimes telling but local or limited roles. Among the latter were the Istanbul mob and the religious school *(medrese)* students *(softa),* who were mobilized as a political force on occasion, usually by the local clergy *(imams).* At the bottom of the heap, of course, came the mass of the peasantry, with the Muslim Turk of Anatolia ordinarily lowest of all.

The requirements for elite status were essentially educational and institutional. To enter the ruling group one needed to "know the Ottoman way"—that is, to have mastered the hybrid language and style of the Ottomans. This usually required education, either in one of the schools of the four main institutions (and it is revealing that each of them had schools) or else through tutoring and the cultural osmosis provided by a privileged family background. One also needed institutional position. Each of the four main institutions of the ruling elite was itself divided into

[5] I do not much like the terms "elitism" and "pluralism" because of their vagueness and evaluative overtones, but there are no ready substitutes. Here I mean by "pluralism" simply a situation in which formerly nonelite elements share in power and, although there may be a contest over each actor's appropriate degree of power, there is acceptance of his claim to a role that is at least significant. For some reservations about the use of the term "elitist," see Frederick W. Frey, "Comment: On Issues and Nonissues in the Study of Power, *American Political Science Review,* vol. 69, no. 4 (December 1971), pp. 1081–82.

[6] See Avigdor Levy, "The Ottoman Ulema and the Military Reforms of Sultan Mahmud II," *Asian and African Studies,* vol. 7 (1971), p. 31.

two groups, the controlling few and their largely inconsequential followers. Not every soldier, every *imam,* every petty official *(küçük memur),* or even every courtier was personally a member of the ruling group; only those at the helms of the grand institutions really qualified. Once in the institution, low birth was not a major hindrance to mobility, although a prestigious family background generally helped. The route to personal power, however, was definitely through institutional position.

Along with elitism, then, some other fundamental Ottoman legacies to contemporary Turkey were a political system in which the four main institutions traditionally wielded power. All of these institutions reflected the *state* in various aspects. No bourgeoisie, hereditary landed aristocracy, or nongovernmental clergy existed as an independent source of power. Even the religious institution, which might superficially seem an exception, was thoroughly involved with government, performing essential judicial, bureaucratic, and educational functions during most of the Ottoman epoch. Thus, the state dominated society, and the four main institutions basically constituted the state. Politics, power, and most of national (as opposed to local) life revolved about the state. What restrained the political elites in their quest for power was more a common loyalty to the state, an awareness of their mutuality of fortune, the power of competitive actors, and the limitations of their own resources, rather than notions of rights inhering in various parties or the illegitimacy of certain political means.

From the eighteenth century on, but most conspicuously in the nineteenth and early twentieth centuries, two distinct groups emerged within the ruling elite, differentiated by their reactions to the inescapable evidence of imperial decline. One group is usually referred to as the "modernizers," "Westernizers," or "reformers." It consisted mainly of younger officers who were products of the new Western type of military schools, bureaucrats who had relatively modern educations and who frequently had diplomatic contact with the West, and some members of the intelligentsia. Much of the history of Ottoman modernization lies in the gradual production of enough of these "new Turks" to provide each other with personal security and psychic reinforcement and then to secure control over crucial segments of two main institutions, the military and the bureaucracy. For this group, the answer to Ottoman debility was modernization—beating the European powers at their own game.

Although lines were often blurred, the opposing camp consisted of a coalition of "traditionalists." For much of the period, the "spearhead" of the resistance to modernization was the traditional contingent within the military, that is, the janissaries and the lower reaches of other military units. Hence, while some results of the destruction of the Janissary Corps in 1826 were quite superficial, its elimination was a major advance for modernization in the Ottoman state.

Even more influential in the traditionalist cause, however, were the clergy. "The main driving force behind the opposition were the *ulema,*" as Avigdor Levy points out.[7] Although the *ulema* were divided, and although an aristocratic element in its leadership sometimes supported specific reforms, in general it furnished the ideological justification for opposition, while the local *imams,* with their capability for

---

[7] Ibid., p. 13.

citing the urban masses, provided the muscle. Moreover, the apparent cooperation of the *ulema* in many specific reform moves often had an eviscerating and enervating effect, subtly depriving them of their progressive content.[8]

In general, then, the last two Ottoman centuries—years of galling defeat for the empire—saw the development of severe intra-elite conflict between modernizing sectors of the military and bureaucracy together with the new intelligentsia on the one hand, and a conservative coalition of the religious institution and other sectors of the military and bureaucracy on the other. The sultan and his court played modernizers and traditionalists off against one another in an attempt to maximize the power and security of the throne. This vital conflict over modernization was still another fundamental legacy left to the Turkish republics by their Ottoman predecessors.

An inspection of structural and institutional aspects of the Ottoman legacy cannot conclude without noting certain features that are often taken for granted. One tends to focus on the most distinctive and perhaps the most troublesome aspects of the Ottoman political system. Elitism, militarism, statism, severe conflict over reform, urbanism, and so on are the features that stand out when we hold the Ottoman system up against a mental template of "normal," "effective," or generally expected political characteristics. Such a view is useful, however, only if one understands its inherent biases. The important point is that other, more positive, and no less important structural characteristics of the Ottoman legacy must not be overlooked. The Ottomans, for example, ruled a potent state for half a millenium and organized what was for at least two hundred years one of the most effective political systems known to man—and in its own way one of the most tolerant and enlightened of its time. The Ottomans developed notable skill at political and military organization and displayed great adaptability, courage, discipline, and endurance. Even in their long decline (and it took a kind of genius to prolong the collapse for so long), they frequently exhibited astute political realism and shrewdness in internal and external political manipulation. They were masters in their own house for centuries, solving the standard problems of statecraft quite effectively and creating durable institutions and structures. The organizational capacity to form and maintain an army, a bureaucracy, or a political party was part of their legacy. This more positive aspect of the Ottoman structural impact on republican Turkey must also be appreciated.

Political culture. The political legacy of the Ottomans to the Turks, however, was not only structural and institutional. The Turkish republic also inherited a political culture that was the psychic starting point from which further political developments have sprung. Hence, it is also useful to examine the preferred strategies and tactics as well as the habitual outlooks and expectations typical of the Ottoman approach to politics. In many respects these are the attitudinal concomitants of the structural characteristics already described.

In the West, the "Turks" (a term that was often used to refer vaguely to Levantines, Arabs, Muslims, or even Persians as well as to the Ottomans) historically had a reputation for cruelty and fearsomeness. This reputation was partly due to the basic human tendency to vilify an opponent; the Ottoman Turks were, after

[8] Ibid., p. 38.

all, a drastic threat to Europe for centuries. Partly it was due to religious conflict and its associated ethnocentrisms, and partly, also, to political expediency—witness Gladstone's oratorical invectives against the Turks as he campaigned against Disraeli over the "Eastern question." In any case, the term "Turk" is one of the few national names to have entered Western dictionaries as an adjective, albeit now archaic, referring to one who is "cruel, hardhearted, or tyrannical." From Shakespeare and Machiavelli on, the West has thought of "the terrible Turk."

One need not accept such prejudicial labeling, however, to observe that a relatively distinctive characteristic of the Ottoman approach to politics (though not of the Ottomans alone, surely) actually was a readiness and facility for the use of force against enemies. Notwithstanding the chivalrous tradition of the *Gazi* warriors and the noble clemency they often showed the compliant vanquished, the Ottomans' greatest expertise for much of their history was in the use of force. On the whole, one forms the impression that force, though latent and implied much of the time, was an appreciably more fundamental part of the uses of power in the Ottoman system than in most others. The Ottomans were relatively less reluctant to use force, had greater skill in its forms, and showed a keener appreciation of its nuances and applications.

Dankwart A. Rustow has remarked that "the Ottoman state . . . was essentially a military camp and an educational institution." [9] Though a deliberate oversimplification, his formulation is particularly useful for present purposes since it brings out two other related aspects of the Ottoman political outlook: it tended to be (1) authoritarian and (2) didactic. As previously indicated, power was mainly wielded by a small ruling group. There were complex reciprocal relations within this group and even some between it and mass elements. The system was by no means an "oriental despotism." But the ruling elite tended in general to act in an arbitrary and self-assured fashion. The special status of the *devsirme* functionaries as personal slaves of the sultan, even while occupying the highest offices of government, was one reflection of this tendency. Another was the institutionalized solution of the succession conflict, first by royal fratricide and then by "caging" prospective heirs (isolating them in the *harem*). The frequent use of confiscation of property, strangulation, exile, and so on also reveals this syndrome.

Of course, all societies contemporaneous with the Ottoman displayed many similar traits. So do our own. The differences are in extent, degree, emphasis, and the amount of self-consciousness. Whether the Ottoman system was actually extreme in these respects is a judgment for which adequate scientific tools are lacking. On balance, however, it seems that it was, and that fact is critically important to an understanding of Turkish political culture today. Although Turkish political culture is not a mere continuation of the Ottoman, it is a product of the Ottoman past and needs to be understood from that perspective.

In the Ottoman system there was a singularly strong nexus between religion and regime. This union of faith and state encouraged an especially potent form of statism. The state became the focus for all important activity, the main measure of all achievement. Loyalty to the state, combining government and religion as it

[9] Dankwart A. Rustow, "Turkey: The Modernity of Tradition," in Lucian W. Pye and Sidney Verba, eds., *Political Culture and Political Development* (Princeton, N.J.: Princeton University Press, 1965), p. 197.

did, became the paramount concern for the ruling group. Conflict with the state was viewed as the severest turpitude and treason. Political opposition was thus easily defined as resistance to both temporal and spiritual authority.[10] A compelling ruler-subject orientation emerged that permitted the rulers to act with great boldness and the society to display great discipline at times, but which also encouraged peremptory, secretive, and even rigid behavior at other moments.

The merging of state and faith, together with the absence of well developed, independent commercial and social interests, funneled almost all significant talent and attention into politics and onto the state (regime and government). The state was the sole determinant of national political life. Politics at this level was a dramatic, risky, often clandestine competition for power in and over the state. A single national arena predominated, rather than several divergent arenas as found in many other systems. Problems were to be solved by the mechanisms and interventions of the state, rather than by more private, decentralized, and immediate means. In the later years of the empire, indeed, the prime problem *was* the state, which further exaggerated this tendency toward state monopoly of attention, talent and power and to perceive state action as the necessary vehicle for solving all serious problems. The state-centeredness of political life was a crucial feature of the Ottoman outlook.

A final aspect of the cultural legacy of the Ottoman Empire for modern Turkey was pride and self-determination. The Ottomans created a great empire with astounding rapidity. They developed great pride in their skill at arms, their courage and dedication, and their confidence. They believed that the deity was on their side, and displayed obvious condescension toward foreigners. The "capitulations," which granted privileges to foreigners in the Ottoman Empire and became such a negative symbol in the empire's dying days, were originally an arrogant and magnanimous Ottoman concession to Europeans. A bone was tossed to the supplicants, only later to become a "bone of contention." The long refusal to send ambassadors to European capitals expressed the same posture of superiority. For such a people, the long imperial decline, obvious foreign interferences, the sobriquet "the sick man of Europe," et cetera, must have been particularly disturbing. They reacted with extreme concern for national dignity and prestige and developed keen sensitivity to foreign opinion and interventions, especially in late Ottoman times. For many Ottoman and Turkish modernizers, these preoccupations were temporarily superseded by the need to borrow from the West and their struggle against the traditionalists. But once the modernizers clinched their position, the resentment built up through years of frustration might have been expected to resurface. In any event, deep concern for national pride, dignity, prestige, and honor constitutes another cardinal feature of the political culture inherited by the Turkish republics.

Situation and problems. When Mustafa Kemal (Ataturk) wangled his assignment as inspector general of the third army, escaped from occupied Istanbul, and landed at Samsun on May 19, 1919, to start the "Turkish Revolution," the situa-

[10] Probably the most graphic and grisly illustration of this was the demise of the progressive Grand Vezir Halil Hamid (1782–1785). Driven from office by the "conservatives" and then killed, a sign was put on his corpse denouncing him as an "enemy of *seriat* (religious law) and state." See Davison, *Turkey*, p. 70.

tion left him by late Ottoman (Young Turk) policies was dismal. Turkey had suffered a costly defeat in World War I, after fighting continuously for about a decade. It had lost all but the Anatolian heart of the empire and a small piece of Thrace. Even Anatolia had been carved up into various spheres of influence and occupation by secret agreements among the Allies. Four days before Kemal's landing at Samsun on the Black Sea coast, the Greeks had invaded Aegean Turkey with the support of Allied naval forces. The "sick man" seemed to be on his death bed.

The problems facing Kemal and the various "Defense of Rights" groups which grew up spontaneously in unoccupied parts of Anatolia were first to save the system from dismemberment, and then to erect some kind of viable structure out of the ashes of the old order. In one respect, the Kemalists had a tremendous advantage. Events had at long last freed them from the incubus of empire. It is possible for political systems to work themselves into self-destructive impasses, and the Ottoman Empire had done so. The crux of the problem was that Ottoman political culture would not permit any leadership to relinquish the empire and retreat to the more viable realm of an Anatolian Turkish nation-state, while conditions in the rest of the world (great power pressures, burgeoning nationalism in subject areas, and so on) would not permit maintenance of the empire. The Ottomans could not hold on and would not let go. Perhaps the only way out of such an impasse was a severe national defeat which indelibly impressed on the Turks the impossibility of maintaining or regaining the empire. They had to be convinced that neither Ottomanism (loyalty to a supposedly multi-ethnic system and its dynasty), pan-Islamism (loyalty to the Muslim religion), nor pan-Turanism (loyalty to Turkic culture) could provide a basis for continued Ottoman hegemony over a diverse collection of peoples. The Balkan and Arab defections and the debacle of World War I finally showed them this, though nearly at the expense of their own sovereign existence.

The culminating defeat, however, raised tremendous problems. Outstanding were three: (1) finding an appropriate national identity, (2) determining a viable political structure compatible with that identity, and (3) resolving the issue of modernization. The essence of the Kemalists' "Angora Reform" is that it solved these three vital problems. The national identity was irreversibly conceived as Anatolian Turkish, the political structure was cast as republican and, more tentatively, as democratic, and the commitment to modernization, at least for the generalized elite, was resolutely made.

Elite Developments in Republican Turkey. The half century of republican Turkey has seen deep transformations in society and politics. In 1919–1920, the Turkish trunk of the once mighty Ottoman Empire was fighting what seemed to be a forlorn "national struggle" to preserve some semblance of sovereign identity. After a brief but very critical period, Mustafa Kemal succeeded in organizing the diverse local resistance units into a more coherent, though still quite heterogeneous, Association for the Defense of Rights of Anatolia and Rumelia (European Turkey). Its antagonists were not only the invading Greeks sent by Premier Eleutherios Venizelos with plans for a "New Ionia" in Aegean Anatolia, but also fellow Turks still loyal to the "captive" Sultan-Caliph (Mehmet VI, Vahdeddin) and his government in Istanbul. Under the truly brilliant leadership of Kemal and his associates, the rebel Association for the Defense of Rights became a national legislature (the Grand National Assembly), legitimizing itself through the doctrine—novel for Turkey—that sovereignty flows from the people. The executive committee of this assembly in turn became a national government, which successfully waged a major war to eject the Greeks and their Allied supporters, and which united the beleaguered remnants of the Ottoman Empire into the Turkish nation.

Having preserved Turkish autonomy, the Kemalists proceeded to dispense first with the sultanate (1922) and then with the other face of monarchy, the caliphate (1924). They constructed a single-party, tutelary government, which tried to drive, prod, lecture, lead, and sometimes even cajole elite segments of Turkish society into that modernity which would guarantee its security and redeem its self-respect. At the same time, the twin themes of democracy and economic development increasingly colored the Kemalist outlook and were imbibed by new generations of Turkish youth, reared under the republican system and publicly assigned the responsibility of being "guardians of the regime."

Mustafa Kemal Ataturk died in 1938, by which time the Kemalist revolution was thoroughly under way in resurgent Turkey. The Kemalist elite was sufficiently united to ensure the peaceful succession of Ataturk's chief lieutenant, Ismet Inönü, who remained the head of state throughout the late Kemalist years, World War II, and the crucial postwar period from 1946 to 1950 when a more democratic multiparty system was established in Turkey. In 1950 the initial acid test of Turkey's move toward democracy was passed when, in the first scrupulously fair and open national election in the history of the republic, the People's party of Ataturk and Inönü was defeated. Resisting pressure to remain in office by force, it honorably relinquished power to the Democratic party of Adnan Menderes and Celal Bayar.

After three or four years of good feeling, political life in Turkey grew increasingly tense and bitter. The necessary political competition between government and opposition began to degenerate into conflict and then into unrestricted warfare. The government claimed obstruction while the opposition charged oppression. It gradually appeared that the Democratic party leaders were pursuing a path that could only lead to a reversal of hard-won democratic progress and a return to authoritarianism. Increasingly stringent press laws were passed and many offending journalists imprisoned. Election laws were altered for partisan advantage. Political pressures were placed on universities and the judiciary. The right to assemble for political purposes was increasingly curtailed.

Violence erupted in the late fifties, and the government began to use the military to put it down. Finally, a one-sided parliamentary commission was established which appeared to have as its objective the abolition of the People's party. Out of such conditions, coupled with severe inflation and other economic difficulties, came the military take-over of 1960, the "gentle coup," a marvelously efficient maneuver which may well have prevented civil war in Turkey, but which ended a unique forty-year period of gradual military withdrawal from politics. The new and tender tradition of military abstention from political interference had now been violated.

The military initially expected their take-over to be brief, but found it necessary to remain in power for more than a year. During this time they convened the

Representative Assembly, which drafted a new constitution. Designed to prevent the great formal concentration of power of the previous constitution, the new document went to the other extreme. It provided for a bicameral legislature, the upper house of which (the Senate) was both elected and appointed. The president of the republic was to be elected by the legislature, but for a seven-year term not coincident with that of the assembly. An independent judiciary, appointed in a complex fashion, was given the power to declare acts of parliament unconstitutional. And, finally, proportional representation rather than a single-member-district system replaced the previous unit-rule list system. The result was a formal structure which seemed to go almost as far toward fragmentation of power as its predecessor had gone toward concentration.

A referendum on the new constitution was held in the summer of 1961, in which it received roughly 60 percent approval. The surprisingly large negative vote was a harbinger of things to come, for it revealed considerable opposition to recent developments—despite the fact that no organized campaign against the constitution was permitted. Furthermore, close analysis of the distribution of negative votes indicated that they followed earlier patterns of regional support for the now outlawed Democratic party. Though the leaders of that party had either been hanged (Premier Menderes and two others) or imprisoned (all other deputies), its support among the electorate, even under adversity, remained surprisingly strong.

A national election under the new constitution was held in October 1961. Under the prevailing conditions, many observers expected a landslide for the People's party. In fact, however, though winning a plurality, they received only about 37 percent of the vote, compared with 35 percent for the not yet fully organized Justice party, which seemed the probable ideological successor to the Democrats. The other party that purported to succeed the Democrats, the New Turkey party, came in third with 14 percent of the vote. Hence, from one perspective, the People's party was actually a minority party.

Turkey was now in a political quandary. If the People's party had won a clear majority, there would have been no problem, for they were acceptable to the military. But the party could not even form a government commanding a parliamentary majority without bringing into a coalition some element tainted by sympathy for the Democratic party. However, there was great uncertainty as to whether the military would permit any Democratic party successor elements to partake of power, for it feared revanchism and still strongly needed to justify its political intervention. The military finally made up its own mind and military pressure helped politicians, after much milling around, to form an improbable coalition of the People's and Justice parties under the premiership of Ismet Inönü. Not surprisingly, this lasted only seven months. It was replaced by a coalition of the People's party and two minor parties, the New Turkey party and the Republican Peasant Nation party. This second coalition government limped along until 1964, while the Justice party made steady gains in local and senatorial elections. It was succeeded in turn by a last-resort coalition of the People's party and some nonaligned independents that lasted until the Justice party mercifully took power shortly before the elections of 1965.

In one sense, the weak coalition period from 1961 to 1965 was an interregnum permitted by an act of self-sacrifice on the part of Inönü and his party. Time was needed to resolve military doubts about the Justice party. Moreover, if the Justice party achieved power, everyone knew it would have to confront the disruptive issue of amnesty for the imprisoned former Democratic party leaders. If the Justice party decided to let them out, it might provoke another military coup. If it did not, it might split its own ranks irremediably. The risks of a Justice party government were thus too great, one way or the other, and so an interregnum was essential to Turkish political stability. Inönü's willingness to assume responsibility for an inevitably weak coalition in times of stress, even though this would be harmful to his party, was critical for the Turkish political system at that time.

The Justice party won a decisive victory in the national elections of 1965, receiving 53 percent of the vote in contrast to but 29 percent for the declining People's party—still, however, clearly the second largest party in the nation. This time the Justice party assumed power under Prime Minister Suleiman Demirel and managed to walk the tightrope between an ever-watchful military and its own potent right wing of hardliners. Between 1965 and 1969, Turkish political life was as open and free as it had ever been. Significant economic development also occurred, which took some of the edge off political conflict. These positive developments, however, were more than offset by three related factors: (1) a sharp increase in ideological tension in Turkish politics, accompanied by (2) growing violence and attraction toward "extra-parliamentary" means of obtaining power, and (3) a marked rise in anti-Americanism, which served to exacerbate conflict and obfuscate many issues. The People's party moved "left of center" while the Justice party was threatened by right-wing defections. Under these disturbing conditions, the general elections of 1969 nevertheless produced another Justice party victory, this time with about 47 percent of the vote against 27 percent for the People's party.

After 1969, electoral failure, organized political agitation, international events, and other factors to be discussed later combined to stimulate both left- and right-wing violence in Turkey. The Demirel government's response was, on the whole, consistently moderate—in fact, too much so for the military, who felt that things were again getting out of hand. In March 1971, the military issued an ultimatum that effectively deposed the Demirel government, replacing it with a neutral administration led by technocrats. Nihat Erim, a relatively conservative People's party parliamentary deputy and a former university professor, resigned his party membership to become premier. In the cabinet with him were five Justice party deputies, two from the People's party, one from the Reliance party (which split off from the People's party in 1967), and fourteen nonpartisan technocrats.

This arrangement lasted for about one year. Caught between the military and the politicians, Erim resigned in April 1972. He was replaced by Ferit Melen, defense minister and an old-time People's party deputy who had switched to the Reliance party in 1967 along with others from the more local and conservative People's party leadership. Just prior to Erim's resignation, the military, through President Cevdet Sunay, a former chief of the Turkish General Staff, asked for constitutional power to permit the government to avoid parliament and rule by decree, accusing the politicians of "bad habits, bad behavior and obstructionism." Despite indirect military intervention for over a year, he maintained that the economic and social reforms the military had demanded had not been carried out.

The political parties, however, were able to resist rule by decree and the military's position grew increasingly awkward. Basically, the armed forces apparently did not wish to or did not feel capable of completely taking over the government without regard for democratic procedures. They therefore had to depend on a significant degree of cooperation from the parties and politicians, who grew steadily more restive under military interference. Moreover, the military's harsh pursuit of what they regarded as disruptive elements and leftists led to the imposition of martial law in many parts of the country, imprisonment of thousands of suspects, and even torture and several dozen deaths. To many of Turkey's convinced democrats and intellectuals the nation seemed only to have shed one kind of terrorism and lawlessness for another.

Throughout this interregnum, as during that of a decade earlier, it was generally assumed that elections would be held as soon as some kind of "order" had been restored. The fundamental and legitimate political structure of the nation was still overwhelmingly presumed to be democratic. The force of this presumption, cleverly directed pressures from the political parties, and elite aversion to military excesses finally led to the announcement that new general elections would be held in the fall of 1973. The military also was rebuked when the Grand National Assembly rejected a candidate for president of the republic whom the military had put forward and when an apparent attempt by the military to place military men in the most prominent political parties similarly failed.

The election of October 14, 1973, revealed further fragmentation of Turkey's political party system. Eight parties competed, none receiving more than one-third of the vote. The People's party rose from a nadir of 27 percent in 1969 to 33 percent, becoming the largest party. The Justice party, beset by splintering, obtained only 30 percent of the vote, many of its former supporters having moved to the new Democratic party (12 percent) and to the National Salvation party (12 percent). Of the remaining parties, each secured less than 6 percent of the valid votes cast.

With such fragmentation, no government could be organized until more than three months after the election. Finally, the left-of-center People's party and the reformist but extremely religious National Salvation party formed an improbable government under People's party leader Bulent Ecevit. Before the clear contradictions in policy between these two governmental parties could surface, the Cyprus crisis broke and Turkey achieved a temporary unity in response. Following Turkey's military success and resistance to external pressures, Ecevit's popularity became extremely high. He appeared to want to take advantage of the situation to increase his party's parliamentary position by holding new elections as quickly as possible. This prospect was unpopular with many politicians who had just been through a strenuous campaign and who did not relish the idea of the People's party profiting from the crisis.

Whether prompted by Ecevit or by the National Salvation party, the dubious governing coalition disintegrated in mid-September 1974. Once again a governmental crisis ensued in which no government could be formed. In mid-November a caretaker cabinet of technocrats and a few politicians from the small Republican

Reliance party formed a government under an independent senator, Sadi Irmak, but it did not obtain a vote of confidence from the Assembly.[11]

All in all, the contrast between the instability and weakness of the past fifteen years and the unity and leadership of the preceding thirty-five years is striking, to say the least. Foremost among the questions provoked by these events is whether Turkey is merely experiencing the unavoidable growing pains of political transition or whether there is something fundamentally amiss in the nation's political structure or culture.

The Social Backgrounds of the Parliamentary Elite

An important perspective on political dynamics in republican Turkey is provided by analysis of the social backgrounds of the parliamentary elite. This group is of special interest because for the past fifty years the main forum for Turkish politics has been the national legislature—the Grand National Assembly. It included the leading politicians of the country and was the main arena in which they interacted. During the First Republic (1923–1960), the unicameral Assembly elected the president of the republic. The president then appointed the prime minister who, in turn, designated the rest of the cabinet from among the deputies. Thus, all offices from the president on down were normally held by deputies to the Assembly.

In the current Second Republic (1961–), the president is elected jointly by both houses of the now bicameral Assembly from among their own members, though he resigns any party affiliation upon being elected. The prime minister is appointed by the president, whose role in this matter is rather similar to that of the monarch in the British system. Cabinet officials are selected by the prime minister and do not have to be deputies, but most are. All these proceedings are, of course, basically shaped by the political parties' relative strength in the Assembly, particularly in the lower house. Although the situation is more diffuse under the Second Republic than under the First, it is still fair to say that the prime focus of national political life and leadership is the Grand National Assembly.

Main political stages of the republican era. Familiarity with the major stages in the development of political life in republican Turkey will help in interpreting the social background data to follow. The major stages are these:

1920–1923, the first Grand National Assembly. This was a *régime d'assemblée,* a heterogeneous, divisive, cantankerous collection of individuals elected under procedures that Mustafa Kemal had been unable to control. Only Kemal's determined leadership and a common hostility to occupation held them together; but interestingly enough, many developments of later years were portended during this period.

1923–1938, the Ataturk era. During this period the solid Kemalist phalanx was formed and single-party leadership reached its height. The landmark reforms—from the proclamation of the Republic, abolition of the Caliphate, and establishment of the Constitution of 1924, through suppression of the

[11] As of this writing, Suleiman Demirel had just formed a coalition government.

dervish orders and secularization of law, to language reforms, women's suffrage, and compulsory adoption of family names—were all pushed through.

1938–1946, the Inönü era. This was the late single-party period, interrupted by World War II. The new forces stirring in the land were first heeded within the continuing tutelary framework.

1946–1950, the transition to a multiparty system. This was a crucial watershed in which a more open, democratic system was clearly introduced, even though the People's party remained in power. The new lines of competitive cleavage became much more apparent.

1950–1960, the democratic era. For the first time in the history of the republic, power was democratically transferred to an opposition party. A new and fundamentally different regime was established. It operated successfully for a few years, and then fell victim to partisan excesses and increasing authoritarianism. The military coup of May 27, 1960, terminated the First Turkish Republic.

1960–1961, the military coup and interregnum. The National Unity Committee of military officers took over the government, imprisoned and tried former Democratic party leaders, and formed the Representative Assembly, which drafted a new constitution. Fourteen younger officers within the unity committee who wanted the military to remain in power for a long period were defeated by the more moderate members, but their opposition revealed divisions and political ambitions within the military.

1961–1965, the era of weak coalitions. The Second Turkish Republic began with a disturbing 40 percent vote against the new constitution and with the failure of the People's party to gain a majority in the Assembly. Three weak coalitions followed. The tension between the military and the Justice party prevented a more rational arrangement until just before the 1965 elections. Two abortive military coups were attempted by Colonel Talat Aydemir, commandant of the War College, with support from his cadets.

1965–1971, the Justice party era. The Justice party won a strong victory in 1965 and a reduced victory in 1969, under the leadership of Suleiman Demirel. It followed a seemingly moderate course amidst increasing ideological polarization, anti-Americanism, and violence from left and right extremes. Disillusionment with these developments and perhaps even with the electoral process upset many intellectuals and, apparently, the military, who issued an ultimatum deposing the Demirel government in March 1971.

1971–1973, the second military intervention. A government of technocrats and tame politicians acceptable to the military ostensibly attempted to eliminate violence and enact reforms. Martial law was proclaimed in many areas, houses searched, thousands imprisoned, and dozens tortured and killed in a widespread military effort to root out presumed subversives. Since the military declined to make, or realized they were incapable of, a full and lasting governmental take-over, they were dependent on cooperation from the parties, who cleverly used this leverage and an increasingly alienated public opinion to pry the military away from its second major intervention in the political life of the republic.

1973 to the present, the second era of weak coalitions. After the general election of October 1973, none of the eight political parties held a commanding position. Following three months of attempts to form a government, an unlikely coalition of the People's party and the National Salvation party was established with People's party leader Bulent Ecevit at the helm. The Cyprus crisis and Turkish successes led to increased popularity for Ecevit, who resigned to capitalize on the situation and obtain a stronger governing group. The other parties, however, were able to forestall new elections and another political crisis ensued, with no party or coalition able to form a government. The crisis remains unresolved as of this writing.

Occupational and educational characteristics.[12] The major occupational and educational characteristics of the deputies are summarized in Figure 1. Several key observations can be made immediately. The distinction between the single-party and multiparty periods is vividly revealed by changes in the occupational backgrounds of the deputies. During the single-party era the "officials" (military men, bureaucrats, and teachers, all agents of the state) were the largest contingent in the Assembly. During the multiparty period the "professionals" (doctors, engineers, and especially lawyers) became the largest occupational group. The "economic" element, consisting of businessmen, merchants, traders, bankers, and a few agriculturists, also improved its position slightly in this period. In short, the fundamental change in the structure of the political system was accompanied by a no less fundamental change in the social backgrounds of the personnel. As the system moved from a structural emphasis on tutelary control to a more open and competitive system, the specialists in force and administration declined while the lawyers and other professionals—specialists in advocacy and technology—increased. As the polity took on the institutional characteristics of the West, its personnel also came to resemble that of the Western systems.

Additional items of interest from Figure 3–1 illustrate the single-party period. It is especially revealing to look at deviations from the basic curve and at points of inflection, when the slope of the curve changes. Take the "official" group, for example. There are three points when the representation of the "official" element is comparatively low: the First Assembly, the Fourth Assembly, and the Eighth Assembly. These deviations fit a clear pattern. The First Assembly was pre-Kemalist. The elections took place before the People's party had been founded

[12] A much fuller treatment of the social background characteristics of deputies during the First Republic is presented in Frederick W. Frey, *The Turkish Political Elite* (Cambridge, Mass.: M.I.T. Press, 1965). In several portions of this essay the author has drawn extensively on this larger work. The data for the Second Republic are calculations which the author made from Frank Tachau's article, "The Anatomy of Political and Social Change: Turkish Parties, Parliaments, and Elections," *Comparative Politics,* vol. 5 (1973), pp. 551–73. Since his coding scheme and the author's were somewhat different (he permitted multiple classification of an individual while the author did not), the percentages for the Second Republic given here had to be estimates and extrapolations. However, they should not be more than a few percentage points in error at worst, compared to what would have been obtained if the original coding scheme had been used throughout. The author is grateful to Professor Tachau for permitting him to see an advance copy of his article and happily exonerates him from any responsibility for the further kneading of his data.

Figure 3–1

EDUCATIONAL AND OCCUPATIONAL BACKGROUNDS OF TURKISH DEPUTIES, 1920–1970

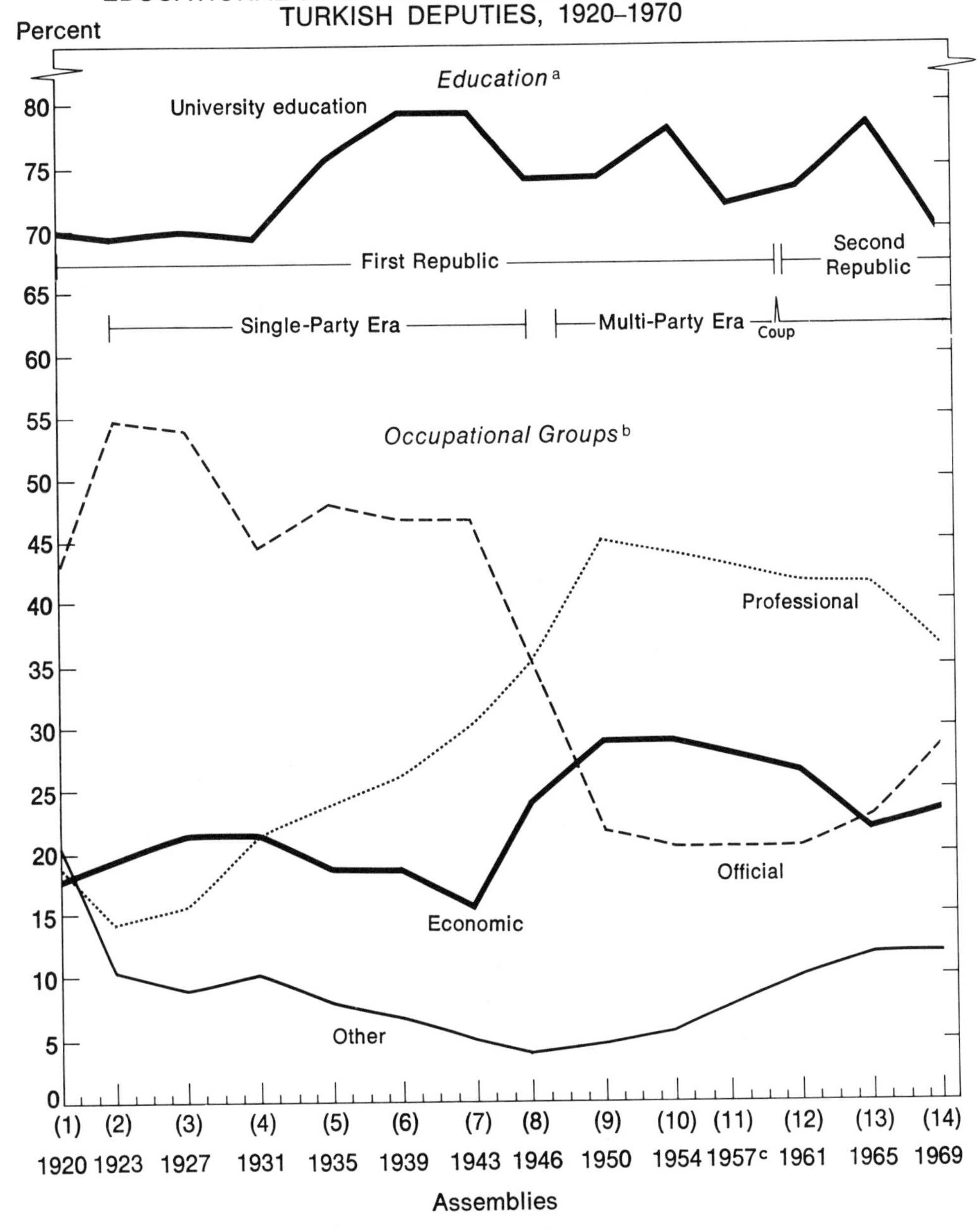

[a] Percentage of deputies with university-level education.

[b] Percentage of deputies in each of four occupational groups: official (military, bureaucrats, and teachers), professional (lawyers, doctors, engineers, et cetera), economic (business, commerce, trade, and agriculture), and "other" (religion, journalism, et cetera). For full description of categories, see Frey, *The Turkish Political Elite,* pp. 78–79.

[c] Data for the occupational groups in 1957 are lacking, and the lines drawn are merely interpolations connecting 1954 and 1961.

Source: See note 12, page 56.

and before strong Kemalist control over selection to the Assembly had been established. In some ways, therefore, the First Assembly was a much better reflection of the distribution of political orientations in the country than subsequent parliaments, though even it was not a truly accurate mirror. One particularly intriguing component of the First Assembly is buried in the "other" group: most of this group—17 percent out of 21 percent—consisted of religious personnel. Next to the bureaucrats, they were the largest specific occupational contingent in the Assembly, a most significant vestige of the Ottoman power structure.

But what happened to those occupational groups in the Second Assembly, which was elected when Kemal and his associates controlled nomination and election to parliament? Virtually the entire religious element was weeded out, dropping from 17 percent to less than 1 percent! The professional group was also pruned, though less severely. Conversely, the "official" element in the Assembly, already high, rose sharply to become an absolute majority (this despite the fact that the classification scheme employed here is deliberately conservative in assigning people to that category). Thus, the Kemalist legislative phalanx that pushed through the great reforms of the twenties and early thirties was predominantly composed of former officers and officials, the same group that had been the institutional core of the modernizing coalition throughout Turkish history.

"Official" representation declined in the Fourth and Eighth Assemblies of the single-party period of People's party control. Both cases are most instructive. The drop in the Fourth Assembly occurred after Kemal had been forced to put down the second attempt to form an opposition party within the single-party years, namely, the Liberal Republican party. The Progressive Republican party of 1924 had been the first attempt at partisan competition. It included a number of very prestigious military officers and intellectuals, and thus seemed to pose a real threat at the highest level to Kemalist control, resulting in its suppression. By contrast, the Liberal party of 1930 was stacked with staunch Kemalists at the top, most visibly Kemal's boyhood friend, Fethi Okyar, and his sister, Makbule. But the party attracted surprising and alarming enthusiasm from "reactionary" quarters of the public, and it, too, had to be terminated. As partial recompense, a few dozen deputyships to the Fourth Assembly were left open for popular nominations and an attempt was made to respond to popular forces by including a few deputies of different background. These minor efforts are reflected in the occupational profile by a slight drop in the percentage of "officials" and a relative rise in the number of "professionals" and "others."

Essentially the same tendencies were displayed in the Eighth Assembly, after the slightly tainted but relatively open election of 1946. An acute decline occurred in the representation of "officials," and there were correspondingly marked rises in the percentage of "professional" and "economic" deputies. The essential point is that, as social background data in other countries often indicate, "the dam leaked before it burst." A latent "professional" and "economic" counterelite to the Kemalists could be perceived long before it burst onto the scene as the Democratic party. In fact, the Kemalists themselves seem to have seen this, as is shown by the representational adjustments they made in the Fourth Assembly and in other modifications in the Sixth and Seventh Assemblies not described here. The alterations in the social composition of the political elite that were to occur in the multiparty period were presaged in the single-party era by minor deviations from dominant patterns.

The educational characteristics of these politicians are also revealing. In contrast to the striking fluctuations in occupational backgrounds, the deputies' level of education remained uniformly high. Over the fifty-year period of both republics, roughly 70 to 80 percent of the deputies were university educated—this in a country where approximately the same proportion of the population was illiterate! Education, clearly, was the hallmark of the elite.

Localism. Figure 3–2 shows the percentage of deputies born in the constituencies (provinces) they represented. There has never been any legal requirement that a deputy live in his constituency, let alone have been born there. Rather, the representational philosophy in Turkey has always been Burkean—that each deputy represents the nation rather than a specific geographic constituency. Thus, the incidence of deputies born in their constituencies seems to reflect quite well the tendencies toward "localism," that is, having deep roots in the constituency and commitment to its interests and views.

In the First Assembly, the incidence of "localism" was high. Over three-fifths of all deputies had been born in the provinces they represented. With the Kemalist consolidation of power, however, localism declined rather precipitously, reaching a nadir of 34 percent in the Fifth Assembly, during which Ataturk died. In the Inönü era it rose somewhat and then sharply accelerated with the advent of the multiparty system. That rise was interrupted in the Thirteenth Assembly, when a secure victory was gained by the Justice party. But in the Fourteenth Assembly, "localism" climbed to a new high. Over three-quarters of all deputies were born in the provinces they represented. A major consequence of competitive party politics has apparently been strong pressure toward greater representation of local interests among elected political leaders.

These main social background characteristics, along with others not discussed here (such as knowledge of foreign languages, age, reelection rates, first election at a by-election, and so on) expose a major aspect of Turkish political life. The Kemalist revolution was both the continuation and the culmination of Turkey's historic struggle over elite modernization. It resulted in the victory of the modernizers and effective general modernization of the national elite. Ataturk brilliantly undermined the strongest institutional resistance to elite modernization, namely, the religious institution. This was carried out in a tactical masterpiece of moves. Always careful to maintain crucial military support and always carrying sufficient bureaucrats and intellectuals with him, he abolished the caliphate, outlawed the dervish orders, proscribed the wearing of religious garb outside mosques, and terminated the *Seyülislam* in favor of a Directorate of Religious Affairs under the prime ministry. Above all, he removed education from religious control and cut off the younger generation's easy contact with traditional inspiration by replacing the Arabic script in which Turkish had previously been written with the Roman script. All in all, it was a brilliant job of extirpating institutionalized religious influence to clear the way for modernization.

Awareness of the basic power patterns within the Ottoman ruling elite helps explain the relative celerity of Turkish modernization in the Ataturk era. The

Figure 3–2

PERCENTAGE OF TURKISH DEPUTIES
BORN IN THE PROVINCE
THEY REPRESENTED ("LOCALISM"), 1920–1970

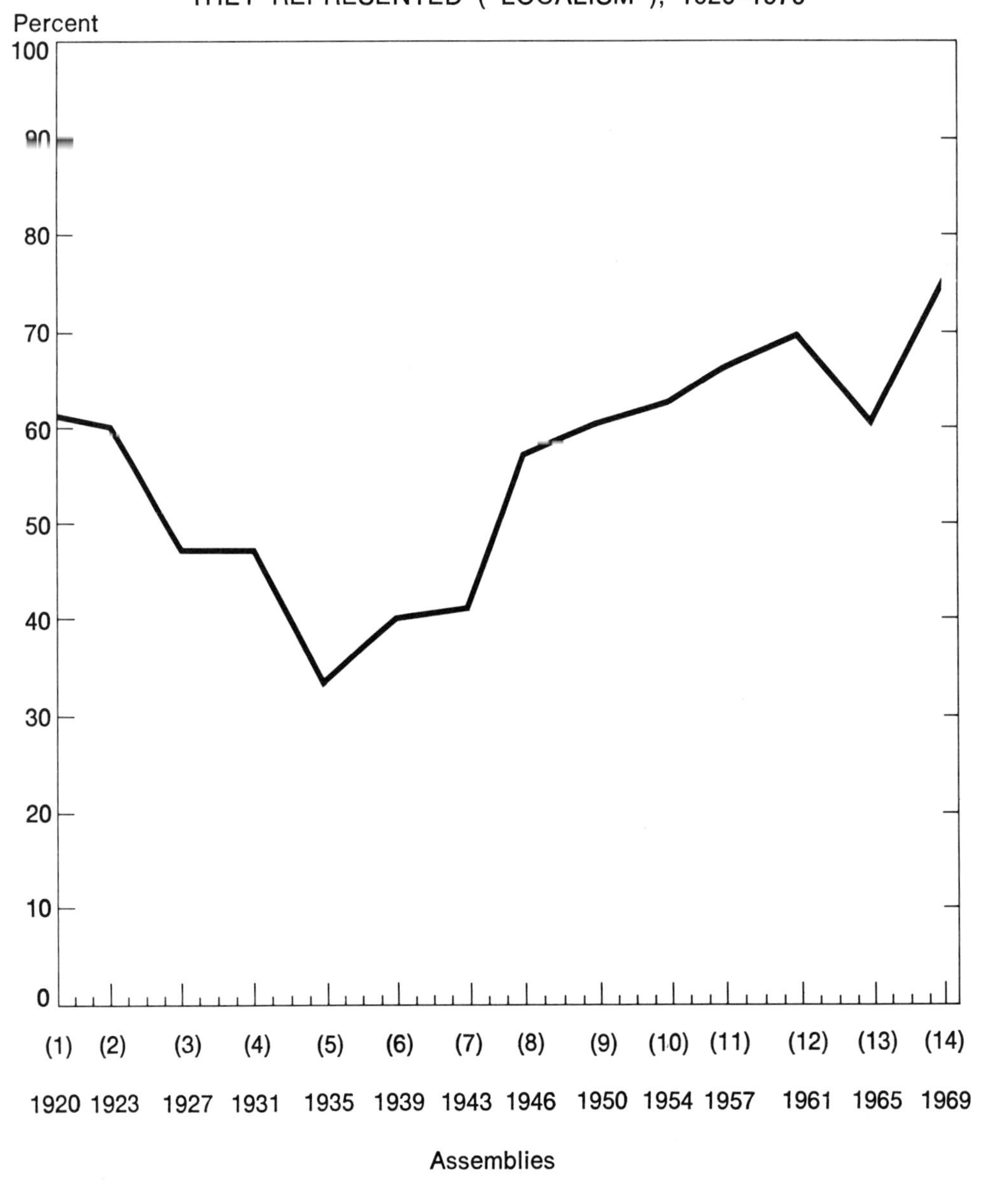

modernizers were extremely well placed in the uppermost levels of the power structure. Having gradually won control over the lower and middle levels of the officers corps and the national bureaucracy in the long years of struggle over modernization, they had mainly to vanquish the traditional elements of the religious institution and consolidate control over the upper reaches of officialdom. This the Kemalists accomplished, ending the bitter intra-elite conflict that had plagued the late Ottoman Empire. The modernizers had finally won at the elite level, and the new Turkish nation experienced about thirty years (1923–53) of apparent stability and harmony as a result.

National elite and local notables. Three criteria seem to have counted most in the selection and retention of deputies during the single-party period. In order of importance, as inferred from reelection rates (being reelected more often) and from election under preferred conditions (such as, at a by-election), these were: higher education, official occupation, and the possession of important local influence. A few deputies satisfying all three of these criteria were most preferred of all, but the majority clustered into two subgroups. One consisted of deputies possessing intellectual and official status, while the other consisted of deputies with primarily provincial and local connections. The former group was more national, international, reformist, secular, cosmopolitan, and statist in its orientation, while the latter was more local, traditional, parochial, conservative, and pluralistic.

An alliance between these two groups made eminent sense. Both had much to gain and little to lose. The national elite occupied the central institutions of power and control, the military and the bureaucracy. However, its apparatus was often weak outside the main urban centers. It needed support at the grass-roots level and found it through the local notables. These were persons of great sway in their local areas, wielding influence based on landowning, tribal position, familial prestige, and so on. The two groups, national elite and local notables, converged in the People's party. By allying themselves with the increasingly potent government, the notables added bureaucratic influence and urban connections to their other sources of power, while the national elite found its new grass-roots connections politically and administratively very valuable. Since the Kemalist revolution concentrated on urban elite modernization, leaving the rural sector largely unaffected, no pronounced conflict of interest between the two groups emerged during most of the single-party era.

Like many successful regimes, however, the Kemalists were overtaken by their own achievements. Their educational and cultural reforms produced fundamental alterations in the general Turkish elite. Ever watchful on one flank for signs of religious revival, they failed to appreciate the significance of an alternative elite developing on their other flank. This was the cadre of free professionals and businessmen whose rise was charted in Figure 1. This new alternative elite was as fully committed to most aspects of modernization as the officers and officials of the Kemalist group, and just as highly educated. Kemalist doctrine had led them to expect to be taken into the halls of power. Instead, they were excluded—or were incorporated far too little and too late. Bitterness resulted, producing an inclination toward organized resistance rather than individual cooptation. The clash was aggravated by the one critical social background difference between the two groups: the alternative elite was much less official in its orientation than the Kemalists. In fact, its leadership included many who chafed under the decided state-centeredness of the Kemalist system. Rigidities and abuses to justify their opposition were easy to find. From such basic elements grew the resurrection of virulent intra-elite conflict in Turkey that later shattered the bright prospects for smooth political development.

Elites within the elite. The preceding analysis is reinforced by close scrutiny of the distribution of power and position within the parliamentary elite. Ratings by a panel of informed specialists were used to assess the relative power associated with the formal offices of the Assembly during the First Turkish Republic.[13] Separate ratings were obtained for each of four periods: the First Assembly, the Ataturk era, the Inönü era, and the Democratic era. Interesting differences in the structure and influence of these top formal positions of the government and Assembly were discovered, but underneath the differences a consistent basic pattern emerged. During most of the First Turkish Republic, national elective leadership formally exhibited eight distinct levels of power. These were as follows:

> Level 1. This was the "pinnacle post" of Turkish politics, formed by a single individual's simultaneously holding the two posts of leader of the dominant political party and head of state (president) or government (prime minister). Leadership of the party seems to have been the more dynamic office.
>
> Level 2. This was a less stable "chief lieutenant's post," occupied by the man who held simultaneously the second highest positions in both party and government. Under the multiparty system the leader of the main opposition party was also placed at this level.
>
> Level 3. A "sublieutenant's level," it was usually occupied by the two people who were, respectively, general secretary of the People's party and president (speaker) of the Grand National Assembly. At this level the party and governmental officeholding usually began to diverge.
>
> Level 4. This was the "top ministerial echelon," comprising the ministries of finance, foreign affairs, interior, and defense. The relative importance of these within the grouping varied quite significantly from era to era. In general, the period as a whole saw the rise of the finance ministry and the decline of the interior ministry, as economic development began to outweigh administrative control.
>
> Level 5. Composed of most of the remaining ministries and some of the leading posts in the parliamentary groups of the parties, this was the "ordinary ministerial level."
>
> Level 6. What might be called the "weak ministerial level," this consisted of the least prestigious ministerial positions, such as customs and monopolies or transportation, as well as a few party and Assembly positions.
>
> Level 7. The intermediate party and Assembly positions constituted this level.
>
> Level 8. This comprised minor party and Assembly positions, shading off into the ordinary backbench.

Unfortunately, no comparable study of the Second Republic has yet been attempted.

[13] See Frey, *Turkish Political Elite,* chap. 9.

Ratings of these offices, along with similar ratings of the power of all parliamentary committees, were used to compute a formal power score for each deputy. On the basis of these scores, deputies were classified into four leadership groups: top leaders, middle leaders, backbenchers, and inconsequentials. Within the top leadership group, cabinet officers were distinguished from less important top leaders.

The findings from these analyses were quite consistent. Top leaders tended to enter the Assembly at a younger age than middle leaders, who, in turn, were younger than the backbenchers on first election. In terms of average age at any given moment, however, the middle leaders were younger than either the top leaders or the backbenchers. The middle leadership seemed to be a transitional group, from which deputies either went on to top leadership status or fell back into the body of backbenchers. Deviant voting behavior was more likely to come from the middle leader ranks than from either of the other two groups.

The three leadership levels were markedly different from one another in formal education. Top and middle leaders were conspicuously better educated than backbenchers. As in the more general analysis summarized in Figure 3–1, occupational patterns varied widely and revealingly across leadership levels, while educational patterns remained relatively stable. The "officials" were most concentrated in the top leadership echelon until the Democratic victory in 1950. Thereafter, "professionals" replaced "officials" as the most disproportionately powerful group in positional terms. Lawyers led the rise of the "professional," while military men suffered the severest losses in the decline of the "officials." The "economic" contingent increased its overall representation, as we have seen, but failed to penetrate the highest circles of power. And, although "localism" was clearly related to preferred recruitment to the Assembly, it was *not* associated with promotion to higher leadership status within the elite group. In fact, through virtually the entire period, cabinet ministers were much less likely to have been born in the constituencies they represented than were average deputies.

On the whole, analyses of promotion to various leadership levels within the Turkish parliamentary system indicate that waves of change in the social characteristics of politicians do not hit the Assembly broadside, affecting all power levels equally. Rather, a sort of capillary absorption occurs. The lowest levels of formal power are affected first; if the pressure continues, the middle leaders are affected; only after a noticeable time-lag is there a seepage of new kinds of personnel into the highest levels of leadership. A group's decline is obversely patterned, so that its overall size of representation is conspicuously lowered before its representation at the highest levels is significantly reduced. Such a personnel process is in general conservative and slow. This is probably valuable to a political system in ordinary times, since it promotes continuity and reduces strain, but it can be too sluggish a process under more challenging conditions, impairing the system's adaptability and increasing the frustration of aspiring groups.

Under the multiparty system (since 1940), there seems to have been a stabilization and convergence in the social background characteristics of Turkey's national politicians. About 40 percent of the Assembly has usually been "professional." The "officials" have certainly not been eliminated, although military representation has been very distinctly reduced. In general, the "officials" have been diminished to approximately half strength compared to the single-party years, but they still make up nearly a quarter of all deputies. The "economic" group has been about the same size as the "officials," somewhat larger until the Justice party era and then slightly smaller. Finally, the residual contingent of those with "other" occupations—mainly journalism—has risen moderately throughout the period. The national election in 1969 produced a decline in the "professional" category and a corresponding increase among the "officials," but it is impossible now to tell whether this is a portent of a new trend or merely a minor fluctuation consistent with previously established patterns. The Assembly produced by the most recent election in 1973 has not yet been analyzed.

Political parties. When the Democratic party first challenged the People's party in the Eighth Assembly (1946), extremely significant differences in social background distinguished the two parties. Substantially fewer Democratic deputies were "officials" (6 percent versus 39 percent) and more were "local" (67 percent versus 56 percent). The same differences were also apparent, though to a lesser extent, in the Ninth Assembly, elected in 1950. Since that time, however, democratic competition for votes has made the main parliamentary parties more similar in social composition. From the Tenth Assembly on, few striking social background differences can be found between the major parties.[14] The delegations from the minor parties are commonly too small to permit confident analysis. The main pressures acting on all parties have been toward increased "localism" and the prominence of the lawyer.

Key Aspects of Elite Political Culture

An understanding of elites in Turkish politics cannot be based solely on information concerning their social backgrounds, valuable as such information is. Without an understanding of certain key aspects of elite political culture in contemporary Turkey the significance of the social background data cannot be grasped.

The notion of "political culture" is still fairly elusive. It often refers to the orientations toward politics widely shared by a group, though sometimes it refers to all orientations toward politics held by group members, regardless of the degree of sharing. In this discussion I shall use the former meaning. The focus is on some of the most distinctive and extensive cultural underpinnings of elite political behavior in Turkey.

Hard data on the distribution of the attitudes to be discussed are woefully lacking. The analysis, therefore, is unavoidably subjective and even potentially invidious. It is based on a few relevant surveys, the impressionistic literature, and personal observation. Hence, it is offered quite tentatively. Still, most authors have skirted or ignored the topics here discussed, so that the available literature seems seriously misleading. It is better, surely, to broach this crucial topic even in an exploratory way than to continue to neglect it. For if this piece of the picture is lacking, then the rest of the political mosaic is likely to be badly misinterpreted.

[14] See Tachau, "Anatomy of Political and Social Change," pp. 551–73.

There are obviously many important values and perceptions that Turkish political elites hold in common with most other people in most other societies. I shall not attempt to deal with these, though their existence must be recalled. Rather, I shall concentrate on selected cultural characteristics which seem to be both distinctive and of unusual political import. Moreover, I shall focus on characteristics which, though never totally shared by all members of the political elite, are nonetheless general rather than specific to some subgroup within the elite. The military, the bureaucrats, the entrepreneurs, or the intelligentsia may additionally have their own particular orientations. But here the spotlight will be on general characteristics of political culture shared by many members of all elite subgroups, recognizing, of course, that there are always counter-currents and exceptions and that the description is more true for some subgroups than for others. Only a general, selective, and primarily pathological gestalt is attempted.

Finally, the characteristics presented are regarded not as an accidental collection of tendencies, but rather as an organized, integrated syndrome. Each of the basic orientations adumbrated below accommodates and reinforces the others in numerous ways, some obvious and some quite subtle. All or even most of these interactions cannot be discussed here, but the principal point must be stressed that these orientations are conceived as a characterological system.

Ingroup-Outgroup Orientation. Possibly the most striking and important characteristic of elite political culture in Turkey is a pronounced tendency to view the world in ingroup versus outgroup terms. Not far below the surface is usually an inclination to see things as "us against them." Interestingly enough, in traditional Islam the world was dichotomized into two elementary realms, the "realm of Islam," where the true way is accepted, and the alternative "realm of War." How much influence this historic ethnocentrism has had upon contemporary Turkish political culture is difficult to say, but it is at least analogous to a telling aspect of contemporary elite orientations.

The ingroup-outgroup orientation is manifested both in foreign affairs, where for example there seems to be a predilection toward an "all or nothing" interpretation of alliances, and in domestic politics where, as Nermin Abadan notes, "criticism will tend to be evaluated within the context of a *Freund-Feind* (friend-foe) frame of reference. . . ." [15] Thus, this is not merely xenophobia, but an outlook that pervades all political encounters, internal as well as external. Indeed, over the past century its internal manifestations seem to have been more significant than its external manifestations. The main impact of this slant on political life has been the chronic degeneration of all attempts at open and legitimate political competition into outright, no-holds-barred political war.

There have been three momentous illustrations of this tendency in the twentieth century: (1) the deterioration of the Young Turk revolution of 1908 into the Committee of Union and Progress' dictatorship of 1913, (2) the tragic erosion of the multiparty system of the early 1950s, leading to the military coup of 1960,

[15] Nermin Abadan, "Turkey," in Michael Steed and Nermin Abadan, "Four Elections of 1965," *Government and Opposition,* vol. 1, no. 3 (May 1966), p. 344.

and (3) the decline from the open politics of the 1960s to the contemporary extremism, violence, offstage military rule, and party fragmentation. Less momentous, but still important, illustrations of the ingroup-outgroup psychology were the First Group/Second Group skirmish in the First Assembly, the appearance and forced termination of the Progressive Republican party in 1924, the rise and demise of the Liberal Republican party in 1930, the abortive coups of the early 1960s, and so on.

The general bias toward excessive commitment to the ingroup and ready hostility toward the outgroup incorporates many lesser tendencies and predilections. This attitude produces heightened involvement, dedication and sharing within the elite membership group. Loyalty and solidarity are attributes which the Turks strongly value and strongly display. Camaraderie and relative egalitarianism are conspicuous within the group. The Turks regard hospitality as one of their most distinctive qualities. The language of kinship that is widely employed in speaking of non-kin ingroup relations is not mere rhetoric or custom. The term *kardesim* (my brother) that ingroup peers readily use among themselves and *oglum* (my son) that ingroup authorities commonly employ toward younger members have much more conviction than their equivalents in most other cultures. Similarly, a profoundly paternalistic bent in Turkish political culture pervades the bureaucracy, political parties, educational system, and other institutions.[16]

Another manifestation of the same ingroup-outgroup orientation is the continuing strength of "old boy" networks, patron-client clusters, fictive kinship linkages, et cetera. Rustow has commented that "above all, the system puts a premium on 'connections.' "[17] In a political world perceived as "us against them," in which other actors tend to be seen as "either with us or against us," such offensive and defensive ties are essential.

The involvement, warmth, commitment, and sharing displayed in ingroup interactions are, however, balanced against almost antipodal tendencies displayed in outgroup interactions. Any ordinary opponent easily becomes regarded as *düsman,* the enemy. Political competition becomes polarized, almost automatically, and that polarization deprives the "vital center" of all vitality.[18] Heavy-handed use of power against opponents provokes equally heavy-handed revanchism by those who can regard themselves as abused. An inclination toward secretive, clandestine operations becomes strongly ingrained, indeed, increasingly necessary in an atmosphere of growing hostility.

Several recent writers have touched on these tendencies in Turkish politics. Michael P. Hyland speaks of "majority tyranny" and "intellectual despotism," Mardin of "overzealous functionaries" and "pathological vehemence," George

[16] See, for example, Frederick T. Bent, "The Turkish Bureaucracy as an Agent of Change," *Journal of Comparative Administration,* vol. 1, no. 1 (May 1969), pp. 47–64.

[17] Rustow, "Turkey: The Modernity of Tradition," p. 190.

[18] Osman Nur Yalman, speaking of such polarization in the modernization struggle of "reform" versus "reaction," has commented that it is ". . . almost a matter of national schizophrenia, which, bereft of careful and responsible statesmanship could still lead to a self-destructive civil war." "Notes on Polarization in Turkey," Middle East Institute Twenty-Fifth Anniversary Panel Series, 1970–71, no. 3 (mimeographed), p. 11.

Harris of "the profound intolerance of each political faction for its rivals," Joseph S. Szyliowicz of "unscrupulous" contention for power, and so on.[19]

The only extensive discussion of this orientation until now has been presented by Mardin in "Opposition and Control in Turkey."[20] He notes the tendency of each group to accuse others of "evil designs" and "trying to divide the Turkish nation." He contends that from scrutiny of these tendencies "we can deduce that there is an element in Turkish political culture to which the notion of opposition is deeply repugnant."[21] At the root of this intolerance toward opposition Mardin sees a fundamental "divisiveness anxiety." Moreover, he observes that "the fact that the Turkish social structure does not reveal the so-called 'objective' factors leading to divisiveness which [produce justifiable fears in certain other nations] and the fact that 'national unity' is very far down the list of Turkish problems, gives rise to the suspicion that we are faced here with a 'subjective' factor. . . ."[22]

Our analysis suggests that such insights are well drawn and crucial. We would go further still to regard this "divisiveness anxiety" as a manifestation of the more fundamental ingroup-outgroup orientation. Moreover, at a deeper level it may not be so irrational after all, although it is usually quite latent. If the tendencies toward a friend-foe outlook are as basic as we suggest, and if the other main aspects of the elite political culture have the characteristics we describe, then the Turks may have good reason to fear divisiveness, not objective reasons in the form of external threats or an extremely heterogeneous society, but valid reasons deriving from an awareness of their own psychological tendencies toward extremism in commitment and contention. It may be, as Mardin proposes, that even this ingroup-outgroup bias is itself a reflection of a still broader "cognitive rigidity," but that is much more difficult to substantiate. For present purposes it is enough to note the grave significance of the friend-foe bias that pervades Turkish political life and leads to a recrudescence of virulent intra-elite conflict every time the system is opened up to democratic competition.

The Group over the Individual. A second and plainly related cultural tendency among Turkish political elites is to elevate the group's interests over the individual's. In many respects this tendency has been one of Turkey's significant assets. Its people, compared to many others in the Near East and elsewhere, have been willing and able to organize, accept discipline, and sacrifice immediate self-interest for suprapersonal goals. Such abilities have played no small part in Turkish governmental and organizational success in the past.

However, the capacity to subordinate the self to the group can be unfortunate if carried to an extreme, as seems to occur frequently in contemporary Turkey. An extreme commitment to hierarchy and discipline can lead to rigidity and institutional excess. For instance, the story that the devil could get a Turkish soldier

---

[19] Michael P. Hyland, "Crisis at the Polls: Turkey's 1969 Elections," *Middle East Journal,* vol. 24, no. 1 (Winter 1970), pp. 1, 3; Mardin, "Opposition and Control in Turkey," p. 378; George Harris, "The Cause of the 1960 Revolution in Turkey," *Middle East Journal,* vol. 24, no. 3 (Autumn 1970), pp. 438–39; Joseph S. Szyliowicz, "Students and Politics in Turkey," *Middle Eastern Studies,* vol. 6, no. 2 (May 1970), p. 159.

[20] Mardin, p. 378.

[21] Ibid., p. 380.

[22] Ibid., p. 379.

to bayonet his own grandmother by simply donning a Turkish corporal's uniform and issuing the necessary order is calumnious, but it is indicative of the pathological aspect of this quality.[23]

When this bias toward elevating the interest of the group over the individual is centered on the nation, the overall result is possibly fortunate. It contributed greatly to the success of the nationalist movement, despite occasional degeneration into chauvinism and jingoism. But it also tends to make the Turkish public easy prey for political propaganda denouncing foreign interference, and it is one factor lying behind the strong appeal of statism for many elite groups. In fact, given this predilection, one might maintain that the elite political culture of Turkey makes it likely that the Turks would have particular success during the tutelary phase of political development but have corresponding difficulty during the democratic phase. The degree of individualism seemingly necessary in a democratic system appears to come very hard to the Turks.

During times when the nation is not clearly threatened from without, the tendency to subordinate the individual becomes, paradoxically, more dangerous. It operates within specific parties, groups, and factions, suppressing individual rights, compunctions, and interests in the name of loyalty, discipline, and duty. The only recourse for the principled deviant in a group is to break away completely and join or form another group; this group, although different, will be no less superordinate and demanding. Carried to an extreme, the tendency toward self-subordination strangely enough becomes quite divisive, especially when combined with the Turkish predisposition to adulate toughness and martyrdom (another form of self-subordination) and to regard other groups as enemies.[24]

A corollary of the elevation of the group over the individual is elite domination of other members within the group. Ziya Gökalp, the theoretician of Young Turk and early Kemalist times, urged that "the nation was the highest moral authority and the intelligentsia were the natural leaders of the nation." [25] The same pattern obtains in lesser groups as well. The group is the supreme authority for its members and the leaders of the group interpret and express its authority. The idea of "democratic centralism," for example, is quite attractive to Turkish elites, especially as it is more centralist than democratic. Similarly, many elite elements seem at least privately to favor a kind of Bismarckian policy which would grant welfare to the masses but not power. Elites which successfully claim to speak for a group are the last to relinquish the superordination of the group over the individual.

The Emphasis on Strength. Turkey is still very much what Macaulay would call a "courage culture." For example, when asked to name the two main characteristics of Turks as people, two-thirds of a national sample of lycee-level students surveyed 1959 answered in terms of "strength and heroism," by far the most frequent

[23] See Geoffrey Lewis, *Turkey* (London: Ernest Benn, 1955), p. 66.

[24] Mardin, "Opposition and Control in Turkey," p. 384, makes an analogous argument concerning the lack of legitimacy of opposition and yet the support for opposition parties, which are regarded not as oppositions but as "ideal" governments not yet vouchsafed power.

[25] Szyliowicz, "Students and Politics in Turkey," p. 151.

type of response.[26] The Mediterranean version of machismo, with a special Turkish flavor, is conspicuous at all levels of society. One reflection is in the very names many people bear. The adoption of last names was legally compelled in 1934. Some of the names taken were ancient patronymics, some reflected places of origin, and some were simply the father's previous single name or occupation. But a large number were names deliberately chosen for their meanings. Among these, symbols of strength and heroism clearly predominate. Demirel (iron hand), Kiliç (sword), Kartal (eagle), Oztürk (essential Turk), Tunç (bronze or shield), Savas (struggle), are examples that come to mind.

This emphasis on strength and courage combines with the ingroup-outgroup orientation to make Turkey, which is a very law-abiding country in general, also a deceptively violent one. In recent years, for example, the per capita rate of murder convictions in Turkey was higher than the rate of known murders in the United States, also a rather violent society. This is surprising to most people, since the violence in Turkey is not organized or reported extensively in the mass media. Much of it seemingly emanates from altercations among males which quickly get out of hand and become, literally, death struggles or blood feuds. Other illustrations of violence are easy to find, even at the highest levels of politics. For instance, pistols have been brandished on several recent occasions in the Grand National Assembly, where fistfights and near altercations are also far from rare. The recent terrorism, rioting, and street fighting hardly come as a surprise; in fact, in retrospect the relative quiet and harmony of the 1923–1953 period may indeed seem the anomaly.

Extremism and a tendency to exalt ends over means are also part of this pattern. In political competition, every possible advantage is exploited for all it is worth by many participants, with the result that the strife of political life is quickly exacerbated and reasons for hostility and enmity are amply available even to those without strong tendencies in that direction. Moreover, the courage-culture tends to foster a kind of *plus outré* psychology, especially among young men. If one group accomplishes some particularly aggressive action, the others are inclined to ask "Can we do less?" This tendency has been a factor behind the emulation of foreign student demonstrations and extremist tactics and of the Tupamaros and Arab fedayeen models by certain Turkish youth groups. Indeed, although there are countervailing forces in Turkish society and political culture that work against the extremist tendencies here described, the Turkish polity may be particularly vulnerable to the creation of a "culture of revolution" and violence that some Turks would wish to establish as a prelude to the anarchy that leads to fascism or, ultimately, to the communist-socialist revolution.

The Need for a Comprehensive Ideology. Political thought has never been one of Turkey's glories. In keeping with the overall syndrome being sketched, the Turkish genius seems to have been more for action and practical affairs than for analysis and lucubration—certain conspicuous exceptions aside, of course. The Turks have been more renowned as doers than thinkers, especially politically. However, two

[26] Frederick W. Frey, "Socialization to National Identification among Turkish Peasants," *Journal of Politics,* vol. 30 (1968), p. 945. Elite and peasant youth differ strikingly in this respect, for the peasant percentages were less than half this level.

aspects of their ideological orientation warrant special mention. The first is that, as one Turkish educator said recently at an informal conference, "Turkish intellectuals look for strong men or strong theory [ideology]," the former, presumably, if they lean politically toward the right and the latter if to the left. In any event, informed students have commented on the Turk's apparent need for comprehensive answers, their preference for organic theories of the state and society, and the attractiveness of Islam to the Turks for this type of reason.[27] Comprehensive and confident ideological assertions seem so attractive to them that one wonders whether, if inescapable national interests had not led to conflict with Russia and thus to deep suspicion of that society, most elite Turks might not have found the scope, certainty, and inevitability claimed by Marxism-Leninism to be extremely attractive. The aforementioned tendency to be *plus outré,* however, probably means that the moment for Marxism-Leninism has passed and that Maoism, Cheism, and successor vogues will have more popularity, albeit shifting and ephemeral.

The second ideological consideration arises from the first. Consider the notion of a "political paradigm"—that is, an ideological and political stance that serves as a basic, ordering framework. The concept of a political paradigm is analogous to a Kuhnian paradigm in science. On several counts one might regard the current condition of Turkish politics as an example of what happens when a political culture has exhausted its paradigm, recognizes that fact dimly, but has no replacement as yet. In a sense, though it was by no means a profound or polished political philosophy, Kemalism was an effective political paradigm for Turkish society. It clearly and convincingly told the society what its goals were and furnished guidelines for achieving them. However, the Kemalist paradigm, one can argue, pertained primarily to the first stage of the modern Turkish Revolution—the stage of elite modernization. It really had very little to say about the second stage—that of bringing mass elements into active participation. Thus, one might argue that part of the current malaise in Turkish political culture is due to the fact that the Kemalist paradigm is exhausted, that this is obscurely recognized, and that no successor has been accepted. When paradigms are exhausted and new ones lacking, one tends to find the phenomena of the absurd. There is thrashing about, disquiet, resistance to previous authority, extremism, and so on (which, incidentally seems also true for the United States and various other countries in the same situation). In short, contemporary Turkey seems to have outgrown but not replaced the Kemalist paradigm and hence confronts its own version of the "politics of the absurd."

Pride and Insecurity. The Ottoman legacy of profound national pride is still very real. National sensitivity, determination, and similar qualities continue to prevail. The psychological consequences of this orientation at the individual level for some elite intellectuals are extremely important. One cannot well understand the political culture of Turkey or most other developing societies without recognizing the inherent psychic problems caused insecure indigenous elites by the very process of development and technical assistance.

[27] Kemal H. Karpat, "The Turkish Left," *Journal of Contemporary History,* vol. 2 (1966), pp. 169–86; Mardin, "Opposition and Control in Turkey," pp. 380–81.

Put in simplest terms, the disrespect of the West, especially of many Western intellectuals, for the elites of developing societies is an almost tangible and extremely distressing thing for the latter, even though, from bravado or repression, they may deny it. As we know, no matter how accurate, simply being labeled nationally "underdeveloped" is irksome. One at least partly mollifying response is to identify with one Western culture in particular and to absorb that culture's contempt for other competitive Western cultures. Thus, if a Turk identifies with the United States, he is likely to find some gratification in absorbing American prejudices against the Russians, the French, or the British. Similarly, and more to the point for Turkish politics, if he identifies with French culture he is likely to pick up and find psychically gratifying all the supercilious anti-Americanism of Left Bank intellectuals. Indeed, through such identification he is likely to become even more extreme than the French, because the most grating foreign presence in Turkey for so long has been Americans.

It should come as no surprise, then, that a highly disproportionate number of leaders of the Turkish left are French-educated, anti-American intellectuals.[28] In fact, to take another example, one cannot fathom the internal politics of certain Turkish ministries, such as education, without grasping the rivalry that exists between American-trained and French-trained officials. In Turkey, as in most developing countries and perhaps most developed societies, an understanding of politics depends partly on insight into the ego-needs of the key participants and their efforts to meet them. The need to assuage wounds to their self-esteem is particularly strong among intellectual elites in proud but poor countries like Turkey. It tacitly governs much of their behavior.

The Democratic Impulse. This discussion of elite political culture in Turkey has deliberately concentrated on the negative aspects. There are several reasons for this. One is that after a period of brilliant success, Turkey has experienced marked troubles in the past one or two decades. Hence, our attention is more urgently directed to what is going wrong than to what is going right. Moreover, scholars in the past may have overemphasized what was going right and neglected many of the problems discussed here. Hence, we may simply know more about what has gone right than about what is going wrong.

Nevertheless, we should not conclude without at least mentioning certain counterpoises to the discouraging tendencies analyzed above. After all, Turkey is certainly surviving as a nation and will surely develop some solution to her current ordeal, whether or not most parties like it and its costs. One major feature of Turkish politics that must be noted is a deep democratic impulse. This democratic impulse ebbs and flows, rises and declines, but even at its lowest ebb it is still profoundly significant. In the very long run it seems unlikely that Turkey will abandon its democratic quest. The positive side of the situation, and especially this democratic aspect, must not be overlooked.

The somewhat pathological focus of this section was intended to provide a corrective understanding of the nature and difficulty of the problems that Turkey is

[28] See Kemal H. Karpat, "Socialism and the Labor Party of Turkey," *Middle East Journal*, vol. 21 (1967), p. 159, n. 4; Rustow, "Turkey: The Modernity of Tradition," pp. 189, 193; Ismet Giritli, "Turkey since the 1965 Elections," *Middle East Journal*, vol. 23 (1969), p. 354.

trying to solve these days. It is too easy to get frustrated or exasperated—to see the Turks merely as perversely squandering bright prospects in elite infighting—unless one grasps the complexity and difficulty of what is confronted and attempted. Even at elite levels there is still much in Turkish political culture that is basically hostile to open and competitive politics. The Turkish task is not easy. They must find some way to dilute virulent political conflict. They must come to terms with recrudescent elitism. They must dampen extremism without resorting to authoritarianism. They must prevent the more puerile aspects of their political culture (which every nation has)—militarism, chauvinism, machismo—from having damaging effects. And they must somehow do these things while engaged in momentous social change and economic development. Moreover, they must alter certain aspects of their elite political culture, if they can, unaided by any real understanding offered from the research community (which is rather weak, in general) of *why* these cultural traits are as they are.

As stressed earlier, this diagnosis has been largely impressionistic and subjective. It may be wrong in various respects. Even so, we know much more about the salient features of Turkish elite political culture than we know about what causes those characteristics. Presumably, the ingroup-outgroup orientation, the exaltation of the group over the individual, the emphasis on strength and heroism, the yearning for a comprehensive ideology despite a traditional pragmatism, the excessive pride and sensitivity, and also the basic impulse to democracy despite underlying tendencies toward authoritarianism, are all strongly influenced by familial and school socialization and by the constraints of Turkish social structure. Much effective research could be done to help understand these vital matters, but not the least of Turkey's problems is that little research of this type is under way and the climate for research is extremely poor. Inquiry is as much affected as politics by the cultural conditions described.

Elite-Mass Linkages

From a broad historical perspective, the process of political development seems to have two major phases, although these phases overlap and blur at the margins. The first is an integrative and concentrative phase. The strands of power in the society are increased, producing some kind of central control over elements that previously had been virtually unaffected by central authority. Simultaneously, power becomes more concentrated (centralized) in one or a few agencies such as the monarchy, the party, the administration, the military, or an economic elite. In this first phase, significant political interaction remains predominantly within the overall political elite. Although some new actors are rather grudgingly admitted to the elite, they adopt an elite outlook upon entry. Hence, their inclusion does not constitute an extension of significant political activity to nonelite actors, but is rather the incorporation of additional actors, who, on inclusion, come to think and function in essentially elite fashion.

The second phase of political development is basically extensive and distributive in nature. Power is increasingly acquired by nonelite actors such as unions, ethnic groups, shopkeepers, the new mass media, peasants, workers, voluntary associations, and so on. These actors enter the power arena as influencers, not as mere on-lookers, but they retain their nonelite status and orientation. They are not essentially coopted into elite status, as was true for the actors newly obtaining significant power in the first phase. This newfound power of nonelite actors engenders novel and anxious problems for the established elite. Much of the story of contemporary political development revolves about the new kinds of elite-mass interaction that result. The style of elite—and nonelite—response to nonelite intrusion into the elite's prior preserve really becomes the focal drama of politics in this phase of development.

As we have seen, the modern "Turkish revolution" has also had two more specific developmental phases. The first or Kemalist phase was the final act of the broader first phase of political development described above. It involved the final, secure, establishment of elite modernization in Turkey, not in the sense that elite modernization was complete, but in the sense that the modernizing elements within the elite had clearly obtained the upper hand and that elite modernization would not be reversed.

The second phase of the Turkish revolution involves bringing the Turkish masses, primarily the peasantry, into more active political, social, and economic participation in the society. Since 1950 at least, Turkey has been in this second phase, although thin but important roots can be traced back to earlier eras. That this second phase of the Turkish revolution unmistakably introduces the second or distributive phase of the basic process of political development indicates the gravity of the problems faced. They include a sea-change in the political climate that has everywhere proven extremely traumatic.

One of the primary features of the second phase of political development is that reciprocal elite-mass linkages now become crucial. Formerly, mass elements could conveniently be ignored or dominated by the elite. Intra-elite relations were decisive. But, in the second phase of political development, elite-mass relations become critical and elite-elite relations are compounded and often confounded by this fact. Hence, the quality of the elite-mass linkages must be examined as part of any serious elite analysis.

In this final section, therefore, we shall consider a very few basic facets of elite-mass linkages in Turkey. Even these few should illustrate some of the most significant problems of Turkish politics. The three aspects considered are: (1) the general administrative control system, (2) a vital elite-mass link in the bureaucracy, the prefect and the headman, and (3) the electoral link.

The Administrative Control System. One of the gravest political problems of a transitional nation like Turkey is rooted in its political culture—or, to be more precise, political cultures. At the most general level this can be labeled an audience problem. The elite-mass bifurcation implies that appeals to which one sector responds may mean little to the other. Goals that are salient to one sector are irrelevant to the other, and rights that are vital or sacred to one seem trivial to the other. It is difficult to make a domestic appeal to which the entire population will respond, and each sector may so little value the concerns of the other that true threats to vital interests may become common.

A specific instance of this type of difficulty is found in developmental administration. Historically, there seem to be three main types of administrative control systems that have been used by states. The earliest and most limited control system was the venal. It was a response to drastically limited communication systems. A provincial governor or other state official far from the capital was induced to behave in the way the dynasty wanted by making it in his venal self-interest to do so. Through mechanisms such as tax farming, rake-offs on licensing, grants of monopolies, et cetera, the official was permitted to exploit his position for personal gain as long as he forwarded to the dynasty the expected proportion of his gains. In return he received a certain amount of legitimacy and protection. Thus, in the Ottoman and other empires, the percentage of tax revenues collected that was actually remitted to the capital declined directly with the distance and difficulty of travel and communication.

Some historic systems perceived the severely limited nature of the venal control system and developed an alternative approach where possible. They recruited relatively malleable people, usually the very young, and indoctrinated them to loyalty to the regime and an outlook that led them to make the kinds of decisions the regime preferred. Then, even though they were far from central scrutiny, they could be trusted to do what was basically desired by the regime. The mandarin system in China, the British public school system in the nineteenth century, and the Ottoman Palace School are all illustrations of this type of programmed control system. The approach was quite effective as long as the élan of the socializing agency could be sustained and the environment did not present novel problems. However, such a system was very rigid in the face of new and unanticipated demands.

Finally, modern communication systems permit top decision makers and their representatives in the field to be in nearly constant communication. Policy makers send appropriate 'decisional premises" to their representatives while these in turn keep policy makers informed about the local conditions they are encountering. Through such feedback a common grasp of goals, resources, and strategies is obtained, but the feedback control system depends on excellent communication channels up and down the line.

Parallel to these three basic differences in administrative control systems were differences in regime goals. The venal control system featured essentially exploitative dynastic goals, the programmed control system tended to follow regulatory goals, while the feedback control system has been associated with developmental and welfare goals.

A major problem of elite-mass interaction in Turkey is that, administratively, it must operate simultaneously in each of these three very different control systems or cultures. At the highest level, the cabinet and top planning agencies use and assume a feedback control system with developmental goals. In other agencies even at the center, such as the Ministry of Justice or the Ministry of the Interior, the system bears a much closer resemblance to the programmed control system, while out in the provinces, towns, and villages one quite often encounters an unregenerate venal control system with exploitative goals at the local level. This is especially likely in the eastern regions. Frequently, actors in one control system do not realize that others may be in a different system, giving rise to severe misunderstandings. From the capital, the peasant often looks perverse and hostile to sincere developmental efforts, but locally the peasant may be dealing most often with a venal control system whose motivation he suspects. Any policy that is truly national and profound must be implemented in each of these three distinctive administrative control systems, and breakdowns regularly occur where they intersect.

A Crucial Link: The Prefect and the Headman. In many Turkish institutions one can designate rather clearly the point at which elite meets mass, the critical link between the lowest elite member and the highest mass member. In internal administration this is the link between the county prefect *(kaymakam)* and the village headman *(muhtar)*. The prefect tends to be the focus of the central government's activities in the rural areas, while the headman is the elected chief representative of the village. Together they constitute a crucial link in Turkish development administration.

A basic hypothesis concerning elite-mass linkages is that breakdowns in power and communication are most likely to occur where the status gap between connecting points is most severe and where reference groups are most discrepant. The prefect and the headman provide a conspicuous illustration of such a linkage over a wide status gap and featuring divergent reference groups, so one might expect problems at this juncture. No definitive study exists of the relations between prefect and headman in Turkey, but an analysis by the author and Leslie L. Roos (1967) is highly suggestive.[29] They obtained survey data from samples of male villagers, village headmen, and the prefects who had been in charge of the counties in which the roughly one hundred villages studied were located. All three groups had been asked what they perceived as the main problem facing their villages. Fifty-one percent of the villagers said either roads or water, and this was also the opinion of 49 percent of the headmen; but, in contrast, only 4 percent of the prefects saw roads or water as the main village problem. Correspondingly, 60 percent of the prefects designated lack of education or poverty as the main village problem, while only 15 percent of the headmen and the male villagers saw things that way. Thus, a striking discrepancy emerged between connecting elite and mass agents in the very diagnosis of the villages' main problems.

This discrepancy becomes even more illuminating if we pursue it one step further. Within the sample of county prefects, some were from village backgrounds and some were not. Those with village origins were significantly more likely to see roads and water as the main village problem than were those with urban origins. And if we add to this comparison responses from a sample of foreign service officials, we find that nearly three-fourths of this last, very urban group designated education and poverty as the main problems of Turkey's villages, while almost no one mentioned roads and water. Thus does the view from elite posts in the capital contrast with the view from behind mud walls.

In short, a formidable breakdown in the elite-mass linkage seems to occur between the prefect and the headman. The former is near the bottom rung of the national administrative elite. Frequently urban in background and outlook, he is oriented upward, intent on working his way higher in the Ministry of the Interior.

[29] Frederick W. Frey and Leslie L. Roos, "Social Structure and Community Development in Rural Turkey: Village and Elite Leadership Relations," Report No. 10, Rural Development Research Project (Cambridge, Mass.: Center for International Studies, M.I.T., 1967).

His values and his cognitions are very different from those of the peasant, making communication between them difficult. Although there are many extremely dedicated and conscientious civil servants in Turkey, it has often been noted that there are also many who display a clear disdain for the peasant masses, who are almost ingenious at avoiding having to visit the villages, and yet who profess with great confidence that they know and sympathize with what the villager needs and thinks, and how he behaves and suffers. And even when the prefect or other official has the knowledge and inclination to provide developmental leadership, his communication and influence position vis-à-vis the villager minimizes the opportunity. The villagers do not look to him for leadership and are not often in direct or indirect contact with him.

The village headman, on the other hand, is oriented downward. He is mainly responsive to the villagers who elect him and in whose midst he lives. While he is usually slightly more "modern" in his outlook than they, the difference is insufficient for him to provide any real impetus toward meaningful change. The prefect is primarily interested in quiet in the village so that in his short stint in that area (too short for any real developmental influence which will redound to his credit) nothing will happen that will blemish his chance for advancement. Missed opportunities are difficult to establish, while visibly untoward occurrences are professionally disastrous.

This situation often suits the headman very well. He is concerned to get what he can from the prefect for his village, and pressures in this direction are increasing, but he is even more concerned to keep that prefect "off his back." Even today, most elite-mass contact is probably rather negatively evaluated by most villagers. The peasant's governmental contacts with gendarmes and tax collectors are still more frequent and regular than contact with developmental or welfare agents. Peasant relations with private landowners, crop brokers, merchants, and so on may also occasion more anxiety than satisfaction. The result very often is a tacit collaboration in maintaining the status quo and the negation of opportunities for development. Elite-mass breakdowns of this type comprise a fundamental developmental problem for nations like Turkey.

The Electoral Link. In a democratic system, which Turkey has taken as its model, the most crucial formal linkage between elite and mass is electoral. Through this link, the masses and elites together presumably decide who shall govern them. This vital elite-mass nexus is supported and amplified by many other linking institutions such as political parties, mass media, voluntary associations and interest groups. We cannot here examine all these manifold elite-mass connections, nor even any one of them, in full depth. Nonetheless, it is instructive to inspect certain basic features of the electoral process, namely, the degree of participation and the nature of the electoral support obtained by the leading parties. These two characteristics indicate some of the underlying quality, trends, and problems of elite-mass interactions in particular and Turkish political life in general.

Participation. By virtually any standard, elections have taken strong hold among the Turkish population. It would be quite disruptive and difficult for elites now to sever this link with the masses. Since the first truly open and fully competitive national election in 1950, the Turkish electorate has gone to the polls seven times at roughly three- or four-year intervals. Nearly two-thirds or more of all those entitled to vote actually did vote in each of these national elections. Turkey has long had political parties with extensive national and grass-roots organizations. For example, village party cells have been prohibited since 1961 (in favor of the next larger organizational level), but just prior to their prohibition two-thirds of the Turkish peasantry lived in villages which had at least one party cell each, and nearly 90 percent of those who lived where there was one party cell also found the local organizations of one or more other parties in their village. Hence, we see that the degree of formal voting participation and the pervasiveness of political organizations are both generally high in Turkey. In this respect, the elite-mass linkage seems relatively good.

Two negative considerations must qualify this picture, however. One is the fact that in certain places, certain types of people seem to be more voted than voting. In parts of eastern Turkey, for example, careful analysis of voting data suggests that there is a good deal of bloc voting. There are numerous situations in which an *aga* (large landowner), tribal leader, or similar local notable makes the basic voting decision, and the masses connected to him then vote as he directs, themselves making no individual party or candidate evaluation. In these areas one finds such phenomena as party cross-overs by entire villages at successive elections, imperviousness to national electoral trends, and relatively unusual and sudden success for independent candidates. Survey findings from 1962 reflect the same phenomenon, showing conspicuous regional variations in the percentage of peasants able to name any political party (75 percent in the Aegean region versus 45 percent in the east-central region) and a majority of peasant women over fifty years old who appeared to have voted in the preceding election but could not name a single political party. Of course, these findings should not be interpreted to mean that the act of voting is not symbolically important, even for those who have not yet joined the majority of more politically sophisticated Turks. But the individual meaning of the vote may vary sharply within the electorate.

The other qualification regarding general political participation is that the overall percentage of the eligible electorate actually voting in national elections has declined precipitously over the past quarter-century, from nearly 90 percent in 1950 and 1954 to about 65 percent in the two most recent elections of 1969 and 1973. The only redeeming feature is that the 1973 election showed a small upturn from the preceding pattern of largely unrelieved decline. Of course, what this drop means—whether nonparticipation is a sign of dissatisfaction, acceptance, or disinterest—is not yet clear. The phenomenon of decline has been sufficiently sharp, however, that even Turkish premiers have commented on it and tried to explain it.[30]

Partisan support. One of the very best clues to understanding not only elite-mass linkages in Turkey but also the basic thrust of the entire political system, is an analysis of the popular bases of support for the major political parties. The

[30] Frederick W. Frey, "Themes in Contemporary Turkish Politics: General and Empirical Views" (Paper delivered at the Center for Middle Eastern Studies, Harvard University, January 8, 1970). See also Ergun Ozbudun, *Social Change and Political Participation in Turkey* (Princeton, N.J.: Princeton University Press, forthcoming).

general fortunes of the various parties can be discerned from Table 3–1. One striking aspect of these data is the secular decline of the People's party. The bad days of the fifties were followed by the terrible days of the sixties, halted by a possibly portentous upturn in 1973. On the whole, however, one of the most revealing observations to be made about Turkish politics is that in the last quarter-century the formerly dominant People's party has never come close to winning support from a majority of the Turkish electorate, and has not even obtained 40 percent of the vote since 1957.[31]

The second line of Table 3–1 portrays the no less important recent history of the Democratic party and its successor, the Justice party. Until the 1973 election, the essential picture was one of relative stability around a level of roughly 50 percent of the vote.[32] In 1973, however, we see the collapse of the coherent Turkish right as the Justice party, under extremist, military, and other pressures, fractured into three parties: a continuing Justice party, a new Democratic party, and a somewhat variant National Salvation party. Nonetheless, assuming that these three parties can be regarded as representing the political right (and this is least certain for the

[31] Cf. Hyland, "Crisis at the Polls."

[32] In 1961, the Justice party was organized in only about two-thirds of the country at the time of the election. Fuller organization would probably have led to an electoral performance very much in the pattern of other elections.

Table 3–1

PERCENTAGES OF TOTAL POPULAR VOTE OBTAINED BY POLITICAL PARTIES

	Grand National Assembly Elections						
Political Parties	1950	1954	1957	1961	1965	1969	1973
People's party	40%	35%	41%	37%	29%	27%	33%
Democratic/Justice party [a]	54	58	48	35	53	47	30
Nation/Republican Nation/ Republican Peasant Nation [b]	3	5	7	14	6	3	1
Freedom party	—	—	4	—	—	—	—
New Turkey party	—	—	—	14	4	2	—
Republican Peasant Nation/ National Action [c]	—	—	—	—	2	3	3
Turkish Labor party	—	—	—	—	3	3	—
Reliance Party/ Republican Reliance party [d]	—	—	—	—	—	7	5
Unity party	—	—	—	—	—	3	1
Democratic party	—	—	—	—	—	—	12
National Salvation party	—	—	—	—	—	—	12
Independents	3	2	0	0	3	6	3
Total	100%	100%	100%	100%	100%	100%	100%
Number of political parties	3	3	4	4	6	8	8

[a] Democratic party through the 1957 election, Justice party thereafter.
[b] Nation party in 1950, 1965 and 1969; Republican Nation party in 1954 and 1957; Republican Peasant Nation party in 1961.
[c] Republican Peasant Nation party in 1965; National Action party in 1969 and 1973.
[d] Reliance party in 1969, Republican Reliance party in 1973.

National Salvation party), we see that the right still commands the allegiance of roughly half the electorate, while the center holds perhaps another 10 percent and the left about a third or more.

The third general observation prompted by Table 3–1 concerns the fragmentation of the party system in Turkey. The right and the center are both obviously splintered at present, and the left, occupied by the People's party and the tiny Unity party, presents a possibly misleading coherence, since the Turkish Labor party has been proscribed and other parties that one might expect to the left of the People's party have not yet fully developed. The general situation is thus one of flux and transition, and there are many signs that Turkey is now in the midst of what some American political scientists call a "critical realignment." [33] This is best revealed by analysis of the social support for the main parties.

Statistical analysis of Turkish voting behavior started by the author and continued by a Turkish scholar, Ergun Ozbudun, has produced the correlations, for all national elections from 1950 through 1969, of the percentage of the popular vote in each province obtained by each of the major parties and a number of provincial socioeconomic indicators such as urbanization, literacy, income per capita, proportion of the work force in agriculture, education, and so on. The patterns revealed by this analysis are essential to an understanding of general and elite politics in contemporary Turkey.

In the 1950s, the Democratic party rested primarily upon the twin supports of the more developed part of the peasantry and an urban coalition of business and free professional elites, together with many working-class people of various types. Its appeal was to the more modern regions of the country and the more privatistic and enterprising elements therein. The statistical manifestations of these tendencies are the consistent, if moderate (0.1 to 0.3), positive correlations between provincial Democratic party voting percentages and such indicators as literacy, all-weather roads, radio receivers, national taxes collected, and so forth.

These correlations between indices that seem to reflect provincial modernization, especially rural modernization, and Democratic party voting changed in the 1960s, with the succession of the Justice party. They did not change in kind, but rather strikingly in degree, becoming much stronger, often moving up to the 0.5 or 0.6 level. By the 1965 and 1969 elections, literacy, for example, was correlated with Justice party voting percentage at 0.667 and 0.640, respectively. Thus, it seems that the Justice party strengthened the Democratic party's solid foundation of socioeconomic support, consisting primarily of the more developed sector of the peasantry, the more privatistic sector of the urban elite, and a more loosely tied but still important segment of the urban working classes. Although one could anticipate some inconsistencies in policy orientation among its main supporting elements, especially the urban working classes, it was a party—in either its Democratic or Justice form—that had an essentially plausible and solid popular base rooted in socioeconomic interests and affirmed in well understood ideological stances.

[33] See Walter Dean Burnham, *Critical Elections and the Mainsprings of American Politics* (New York: Norton, 1970), and Ergun Ozbudun and Frank Tachau, "Social Change and Electoral Behavior in Turkey: Towards a 'Critical Realignment'?" (Paper presented to the annual meeting of the Middle East Studies Association, Boston, Massachusetts, November 6–9, 1974).

When we similarly examine the support bases of the People's party, an opposite picture emerges—opposite not in the sense of revealing an equally firm appeal but to different strata, but in the sense of revealing no plausible foundation in socioeconomic interests at all! In the 1950 election results one can perceive some differential People's party support from the more backward and eastern provinces, but this is explainable in terms of the bloc voting phenomena previously mentioned and the locations of the constituencies of a few top People's party leaders. After 1950 and until 1969, however, one finds no significant correlations between any major socioeconomic indicators and differential provincial support for the People's party. Although it could be argued that the People's party was, therefore, a truly national party not resting on more limited socioeconomic support from particular classes or strata, a more plausible hypothesis is that it had become something of an anachronism, a vestigial organization living primarily off the memories of its more dynamic and effective past. Except perhaps for the functionaries, the party had little appeal to the strongly felt interests of any class or stratum in Turkish society. Most significantly of all, it seemed to have very little appeal to the peasantry.

The party seemed to adapt very poorly to a power situation where it had to compete for the favor of a mass electorate. Its elitist posture and its internal division between national intellectuals and local notables both hindered such adaptation. The very idea of catering to the masses and styling policy to meet their ideas of what they wanted rather than elite ideas of what they should have was repugnant to many of the national intellectuals. On the other side, the kinds of policies that electoral competition for peasant votes would require tended to be threatening to the position of the local notables. So both main elements in the People's party found adaptation to democratic electoral competition extremely difficult. And the peasants, sensing these difficulties and the reasons behind them, found even the party's more sincere appeals unconvincing.

As described earlier, the People's party eventually, if slowly, began to confront its new situation and its poor linkage to mass elements, going through a most revealing internal spasm in the process. The successful left-of-center démarche is especially interesting in this connection. It has been, uncharacteristically, a major attempt at adaptation, something neither electoral failure nor even the defection by the party's contingent of local notables and conservatives, led by some of its best known leaders, could produce. What caused it? The answer would seem to be primarily the inroads made into the party's elitist intellectual support by the Turkish Labor party and the rise of socialist ideology in Turkey. The elitist intellectual stance of the People's party is nowhere better displayed. Impervious to all sorts of strong pressures from other quarters and events, when the intellectual elite showed signs of straying from the fold a drastic and prompt response was forthcoming from the party. As Turkish intellectual thought in general moved leftward in the sixties and a real political threat from the left confronted the People's party, it adjusted its program and posture to a degree that pressures from other quarters —notables or peasants—could never effect.

The left-of-center move by the People's party, under the able leadership of Bulent Ecevit, has already managed some signal accomplishments. Probably most significantly, it reversed the continuing decline in the party's electoral fortunes, moving from 27 percent of the vote in 1969 to 33 percent in 1973, and reversed its accumulating image of drift, opportunism, and staleness. The party has become more dynamic and seemingly more principled. Our correlational analysis indicates that this change began even in the 1969 election, when the party appeared to be at its nadir. Through 1965, there were virtually no significant correlations between socioeconomic indicators and People's party voting. In 1969, however, for the first time in nearly twenty years, signs of a successful appeal to interests by the party appeared. Positive correlations between People's party voting and almost all of the measures of socioeconomic modernity were found, correlations that very closely paralleled the Justice party's pattern but were usually somewhat weaker. In short, the People's party seemed to be appealing differentially to the same relatively modern sectors of the Turkish population that the Justice party appealed to. The main difference between the two appeals that is reflected in various voting statistics carefully analyzed is that the People's party appeals more to the urban populations in the more modern areas, while the Justice party is stronger among the more developed rural sector. The most backward areas of Turkey are regions in which both of the formerly major parties do rather poorly; the lesser parties are the ones that do relatively better in the disadvantaged provinces, as do independent candidates.

These data point to one of Turkey's crucial political problems. For the People's party, the question is first whether it can mount a successful electoral appeal to a large part of the Turkish peasantry or whether its recent gains are based mainly on urban appeals and come close to the limit of growth that is to be expected from that quarter. Assuming that the party can make a reasonably competitive appeal to the peasants in the more developed areas, especially to the poorer villagers in those areas, as would be appropriate for a left-of-center party stressing social justice, the second question that arises is whether this strategy could ever be enough to secure majority status for the party. Could a coalition of urban intellectuals and workers and the more disadvantaged peasants in the more modern areas ever be large enough to produce a People's party government? If not, it is quite possible that the People's party may work its way up to about 40 percent of the vote under its present strategy and then get no farther. That degree of People's party strength might possibly be sufficient to reunite the right, but if it did not, it might doom Turkey to a continuation of weak coalition governments.

One might argue, on the contrary, that a truly left-of-center party like the People's party cannot in good conscience abandon the most deprived part of the Turkish population, the peasants of the more backward eastern regions. Surely the addition of these would be ideologically appropriate and electorally significant, possibly pushing the party over the hump to majority status. Why not also gear the party's efforts to them? Here, however, surfaces one of the fundamental political dilemmas of contemporary Turkey. The People's party finds this appeal to the backward East very difficult, not only because of residual elitist tendencies within the party, but even more because of the bloc voting characteristics of the East and because of the greater salience of religion and traditionalism in that area. Thus, to deal effectively with the East, the party would have to deal with local leaders whom the party's intellectual leaders find ideologically unsavory. It would also have to soft-pedal its secularism and its modernizing tendencies to an appreciable extent, and this would be very disturbing to some of the most dynamic intellectual elements in the party.

The situation is quite similar in principle to that of the Democratic party in the American South under Franklin Roosevelt. From an economic perspective, the South—poor white southern farmers in particular—should have been one of the most liberal or radical areas of the country. But every time a successful economic appeal to the have-nots of the area seemed to be launched, the racial question, on which the same farmers were ultraconservative, was raised to counteract the economic appeal. An area that might potentially have been a strong support for liberal programs was thus denied, although the liberal coalition formed in the rest of the country proved at least temporarily viable. In Turkey it remains very much to be seen whether a reformist coalition of majority strength can be formed without effective People's party appeal to the more backward areas. In any event, this is one of the key features of Turkish politics to watch in the forthcoming elections. If the elite-mass electoral link between Turkey's less developed regions and its major political parties remains poor, the implications for the country's pattern of development are potentially alarming. The neediest and most difficult areas would be disproportionately represented by the smallest and most extreme or personalized parties.

Conclusion

Throughout much of its recent history, Turkish modernization was fostered and led by its political elite. Indeed, that elite probably constituted the nation's greatest developmental asset. Today, however, one can seriously question whether this remains true. In fact, one is even prompted to ask whether the dogmatic and extremist portions of that elite have not become an active liability in the nation's quest for further growth. Erstwhile strengths often can turn into subsequent weaknesses under circumstances of pervasive change.

In any case, the preceding analyses suggest that continued elitism, an ingroup-outgroup psychology, virulent intra-elite conflict, and inadequate elite-mass linkages are now among the most salient patterns of elite politics in Turkey and are among the nation's pressing political problems. Whether and how these patterns change, and what new patterns take their place, will go far toward determining the political future of Turkey and the region.

IV. PATTERNS OF ASSOCIATION IN THE EGYPTIAN POLITICAL ELITE

Robert Springborg

Politics without Organized Groups

At the heart of the Western political process are organized groups. Policies result from the clash of group interests; individuals are integrated into political action through groups; and political identifications are formed through group membership. Because groups are central to Western politics, and because a realistic account of Western political processes can be offered by relying on groups as the key unit of analysis, it has been assumed that groups are equally important in the political processes of African and Asian states, and that the notion of group is a useful concept in formulating theories of comparative politics.[1]

The case of Egypt suggests, however, that groups may not be indispensable to the political process. "Egyptians do not act politically primarily through organized groups. . . ." [2] Furthermore, several recent accounts of non-Western politics indicate that Egypt is not a unique case. Other African and Asian nations share in this political individualism.[3]

The absence of categorically based, organized groups is, in Egypt, not a recent

I gratefully acknowledge support from the Center for Research in International Studies of Stanford University, which made the research for this article possible, and the American Research Center in Egypt, of which I was an honorary fellow in 1971–72. I would also like to thank Clement Henry Moore for sharing with me his detailed knowledge of Egyptian politics and for commenting on an earlier draft of this article.

[1] See, for example, Gabriel Almond and Bingham Powell, *Comparative Politics: A Developmental Approach* (Boston: Little, Brown and Co., 1966).

[2] Clement Henry Moore, "Authoritarian Politics in Unincorporated Society: The Case of Nasser's Egypt" (Paper delivered to the annual meeting of the American Political Science Association, Washington, D.C., September 1972), p. 18. A revised version of this paper appears under the same title in *Comparative Politics,* vol. 6, no. 2 (January 1974), pp. 193–218.

[3] That horizontal categorical groups are irrelevant for politics is suggested in the following works:

On the Middle East and North Africa: P. J. Vatikiotis, *Conflict in the Middle East* (London: Allen and Unwin, 1971); David and Marina Ottoway, *Algeria: The Politics of a Socialist Revolution* (Berkeley: University of California Press, 1970); James A. Bill, "Class Analysis and the Dialectics of Modernization in the Middle East," *International Journal of Middle East Studies,* vol. 3, no. 4 (October 1972), pp. 417–34; John Waterbury, *The Commander of the Faithful: The Moroccan Political Elite—A Study of Segmented Politics* (London: Weidenfeld and Nicholson, 1970).

On Africa: Aristide R. Zolberg, *Creating Political Order: The Party-States of West Africa* (Chicago: University of Chicago Press, 1966); Jean-Claude Williame, *Patrimonialism and Political Change in the Congo* (Stanford: Stanford University Press, 1972); René Lemarchand, "Political Clientelism and Ethnicity in Tropical Africa: Competing Solidarities in Nation-Building," *American Political Science Review,* vol. 66, no. 1 (March 1972), pp. 68–90.

On Asia: F. G. Bailey, *Stratagems and Spoils: A Social Anthropology of Politics* (Oxford: Oxford University Press, 1969); James C. Scott, "Patron-Client Politics and Political Change in Southeast Asia," *American Political Science Review,* vol. 66, no. 1 (March 1972), pp. 91–113; Lloyd Rudolph and Susanne Rudolph, *The Modernity of Tradition: Political Development in India* (Chicago: University of Chicago Press, 1967).

development. Corporateness has never taken hold in Egyptian society for at least two main reasons. First, the economic system is only now beginning to give rise to a stable class structure. Over the centuries, economic power has been subordinate to political power. The constant upheavals in land tenure, which came with shifts of power in the central government, frustrated the rise of an entrenched class of feudalists during the Ottoman-Mamluk period.[4] The feudal aristocracy eventually created by British-inspired land tenure policies in the nineteenth and twentieth centuries was virtually destroyed as a class by Nasser's agrarian reforms. The seedbed of mass political organization in Europe, the bourgeoisie, constituted a smaller percentage of the population in the traditional Islamic state than it did in preindustrial Europe.[5] When the Egyptian bourgeoisie began to expand rapidly in the late nineteenth and in the twentieth centuries, it was composed largely of individuals who were not native Muslim Egyptians.[6]

Objective economic conditions and especially the narrow scope of industrialization have not been conducive to the rise of a proletariat. Small shops, a relatively high degree of upward mobility among craftsmen, and the social status attached to small-scale ownership,[7] hindered the formation of a "unified and egalitarian working class." [8] While domination of the domestic manufacturing economy by artisans and craftsmen has now become a thing of the past, the legacy of entrepreneurship lives on in Egypt as is does elsewhere in the Arab world.[9] In an Egyptian's thinking, being in the employ of someone else exposes one to exploitation without affording the prestige or possibility of accumulating wealth provided by having one's own business, however small. That an individualistic orientation toward economic activity persists is in part a function of Egypt's close proximity to its medieval past. The transformation of even the lowest strata of urban workers from entrepreneurs into wage laborers did not begin until the last years of the nineteenth century. The guild of water carriers in Alexandria, for example, was abolished as a consequence of an 1894 decree that fixed prices for water and wages for its carriers and, in effect, transformed the carriers from individual businessmen into wage laborers. Prior to the issuance of the decree, they had purchased water from the Alexandria Water Company and sold it for whatever price they could obtain.[10] There still are in Cairo and Alexandria, however, countless niches in the economies that provide scope for the entrepreneurial ambitions of Egyptians and continue to frustrate the rise of working-class consciousness.

Economic conditions, though, do not provide a complete explanation of the absence of cohesive political organizations in modern Egypt. There are also cultural factors that have prevented the establishment of categorical ties. While the absence of strong ethnic identities and the persistence of intense familial loyalties are of

---

[4] See, for example, Manfred Halpern, *The Politics of Social Change in the Middle East and North Africa* (Princeton: Princeton University Press, 1963), pp. 43–44.

[5] Ibid., pp. 45–46. See also S. D. Goitein, *Studies in Islamic History and Institutions* (Leiden: E. J. Brill, 1966), p. 218.

[6] Gabriel Baer, *Population and Society in the Arab East* (New York: Praeger, 1964), p. 205.

[7] Goitein, *Islamic History,* pp. 277–78.

[8] Ibid., p. 277.

[9] For an analysis of entrepreneurial behavior in Morocco, see John Waterbury, *North for the Trade* (Berkeley: University of California Press, 1972).

[10] Gabriel Baer, *Egyptian Guilds in Modern Times* (Jerusalem: Israel Oriental Society, 1964), pp. 143–44.

importance, the chief factor is that Islam, unlike Christianity, was never effectively institutionalized. Islam has never provided a counterbalance to arbitrary rulers nor checked their ambitions by imposing a clearly delineated theoretical guideline to circumscribe the exercise of secular power. The Muslim community of believers has functioned without formal, organized religious authority. Unorganized and, according to Moore, "born reformed,"[11] Islam could not give rise to a Reformation. In the West, the dialectical response of Puritanism to institutionalized Catholicism provided an organizational model which was later incorporated into politics.[12] However, in the Arab world dialectical growth of a reform-minded, religious institution was impossible, since there was no institutionalized religion against which to react.

In the absence of cohesive categorical ties extending either horizontally through a class or vertically through an ethnic, linguistic, or other minority community, or through the ranks of the faithful, formal organizations have traditionally been condemned to political obscurity. Only when the central government was torn by internal feuding or weakened by events beyond Egypt's borders were organizations composed of native Muslim Egyptians capable of participating in the king-making process or of influencing governmental policies, but these opportunities were rare.[13] The essence of the history of traditional secular organizations (the strongest of which were guilds), of established Islam, and of the Sufi brotherhoods (notoriously rebellious in most Islamic societies) is that of obsequiousness in the face of authority.[14] Even in periods of elite turmoil and the flourishing of organizations, the most that members of guilds, Sufi orders, or the mass of believers could hope for was control over the selection of their leaders. Even then, the role of *ulama* and Sufi and guild *shaykhs* was not primarily that of spokesmen for group interests. Instead, the task of *ulama* and *shaykhs* was to serve as brokers between their followers and the Mamluk, Ottoman, or Albanian ruling caste.[15] In return for the patronage bestowed upon them by the political elite, a portion of which they passed down through the ranks, *ulama* and *shaykhs* were expected by the elite to extract resources for the state and to placate their followers.[16] The leadership role that therefore became institutionalized was that of benevolent patron. Guilds and Sufi orders sought as leaders patrons who were of elite status and close to the

---

[11] Clement Henry Moore, "On Theory and Practice among the Arabs," *World Politics* (October 1971), p. 113.

[12] See Michael Walzer, *The Revolution of the Saints* (Cambridge, Mass.: Harvard University Press, 1965).

[13] The brief period in the beginning of the nineteenth century between the evacuation of Napoleon's expeditionary force and Mohammed Ali's consolidation of power was, because of disarray and attrition in the ranks of Mamluks, the time at which *ulama* were able to exert their greatest political influence. Even then, however, they failed to gain significant concessions from the ruler. See Daniel Crecelius, "Nonideological Responses of the Egyptian *Ulama* to Modernization," in *Scholars, Saints and Sufis: Muslim Religious Institutions in the Middle East since 1500,* ed. Nikkie Keddie (Berkeley: University of California Press, 1972), p. 174 and passim.

[14] See Baer, *Egyptian Guilds in Modern Times;* and Afaf Lutfi al Sayyid Marsot, "The *Ulama* of Cairo in the 18th and 19th Centuries," in Keddie, *Scholars, Saints and Sufis.*

[15] For a succinct explanation of why Arab elites have historically adopted brokerage roles, see Albert Hourani, "Revolution in the Middle East" in P. J. Vatikiotis, *Revolution in the Middle East and Other Case Studies* (London: Allen and Unwin, 1972), pp. 65–72.

[16] Marsot, "*Ulama* of Cairo," pp. 152–53.

source of patronage, such as members of the royal household.[17] Unable to thrust leaders charged with representative obligations into the political elite, secular and religious organizations chose as leaders those who would serve as conduits for goods and services flowing from the elite down into the rank and file.

Since *ulama* and guild *shaykhs* were not representatives of institutionalized and autonomous power, they were, in the final analysis, dependent upon the good will of the absolute ruler. This patron-client relationship was subjected to a ceaseless process of erosion as a consequence of Mohammed Ali's program of modernization, which included the creation of a bureaucracy and thereby rendered redundant the inefficient extractive capabilities of *ulama* and *shaykhs*. Mohammed Ali's economic modernization and his industrialization efforts also led to the gradual decline of guilds. So from the beginning of the nineteenth century, both *ulama* and guild *shaykhs,* having been unable to circumscribe the power of their rulers, became increasingly impotent, and patronage was directed away from them and their organizations.

Formal organizations have sprung up since that time but have not enjoyed substantially greater success in winning autonomy from the whims of succeeding rulers. Contemporary voluntary associations are not more successful than their medieval forerunners in inculcating strong horizontal loyalties between their members. Nor have their leaders carved out new roles for themselves. These leaders, too, are brokers between the ruler and their organization's membership, and are evaluated by their followers largely in terms of the amount of patronage they funnel down into the organization. The process by which they are selected is similarly reminiscent of historical experience. During the period of strong rulership embodied by Gamal Abdul Nasser, virtually all leaders of political, economic, social, and religious organizations were, if not chosen directly by him, subject to close scrutiny by the top members of his regime. As the Nasser regime has decayed since its founder's death and since its inheritance by a weaker individual, it has been forced to grant greater subsystem autonomy by allowing organizations more freedom in selecting leaders. Since this freedom resulted not from a basic change in the character of those organizations, which remain weak, but from the diminished power and authority of the executive, renewed vigor and strength at the top would undoubtedly once again be at the expense of voluntary associations.

Egypt's rulers continue to exercise the prerogatives of leadership unfettered by the constraints of organized constituencies. While the rulers themselves may appreciate their relative freedom of action, the organizational vacuum over which they preside actually sets real and narrow limits on their governing scope. Egyptian rulers can be authoritarian but, in the absence of any means of organizing mass behavior on a permanent rather than a temporary basis, they are incapable of establishing either totalitarian government or government based on a system of checks and balances between institutions. The symbolic trappings of modern government,[18] which Egyptian rulers import much like manufactured goods that cannot be produced locally, are not congruent either with their personalized styles of leadership or with other aspects of the indigenous political culture.

---

[17] Crecelius, "Nonideological Responses"; Baer, *Egyptian Guilds in Modern Times,* pp. 13–15 and passim.

[18] Government based in at least semi-institutionalized mass participation.

For example, Nasserism, a political ideology constructed not by the leader himself but by theoreticians who sought to give ideological continuity to his ad hoc decisions, and the political structures that Nasser attempted to create foundered because they required horizontal linkages between individuals. Socialism cannot be built without socialists, as critics of the Nasser regime lamented. Informed more by Western political thought and action than by Egyptian experience, Nasserism remained an expressive ideology.[19] It could not become a practical guide to action before those who espoused it came to grips with the nature of political association in Egypt. The main ties that bind Egyptians together in mutual political activity are those that cement clients to patrons. The horizontal bonds which do exist give rise to cliques and factions but not to effective mass political organizations.

Political Clientelism

Political clientelism was the glue that held the political system together under the Mamluks and their Albanian successors, and it continues to be the most effective adhesive in Egyptian politics. Further, the basic discontinuity in political clientelism is as evident in contemporary Egypt as it was in previous centuries. In other words, clientelism effectively integrates those on the political periphery but, by its very nature, it cannot provide sufficient cohesion within the elite. Because clients look to their patrons to solve political disputes, conflict can be resolved only at the pinnacle of the system. The decision-making load, therefore, is comparatively burdensome for the elite in a clientage-based system, but ironically, instead of enhancing the elite's ability to resolve social conflict, clientelism actually detracts from it. Fragmented into competing clientage networks, members of the elite lack the unity and shared dedication of purpose necessary to provide dynamic leadership.

Mamluk Egypt provides a clear example of the two faces of political clientelism. On the periphery, Mamluks were easily able to contain *ulama,* the one native Egyptian elite posing a threat to Mamluk rule, by appointing them to a variety of administrative and political posts and by granting them lucrative religious trusts *(awqaf).*[20] As clients of their patron rulers, the *ulama* also acted as patrons to the community of believers, thereby providing the necessary linkage between rulers and ruled. As Crecelius points out, "It would not be exaggerating to note that the entire religious structure was dependent upon the favors and support of the ruling elite."[21] Although Islam in Egypt was not institutionalized, the community of believers did provide a framework within which clientage networks, stretching from the Ottoman-Mamluk rulers through the *ulama* and down to the masses, could be established. Informal, personalistic, and relatively inefficient as a means of winning support and extracting resources from the populace, clientelism nevertheless provided a sufficiently strong quasi-organizational skeleton to give political shape to the amorphous religious legitimacy.

Similarly, personal alliances within the Ottoman-Mamluk elite were based on patron-client relationships, but the consequence of clientelism at this level was

---

[19] See Moore, "On Theory and Practice among the Arabs," esp. pp. 106–7.
[20] See Marsot, "*Ulama* of Cairo," p. 153.
[21] Crecelius, "Nonideological Responses," p. 171.

fragmentation rather than integration, instability rather than stability. Violent struggles for power remained the hallmark of Mamlukian political behavior. According to P. M. Holt:

> . . . the grandees of Egypt in the seventeenth and eighteenth centuries founded complex patronage-groups the members of which might be linked to the founder by any of three ties: that of servitude, as a mamluk; that of maintenance, as a sarraj; and that of natural kinship, since in some cases sons of grandees were also notables. Furthermore, since dependents in many cases became in course of time founders of their own patronage-groups, 'clans' came to be formed, which in times of crisis were transformed into political factions.[22]

Ottoman Egypt suffered from chronic elite factionalization, which contributed to the downfall of the Mamluks at the hands of Napoleon and then Mohammed Ali. Successive regimes have had the same problem, for they too have been based on relationships between patrons and clients. The persistence of this mode of social organization, plagued as it is by inherent susceptibility to fragmentation, deserves comment.

The Tenacity of Clientelism. The tenacity of clientelism in Egypt is due in large part to its adaptability in the face of modernization. Modern political and administrative organizations, including political parties and bureaucracies, provide fertile breeding grounds for patron-client relationships. James Scott's observation on how modernization has reinforced clientelism in Southeast Asia is equally appropriate in Egypt. According to him,

> New resources for patronage, such as party connections, development programs, nationalized enterprises, and bureaucratic power have been created. Patron-client structures are now more closely linked to the national level with jobs, cash, and petty favors flowing down the network, and votes or support flowing upward. In the midst of this change, old style patrons still thrive.[23]

Patron-client linkages may be cemented with a variety of resources, and the intensity of the relationships may vary without changing their basic character. Nasser's reforms, for example, did not reduce the scope of clientelism, but they did change it. More equitable economic distribution generally and the demise of agrarian feudalism specifically have led to a decrease in the imbalance in the relationship between patrons and clients. Land ownership and other forms of material wealth continue to provide some Egyptians with a resource base for attracting clients, but their importance varies in direct proportion to the distance of the clientage network from the political center. As one moves up through the layers of political stratification, resources of land and capital give way to strategic contacts with other people as the basis of clientelism. But both at the center and on the periphery of the political system, the degree of asymmetry in patron-client relationships is much reduced from that prevailing under preceding regimes. Patrons

[22] P. M. Holt, *Studies in the History of the Near East* (London: Frank Cass, 1973), p. 237.
[23] Scott, "Patron-Client Politics," p. 105.

no longer possess sufficient material or brokerage resources to guarantee a stable, loyal clientele and, as Lemarchand and Legg state, "The less asymmetrical the relationship, the greater likelihood of the obligation remaining open-ended." [24] The duration of patron-client relationships, while still lifelong in the most remote and inaccessible rural areas, may, within the administrative and political structures, be as short as months or weeks. Affective ties, which supplemented the instrumental bonds linking peasants to their landowner patrons and increased the longevity of their relationships, play a very secondary role or are entirely absent from patron-client relationships within the elite. Clients abandon patrons whose star is visibly falling in the political/administrative galaxy and seek attachment to a new, more conspicuously placed patron.

Clientelism on the Periphery of Contemporary Egypt

Patrons on the outer fringe of the political elite, including some large landowners and most urban bosses, generally have relatively little influence on national policy making. The main political function performed by those large landowners who are not entrenched in the national elite and by urban bosses is to provide communal solidarity and social integration through the construction of clientage networks.

Egypt's urban patrons have been weak in comparison to their counterparts in some other Arab countries. Fassi notables, for example, have long been key actors in Moroccan politics,[25] and the *Zuaama* of Beirut and Tripoli assumed an important role in Lebanese politics after World War II.[26] But in Egypt's predominantly agricultural, peasant society, the city has been sandwiched between national political power and rural clientage networks based on land ownership. Cairo is the seat of central government and is the site of most mass political activity, but only rarely has it provided a base for a political boss to catapult into national politics. Clientage-based political machines encompass a smaller percentage of Egypt's urban population than do the machines of urban Lebanese *zuaama*. Nevertheless, significant numbers of Egypt's urban poor are loosely organized within clientage networks, and as the urban population continues to swell, the scope, if not the density, of these networks can be expected to increase. The incongruity between the local importance of urban bosses and their impotence on the national scene is, moreover, potentially unstabilizing. The regime, as yet unwilling to admit the big fish of local ponds (both urban and rural) into the decision-making elite or to decentralize power, is not only deprived of the support base of urban machines, but it earns the antipathy of urban bosses and their clients.

The career of Sayed Gallal, the most popular and powerful of Cairo's bosses, illustrates both the integrating role played locally by urban clientage networks and

---

[24] René Lemarchand and Keith Legg, "Political Clientelism and Development," *Comparative Politics* (January 1972), p. 155.

[25] Fassi notables are not, however, bosses in the true sense of the word. Rather, they are a blue-blooded elite whose political influence rests primarily on their well-established social and economic status.

[26] See Samir Khalaf, "Primordial Ties and Politics in Lebanon," *Middle Eastern Studies* (April 1968), esp. pp. 254–57. See also Arnold Hottinger, "Zu'ama in Historical Perspective," in *Politics in Lebanon,* ed. Leonard Binder (New York: John Wiley and Sons, 1966).

the government's hostility toward them. Gallal is a self-made man, who acquired considerable wealth by his commercial acumen. He now controls a major percentage of wholesale and retail foodstuff outlets in the Cairo *baladi* district (old native quarter) bordering Al-Azhar. His financial empire is paralleled by an extensive clientage network which extends down into the impoverished citizenry of the district, who look up to Gallal as the benevolent provider of welfare and occasional protection from the whims of interfering bureaucrats. The ties binding clients to Gallal are not simply instrumental; he is looked upon as a devoutly religious man and as a spiritual leader, and he has reinforced this image by financing the building of mosques in his district. His religious commitment is apparently genuine, for he risked his career in the National Assembly by strict adherence to what he considers to be a principle of Islam. Having won election to parliament in 1957, he became identified as the leading critic of the government's efforts to improve the status of women. His vehement objection to the inclusion of women in the country's political organizations caused the government to prevent him from offering his candidacy for reelection to the Assembly in 1969, and Dr. Hassan Mahmoud Kalifa was imposed by the government on the district's reluctant constituents. Despite the very audible grumbling of Gallal's clients and their effective boycott of the elections, the government refused at first to give ground, assuming that Gallal's following would dissipate when it became apparent that he had no friends in the government.[27] But Gallal could not be dispatched to political obscurity so easily, and in the 1971 parliamentary election the government, having recently been purged of Gallal's main enemies (namely, Ali Sabry and his supporters), permitted him to run. He won by a landslide.

Gallal, easily the most powerful of Egypt's urban bosses, is not an important figure in national politics. While he cannot be shaken out of the government, those in power do not have to let him climb higher. His and other urban machines do not effectively and continuously articulate demands on the government. Their role is that of enhancing communal solidarity by providing welfare services, frequently augmented by spiritual guidance, in a fashion not dissimilar to that of American ethnic-based political machines of a bygone era. But unlike the ethnic mosaic upon which American political machines were based, Egypt's relative homogeneity provides few supplementary ethnic ties.

The degree of integration and stable community politics achieved in Egypt is due largely to patron-client relationships. The absence of categorical horizontal ties and, therefore, of political groups does not seem to cause a generalized frustration, even in the face of social mobilization. Vertical loyalties in informal authority structures provide Egyptian urban politics with an adequate functional substitute.

Clientelism in the Contemporary Political Elite. Any reasonable criterion for defining the Egyptian political elite leads to the conclusion that it is large and poorly

[27] This reasoning would have been correct had Gallal not had an independent resource base in his chain of grocery stores, which the government could not sequester because Gallal vested formal ownership in his managers while personally retaining de facto ownership. Most other aspiring politicians are not so well provided for, and were they to lose access to their main resource of control over allocation of government jobs, their clients would quickly abandon them.

integrated.[28] Members of the elite do not pass through well-defined and rigid channels of recruitment; nor are they all personally acquainted. There are no geographically distinctive areas, no cohesive ethnic groups, and no elite schools which contribute a disproportionate and identifiable share of Egypt's top decision makers.[29] The party, far from being an effective structure for the recruitment of elites, fails to screen out elements actively hostile to it. The elite is at once homogeneous in that it is not factionalized along ethnic, religious, linguistic or other categorical lines, and heterogeneous in that it lacks a cohesive political ideology and a shared dedication of purpose. Precisely because the elite is an undifferentiated lump that lacks any leavening agents, it is honeycombed with constantly shifting cliques and factions. There are no restraints on alliance formation and disintegration other than those dictated by short-term tactics. Identifiable variations in occupational background and social origins, such as civilian versus military and landed upper class versus urban middle class, do not provide fault lines that run through and permanently divide the elite. Civilians and officers, pashas and bureaucrats, work together and against one another in a way that belies categorical loyalties.

There is, however, some method to the madness. Cutting through the elite are clientage networks that provide the chains of command through which Egypt is ruled. In addition to vertical relationships between patrons and clients, horizontal ties among equals influence recruitment and serve as the basis for shifting factionalism. Nonetheless, the recruitment process itself and the political muscle of cliques and factions ultimately depend upon vertical and not horizontal solidarities. Relationships among equals are supplementary to clientelism in that they provide channels of mobility between clientage networks. Also, patrons of competitive clientage networks may forge temporary alliances in pursuit of mutual interests. For these personal alliance systems to be formed and maintained, a plethora of formal and informal organizations is required, in which politically relevant personal relationships may be established. Before examining these patterns of association, let us first take a closer look at the structure of the elite under Nasser and under Sadat.

The political elite under Nasser was stratified into two distinct layers. The top stratum consisted of Nasser himself and a handful of his closest advisors, almost all of whom were members of the original Revolutionary Command Council. Membership in this inner core fluctuated as a consequence of interpersonal rivalries among Abdul Hakim Amer, Zakaria Mohieddin, Abdul Latif Baghdadi, Ali Sabry, Sami Sharaf, and so forth, and as a result of Nasser's personal political power requirements. Of Nasser's closest advisors, only Amer remained continuously within the inner core during the entirety of his political life. Other key figures circulated from the bottom to the top layer of the elite and back down again, or vice versa, at a pace which indicates a moderate degree of rivalry, hostility and disagree-

[28] Because power is not institutionalized, role incumbency is not a good indicator of elite status. Nevertheless, because it is the only readily available definitional criterion, it may be used as a rough indication of what types of individuals may be powerful in Egyptian politics. The roles of greatest importance are the presidency, presidential advisors, cabinet ministers, top-ranking officers, governors, high ASU officials, leaders of the People's Assembly, editors of the leading daily newspapers and weekly magazines, and chairmen of the boards of the largest state companies and holding companies.

[29] These conclusions are based on data on the social backgrounds of the Egyptian political elite as presented in R. Hrair Dekmejian, *Egypt under Nasser* (Albany: State University of New York Press, 1971), pp. 176–204.

ment within the elite, but not fratricidal intra-elite conflict. For most players, the stakes of the game were not all or nothing, but were gains or losses proportional to the limited scope of the ventures they were willing to undertake.

Since very few players were forced into total retirement, the size of the elite continued to expand as the number of those entering the rotation system in the inner core and on the periphery of the elite increased. What began as a small coterie of fellow colonels and majors rapidly became an amorphous, sprawling elite of officers, bureaucrats, professors, *ancien régime* politicians, and others who had to be brought into the picture as Nasser and his comrades were faced with the tasks of ruling. Nasser believed that new directions required new personnel, and his shotgun blast at modernization brought into the fold vast numbers of idea men and administrators who could not later be ejected when their ideas proved unsound or their administrative fiefdoms were kidnapped by members of succeeding waves of entrants to the elite. While the colonels and majors were bound together ideologically only by loyalty to the army and to the nation, the proliferation of the elite and Egypt's de facto independence severed even those bonds of elite cohesion.

Sadat inherited an unwieldy command structure further neutralized by poor integration of his commanders. The two-tiered elite system, still intact at Nasser's death, could not be handed down because those in the inner core at the moment of transition, including Ali Sabry, Sami Sharaf, and Shaarawi Gomaa, were all implacable enemies of Sadat. Most other prestigious members of Nasser's inner core had been put on the shelf several years earlier, and Sadat had no desire to dust them off and bring them back as equals or even as clients. This left Sadat with only a handful of moderately prestigious civilians, such as Mahmoud Fawzi, Aziz Sidky, and Sayed Marei, whom he could push into the limelight and thereby hope to win some legitimacy for his regime. In the meantime he secured the crucial military prop by promoting his comrades from officer school days into vital command positions; but neither step could provide the semblance or the reality of an inner core of advisors on whom Sadat could lean and through whom those further removed from the top could approach the president. Thus both the legitimacy provided by the prestigious inner core, especially before 1967, and the effective performance of the demand articulation function through the president's clients were reduced substantially by the replacement of an inner core with a personnel vacuum. Sadat has further homogenized the elite by recruiting political unknowns as cabinet ministers and Arab Socialist Union (ASU) stalwarts, causing many Egyptians to wonder by whom they are being governed.

Sadat's unwillingness to recruit prestigious figures for active roles in the government or party arises from his fear of a possible challenge to his own authority. Ironically, it has caused power to ebb down into the elite. Formal structures, the foremost of which is the People's Assembly, and informal cliques and factions even at the edge of the elite have acquired additional veto power, which they possessed only in small measure under Nasser, and some actual power over decision making, a real change from the days of rubber-stamp democracy under Nasser. While power is still highly centralized and ultimately vested in the presidency, Sadat's clientage network is too poorly delineated to draw all political decision making into its channels and hence upward into the hands of the president and an inner core of his closest clients. This may, however, be only a temporary state of affairs, for if Sadat successfully consolidates his power, decision making will revert to the exclusive arena of the president's clientage network.

While the specific pattern of clientelism in the elite has been modified as a result of Sadat's succession, the organizational form itself remains intact. Similarly, the units of organization that facilitate communication within and between clientage networks have remained unaltered. They are key elements in the Egyptian political system, and little short of a transformation of the political culture would seriously affect the vital role they play. The remainder of this paper will be devoted to an analysis of these units of informal and formal organization.

Units of Informal Organization in the Elite

The Family. The family is the most easily identified unit of informal political organization, but it no longer has the overwhelming importance it once had. Prior to 1952, recruitment into and politics within the elite were based almost exclusively on ties of kinship and marriage. Wealthy landowners with extended clientage networks based on material wealth monopolized top political posts. The most universal and effective adhesive for binding two or more families together and uniting their clientage networks was marriage. Cliques, factions, and political parties were vehicles of family interest.

This domination of politics by relatively few extended families was terminated by Nasser's seizure of power. The right to participate in politics was denied to many of the leading members of the *ancien régime,* while the economic basis of their political power was attacked through agrarian reform. The party system, which had provided a convenient structure within which family-based politics flourished, was also abolished.

However, the role of the family as a unit of political organization was not destroyed by Nasserism. While economic reforms have undermined material resource bases for clientelism, and while the dramatic increase in the size of the elite has demanded additional social units for elite integration, the family was not so weakened as to be shouldered aside by either the formal or informal structures that have emerged since 1952. In the first instance, those units of intra-elite political organization that have emerged do not provide stiff competition for familism. All formal structures are weak, and nonfamilial informal groupings, such as *shillas* and *dufaas* (see below), are not structurally superior to families in the sense of being able to unite really large numbers of people for concerted political activity. Nasser's political creations have been supplements to familism, not replacements.

This may well be as Nasser himself desired it. There is no evidence to suggest that he was bent on destroying the family as a unit of political organization; he simply wanted to purge those families whose politics he could not stomach. He was perfectly willing to recruit into his cabinets and into the ASU reform-minded *ancien régime* politicians from prestigious families as long as they could provide him with administrative expertise or political connections to segments of the articulate public. Furthermore, Nasser himself did not refrain from using family connections in pursuit of personal ambition. He was refused admission to officers school on his first try, but his second application succeeded because of the intervention of General Haidar, Abdul Hakim Amer's uncle. Years later, Nasser's Free Officer organization included several officers from leading families, including Amer, Ali Sabry, Khaled Mohieddin, Wagih Abaza, Salah Dessouki, and others. Nasser was a realist who accepted the political role of the family and sought not to destroy it, but rather to use it for his own purposes.

The importance of the family in the recruitment process has been maintained despite a basic change in the nature of clientelism. Before 1952 clientelism was based mainly on material wealth, and elite status was guaranteed for wealthy landowners. The transition from land to strategic personal contacts within administrative and political structures as the main basis for clientelism made the family into one of several units through which profitable personal contacts could be secured. The family is no longer a political unit with a corporate identity. It is a communication center in which one member's linkages become available to all on an individual, and not on a group, basis. The Hassanein, Marei, Tarraf, Borolossy, Zayyat, and other families with several brothers and cousins within the elite are more akin to small instrumental friendship groups than to political dynasties. The political welfare of members of nuclear or extended families is no longer automatically more compelling than other personal alliances.

Families whose members move up in the elite and enjoy greater longevity than average at the top are usually those with wide-ranging contacts. If all members of the family are entrenched in the same ministry or are otherwise locked into one structure or one profession, their contacts will be fewer and their careers will be subject to more fluctuations and overlap. A family spread more thinly across several governmental structures and professions and active in a variety of voluntary associations will have more linkages to exploit. In the Marei family, for example, one brother (Marei Ahmed) was a business success and is now director of the chemical *mouassassa* (a state holding company); another (Hassan) as an engineer and former minister of industry has excellent ties to the industrial community; and a third (Sayid) is an agronomist with a firm base of personal connections among agricultural engineers. The Mareis, by virtue of their father's activities in the Wafd and Sayid's in the Saadist party, have useful political ties to former leading families which produced young, bourgeois nationalists. From the outset of the Nasser era they have had ties to officers in the regime through their cousin, Ali Sabry. Thus the Mareis, while having numerous enemies in and out of the elite, have sufficiently wide-ranging ties to be immune to efforts to oust them from the elite. While the Marei brothers fall back on the family in times of need, each also has other personal connections and loyalties that are equally important for his political career.

While recruitment is more a function of mutual contacts shared by members of a family than of direct intervention by one member of a family on behalf of another, there are cases of influence-peddling on the basis of family name. Even Nasser was not able to prevent his relatives from using his name for personal, pecuniary interest. The activities of Nasser's brother in Alexandria eventually became so notorious that Nasser was compelled to purge him from the National Assembly and to have his wheeling and dealing curtailed. Relatives of other members of the inner core also cashed in on family connections. Mohammed Baghdadi,

Abdul Latif Baghdadi's brother, assisted his friends by giving them calling cards with a brief, handwritten note of introduction, a service for which he charged £E50. Sadat, whose abhorrence of corruption and the feathering of family nests is considerably less than was Nasser's, is willing to operate more directly through those related to him by marriage. One of Sadat's key henchmen in the People's Assembly is Abu Wafia, the husband of his wife's sister. In the SUMED (Suez-Mediterranean) pipeline scandal of 1972, many suspected Wafia of covering the trail of graft which was thought to lead to Sadat himself.

Nasser's fear of having his regime tainted by scandals growing out of family interest, along with his purge of the country's leading political families, his attack on the basis of family wealth, and the proliferation of the elite under him reduced but did not destroy the role of the family as a unit of informal organization within the elite. Ingrained in traditional political culture as the sole unit within which relationships of mutual trust could be established, the family has remained important as a symbol of unity and trust. The ultimate symbolic step in cementing a political alliance is still interfamily marriage. In 1966 for example, after the passage of three years had healed the wound in the Nasser-Amer relationship caused by the dispute over control of the armed forces, Nasser and Amer celebrated their reunion as political comrades by marrying Nasser's brother to Amer's daughter.[30]

In addition to the symbolic role of marriage in uniting long-time political allies, ties of kinship and marriage still operate alongside patron-client linkages and horizontal ties in binding together members of the elite. The manifold ties holding together the amorphous group that allegedly sought to overthrow Sadat in May 1971 illustrate how widespread family ties are in the elite and how they are employed with other linkages in the formation of cliques and factions. The three leaders of the anti-Sadat forces were Ali Sabry, Sami Sharaf, and Shaarawi Gomaa. These three men were bound together by their mutual antipathy to Sadat, but by very little else. Until Nasser's death, in fact, Sharaf and Sabry had been antagonists, in part because Nasser had relied on Sharaf to police Sabry's activities. But Nasser's death and Sadat's rise to power altered the situation dramatically and made temporary friends of these one-time enemies. Each of the three had extensive clientage networks within the structures over which he had formal authority. Sabry, former first secretary of the ASU, had a network of clients in the ASU; Gomaa, minister of the interior, had entrenched his clients in the Ministry of the Interior and the security organs under its jurisdiction; and Sharaf, director of Nasser's personal security service, had clients within this force and, by virtue of his close daily contact with Nasser and his control over access to the president, he had been able to establish ties over a broad front. Other members of the anti-Sadat faction were brought into the fold as a result of kinship or marriage ties to Sabry, Gomaa, or Sharaf, whereas still others were anti-Sadat because of kinship or marriage ties to clients of the faction's leaders. The failure of the faction to achieve its aim of ousting Sadat was perhaps due to its Byzantine complexity, which would have made a well-timed, carefully coordinated strike difficult and security leaks inevitable.

---

[30] The marriage was not enough, though, to prevent the final break between Amer and Nasser as a result of disaster in the 1967 war.

Although the entire network of kinship ties within the faction is so complex that it is impossible to sort out, some idea of the role these ties played may be obtained by looking at the tip of the iceberg. Mohammed Faik, minister of communications at the time of the purge, is married to Ali Sabry's niece. Two other cabinet members who joined the faction, Saad Zayed, minister of housing, and Hilmy Said, minister of electricity and the High Dam, are married to two daughters of Morsi Farahat, a lawyer and ex-Wafdist minister of supply in the 1950 cabinet. Farahat's third daughter is married to Shaarawi Gomaa. These ties are further reinforced through the marriage of one of Hilmy Said's brothers to Saad Zayed's daughter and of another of his brothers to Shaarawi Gomaa's daughter.

Mahmoud Riad, minister of foreign affairs then and now secretary general of the Arab League, came within a hair's breadth of being purged during the "correction of the revolution." He is related to former Minister of War Mohammed Fawzi, who apparently joined the anti-Sadat faction just prior to Sadat's roundup. Riad is also related to Sharaf's wife, who is in turn a close friend of two sisters, one of whom is married to Ali Zein Abidine, ex-minister of transport, former president of the engineer's syndicate, and a member of the anti-Sadat faction. The other sister is married to Ahmed Muharrem, a former minister of housing who has long been a *shilla* [31] copartner with Osman A. Osman, Egypt's leading building contractor, a close friend of Sadat's and currently a cabinet super-minister. The Muharrem-Osman *shilla* is cohesive and withstood the comparatively minor centrifugal force of Muharrem's distant family tie to the "conspirators." Although important, family connections are not always compelling.

On the periphery of the faction, membership was mainly a result of patron-client linkages; but in some cases clientelism was reinforced by marriage bonds or by kinship. Hashem al-Ashiry, for example, assistant secretary general of the Cairo ASU branch before being jailed by Sadat, is a distant cousin of Sami Sharaf, and his brother, a police officer, is married to Sami Sharaf's daughter.

Obviously, family ties are still vital for intra-elite politics. They are not, however, the sole means of organizing political activity, and they are not so important that they cannot be ignored. Because there are alternative units in which politically efficacious relationships may be established, loyalties are not exclusively familial. Mahmoud Riad, for example, while thoroughly entangled in the web of family ties that pulled the anti-Sadat faction together, apparently never committed himself to the cause of ousting the president. Similarly, Ahmed Muharrem, while tied to the faction through his wife's sister's husband, Ali Zein Abidine, also maintained connections to Sadat through his association with Osman A. Osman. There are other cases of family ties being overridden by cross-cutting loyalties. Ali Sabry went out of his way to create problems for his banker uncle, Ali Shamsi Pasha, possibly because Sabry believed this would raise his political stock with Nasser and/or among leftists, for whom he was attempting to pose as a champion. Similarly, Sabry and Sayed Marei, while first cousins, have helped one another only rarely.

[31] A *shilla* is a group of two to about ten members who work together in the pursuit of individual goals. The role played by *shillas* in the Egyptian political elite is more or less the same as that played by *dawrahs* in the Iranian elite. (See James Bill, *The Politics of Iran: Groups, Classes and Modernization* (Columbus, Ohio: Charles Merrill, 1972), pp. 44–49; and Marvin Zonis, *The Political Elite of Iran* (Princeton: Princeton University Press, 1971), pp. 238–41. *Shillas* will be discussed below at greater length.

More frequently, the different loci of their extrafamilial connections, Sabry's in the military and the ASU and Marei's among agronomists and political conservatives generally, have forced them to take different stances on issues and, on occasion, to personally oppose one another.

Ties of kinship and marriage therefore provide one of several guides to an individual's status *vis à vis* shifting cliques and factions within the elite, and also may explain his presence in the elite in the first instance. But family members are outward- rather than inward-looking. If other ties prove to be more efficacious than those of kinship, politicians will pursue them and abandon the family as a political base. Families are preeminently junctions of personal communication networks, which multiply their members' opportunities for establishing useful contacts.

The *Dufaa*. The Egyptian equivalent of the old boy network is the *dufaa*. Literally *dufaa* means a pushing out; colloquially it refers to a graduating class in a single faculty or subject from a university, technical or military institute, or secondary school. Similar to an informal alumnus organization, the *dufaa* generates somewhat stronger loyalties and mutual obligations than do its Western counterparts. Its important role in the recruitment process stems from the intimate connection between higher education and vocational opportunities within the civilian, military, and public sector bureaucracies. Because the *dufaa* provides an ascriptive channel within which recruitment into government jobs is effected, and because the majority of the political elite is recruited from the civil service, military, or the public sector, the *dufaa* is in turn a vital unit for recruitment into, and an informal unit of organization within, the political elite. Its importance is further enhanced by the absence of a political party effectively performing recruitment and decision-making functions.

Virtually all ministries, governmental institutes, public sector companies and holding companies *(mouassassas)*, as well as the military, are arenas of intense inter-*dufaa* competition. Cleavages between *dufaas* are on the basis of year and place of graduation and academic subject. In specialized ministries and institutes, such as the Ministry of Agriculture, where virtually all employees are agronomists and hence interacademic rivalries are avoided, *dufaa* connections nevertheless are important for the functioning of the ministry. They are, moreover, becoming ever more vital as the bureaucracy swells. From the early part of this century until the 1940s, *dufaa* rivalries within the Ministry of Agriculture were confined almost exclusively to a sort of friendly competition between those who had taken graduate degrees in America and those who had taken them in Great Britain. There was only one faculty of agriculture in Egypt until 1944. All agronomists were members of a Cairo University agricultural faculty *dufaa* and virtually all agronomists knew one another personally. The establishment of a faculty of agriculture at Alexandria led to a Cairo University/Alexandria University cleavage within the ministry and this, along with the expanding size of the ministry and the ever-increasing number of agronomists, began to make *dufaa* ties important for recruitment. This process was speeded up under Nasser. The vast expansion of higher education, including new faculties of agriculture and agricultural higher institutes, and the limitation of employment opportunities to the civil service enormously increased the competition for government jobs. The *dufaa* became the main unit on which aspiring graduates could rely for favorable appointments. Its importance to these fresh recruits was further reinforced by their lack of other career-relevant personal ties. Unlike their predecessors, who were generally of high social status and who enjoyed excellent family connections, graduates since World War II, and particularly since 1952, have been more broadly representative of the society. Lacking family connections or well placed patrons, they must rely on other members of their *dufaa* for mutual assistance.

In those ministries, institutes, companies, and holding companies in which more than one specific professional skill is required, the *dufaa* has become even more important. Whereas in the Ministry of Agriculture it is only agronomists who are struggling for upward mobility, in other arms of the bureaucracy competition is more complex because engineers, accountants, economists, scientists, and others can all make a case for the occupational relevance of their skills. There is intense rivalry for management positions, for example, between graduates of the commerce faculties and engineers, both groups claiming that their educations better prepare them for management tasks. Normally the deciding factor in recruitment and promotion is not achievement, but rather the operation of *dufaa* networks.

While *dufaas* are vital for recruitment, they are too large for all members to be on close personal terms. The *dufaa* is not a cohesive unit whose members share a one-for-all and all-for-one spirit. There are mutual expectations of assistance in obtaining jobs and promotions, and other favors are exchanged, but the expectations are those appropriate to casual friendship based on the old-boy tie. Great personal sacrifices are not expected and usually are not made. One puts in a good word for a member of his *dufaa* but does not ruthlessly twist arms for him.

The politically important function performed by the *dufaa* is that of providing a setting within which closer personal relationships may be established, relationships which do call for arm-twisting. It is in this role as a communication network that the *dufaa* takes on added importance for recruitment at higher levels in the bureaucracy and into the elite and for intra-elite politics. Friendships established within *dufaas* may weld together a small group of fellow graduates whose personal loyalties run deep and expectations of mutual assistance are great. Such a friendship unit, whether established in a *dufaa,* as a result of family connections, or as a consequence of activity in voluntary associations or other formal organizations, is referred to as a *shilla.*

The relative importance of the *dufaa,* the family, and formal organizations as networks within which individuals establish *shillas* and patron-client relationships varies. Any one may be the crucial unit within which the necessary contacts are made. For those of higher social status—and especially those who were active, or whose families were active, in politics before 1952—the family is normally of greater importance than the *dufaa.* The expansion of the elite and its absorption of a broader spectrum of the populace, as well as the demise of many of the leading political families due to direct prohibition of their political activities and through the undermining of their economic base, has operated to enhance the importance of the *dufaa* at the expense of the family. Lacking extensive family connections, the technical specialists recruited into the elite by Nasser and Sadat have depended far more heavily on their university and professional connections than did their predecessors.

Since 1952 the *dufaa* has been of significance at the pinnacle of the elite. The Free Officers who overthrew King Farouk were members of the first *dufaas* of the military academy after formal independence had been granted in 1936 and of the 1948 *dufaa* of the staff college. The *shillas,* which were later to contend for power and influence in the elite, grew out of these *dufaas.* Although the civilianizing of the regime resulted in the Free Officers expanding their contacts and eventually in the formation of *shillas* and clientage networks including both officers and civilians, *dufaa* ties and inter-*dufaa* hostilities dating to the late 1930s and early 1940s are still alive. Sadat has systematically installed surviving members of his officer school *dufaa* in top command positions in the armed forces, culminating with the appointment of Ahmed Ismail as minister of war. These senior officers had been victims of former Commander-in-Chief Abdul Hakim Amer's recruitment practices. Amer, who was younger than Sadat and Nasser, refused to appoint officers older than himself to top posts. He preferred to recruit those of later graduating classes, whose dependency status could not be doubted.

Like families and formal organizations, *dufaas* do not possess an organizational character, and they do not articulate or aggregate interests. Families, *dufaas,* and formal organizations are important for analyses of Egyptian politics, not because they provide clearly delineated boundaries of political action, but because they provide clues to the personal loyalties and hostilities that influence the performance of all political functions. Knowledge of an elite member's family, educational background, and organizational activities is necessary, but it is usually not a sufficient basis on which to predict or account for his behavior. In order to understand why a politician behaves as he does, it is necessary to determine where he stands within clientage networks and in the complex of constantly shifting and overlapping circles of equals. These circles, or *shillas,* are the largest effective unit of horizontal political organization.

The *Shilla*. A *shilla* is a small group of friends who work together to obtain individual goals and particularly career advancement in the civil service, military, public sector, and/or the political elite. *Shillas* may survive in the absence of affective ties, but will die away if their instrumental value evaporates. They are usually, however, more than just temporary coalitions of individuals within their roles of bureaucrats, officers, managers, or politicians. A *shilla* relationship normally requires a diffuse and generalized commitment. Members of a *shilla* socialize with one another; they do not just conspire together in the corridors of Abdin palace. For example, the ringleaders of the anti-Sadat faction shared neighboring beach cabañas at Montezeh, a Mediterranean playground for wealthy Egyptians, where they and their families romped on weekends. In the meantime, members of other *shillas* were combining politics and family recreation at other locations.[32]

Shillas may result from acquaintances in *dufaas* or in formal organizations, or from vocational or family connections. Among the elite, *shillas* are more likely to

[32] Literally, most were down on the farm. Most leading members of the elite, if they did not already own farms before achieving political prominence, acquired one or more afterwards. Removed from the public eye of the capital and less prone to the ubiquitous surveillance and bugging activities of the *moukhabarat* and presidential security service, farms have become favorite weekend retreats for political activists.

be formed as a result of a combination of these ties than they are on the periphery. The tendency for multi-associational bases for *shilla* formation in the elite has been reinforced by the decline of familism and by the expanding size of the elite.

***Shillas* in the Bureaucracy.** At the nonelite level, a multitude of connections are not as crucial for upward mobility as in the elite. A *shilla* of five workers in the Ministry of Social Affairs may be as effective if it is composed of five cousins, five members of the same Sufi order, or five members of the same *dufaa* as it would be if it were formed of one or two members from each of the groupings. Because the bureaucratic environment is more stable than that of the political elite, and because *shillas* are more frequently formed within rather than across family, *dufaa,* or organizational boundaries, *shillas* in the bureaucracy are of longer duration than those in the elite. No politically powerful *shilla* persisted throughout the Nasser era, but countless numbers of bureaucratic *shillas* which pre-date Nasser's rise to power still exist today.

The history of one such *shilla* is illustrative. It was formed in 1952 by four recent graduates of Cairo University's special degree course in rural administration. Of similar urban middle-class backgrounds, these men had become friends during their years at the university and, upon their graduation and absorption into the Ministry of Social Affairs, they secured appointments to neighboring combined units in Gharbia Governorate. Over the next eight years they were posted to various combined units in the governorates of Lower Egypt, their geographical movement and professional mobility being identical. In 1960 as a result of the omnibus local government law, the post of village council chairman was created, and all four members of the *shilla* obtained appointments as chairmen in Giza Governorate, close to their homes in Cairo's suburb of Dokki. From that position they began to climb the bureaucratic ladder in the Giza Governorate's executive authority. To speed their rise, two of the four became active in the Arab Socialist Union, eventually succeeding in winning election to the Giza Governorate ASU committee and then to the General National Congress of the ASU in 1968. Another of the *shilla* members had a cousin who was legal officer for Giza Governorate, while the fourth, lacking any powerful connections in the Giza executive or political authorities, rode the coattails of his three comrades. Relationships established within the ASU and the kinship connection to the legal officer were sufficient to provide continuous promotions within the governorate and, by 1971, all members of the *shilla* had risen to grade three in the civil service.[33]

Fortune smiled on the *shilla* again in May 1971 when, as a result of the "correction of the revolution," the governor of Fayoum was purged and replaced by a university professor and former teacher of the four *shilla* members. Within a year all four had received transfers to Fayoum, being promoted to city council chairmen.

The history of this *shilla* illustrates several characteristics of *shillas* within the bureaucracy. First, they are of longer duration than *shillas* in the elite since their members have fewer incentives to jump into other *shillas*. Upward mobility in the bureaucracy, as opposed to the political elite, is usually a laborious process.

[33] All civil service jobs are graded from ten—the lowest—to one. Grade one is further subdivided into three subcategories, and on top of grade one has been placed a ministerial supergrade.

Bureaucrats are confronted with a regular sequence of steps leading upward and, with their attention focused on each succeeding step rather than on how to leap the staircase in one bound, their tactics are appropriately incremental. Remaining within one *shilla* and working for gradual promotion is a more suitable strategy than moving from *shilla* to *shilla* in an attempt to maximize upward mobility. It is in the political elite where the structure is more fluid and careers are more meteoric that *shilla*-jumping not only is useful, but is also a necessary prerequisite for success.

Second, this *shilla* illustrates how a variety of personal connections are relevant to a career. Based in a *dufaa,* the *shilla* depended for its success on kinship linkages, patron-client relationships in the ASU, and on the patronage extended by a former teacher, with whom the members of the *shilla* had kept in touch over the years.

Finally, this *shilla,* which has almost reached the gap separating bureaucrats from politicians, reveals the inherent weakness in bureaucracy-centered *shillas* once they begin to approach the political elite. A long-lived *shilla* that is based exclusively in a *dufaa* and whose members lack personal connections within the elite cannot move as one unit into the elite. The members of that *shilla* must begin to go their separate ways if they are to climb much further. For members of this particular *shilla,* the next step is to become secretary-general of a governorate, a promotion which could be arranged within the network of bureaucratic connections the *shilla* enjoys, but that is the top of the bureaucratic ladder. The next rung is occupied by a political appointee in the sense that appointment as a governor or an undersecretary requires at least one patron who is well placed within the political elite. In order to establish a connection with such a patron, an upwardly mobile bureaucrat would have to be in a *shilla* in which at least one of the members had already established such a patron-client relationship. The *shilla* described here has no such connections. If its members nurse ambitions of becoming undersecretaries,[34] they must look for new *shilla* partners outside the confines of their *dufaa.* All four are members of a Sufi order, and perhaps a connection established within that context could prove to be the crucial one.

***Shillas* in the Political Elite.** The strength of a *shilla* in the elite depends on the personal power and positions of its members. A *shilla* whose members are dispersed broadly throughout the elite offers greater advantages to its members than one in which members congregate in certain political or governmental structures. If, for example, one member of a *shilla* has a high post in the ASU, another holds a ministerial portfolio, and a third is in the president's office (as was the case with the short-lived Sabry, Gomaa, Sharaf *shilla*), then its scope can be extraordinarily wide. A *shilla* may in fact form the basis for a large faction, for each member of the *shilla* contributes his clientage network and family connections to the alliance.

The fluidity of *shillas* in the elite is due to the ebb and flow of political events, both internal and external, to the low level of institutionalization of Egyptian political life, and to a dynamism which is generated by *shillas* themselves. A law of *shilla* balance appears to operate. Strong *shillas* which threaten to upset the

[34] It is highly improbable that they could secure appointments as governors. Only one career local government official has been appointed as a governor since 1952.

equilibrium of the elite give rise to counter *shillas,* and once the threat has been removed, they disintegrate and make room for new combinations. This dynamic is not impaired by other loyalties. *Shillas* are not predicated on political ideologies. They may be based on a shared position on key issues, such as control of the military or redistribution of land ownership, but the position itself is usually dictated by nonideological factors and is not symptomatic of a comprehensive ideology from which tactics are deduced. Political ambition and material rewards are the primary stimulants for *shilla* formation.

That *shilla* commitments are open ended is illustrated by Aziz Sidky's political career. After returning to Egypt with a Harvard Ph.D., his first big job was with the Tahrir Province Organization, where he became friends with the organization's director, Major Magdi Hassanein, a favorite Nasser client. Sidky's friendship with Hassanein paid off in 1956 when, partly as a result of Hassanein's patron-client relationship with Nasser, Sidky was made minister of industry. The Sidky-Hassanein *shilla* was later cemented by Sidky's appointment of Magdi Hassanein's two brothers to directorships of industrial firms in Helwan. But this *shilla,* like most others, did not command absolute loyalty from its members, nor did the relationship require either partner to terminate secondary alliances with the other's enemies. Hassanein remained on close terms with Minister of Transport Mustafa Khalil, who advised Hassanein on investing his mounting fortune garnered through his supervision of coal importation for the newly built iron and steel works, but the Khalil-Sidky relationship deteriorated after 1961. In 1964, when Khalil wrote an article criticizing Egypt's industrial policies, the relationship turned permanently sour, despite the mutual tie to Hassanein and another mutual friendship with Mohammed Hassanein Heikal. In 1970, when Heikal and Sidky were on good terms because of the mounting attack on "technocrats" and "antisocialists," Heikal in his capacity as minister of information appointed Khalil to a key position in broadcasting.

Although the Sidky-Hassanein connection has not been completely severed, its strength waned because Hassanein's political fortunes never completely recovered from the blow of the Tahrir Province scandal, which finally broke into the open during the 1957 session of the National Assembly. Eventually removed from the scene by being appointed ambassador to Czechoslovakia, Hassanein could no longer pull his weight in the relationship, so Sidky sought friends elsewhere. In the mid–1960s he buried the hatchet in his feud with Sayed Marei, arch enemy of Hassanein and the staunchest opponent of the military's involvement in the agricultural sector. Sidky and Marei were forced into each other's unwilling arms by their mutual opposition to the growing role of the military in domains previously exclusively civilian, and later because of their suspicion of Sami Sharaf's ambitions. Equally important for the temporary truce was the fact that Marei and Sidky, of approximately equal stature in the elite, were in noncompetitive positions and hence each was able to assist the other in an area over which he otherwise had little influence. Sidky's network of clients and personal relationships and his formal authority were centered in the industrial sector, while Marei's power was founded in the Ministries of Agriculture and Agrarian Reform and the agriculture sector generally. As long as they remained in noncompetitive positions and the threat to their prestige and importance as civilian technocrats was alive, they remained on reasonably friendly terms, but success ruined their alliance. When in 1971 Sadat removed the threat to "science and faith" and promoted Sidky and Marei to deputy premierships, he effectively destroyed the vulnerable bond between them. In competitive positions in the cabinet, their ambitions were no longer reinforcing. Friendship turned to intense hostility, and in 1972 Sadat was forced to step in and separate the two by making Sidky prime minister and Marei first secretary of the ASU Central Committee. Marei and Sidky continued their personal battle from these command posts.[35]

While mutual threats and opportunities cause *shillas* to be formed and later dissolved, promotions tend to wreck them. When a member of a *shilla* is promoted, it is to his advantage to use his new influence to recruit clients rather than members of his *shilla,* and to jump into a more powerful *shilla. Shilla* obligations are honored only so long as all members contribute an equal share, and even then ambition may destroy the relationship. Upward mobility, which depends ultimately on patron-client relationships, is a constant source of temptation which threatens the stability of *shillas.*

Because *shillas* disintegrate as one or more of their members abandon them for greener pastures, the elite is well-stocked with individuals who are temporarily virtually without functions or responsibilities while waiting for an opportunity to join a new *shilla* which may offer them useful patronage. When one is left to his fate by his upwardly mobile friends, he retains his post and salary; but since authority and responsibility flow from personal connections and not from formal job descriptions, he has no real responsibility. His official grade and salary are his personal property and may not be confiscated. It is almost impossible to be downwardly mobile, although it is highly probable that one will be stationary and without real job responsibilities at various times in one's career. All categories of formal roles have a certain percentage of incumbents who are biding their time, waiting for the opportunity to jump into a new *shilla,* but some roles are almost exclusively parking lots for those temporarily abandoned. Nasser and Sadat have used the post of presidential advisor as one such resting place. A few advisors, such as Sami Sharaf under Nasser and Hafez Ismail under Sadat, have exercised real power, but up to a dozen others have simultaneously drawn grade-one salaries while using their offices for strictly personal purposes. Presidential advisor Sarwat Okasha, benefiting from the scholarly efforts of Magdi Wahba, almost completed a four-volume history of Islamic art before losing his job. He was fired not because of his redundancy but because he was traced as the source of a rumor that his long-time rival Abdul Qader Hatem had pocketed some of the £E6 million lost by the cinema industry in 1971. Ministerial secretaries and even deputy premiers may likewise be coupon clippers rather than active public servants.

Shillas are the strongest unit of organization for those of equal or only slightly

[35] Sidky, in addition to appointing Marei's opponents to cabinet positions, launched a "meet the people" campaign in which he toured the governorates, personally announcing his government's decisions to allocate funds to the governorates for welfare and public works projects. He also succeeded in creating the impression that, far from being a Russian puppet, he was a man of God. At each of his stops, the first order of business was to visit the local mosque. Marei, travelling the country in his capacity a first secretary of the ASU, was left with the task of stirring up enthusiasm for war, a far less popular platform than Sidky's combination of pork barrel and religion.

unequal status, but they are too small and too weak to be a source of durable cohesion in the elite. Their weakness may be attributed to the fact that alliance systems depend primarily on clientelism. Vertical associations cut through horizontal ties. Even among the inner core of the elite, *shillas* are not immune to the patronage power of the president, who can break up a *shilla* by favoring one or more of its members or counter its influence by directing his patronage away from it. If *shilla* ties were stronger, the elite would be less stable. The present fluidity of *shillas* prevents conflict from becoming crystalized and keeps personal hostilities from creating unbridgeable intra-elite cleavages.

Formal Organizations

Functionally, formal organizations are similar to families and *dufaas* in that they serve primarily to expand the personal alliances of their members. Formal organizations are not political groups as that concept is normally understood. They are not based on strong categorical ties, and they are not identifiable actors in decision-making arenas. An investigation of whether or not the most powerful of the professional organizations, the Engineers' Syndicate, "has been able to use its resources—influential members, scarce skills, and technical expertise—to exert influence on government policies," revealed that it has not.[36] The Engineers' Syndicate, like other professional associations, acts as a unit within the policy-making arena only with regard to a narrow range of professional issues, such as pensions, academic qualifications, pay scales, et cetera. Even in pursuit of such limited goals as these, professional associations behave more as medieval guilds than as modern associational interest groups. Inherently weak, they seek as leaders those close to the sources of patronage, such as ministers or ministerial secretaries.[37]

Because the importance of formal organizations is as vehicles through which personal connections are established, organizations which have been formally disbanded but in which strong personal ties had been established may be as, or more, powerful in contributing to policy outcomes than organizations with a formal, legal existence. During the Nasser era, for example, connections established earlier within those political parties banned after 1952 were important for recruitment into and politics within the elite. Nasser himself had close ties to members of *Misr al-Fatat,* and its former members enjoyed considerable influence over policies, particularly those in the agricultural sector. Nasser also had close ties with members of the *Hizb al-Watani* and recruited several of them into cabinets formed in the mid–1950s.[38] While the National Union was the sole legal party at the time, it played a comparatively minor role in recruitment and policy making.

The role of formal organizations as communication centers is enhanced by the nature of the recruitment process. It is personal connections and not organizational

[36] Moore, "Authoritarian Politics in Unincorporated Society," p. 16.

[37] For an analysis of the role of Naquib (president) of the agricultural engineers' syndicate, see Robert Springborg, "The Ties that Bind: Political Association and Policy Making in Egypt" (Ph.D. diss., Stanford University, 1974), pp. 256–62, 299–304.

[38] For example, Fathi Radwan was made minister of state in the first Naguib-Nasser government, and he subsequently held three other cabinet portfolios. Nur al-Din Tarraf, a former member of both *Misr al-Fatat* and the *Hizb al-Watani,* was the perennial minister of health in the 1950s and early 1960s.

loyalties that open the channels of upward mobility. Boundaries between institutions are extremely porous. An individual's path into the elite may lead through the military, the universities, public sector companies, the civil service, and/or the ASU. It is advantageous for an aspiring politician to shift from one to another of these institutions. Lateral movement is generally crucial for upward mobility, partly because it facilitates the expansion of alliance systems, and partly because in each institution the road up is blocked by the superabundance of manpower. There are too many seniors for a frontal assault to be successful, so a move one step sideways from the bureaucracy to the ASU, from the military to the public sector, from the university to the bureaucracy, and so on, usually means two steps up. Lateral movement is made possible through *shilla* or patronage connections, which in turn are generated by membership in *dufaas,* families, and formal organizations. Thus Sufi orders, sports clubs, the Rotary, professional syndicates, and so on are vital, for they provide neutral territory where individuals in various career structures may expand their connections beyond the strict confines of their ministry, company, university, et cetera. Because of the large size of the elite, the lack of integrating socialization experiences, and the absence of a party within which recruitment could be accomplished, formal organizations must facilitate recruitment by providing opportunities for politically relevant personal interaction.

Since formal organizations provide a necessary structure within which personal alliance systems may be established and maintained but do not behave as a collective political actor, it is not advantageous for an organization to be large. A large membership is in fact a liability. An organization's value to its members lies in its nature as a social gathering. If size begins to preclude face-to-face communication among the entirety of the membership, the organization will either splinter into smaller, informal groupings or it will be abandoned by its members. Large organizations necessarily are weak organizations, for either they are riddled with small informal groups which attenuate their members' linkages to the organization as a whole or their members have no commitment whatsoever. Professional syndicates with tens of thousands of members rarely attract more than a few hundred to their annual meetings, but small informal groups of engineers, agronomists, and other professionals manage to meet weekly for political, professional, and social purposes.[39] Individual Sufi orders have flourished under the Nasser and Sadat regimes, but the Sufi movement as an organized whole has stagnated.[40]

Because small groupings are as effective as large organizations or more so, and because organizations are vital as communication centers but valueless as collective actors, there are no criteria by which "political" may be distinguished from "nonpolitical" organizations. Personal contacts established within the Rotary may be as significant for political recruitment as contacts within the ASU. A *shilla* formed as a result of mutual activities in a Sufi order may have a greater impact on decision making than a *shilla* formed of ASU activists or of syndicate loyalists. All social gatherings, formal and informal, are of potential political relevance. The relative political importance of organizations depends less on their size and formal *raison d'être* than on the status of their members.

[39] See, for example, Moore, "Authoritarian Politics in Unincorporated Society," p. 18.

[40] See Morroe Berger, *Islam in Egypt Today: Social and Political Aspects of Popular Religion* (Cambridge: Cambridge University Press, 1970).

Conclusion

Clientelism provides an integrative, stabilizing force on the periphery of the Egyptian political system. Its flexibility has made it capable of adapting to new conditions and has headed off many of the potentially unsettling effects of social mobilization. In rural Egypt clientelism is based for the most part on the first-order resource of land ownership. Clientelism and the traditional solidarities of family and clan are still more important for social and political life than are any new organizational loyalties created under Nasser's or Sadat's tutelage. A clientelism based on the second-order resource of personal connections also is beginning to take hold in rural areas, and while patron-client relationships thus established may be less enduring, they nevertheless will continue to promote rural political stability.

Urban Egypt is expanding at a phenomenal pace—too rapid for its transport, communication, sanitation, housing, and other facilities—but it is not a scene of social or political breakdown. Neither is it a hotbed of associational activity. Anomie is prevented not by group membership but by political integration through traditional structures such as the family, and by clientage networks.

However, while clientelism promotes political stability on the periphery of the political system, it does not provide a sufficient organizational basis for a leader to enforce unity of purpose within the elite, nor for him to reach down effectively into the population to extract or distribute resources. Its shortcomings are based on the fact that loyalties are exclusively personal, effectively circumscribed by the maximum possible extent of face-to-face communication. As Scott argues, it becomes physically impossible for a patron to service relationships with more than about twenty or thirty clients. While a clientage network may be considerably larger than this, most clients are linked to the patron through intermediaries, and "at the periphery of a man's following are those clients who are relatively easy to detach. . . ."[41] Even Nasser, preeminent patron in the Egyptian elite, could not rely on his clientage system as an organizational weapon. Prevented from establishing a direct patron-client relationship with all or even with a substantial percentage of the elite, Nasser had to rely on his most immediate clients, or "client cluster" in Scott's terminology,[42] as intermediaries between himself and clients further from his person. While in theory this extended his patronage throughout the elite, in practice it was a crippling handicap. Members of his client cluster, including Abdul Hakim Amer, Zakaria Mohieddin, Sami Sharaf, Ali Sabry, and so on, short-circuited the connection between their clients and Nasser himself. Having used Nasser's patronage to construct a network of clients in the military, the Ministry of the Interior, the security services, the ASU, and within and across other institutions of the state, they manipulated their personal clientage networks for their own gain, which frequently ran counter to Nasser's interests.

There were real constraints on Nasser's exercise of power. Having delegated power to his clients, which enabled them to build clientage networks, he then had to prevent them from coalescing against him by balancing off one against the other, by withdrawing his patronage from them or, when the occasion demanded it, by

[41] Scott, "Patron-Client Politics," p. 95.
[42] Ibid., p. 97.

shearing from them all administrative and political responsibilities, and simultaneously by bringing in new clients to start the process once again. While he always managed to keep the upper hand because of his extraordinary skill at political infighting, he nevertheless had to yield to his rebellious clients on many issues, lest his balancing act topple over.

Nasser was a prisoner of the authority system by which he ruled. It kept him in power, but it prevented him from legitimating his rule in any procedural, ideological, or structural sense, and it did not provide him with the means for mobilizing the human energies needed to tackle Egypt's pressing economic problems. While it would be premature to pass judgment on Sadat, it appears unlikely at this point that he will develop the organizational weapon essential to the attainment of Egypt's elusive developmental goals.

V. THE POLITICAL ELITE IN IRAQ

Phebe A. Marr

In few countries of the Middle East has the quality of leadership been more crucial to development than in Iraq. Established as recently as 1920 at the behest of the British, Iraq has boundaries which reflect the interests of foreign powers rather than domestic realities. As a result, the country is fragmented among various ethnic and religious communities that share little tradition of cooperation and even less sense of a common national identity. There are no firm and well established political institutions which might hold the country together in times of adversity. Iraq's entire recorded history has been filled with conquest, discontinuity, and control by outside powers. For all of these reasons and despite its favorable resource pattern, Iraq is a notoriously difficult country to govern.

To these fundamental difficulties the revolution of 1958 has added the burdens of rapid modernization and radical social change. Yet if the revolution of 1958 and its aftermath have shown anything, it is that for Iraq the key to progress on any front is good political management. And this, of course, depends on the nature and quality of the country's political leadership, the kinds of men who come to the fore, and the skills, attitudes, and outlooks they bring with them.

For this reason, this study is focused on the political elite. It will seek to discover those factors in the background of the political elite which are relevant to the contemporary political situation. In so doing, it can, it is hoped, shed considerable light on the larger educated elite of which the political elite is the most important and representative segment. The political elite studied here is the group of people who make decisions on national policy. The sample includes the cabinet ministers who have held office since 1958, the three presidents of the republic, and the fifteen men who have been members of the Baathist Revolutionary Command Council since 1968.[1] Altogether this group includes 175 men and 2 women. A comparison between data for this group and broad statistical data on Iraqi society as a whole should yield some definite conclusions about the larger elite emerging in Iraq.

One difficulty hampers such a study in Iraq. There have been four different regimes since 1958, and each has brought about an almost complete turnover of high-level government personnel. This has been taken into consideration. Where there are marked differences in leadership traits between regimes, they have been noted. However, the focus will be on the general characteristics of leadership since 1958 and the most significant trends that have emerged during this period.

[1] A few cabinet ministers in the current Baath regime (1974) have been omitted because of inadequate data, but the current RCC (now reduced to six members) has been included. Under the present regime, the Regional Command of the Baath party, now consisting of thirteen members, has emerged as a much more significant policy-making group than the cabinet. These have not been included in the sample (unless they are also RCC members or ministers), but data on them is used to indicate the characteristics of the newly emerging Baath leadership where it differs from previous regimes.

Historical Perspective

It is impossible to understand the leaders of the new regime without some historical perspective. The outstanding Iraqi politicians of the pre-revolutionary era came to power in the 1920s with the establishment of the British mandate and the enthronement of the Hashemite monarch, Faisal I. They were the first generation of Arab nationalists to work for independence from the Ottoman Turks. At the time of the mandate they were men in their thirties. They had been educated in Ottoman academies in Istanbul; like their present-day counterparts, many were army officers, often from the lower middle class, and considered the radical nationalists of their day. Their cooperation with the British during World War I and British backing for Faisal disposed them to cooperate with the mandate power in achieving independence, rather than to rebel against it. Thus close Anglo-Iraqi ties were forged.

Aside from these nationalist politicians, the three essential pillars of the old regime were the British, the monarchy, and the landed oligarchy. Although the British mandate officially ended in 1932 when Iraq was admitted to the League of Nations as an independent country, the British connection continued in the form of a treaty of alliance. This gave the British the use of two Iraqi air bases and precedence in providing military training, economic assistance, and "advice." When this treaty expired in 1955, Iraq became a member of a new defense agreement, the Baghdad Pact, which included Turkey and later Iran, Pakistan, and Britain. The United States was a member in all but name. The pact ensured continued Western support of the regime.

The second pillar of the old regime was the monarchy. Under the Iraqi constitution, the king had considerable power, including the authority to select the prime minister, to adjourn parliament, to call for general elections and, according to an amendment of 1943, to dismiss the cabinet. Faisal I, a shrewd and canny politician, was able to make himself the chief arbiter of the political scene, but the monarchy declined after Faisal's death in 1933. His son Ghazi, killed in an auto accident in 1939, was young, inexperienced, and unable to play the role his father had. His death ushered in the regency of Amir Abdul Ilah, which officially lasted until 1953 when young King Faisal II, his nephew, attained his majority. In fact, Abdul Ilah, along with Nuri al-Said, perennial prime minister, remained a dominant figure until the end. His unpopularity with the masses and with the nationalists contributed significantly to the revolution.

The third pillar of the old regime consisted of those with wealth. Most important were the rural landlords, many of them also tribal leaders, who had considerable economic, social, and political power over the great majority of peasants. They were joined by the urban well-to-do, a smaller group, which had profited from the free enterprise policy of the old regime and the economic boom of the 1950s. Their strength lay in their control of parliament, which they used to block even moderate social reforms.

Meanwhile a counterforce to these elements, at first weak in numbers but growing in political importance, was emerging: the urban, educated elite. A heterogeneous group, its members had originated in various social and economic strata, but they possessed several distinctive characteristics. First, they had been educated in the new secular schools established under the mandate and later under independent Iraq. Second, they were urbanized. If they had not been born in cities, they had gone to school there (secondary schools were all located in the larger towns) and spent their working lives there, so they were largely cut off from the rural hinterland and the tribal population. Third, they were mainly professional men, the overwhelming majority of them employed by the government. They included the army officer corps, the middle to upper levels of the bureaucracy, the teaching staffs of secondary schools and colleges, and a new group of independent professionals—lawyers, doctors, engineers, and journalists. While some drew income from real estate or business, they did not identify their interests with these sectors.

By the last decade of the old regime, considerable numbers of this new elite had been absorbed into the establishment—the cabinet, the upper echelons of the bureaucracy, and the military. However, they had not yet replaced the handful of older, Ottoman-educated leaders who dominated the command posts of power and were symbolized by the strong man of the regime, Nuri al-Said. Nor had they been able to dislodge the other pillars—the British, the monarch, and above all the landlord shayks who had a dominant voice in parliament. The emerging middle class was less committed to actually assuming power than to having its way in a number of crucial issues on which it opposed the establishment's equally determined position. What were these issues?

First and foremost was the foreign policy of the regime. The treaty with Britain and later the Baghdad Pact were regarded by the opposition as diminutions of national sovereignty, because they tied Iraq to the Western powers, suspect because of their past imperialist policies in the Middle East and for their support of Israel. Moreover, the orientation of the regime toward the West and the "northern tier" countries, the opposition claimed, had alienated Iraq from other Arab countries, especially the new nationalist regime in Egypt. The second issue that opposed the establishment and the middle class was the severe crackdown by the regime on political freedoms, particularly through manipulation of elections, interference with the press, and suppression of opposition parties. These measures had been intensified in the mid–1950s, partly to engineer the passage of the Baghdad Pact by parliament. Third was the refusal of the regime to move more rapidly toward social reforms, especially land reform and diminution of the influence of the landlord shayks in parliament. These issues—most of all, dislike of the Baghdad Pact—were fanned into revolutionary fervor by the Nasser regime in Egypt and propaganda from Radio Cairo. The result was the revolution of July 14, 1958.

The revolution, when it came, was not the work of the civilian opposition, but of a handful of army officers. Disaffection among certain elements in the military had led to the formation of a Free Officers' movement similar to its Egyptian prototype sometime after 1954. A Higher Committee of Fourteen headed by Brigadier Abdul Karim Kassem was formed to plan the revolution. The coup which unseated the old regime, however, was not carried out by this committee (a fact that later alienated many of the Free Officers), but by two men, Kassem himself and his close associate, Colonel Abdul Salam Aref, together with a few handpicked officers. Although some civilian opposition politicians had been consulted beforehand, they played no part in the actual revolt. Thus, although they were later brought into the first government established after the revolution, they could make no claim to revolutionary leadership. Authority was placed firmly in the hands of military men where it has remained, directly under earlier regimes, indirectly under the present Baath regime.[2]

The new military rulers lost no time in dismantling the pillars of the old regime. The regent and the king were killed; parliament was abolished and with it the political power of the landed oligarchs; the leading old regime politicians were rounded up for trial and Nuri al-Said was killed in Baghdad while trying to escape from the authorities. Last came withdrawal from the Baghdad Pact, recognition of the Communist-bloc countries, and a rapid cooling of relations with the West. It should be noted that the support of the Soviet Union for the new regime, including Soviet economic and military aid, did not entirely counterbalance the lost British connection. Soviet influence has never been as strong as that previously exercised by Britain, and Iraqi-Soviet relations have frequently been strained.

It is well known that the Free Officers had come to no clear agreement among themselves on the positive aims to be pursued after the revolution. The result was a serious split on policy, a bitter struggle for power culminating in the Mosul rebellion of March 1959, and the chronic political instability which was the major problem of Iraq until the 1970s.

It is not our purpose here to trace the history of the new regime, but to analyze the men who have governed under it. However, one final point should be made in this introduction about revolutionary transition. It has resulted in a complete change of personnel at all top levels of government and through successive changes in the past fifteen years has now placed in power an entirely new generation of men with few adult memories of the old regime and little practical experience under it. The significant question here is how different they are from old regime leaders. In some ways, particularly in ideological and political orientation, the new leaders do present a contrast to the old; in others, notably in education, occupation, and ethnic and religious background, they do not. What has changed—and this is of prime importance in understanding the new regime's programs and difficulties—is its source of support. If the old regime relied mainly on the monarchy and the landed interests, the new one relies upon the army and, more broadly, the urban educated classes, of which the new leaders are the chief representatives. Regardless of the ideology that is used to justify them, the revolutionary programs of the new leaders have largely been shaped by their need for the support of this new middle class. The fact that this middle class is still small in numbers and far from homogeneous in its aims and interests goes far toward explaining the difficulties of the new regime in achieving a consensus and in implementing its programs. While the silent acquiescence of the peasantry and the small working class (neither of which can be relied on *in toto* to support the regime) may be gratifying to the present rulers, it is of little political consequence.

Who are these new leaders? What kind of education, skills and qualifications

[2] The current Baath regime has managed to isolate the army from politics, but the support of the military is essential if the regime is to survive. For an account of the revolution, see Majid Khadduri, *Republican Iraq* (New York: Oxford University Press, 1969), pp. 18–25.

do they bring to government? Above all, what are their aims, goals and accomplishments?

Educational Background

Education more than any other factor has created and shaped the new leadership and its supporters, the urban professional classes. What has this educational background been and what is its political significance?

Level of Education. First of all, an analysis of the cabinets and the RCC shows that the leaders possess a high level of education relative to the rest of the population. Some 91 percent have had at least three years of higher education, and three-quarters have a bachelor's degree or its equivalent. More surprising, almost half have done one year of graduate work, while a full 28 percent have completed doctorates.

To be appreciated, these figures must be compared with the general level of education in Iraq. In 1965 it was estimated that of a population of about nine million only 20 percent were literate;[3] 8 percent of the population had completed primary school; 2 percent secondary school, and less than .5 percent had received any higher education.[4] Another estimate has placed the college educated population, also in 1965, at not more than 26,000.[5] Among the younger generation these percentages will be higher. In 1971, roughly two-thirds of the requisite school-age population was in primary schools, one-third in secondary, and 6 percent in institutions of higher education.[6]

The reason for these extremely low figures is that education got off to a slow start in Iraq. At the time of the mandate there were probably not more than one or two thousand Iraqis who had graduated from any kind of higher educational institution, almost all of them in Istanbul. In contrast to the Turks, the Egyptians, and the Lebanese, virtually none had attended European institutions. Under the mandate education grew slowly. By 1932 the secondary schools were still only graduating about 170 students a year and the colleges about 50.[7] As the figures below indicate, the real spurt in education came only after the revolution. By the end of the old regime there were only a little over 50,000 students in intermediate and secondary schools, 5,700 in college, and 203 on missions abroad.[8] These statistics indicate why the political leaders can be considered an "elite."

---

[3] Foreign Area Studies, *Area Handbook for Iraq* (Washington, D.C.: Government Printing Office, 1969), p. 115. Hereafter cited as *Handbook.*

[4] These are percentages of the population who sat for final examinations after completing primary and secondary levels. Many failed the examinations. Had only those who passed been counted the figures would be 30 to 40 percent lower. Figures are taken from the Directorate General of Statistics, *Report on Education in Iraq, 1957–1958* (Baghdad: Government Press, 1959), pp. 20–25; Ministry of Education, *Educational Statistics 1964–1965* (Baghdad: Government Press, 1967), pp. 47, 81–85.

[5] Fahim Qubain, *Education and Science in the Arab World* (Baltimore: Johns Hopkins Press, 1966), pp. 290–91.

[6] Ministry of Planning, General Statistical Organization, *Annual Abstract of Statistics, 1971* (Baghdad, 1972).

[7] Directorate General of Statistics, *Report on Education, 1957–1958* (Baghdad: Government Press, 1959), pp. 9, 14.

[8] Ibid., p. 2; Qubain, *Education and Science,* p. 278.

However, caution must be used in evaluating the seemingly high level of education among the leaders. First of all, most of the highly educated men in the cabinets, especially those with doctorates, occupy secondary positions rather than the top policy-making positions.[9] Over 10 percent of the top-level leaders have not completed the equivalent of a college education and only 17 percent have doctorates. Second, there has been a downward trend in the educational level of leaders at the top since the revolution. This is particularly true of the military. Under Kassem, none of the top-level ministers had less than four years of higher education; by the end of the Aref regime, a third had no more than three years.[10] Among the RCC members who have served since 1968, 20 percent have had some graduate-level training; 47 percent have had a college-level degree; 13 percent have not completed college, while another 13 percent have had their college education interrupted. (One of these has since been awarded a degree.) This means that 26 percent had little or no higher education when they came to power.

Kind of Education. More important than the level of education, however, is its quality and content. What kind of education has the leadership received?

At the time the post-revolutionary leaders were in school, the Iraqi education system was divided at the lower levels into three steps—primary (six years), intermediate (three years), and secondary (two years).[11] Throughout, the curriculum

[9] The top-level positions include the presidents, the prime ministers, the ministers of interior, defense, finance and foreign affairs and in the 1968 Baath regime, the RCC.

[10] P. A. Marr, "Iraq's Leadership Dilemma," *Middle East Journal,* Summer 1970, p. 291.

[11] Recently a third year has been added to the secondary level, now making twelve years of schooling in all.

Table 5-1

LEVEL OF EDUCATION OF LEADERSHIP

Level of Higher Education	Kassem		Baath 1963		Aref		Baath 1968 [a]		Total [b]	
	No.	%	No.	%	No.	%	No.	%	No.	%
None	0	0	1	4	1	1	5	8	7	4
3 years	2	6	3	11	15	17	10	17	27	15
4 years	14	41	9	33	22	25	16	27	54	30
5 years	6	17	5	18	16	18	5	8	24	13
6 years or more	12	35	9	33	31	35	19	32	59	33
Unknown	0	0	0	0	3	3	3	5	6	3
Total	34	100	27	100	88	100	59	100	177	100
Addendum: completed doctorates	9	26	5	18	27	30	18	30	51	28

[a] Ministers in the first non-Baathist cabinet, ousted after two weeks, are included in the Baath 1968 figures.

[b] One hundred and seventy-seven individuals were included in this survey. Since some persons served under more than one regime, the figures for the individual regimes will not add up to the total column if added across. There are four such carryovers included in the Baath 1963 regime, fourteen in the Aref regime, and thirteen in the Baath 1968 regime.

was fixed by the central government. On the whole, it was theoretical and academic rather than practical. The primary grades taught religion, Arabic (with emphasis on classical Arabic), arithmetic, geography, history, and civics. English was added in the fifth and sixth grades. At the intermediate levels the same subjects were offered, with the addition of algebra, chemistry, biology, and physics. At the secondary level the curriculum was divided into two streams, literary and scientific. Some language and social science were offered in the science section, and general math and geography were offered in the literary section, but both sections were highly specialized.

Several features of the system deserve mention. The quality of the schools varied widely; it was highest in certain sections of major cities like Baghdad, Mosul, and Kirkuk and very low, especially in foreign language training, in small provincial towns. The curriculum tended to be crowded, with at least eleven subjects taught in primary schools and seventeen in intermediate, most of them non-elective. Finally, each level was terminated by an exam which determined entrance to the next level; the drop-out rate along the way was—and still is—very high.

Table 5-2

GROWTH OF EDUCATION IN IRAQ

	Government Primary		**Government Secondary** [a]		**Higher Education** [b]	**Government Missions**
Year	Schools	Pupils	Schools	Pupils	Students	Students
1920–21	88	8,001	3	110	65	9
1925–26	228	22,712	5	583	140	26
1930–31	316	34,513	19	2,082	119	32
1935–36	590	67,593	35	6,138	279	67
1940–41	735	90,794	44	13,969	1,218	17
1945–46	944	118,487	59	12,173	2,146	114
1950–51	1,101	180,779	95	22,706	4,951	133
1955–56	1,748	332,681	152	44,598	5,448	130
1957–58	2,037	416,603	178	51,504	5,679	203
1965–66	4,345	921,786	424	172,229	29,160	1,227
1970–71 [c]	5,671	1,120,213	1,222	301,104	39,892	—

[a] Includes intermediate and secondary schools. The figures for 1970–71 include public and private schools.

[b] Includes Law College, Education College, Engineering College, Women's College, College of Commerce and Economics, College of Arts and Sciences, Higher Physical Education Institute, Technical Engineering Institute, College of Medicine, College of Dentistry, College of Pharmacy, Police College, Divinity College, Agricultural College and Veterinary College; after 1958 it includes the university branches in Mosul and Basra and the higher institutes.

[c] Includes only those in public and private colleges and universities; students on government missions are unknown.

Source: Statistics from Directorate General of Statistics, *Report on Education in Iraq, 1957–1958,* pp. 8–9, 14, 15, 30; Central Bureau of Statistics, *Statistical Abstract, 1965,* pp. 420, 422, 428, 430, 433; General Statistical Organization, *Annual Abstract of Statistics, 1971,* pp. 516, 517, 521, 535, 545.

Much time was spent on cramming in the last year;[12] even so, only about 50 percent of those taking the baccalaureate exam passed.

When most of these leaders were ready for higher education, opportunities within Iraq were limited. A few young people were sent abroad, but most had to choose among a handful of Iraqi higher educational institutions which included the Law College, established in 1908, the Royal Military Academy (1924), the College of Education (1923), and the Medical College (1927). Until the post-World War II period, the law and military schools produced about 65 percent of all college graduates, and the College of Education produced a quarter. Only about 6 percent of Iraqis with higher degrees had studied liberal arts, all of them abroad.[13] Thus the higher education of the vast majority of post-revolutionary leaders has been narrow and professional. Their last exposure to general education was in secondary school.

Some 28 percent of political leaders since 1958 were educated at the Military Academy, while 22 percent graduated from the Law College. Together these constitute half of all leaders. About a quarter have degrees in liberal arts subjects including economics, while the remainder have degrees in various technical, scientific, and professional fields.

The heavy preponderance of Military Academy and Law College graduates, particularly in top policy-making positions, makes it essential to understand the nature of the curricula at these institutions in the late 1950s and 1960s when the leaders passed through them.

Essentially two educational programs were available to military men. The first was that of the Royal Military Academy (RMA), which offered a three-year

[12] *Handbook,* pp. 212–23.

[13] These estimates have been gathered from the statistical reports cited above and from unpublished figures on the graduates of the Royal Military Academy supplied to the author by previous graduates.

Table 5–3

TYPE OF HIGHER EDUCATION OF LEADERS[a]

Type of Higher Education	Kassem		Baath 1963		Aref		Baath 1968		Total	
	No.	%	No.	%	No.	%	No.	%	No.	%
None	0	0	1	3	1	1	5	8	7	4
Military	10	29	8	29	32	36	15	25	50	28
Law	12	35	5	18	15	17	13	22	39	22
Liberal Arts	8	23	6	22	17	19	14	24	40	23
Medical	3	8	1	4	6	7	3	5	12	7
Engineering	1	2	3	11	9	10	3	5	13	7
Education	0	0	2	7	3	3	1	1	5	3
Agriculture	0	0	1	3	2	2	1	1	4	2
Other	0	0	0	0	0	0	1	1	1	1
Unknown	0	0	0	0	3	3	3	5	6	3
Total	34	100	27	100	88	100	59	100	177	100

[a] See notes to Table 5–1.

course following high school; the second, at the Staff College, was a two-year course usually open to first lieutenants and captains who had completed at least four years of army service. Finally, some officers received training in higher military academies abroad, exclusively British or American with heavy emphasis on the former until 1958. It should be noted that graduation from the RMA would be roughly the equivalent of completion of a junior college level program in the United States; graduation from the Staff College to an American bachelor's degree. Study abroad rarely lasted more than six months to a year.

Students at the RMA followed a military curriculum for three years, with some specialization in the last year. There was some instruction on an ad hoc basis in nonmilitary subjects such as economics, administration, and Iraqi and Middle Eastern history, but these were not taught regularly or consistently—no text was used and no regular examinations were given. Although training in foreign languages was included in the academy's program, it was weak, and most graduates did not have facility in languages. The Staff College obviously maintained higher standards, though the subjects it taught were essentially the same. Students were selected from among the most highly qualified and motivated officers and were required to pass a stiff entrance examination in languages and history as well as military subjects, which suggests that the better officers were expected to study on their own.[14] At the pinnacle of the military education system were the few officers who went on to Camberley in England or Leavenworth in the United States for further training (probably not more than 10 to 15 percent of the total).

Of the military men in the leadership sample, about 44 percent graduated from the Staff College, while only a small proportion (about 12 percent) studied abroad. About 8 percent have had additional training in nonmilitary institutions like the colleges of education and law. The rest were merely graduates of the RMA. It is interesting to note that of a sample of high-ranking officers who occupied positions in the military itself (commanders of divisions or of operations and intelligence, for example) a higher percentage (well over half) graduated from the Staff College. This suggests that politics has not been getting the best-educated officers or, more likely, that instability is weeding them out.

The graduates of the Law College do not rank far above the graduates of the RMA on any scale of quality. Taught entirely in Arabic, the legal curriculum too left its graduates with a low competence in foreign languages, and it also was narrowly professional. Out of thirty semester courses offered in four years, only six were not in legal subjects. These were in economics and administration. In fact, the Law College expected to train students for positions at the bar and bench, but also to staff the upper reaches of the bureaucracy. Many people felt it did neither job well.

The best-educated political leaders are those who have studied abroad or graduated from one of the newer professional colleges in Iraq. Since World War II higher education in Iraq has expanded and diversified. The College of Engineering was established in 1942, the College of Women (liberal arts mainly) in 1946, Commerce and Economics in 1947, Arts and Sciences in 1949, Agriculture in 1952, Dentistry in 1953, and, finally, the University of Baghdad, which now has

[14] Private communication to the author.

Table 5-4

GROWTH OF HIGHER EDUCATION IN IRAQ
(number of students in school)

Year	Law	Education	Engineering	Arts and Sciences	Economics, Commerce	Medicine	Agriculture	Other[a]
1920–21	65							
1925–26	131	9						
1930–31	75	44						
1935–36	242	37						
1940–41	586	321				311		
1945–46	1,081	347	158	89		310		161
1950–51	1,967	718	317	516	681	414	23	315
1955–56	737	962	401	1,119	727	636	216	558
1957–58	562	1,068	364	1,200	493	774	247	689
1965–66	1,768	2,882	1,971	5,612[b]	2,228[c]	2,150	898	2,447[d]

[a] Includes Colleges of Pharmacy, Dentistry, Police, Divinity, and Veterinary Medicine, but not the higher institutes.

[b] Of which 2,342 were in arts, 1,706 in science, and 1,564 undetermined.

[c] Including political science.

[d] Including Nursing School.

Source: Directorate General of Statistics, *Report on Education in Iraq, 1957–58,* pp. 14–15; *Statistical Abstract, 1965,* pp. 20–21.

branches in Mosul, Sulaimaniya and Basra, in 1957. Some of these schools, in particular the Colleges of Medicine and Engineering, have firmer academic foundations and teach many of their subjects in English.

At the same time student missions abroad have increased. Contrary to what is generally supposed, most Iraqis studying abroad, especially recently, have specialized in the sciences and technical subjects rather than in the humanities. A census in 1947 showed that of the 901 students in foreign universities, the largest single group (217) were in engineering. The rest were studying science and math (185), languages and literature (76), agriculture (69), geography and history (62), education (47), and economics (28).[15]

As a result of these trends, the composition of the college-educated population of Iraq as a whole has changed considerably. Graduates of the liberal arts and the newer scientific-technical colleges together have come to outnumber the graduates of the Law and Military Colleges. By 1965 some 22 percent of college-educated Iraqis were graduates in the arts and sciences (about twice as many in arts as in sciences), while about 17 percent had degrees in education, a curriculum itself largely composed of arts and sciences. Together these two groups accounted for almost 40 percent of all college graduates. Next came graduates in commerce and economics (about 7 percent), engineering (6 percent), and medicine (4 percent).

[15] Ministry of Economics, Bureau of Statistics, *Statistical Abstract, 1947* (Baghdad: Government Press, 1949), p. 73.

About 37 percent graduated from the Law and Military Colleges.[16] This trend will be intensified in the future. In 1971 43.3 percent of the university graduates received degrees in science (16 percent in pure sciences, 15 percent in engineering, 8 percent in medicine, and 4 percent in agriculture). The remainder went into human studies, which included law, education and the arts.[17] No figures were available on the graduates of the Military College.

How are these changes reflected in the backgrounds of political leaders? As might be expected, the progress of the graduates of the new scientific and professional schools in the political hierarchy has been much slower than their growth in society at large. Liberal arts graduates are more numerous than they were under the old regime, but they still constitute only 24 percent of the leaders studied. Many of these earned doctorates abroad. Graduates of the Colleges of Medicine, Engineering, and Agriculture, the technocrats par excellence, comprise almost a fifth of the group, usually filling positions connected with their specialties, such as the ministries of oil, agriculture and health. Although some of these new technocrats have been educated abroad, most are now graduates of Iraq's own colleges.

Two points need to be made in connection with this development. The first is, again, that the better-educated cabinet ministers have not yet reached the top levels of power. The second is that there now exists an educational imbalance between the political elite and the educated elite as a whole. While the former continues to be dominated at the top levels by the Military and Law College graduates or by men with little higher education, the educated elite is composed mainly of graduates in arts and sciences, economics, and the new technical subjects. Political friction has already developed between these two groups. One indication of this dissatisfaction is the "brain drain" discussed later.

Place of Education. A high percentage of cabinet ministers and political leaders were educated abroad—an average of about 36 percent. Most of these ministers were the beneficiaries of government missions abroad in the late 1940s and 1950s.

As already mentioned, foreign education got a slow start in Iraq. It is estimated that about 2,600 Iraqis received degrees from foreign (mainly western European or American) universities between 1920 and 1958.[18] Most of these were enrolled in undergraduate programs. Since then the number has increased dramatically. By 1965 there were over 3,500 Iraqis studying in Europe or the United States, about 1,700 in other Middle Eastern countries, and about 1,750 in Communist-bloc countries. An average of 350 were returning each year with foreign degrees.[19] Most of these are now graduate students who have received their bachelor's degrees at home. But despite the enormous expansion of higher education in Iraq, one out of every six students with a higher degree obtained it abroad.

A Western education definitely increases political and occupational mobility—

[16] These averages are based on Qubain's figures (*Education and Science,* p. 291) together with unofficial estimates of military graduates.

[17] *Annual Abstract of Statistics, 1971,* p. 550.

[18] Some 885 returned from government missions. According to Qubain this should be multiplied by three to include those who went abroad at their own expense (*Education and Science*, p. 289).

[19] Ministry of Planning, Central Bureau of Statistics, *Statistical Abstract, 1965* (Baghdad: Government Press, 1966), pp. 421–22.

up to a point. A recent study of the upper levels of the bureaucracy showed a very high percentage of degrees from Western universities, and rapid promotions.[20] The percentage of cabinet members with such degrees is twice as high as the percentage of members of the college-educated population as a whole who hold them.

[20] U.S., Department of State, Bureau of Intelligence and Research, "Survey on Iraqi Elites, 1950–1965" (unpublished), 1966.

Table 5–5

PLACE OF HIGHER EDUCATION OF LEADERSHIP[a]

Place of Higher Education	Kassem		Baath 1963		Aref		Baath 1968		Total	
	No.	%	No.	%	No.	%	No.	%	No.	%
Iraq	21	61	15	57	47	54	32	59	99	58
Middle East	1	3	1	4	4	5	3	6	6	3
Europe	9	27	3	12	8	9	4	8	19	11
Britain	(9)	(18)	(2)	(8)	(5)	(6)	(2)	(4)	(12)	(9)
France	(2)	(6)	(1)	(4)	(1)	(1)	(2)	(4)	(4)	(2)
West Germany	(1)	(3)	(0)	(0)	(2)	(2)	(0)	(0)	(3)	(1)
United States	3	9	7	27	23	26	7	13	13	20
Other Western	0	0	0	0	2	2	5	9	7	3
Unknown	0	0	0	0	3	3	3	5	6	3
Total	34	100	26	100	87	100	54	100	170	100

[a] Does not include individuals shown in Table 5–1 to have had no higher education.

Table 5–6

GROWTH OF STUDENT GOVERNMENT MISSIONS IN IRAQ
(numbers of students)

Year	Middle East	Europe				United States	Communist Bloc	Other
		Britain	France	West Germany	Other			
1921–25	17	4						
1925–30	73	48	1			16		1
1931–35	83	38	11	12		33		6
1936–40	144	46	10	31		30		13
1941–45	88	57	1			24		10
1945–50	296	108	39			250		3
1951–55	57	238	17		22	415		20
1956–58	7	186		52	27	206		6
1958–60		382		34	28	55	740	51
1962–63	54	1,353	3	209	65	348	447	4
1965–66	29	498	1	139	40	304	215	1

Source: Statistics from tables in Qubain, *Education and Science in the Arab World,* p. 278, 280; and Central Bureau of Statistics, *Statistical Abstract, 1965,* p. 422. The table includes only those sent at government expense.

Where are these degrees obtained? Under the old regime and in the Kassem era, two to three times as many Western-educated politicians had graduated from European, primarily British, universities as from American colleges. Since then, the number of American degrees has achieved parity with them and in some cases has pulled ahead. Under the Baath regime of 1963 and that of the Arefs, twice as many ministers had American degrees as European; in the current Baath regime the two are about equal. This trend corresponds to a shift in the flow of students to the West. Prior to the 1950s more students went to Britain than to the United States; thereafter—during a period of increased American money, advisors, and influence in Iraq—more students came to the United States. However, since the revolution this trend has once again been reversed in the British favor, probably as a reflection of worsening American-Iraqi relations. If this continues, there will probably be more British-educated than American-trained ministers in future Iraqi cabinets. After Britain, West Germany now ranks second among the western European countries, training increasing numbers of Iraqis in science, engineering, and technology. Austria ranks third, and France a very poor fourth. French education has played a far less significant role in Iraq than in many other Middle Eastern countries.

Sending students to Communist-bloc countries is new for Iraq. It began after the revolution, and by 1965 about 1,750 Iraqi students—about 25 percent of the total studying abroad—were in Communist countries. Only about 12 percent of these were recipients of Iraqi government scholarships. It is worth noting that more students are sent to the United States alone on government missions than are sent to Communist-bloc countries, and when these are added to those sent by the government to western Europe, the ratio is about four to one in favor of the West. According to most reports, the best students go west, and competition for positions is keen. Their second choice is the Middle East, particularly the American University of Beirut and the University of Cairo, where there is less of a language barrier. Third on the list comes the Soviet bloc. In addition to the

Table 5–7

HIGHER EDUCATION OF STUDENTS ABROAD

Source of Support	**Middle East**	Europe: Britain	Europe: France	Europe: West Germany	Europe: Other	**United States**	**Communist Bloc**	**Other**
Government missions	29	498	1	139	40	304	215	1
Some financial aid	146	95	2	170	32	100	130	0
Personal expense [a]	1,502	680	14	350	320	514	1,000	

[a] These figures may include some financial aid from host governments or institutions. This is almost certainly the case for the Communist bloc.

Source: Central Bureau of Statistics, *Statistical Abstract, 1965,* p. 422.

language problem, the low esteem in which Soviet education apparently is held upon the student's return has increased the unpopularity of Soviet education. Western degrees, even Arab degrees, are preferred by employers to those from the Communist bloc. Moreover, many of the young people trained in Russia or eastern Europe have degrees from technical institutes that are not quite equivalent to university degrees, and hence are considered unqualified for a number of top-level jobs.

It is significant that so far there have been no Communist-educated members of the cabinet nor, apparently, top-level military officers or bureaucrats. While this may be due to the time-lag, it is far more likely a reflection of a cultural preference for the West. There may also be political distrust of Communist-educated graduates. Whatever the reason, political leaders with a Western, especially Anglo-Saxon, education are thoroughly entrenched within Iraq's political elite and are likely to remain so for some time.

However, the influence of Western education on policy should not be overestimated. Again, most of it is concentrated in the secondary cabinet positions. The top positions, usually monopolized by the military or, currently, the Baath party politicians, are almost wholly taken up by men educated in Iraq. Moreover, at this level the influence of foreign graduates has been declining since Kassem's time. Under Kassem a fifth of the top-level leaders had had some kind of foreign education; in the current six-member RCC, none has had such training or exposure.

What conclusions of political significance can be drawn from these educational data? First, while men who have received liberal, scientific, or technical educations, and men educated in the West have held positions in Iraqi cabinets since the revolution, most of them have been civilians of middle or lower rank. The top posts are still controlled by military men or, in the current regime, by Baath party politicians whose education has been more limited and whose exposure to outside environments has been minimal. The best-educated men in Iraq have not reached the top of the political ladder, a fact which has certainly affected the quality of leadership and decision making. While political wisdom can by no means be equated with higher degrees, the kind of education received by leaders, and the degree of their exposure to different cultures and ideas, have a profound effect on their capacity to govern a modern developing state. Moreover, the decline of familiarity with the West among top leaders, especially among the current Baathists, may well be contributing to the pronounced anti-Western sentiment of the regime, as well as to policies which have isolated Iraq from the outside world.

Second, the continuing lower level of education among the top leaders indicates that the situation is not improving. Political instability is reflected in the kind of men who have succeeded in reaching the top and staying there. Since the revolution, these have rarely been highly or broadly educated men.

Third, the political leadership has become increasingly polarized between men who have higher degrees and often considerable exposure to a Western environment and their less well educated counterparts at the top. This polarization has led to a misuse of talent and hampered policy making. Yet a similar imbalance can also be detected between the political elite and society at large. The educated elements within Iraq, who have acquired a wide diversity of skills and knowledge, are faced with political leaders at the top whose educational base is much narrower than theirs. It is worth noting that one of the major complaints of the intelligentsia under the old regime was that its top leaders were men of narrow and outdated mentality. The new regime may be boxing itself into a similar corner.

Educational Problems. Since the revolution Iraq has been faced with two educational problems which plague many developing countries. The first is the problem of absorbing the newly educated groups into useful and productive activity; the second is a brain drain of considerable proportions. While the first may be on the threshold of solution due to increased oil revenues, the second shows no sign of improvement.

The Overexpansion of Education. Between 1958 and 1974, despite the need for talent at all levels of society, education expanded too rapidly for the economy to absorb its new graduates. This was partly due to the education boom of staggering proportions that took place in that time period, particularly at the secondary and college levels, and partly to the stagnation of the economy.

Between 1957–58 and 1970–71 secondary school attendance jumped from 51,504 to 301,104, and enrollment in higher educational institutions inside Iraq from 5,679 to 39,892. This is a 580 percent increase at the secondary level, a 700 percent increase at the college level.[21] The number of graduates of college-level institutions during this period was about 44,000, many times more than the total from the entire period before the revolution, and there is every indication that it has increased since then. Much of the impetus for this increase has come from revolutionary dedication to increased social opportunities, together with oil revenues to finance it.

While there is little doubt that the expansion of education has helped fill a real need (though the quality of Iraqi graduates may have declined in the process), the economy has not kept pace. It is beyond the scope of this study to analyze Iraq's economic difficulties, but every independent observer of the Iraqi economy since the revolution has noted that, despite the country's favorable resources and oil revenue, its economic development has been slow. Writing in October 1970, for example, Howard Ellis stated that, "In recent years, Iraqi economic history has not been prepossessing. Judged from the angle of the most general economic measures —gross national product in total and per capita—there has been a retrogression. . . ."[22] The same conclusion was reached by Jawad Hashim, formerly minister of planning, who estimates that the ratio between GNP and the rate of fixed capital formation deteriorated between 1962 and 1969. Writing in June 1973 the London *Economist* claimed that "the situation since 1969 has, if anything, worsened."[23] Much of this deterioration has been caused by political instability, but some of it was due to the long-standing dispute between the Iraqi government and the Iraq Petroleum Company (IPC), which kept oil production well below its potential and, after nationalization in 1972, drastically curtailed revenue.

---

[21] Ministry of Education, *Educational Statistics, 1964–1965* (Baghdad: Government Press, 1967), pp. 57, 129; *Annual Abstract of Statistics, 1971*, pp. 535, 545.

[22] Howard Ellis, *Private Enterprise and Socialism in the Middle East* (Washington, D.C.: American Enterprise Institute, 1970), p. 41.

[23] *Quarterly Economic Review (QER), Iraq, Annual Supplement 1973* (London: London Economist, Economist Intelligence Unit, 1973), p. 3.

This situation has now changed, however. The settlement of the IPC dispute in 1973 and the enormously increased revenue from oil which the recent price increases will bring Iraq have already given the economy a much needed boost. Revenues from oil are expected to exceed $6 billion in the fiscal year 1974–1975; allocations for development in the same period will almost triple those of the previous year. These increases are already being incorporated into development plans which call for expansion in all sectors of the economy. Given political stability (always a large question) and a reasonable rate of implementation, these conditions should provide jobs for the educated elite in increasing numbers, thus alleviating one of Iraq's major problems. Indeed, the projected economic boom may require the importation of some technical talent. Nevertheless, while the future looks brighter, the period from 1958 to 1974 has been characterized mainly by economic stagnation rather than growth.

In the absence of an expanding economy—compounded, of course, by the decline of the private sector under increasingly socialistic regimes—it is the bureaucracy which has had to absorb the new graduates. As a result, the bureaucracy has grown to unmanageable proportions. In 1966, some 312,000 men and women, or slightly more than one-half of the active urban working population in Iraq, were working for the government, and the figure has undoubtedly risen since.[24] Even so, there are indications that the civil service has not grown fast enough to absorb all the graduates. While this may now change with the increased oil revenues, the expansion of the bureaucracy is already creating problems of its own. Red tape hampers implementation of development projects and may grow worse unless the private sector is also expanded and allowed to assume a share of the management of development.

The Brain Drain. The second problem, closely related to the first, is the loss of much of the skill that the educational system has already produced. A brain drain is taking place at several levels, most seriously among the older, experienced professionals who could man the command posts of the development sector. The reasons for this are many, but chief among them, again, are instability and political mismanagement. There has been a rapid turnover in the top layers of personnel in all branches of government, and too many political appointments have been made regardless of actual competence. At the top of the ladder the problem is no longer the lack of sufficient talent, as it was thirty years ago, but the misuse of the talent which is available and has been so painfully built up in recent years.

Statistical data on the brain drain are not available; still, there are some indications of its proportions. The loss of top-level cabinet ministers, for example, can be roughly charted. Of the old regime ministers, 25 percent are out of the country working in other capacities. Of the ministers appointed under Kassem, about 27 percent have been lost to Iraq through death, arrest, or emigration; for the Baath regime of 1963 this figure is 18 percent; for the Arefs 22 percent. And it continues under the present regime. The men who have left include first-rate oil experts, one of whom is now advisor to the Abu Dhabi government, education specialists, economic planners, and professors by the dozens. Some of these are living and working outside of Iraq; others, still inside the country, are barred from meaningful em-

[24] Ibid., p. 4.

ployment. It is safe to say that at least this rate of attrition would apply to the upper reaches of the army and the bureaucracy. As for the university, of the five presidents appointed between 1957 and 1971, four were dismissed, three are now abroad teaching or advising foreign governments, and the fourth died recently.

It is interesting to note that Iraq's competitors in the oil business have benefited from much of this discarded talent. Many of the top-level advisors and planners in Abu Dhabi and Kuwait are Iraqis. The largest single national group of professors on the staff of Riyadh University in Saudi Arabia in 1970 was Iraqi, and the university's president was busy recruiting more. In Lebanon, Iraqis are so numerous that whole neighborhoods have been taken over by Iraqi families in exile. As for the loss at lower levels, its extent can only be guessed. Not too long ago the government offered to give jobs, virtually rent-free housing, and other privileges to Iraqis with foreign degrees if they would only return—an indication of the seriousness of the situation. There is little indication that many have been attracted by these inducements.

Occupation

Occupation is second only to education in its impact on the ideas and outlook of the revolutionary leaders. Occupational background helps determine what skills and experience leaders bring to the decision-making process and indicates what interests they represent and are likely to promote once they are in office. If the landowners and wealthy merchants who dominated the old regime pursued policies favoring acquisition of wealth, the army officers and civil servants who dominate the new regime are equally assiduous in furthering policies that directly or indirectly benefit the military and the bureaucracy.

The Military. The most striking feature of the new regime, at least until recently, has been the intrusion of the military into politics and the subordination of civilians, regardless of their occupational backgrounds. Army officers initiated the first revolution in 1958, and they have been the prime movers in all of the coups and changes of government which have taken place since. Inevitably, the intermittent substitution of force for political and legal process has had a disastrous effect on political continuity and stability. Since 1958 there have been at least ten coups and attempted coups, two armed rebellions, and a full-scale civil war lasting for ten years (1961–1970) with fighting resumed in the spring of 1974. Every regime since 1958 has depended on support from the army or a critical portion of it, and key positions in the military have been distributed to every regime's supporters. More pertinent to this study are the men who have left the military to devote themselves full time to political work. To what degree have they penetrated the political structure, and what has been the effect of their military orientation?

In all cabinets between 1958 and 1968 men of military background have held between 25 and 35 percent of all posts. More important, they have monopolized from one-half to two-thirds of the top policy-making positions.[25] The three presidents of the republic, all prime ministers except one, all vice-presidents except one,

[25] Marr, "Iraq's Leadership Dilemma," p. 296.

almost all ministers of interior and defense, and many ministers of information have been ex-military men.

Most of these men moved into political positions directly from the military with no intervening experience in civilian government, administration, or political party organization. From 1958 to 1968 their numbers and influence in the political sphere steadily increased. In the first revolutionary cabinet appointed by Kassem in 1958 there were only three officers, including Kassem. The power struggle which took place in the first year and a half of his regime eroded civilian support and, by the end of his regime, officers, mostly Kassem's army cronies, occupied a quarter of all cabinet posts. The coup which brought the short-lived Baath regime of 1963 to power was carried out by military men who were rewarded with political posts in the cabinet. During the Aref regime the military reached the peak of their influence, filling over 31 percent of all cabinet posts.

Military men have also intruded considerably into other civilian spheres. They have held many of the governorships, and always the critical governorship of Baghdad. Military domination of the judicial process reached its height with the notorious Mahdawi trials of 1958–1960, when a military tribunal with no pretensions to legal knowledge, much less judicial impartiality, made a mockery of justice in Iraq. Since then the military has retreated somewhat in this field, but military men dominated the rapid, secret trials of 1969 and 1970 which sentenced almost 100 people to death. In the field of foreign affairs, army officers have held top ambassadorial posts, including those in London, Amman, Kuwait, and Saudi Arabia. Even the economic sphere, furthest from military training and experience, has been affected: military men have been undersecretary of the Ministry of Industry, head of the Industrial Organization, head of a large government-owned textile plant, and so on.

The present Baath regime is an exception to this rule. So far the party has successfully reduced the numbers of military politicians in the RCC and the cabinet and reestablished a considerable measure of civilian control over the military, mainly by the imposition of party discipline over military party members and by the gradual removal of military politicians from positions of real power. Although the president of the republic, Ahmad Hasan al-Bakr, is a former army officer, for the first time since 1958, a civilian, Saddam Hussein, vice-president of the RCC, has equal, if not superior, power. The RCC, which originally consisted of five military men, was enlarged in 1969 to fifteen men, which reduced military membership to a third, the lowest percentage of officers in top office in a decade. Since then three of these military members have been dropped from the RCC (two through death). In the newly elected Regional Command of the party, there are only two military members including President Bakr. In the Council of Ministers, military men fare even worse, and in the reshuffled cabinet of 1974, there were only three or four army officers (among over thirty ministers), including Bakr, who was acting minister of defense, and Ghaidan, who was demoted from minister of interior to minister of communications.

Nevertheless, for almost all of the period since 1958 former military men have dominated politics, and they still play a considerable role, particularly in the area of security. Even the current Baath regime, although dominated by civilians, ultimately depends on the army for support, and it is always possible that dissident groups in the military might oust the civilians from office. What has been the effect of this intrusion of military men into the top offices of state?

First, it has had a deleterious effect on the military itself. There has been a rapid turnover in the top military commands as officers are absorbed into politics or removed for political reasons. Those who remain in the military are often appointed in reward for their political support rather than in recognition of their competence. Currently, loyalty to the Baath regime, although not necessarily membership in the party, is a prerequisite for advancement in the military, and only the Baath party is allowed to recruit army members. These factors have reduced the effectiveness of the military in their own sphere. More important, however, the qualities on behalf of which the military is said to have entered politics—discipline, efficiency, and organization—have been badly eroded within the military itself. Instead of introducing these benefits to public life, the military has lost them. Recently this trend has been checked by the Baath. Its isolation of the military from politics has stabilized the officer corps, which has now, in addition, had active service on the Israeli front in 1973 and in Kurdish areas in 1974 and 1975 to improve its military efficiency. If the current stability can be maintained and the military kept out of politics, professional standards may improve.

Second, the intrusion of the military into politics has been one of the major causes of the decline in the quality of political leadership. Although there is no intrinsic reason why the military should not be able to produce high calibre leadership (there have been very able military leaders in the past), in fact it has not. The reasons for this are several. "The work of doctors, lawyers, engineers, and journalists brings them into contact with all sorts of people; the work of the soldier brings him together only with other soldiers," one authority has written.[26] This has been particularly true of the Iraqi officers who have come to power. Most of them have not been high-ranking generals, but colonels and majors of middle rank. As such, their experience had been almost wholly limited to military operations, and their professional lives have been spent in the barracks or with their units. Often their social contacts had been limited to the company of other military men at the officers' club, the Voice of the Arabs, broadcast from Cairo, their only intellectual diversion. With the notable exceptions of Prime Minister Kassem and Naji Taleb, very few had had any experience with liaison work in the capital or abroad which might have brought them into contact with political realities. Nor, if the evidence is correct, had they read widely or deeply on any subject. None, as far as is known, had been a teacher at the Staff College, as had Nasser. Furthermore, in the past few decades the Military Academy has not attracted Iraq's outstanding students, nor provided cadets real intellectual competition or training. The military, then, has thrust upon Iraq leaders with limited vision, narrow talents, and a relative lack of experience in internal and international politics.

A third, perhaps inevitable, result has been a strengthening of military priorities in government spending and investment at the expense of development. Between 1958 and 1966 defense spending more than doubled, jumping from thirty-four million *dinars* to eighty-seven million, and it has risen considerably since. In the

[26] Malcolm Kerr, "Egypt," in *Education and Political Development,* ed. James Coleman (Princeton, N.J.: Princeton University Press, 1965), p. 192.

same period the sum spent on development remained almost stationary; indeed, between 1958 and 1960 it declined by nine million *dinars,* and thereafter spending rose and fell erratically in relation to the political situation.[27] Another reflection of military priorities has been expenditures on pensions and other benefits for officers. While these began under Nuri's regime, they have been greatly expanded since the revolution.

The Civilians. Civilian leaders are more diverse in occupation and background than their military counterparts. Many have high degrees of talent, skill, and expertise in various fields, especially economics, education, engineering, and medicine. However, three generalizations can be made about them. Almost all of them are professionals; they are increasingly specialized; and most—well over half—have spent their professional lives on the government payroll and tend to identify their interests with those of the government.

The occupational group whose representation in the cabinet and in public life as a whole has risen most remarkably has been that of academicians. Their political rise reflects the enormous expansion of higher education and the prestige it has acquired in recent years. In the last decade of the old regime, only about 2 percent of the cabinet had been college or university teachers or deans. Under the current Baath regime, at least 20 percent previously held university positions, constituting the largest civilian group in the cabinet. Most are in the forty to fifty age bracket, and almost all are specialists in technical fields or fields connected with

[27] J. C. Hurewitz, *Middle Eastern Politics: The Military Dimension* (New York: Praeger, 1969), p. 160.

Table 5–8

OCCUPATIONAL STRUCTURE OF LEADERSHIP[a]

Occupation	Kassem No.	Kassem %	Baath 1963 No.	Baath 1963 %	Aref No.	Aref %	Baath 1968 No.	Baath 1968 %	Total No.	Total %
Army officer	11	32	8	30	31	35	15	25	51	29
Lawyer/judge	4	12	4	15	12	14	7	12	25	14
Civil servant	7	20	2	7	10[b]	11	7	12	27	15
Professor	3	9	3	11	14	16	10	17	26	15
Doctor	3	9	1	4	6	7	3	5	12	7
Engineer	1	3	2	7	10	11	3	5	12	7
Politician	5	15	1	4	0	0	2[c]	3	6	3
Other	0	0	6	22	3	3	5	8	10	6
Unknown	0	0	0	0	2	1	7	12	8	4
Total	34	100	27	100	88	100	59	100	177	100

[a] See notes to Table 5–1.

[b] Includes six specialists such as economists and agriculturalists.

[c] This figure is probably understated since some of those in the "unknown" category undoubtedly have spent their careers working behind the scenes in the party; this would help explain why their careers are unknown. They are also the ones who, with no education beyond high school, would not be equipped for professional careers.

development, especially economics. Few are historians, political scientists, or social scientists by training.

After academicians, the two most important civilian groups are civil servants and lawyers. For present purposes a civil servant is a generalist, usually trained in administration at the Law College, who has worked his way up the administrative hierarchy, particularly in provincial posts in the Ministry of Interior. This group has been declining in relative size. Under the old regime civil servants occupied almost a third of the cabinet posts; they now fill half that percentage. One reason for this is that many of the top administrative posts from which bureaucrats used to move into politics have been reserved for the military. More important, however, is the overall decline in the importance of the generalists. The civil service itself has become a haven of specialists, employing more Ph.D.'s than the university itself.

The decline in the number of lawyers in the cabinet has also been marked. Under the old regime they were the largest occupational group, while today they are only 12 percent. This profession has lost its status as the main avenue to power thanks to the growing diversity of occupations and education in Iraq. Furthermore, law has lost prestige both as a profession and as a stepping-stone to government employment largely because lawmaking, once the function of a large body of parliamentarians, is now undertaken by a very small group of people at the pinnacle of power. It is worth noting, however, that the two top figures in the current Baath regime, President Bakr and RCC Vice-President Hussein, have law degrees. Bakr also has Military Academy credentials.

But the decline in these groups is matched by the rise of the technocrat, here defined as a specialist in some field involving the application of science to human needs. At least 15 percent of the leaders under study have been technocrats—at least twelve of them engineers, fourteen economists, and twelve doctors. But these figures are misleadingly low. If the technical specialists concealed among the academicians are added, this group outnumbers all others including the military. Technocrats have come to symbolize a commitment to economic development, and the presence of so many of them in the cabinet indicates that, at least at a formal level, the new regime has made that commitment. Whether they have been properly used is another question. It also shows the heavy emphasis on scientific and technical skills at the expense of humanistic values.

One of the most striking facts about the occupational composition of the political elite is the omission of certain occupations. Virtually none has had full-time occupational experience in the private sector, either as a merchant, businessman, or landlord. This is not surprising since one of the great aims of the revolution was to remove the wealthy from power. (This has been successfully done, though the wealthy have not necessarily been separated from their money or from their economic power in the countryside.) It should be noted, however, that this trend was well under way in the last years of the old regime. Merchants and landowners occupied only about 11 percent of all cabinet posts, though they held 16 percent of the top posts. Under the new regime, in sixteen years only 1 percent of the cabinet posts and the RCC have been filled by such men. What is significant is not that the wealthy have been weeded out of the ruling elite, but that they have been shorn of their political power in the capital. This has been accomplished by a series of reform measures, including the land reform and the nationalization of industry, but most of all by the abolition of parliament, which was the stronghold of this group.

Another significant omission from the list of occupations represented in the leadership group is that of the full-time professional politician. In the last decade before the revolution, a full 24 percent of cabinet ministers would have fit into this category. Under the new regime this group has virtually disappeared from power. It is important to define what is meant by politician. Under the old regime the politican was a man engaged mainly, if not wholly, in articulating various interests and in reconciling and conciliating various viewpoints, usually through the forums of political parties or parliament. If successful, he was also engaged in the formulation of public policy and the communication of that policy to the public through parliamentary debates, elections, and the press. These institutions malfunctioned under the old regime, but in a rudimentary way the system did provide the means of acquiring and exercising the political skills that are valued in an open society—communication, compromise, and persuasion. The abolition of parliamentary institutions and more open press and elections, without any visible substitute on the horizon, have meant a loss of such skills.

Recently, with the emergence of the Baath party, an entirely new breed of politician has appeared. Some 14 percent of the RCC members who have served since 1968 fall into this group, although at least twice as many have spent at least as much time working in the party as in their chosen occupation. The new politicians are mainly committed revolutionaries whose experience has been in clandestine (rather than public) politics, in the art of conspiracy, and in the process of securing and holding power by any means necessary. They have shown themselves far more adept in the use of political repression than in public persuasion and compromise. However, they may be developing a party organization and discipline which will stand them in good stead. So far, the result of Baath domination has been Iraq's subjection to a period of relentless eradication of opposition, but one of relative stability as well. The 1968 Baath regime has now maintained itself in power longer than any other post-revolutionary group.

What, then, do the civilians contribute to leadership? First, they provide an impressive array of expertise, especially the skill and knowledge to draw up sophisticated economic development plans and to analyze development problems. Most observers agree that the quality of thinking in this area has improved significantly since the old regime. But there have been some egregious losses as well. One is a decline in administrative experience of the kind accumulated by the old bureaucrats who worked their way up the hierarchy and learned how to get things done—often by compromise. Many, if not most, of the new technocrats and academicians come directly to the cabinet with no administrative experience. Moreover, they frequently have a theoretical, rather than a practical orientation. Often educated in the West, they may, in addition, be out of touch with realities in their own country. A recent article attributes the failures of the land reform program to "the management factor, which has been persistently misunderstood during successive political regimes. . . ." The academic administrators, its author claims, "often seem to lack the competence to carry out even the simplest task." [28] While technocrats may produce better plans, they seem unable to put them into effect.

Another loss, unquestionably the most serious of all, is that of political skill. No occupational group has brought political skills to the cabinets of the new regime—not the military man, trained to command; not the technocrat, more at home with the slide rule than with people; nor even the academic, more used to dispensing knowledge from the podium than to listening. Heavy emphasis on scientific and technical knowledge, rather than on the humanities and social sciences, reinforces this tendency. While the new Baath leaders possess political skills of a sort—namely, those calculated to keep them in power—these are clearly attributes of an authoritarian system. Whether they will be able to develop the skills of compromise and practicality necessary for a transition to a more open society is the question. While these factors have not been a major cause of political instability, they have helped to compound it.

Like their military colleagues, the civilian members of the cabinets have policy priorities that are often reflected in the budget. The fact that most of them have been associated in one way or another with the government for some time and look to it for employment helps to account for the domination of "socialist" ideologies emphasizing state control over the economy and the expansion of the public sector to include most areas of activity. Of course, government employment does not automatically lead to socialist convictions. Other factors are much more likely to incline the political elite toward socialism, notably a desire for rapid development, particularly industrial development, a redistribution of income, and increased social mobility, which it is felt only the state can foster. But socialist ideologies are highly compatible with the personal interests of government employees, the people who will benefit from and control the new state agencies and the burgeoning bureaucracy.

This is not the place for an analysis of the accomplishments of revolutionary governments, but a brief review of their most important measures will illustrate the point. The only sector of the economy that showed substantial growth (as a percentage of gross domestic product) between 1958 and 1966 was public administration and defense, which rose from 7.8 percent to 11 percent; all other factors remained relatively stationary.[29] In civilian employment, the greatest growth in the same time period took place in the bureaucracy and in the education establishment. These priorities have also been reflected in budgets. In the fiscal years 1961 to 1965, the amount of public investment in industrialization (which is always said to be a major priority of the revolutionary regimes) was one-third of the sum spent on education and less than one-fifth of the sum spent on defense.[30] By the 1970s the situation had improved somewhat, but the priorities remained. Published figures for the investment and regular budgets for 1971–1972 show that industry received about 70 percent of the allocation of education and 29 percent of that of the military.[31]

---

[28] John Simmons, "Agricultural Development in Iraq: Planning and Management Failures," *Middle East Journal,* Spring 1965, p. 129.

[29] London Economist Intelligence Unit, *Economic Review of Iraq* (December 1970), p. 5.

[30] *QER, Iraq,* no. 1 (1971), p. 4.

[31] *QER, Iraq, Annual Supplement 1973,* pp. 6, 15.

Revolutionary rhetoric is all on the side of the lower classes, yet there have been only two major revolutionary reforms since 1958 and neither has, as yet, brought measurable benefits to the peasants and workers. The first is the land reform, which has been modified many times. Although this program confiscated up to ten million *donums* of land, which are now in state hands (in addition to *miri* [state-owned] land), by 1971 it had only distributed about four million *donums* to the peasants; the rest of the land was leased to them by the state. In 1971 over nine million *donums* were covered by lease arrangements.[32] The current Baath regime has improved the situation of the peasantry somewhat by a revision of the land law, which does not require the peasant to pay for the land actually distributed, but there has been little improvement in the rate of redistribution of land to the peasants. The failures of the land reform have been numerous, as the current government admits. A major one has been the shortage of trained personnel willing to go out to the country to staff the cooperatives and generally perform the management functions of the old landlords. Another is the low level of farming technology. As a result, agriculture, which employs about 60 percent of the population, declined drastically between 1958 and 1961 and has not yet fully recovered. This can scarcely have benefited the peasants as a whole.

The second major reform, which took place in 1964, was the nationalization of twenty-seven large private firms, including banks and insurance companies, and the imposition of a government monopoly on certain imports. In fact, this was the beginning of the end for the private sector, which has been consistently squeezed ever since. Industry has grown only marginally, but government jobs in the Economic Organization created to manage the sector have proliferated. According to official statistics, in 1966 state enterprises employed 44,442 people; private industry, 1,446.[33] With the settlement of the IPC dispute and the increase in revenue, industrial development has picked up, and the employment situation has improved markedly. Up until 1973, however, jobs were not being created for workers in any great numbers. In 1974 the government raised workers' salaries, along with those of government employees, but Baath legislation provides very stringent regulation of the labor force.

Like the military, the civil servants have granted themselves benefits. About 120 housing projects have been built in Baghdad since 1958, the majority for government employees; about 90 percent of these were built on government land. And the burgeoning of the education establishment and the bureaucracy guarantees that this process will continue.

One last critical question must be asked about the role of civilians in government: How much influence do they have over policy? Unfortunately the civilians in the cabinet, like professionals in society at large, suffer from a lack of political muscle. They have no political organization, no large or important constituency, and no independent economic power base from which to exercise leverage on the military, or currently the Baath, politicians. However, they do have the knowledge necessary for development. There is evidence that in times of relative stability,

[32] *Annual Abstract of Statistics, 1971*, pp. 119–121, 123. Statistics on the land reform vary widely and must be used with caution. There is no doubt, however, that considerable portions of this land have so far failed to find their way into peasant hands.

[33] *Handbook*, p. 80.

when good personal relations prevail between top policy makers and the leading technocrats, civilian ministers have influenced policy. As minister of finance, Mohammed Hadid was a major architect of the original land reform program; the nationalization act, though adopted for political reasons, was framed by another technocrat.

The difficulty lies in the fact that stability has seldom prevailed for periods long enough to have development priorities take effect. The careful plans of technocrats can be completely overturned with a reversal of political or personal fortune. The fates of the successive development plans are a good example of this. The plan drawn up under Kassem in 1961 was in effect for only two years, until the government was overturned by the Baath. A second five-year plan was drawn up in 1965 by the Aref regime, but it suffered considerable shortfall. A third was drawn up in 1970 by the Baath, but this was disrupted by the nationalization of IPC. Instability aside, however, the influence of the technocrat is probably weak. A recent article in the London *Economist* cited "insecure leadership of executive ministries" as one reason for the bureaucrats' inability to effect reforms.[34] One leading Western-trained oil engineer admitted in a closed session of a conference in Beirut several years ago that the influence of men like himself on government was nil. On another occasion Iraq's minister of finance, a Western-trained economist, disclosed to the author that any of his decisions could be overridden by political considerations at a moment's notice, and that he always had his letter of resignation ready.

Socioeconomic Background

The data on the occupations of the leaders show, not surprisingly, that most were at least members of the middle class or better by the time of their entrance into the cabinet or the RCC. But what of their origins? How much social and economic mobility is there in Iraq? And what is its significance for policy?

Hard data on the income levels of the families from which political leaders have come are not easy to find. The fathers' occupations are easier to trace and have

[34] *QER, Iraq,* no. 1, p. 8.

Table 5–9

SOCIOECONOMIC BACKGROUND OF LEADERS[a]

Socioeconomic Strata	Kassem		Baath 1963		Aref		Baath 1968		Total	
	No.	%	No.	%	No.	%	No.	%	No.	%
Upper	3	8	1	4	3	3	4	7	8	4
Upper middle	8	23	4	15	12	14	6	10	24	14
Middle	17	50	10	37	42	48	11	19	68	38
Lower middle	3	8	5	18	5	6	9	15	19	11
Lower	2	6	1	4	1	1	2	3	4	2
Unknown	1	3	6	22	25	28	27	46	55	31
Total	34	100	27	100	88	100	59	100	177	100

[a] See notes to Table 5–1.

the advantage of giving a rough idea not only of family income and social status, but also of early formative influences on the future leaders. Hence, the data here is based on fathers' occupation. Even so, there is a high unknown factor, particularly for the current Baath regime, so conclusions are necessarily tentative.

As a whole, the new revolutionary leaders come from middle-class families, rather than from underprivileged groups. In every regime the largest single group (probably half, if the "unknown" figures were known) come from solidly middle-class families, defined here as middle-level landowners, merchants, religious leaders, professionals and bureaucrats. In each regime, except for the current Baath regime, a higher proportion of leaders came from upper middle-class or distinctly wealthy families than from lower middle or poor ones. Some 14 percent had fathers who were high-level officials and army officers, well-to-do landowners, merchants, and real estate owners, while 4 percent came from families which can only be described as wealthy and prestigious. Only about 11 percent came from the lower middle class defined here as small landowners and so on. Members of poor families have had little access to the political elite as yet.

The current Baath regime represents a distinct difference here. Data available for half of the sample (exclusive of ministers who served only for two weeks in June 1968 and who are included under the Baath in Table 5–9) indicates a shift toward the lower end of the economic spectrum. Some 45 percent of those on whom data is available come from middle-class families, 27 percent from lower middle-class, and 9 percent each from the lower, upper, and upper middle-class ends of the spectrum. The trend is even more pronounced among the fifteen members who have served on the RCC. None has come from upper or upper middle-class families, while at least 13 percent are from poor families. Since 1968, then, power at the top has shifted to the lower middle- and middle-class elements.

This is the overall picture. However several provisos must be made. First, a few men of definitely lower middle-class, if not poor, origin have played a dominant role in all regimes. Abdul Karim Kassem came from a lower middle-class family at best,[35] while the two Aref brothers were the sons of a relatively poor *mulla* and artisan. In the present Baath RCC, several members come from poor families. These men have exerted influence out of proportion to their numbers.

The second proviso is that the cabinets, particularly the more important cabinet posts, have become more and more middle-class—even lower middle-class—at the expense of the upper middle class. In the present regime, for example, President Ahmad Hasan al-Bakr and Baath chief Saddam Hussein, both from Tikrit, a small town on the northern Tigris, come from modest families. While their families might be viewed as middle-class in Tikrit, they are probably lower middle-class by Baghdad standards.

Education and urbanization have been the main causes of social mobility. In 1942 there were only 45 intermediate and 15 secondary schools in Iraq, the latter located only in the *liwa* (provincial) capitals; two *liwa*s had none. By 1965 there were 430 such schools spread through every *liwa*.[36] Meanwhile, internal migration, mainly to Baghdad, but also to provincial cities, has grown at a phenomenal rate.

[35] Uriel Dann, *Iraq under Qassim* (New York: Praeger, 1969), p. 21.

[36] *Statistical Abstract, 1947;* Bureau of Statistics, *Statistical Abstract, 1965* (Baghdad: Government Press, 1966).

The population of Baghdad jumped from 665,000 in 1947 to 1.7 million in 1965. Provincial cities have also grown. It is only in cities that opportunities for social mobility—schools, white-collar jobs, and political contacts—exist.

What do these trends mean for the future? Undoubtedly they will help give Iraqi society a clear egalitarian cast and make reversion to an elitist policy difficult. Indeed, this has been a major aim of the revolution. It should be noted, however, that Iraq has always had considerable social mobility; many old regime leaders, including Nuri al-Said and a number of prime ministers, originally came from middle- and lower middle-class families. Social mobility should also contribute to the social integration of Iraq's various communities, which is still far from complete. Social cleavages—along with intense conservatism—remain the major features of Iraqi society, despite the revolution. Finally, it should be emphasized again that increased mobility without corresponding social and economic rewards will create enormous pressures and difficulties for future regimes. While the increased revenues from oil in the future will certainly provide the means to overcome these difficulties, if these funds are not soon translated into opportunities for economic advancement, higher standards of living and other benefits such as travel and a more open society, the regime may find itself in even greater difficulties. The revolution of rising expectations is already well under way.

A second and perhaps more important question is whether the new members of the political elite, who originate in lower socioeconomic strata, will affect the political orientation of the government, specifically whether they will make it more radical. Here several cautions must be exercised. First, although the term radical is often applied to Iraq, its meaning is not clear. If a virulently anti-Western policy, authoritarian government, and militant pronouncements constitute radicalism, Iraq's recent regimes have indeed been radical. But if radicalism implies a real redistribution as well as a wide diffusion of wealth and power in society, then Iraq is much more conservative. As indicated, while wealth and power have been redistributed from the upper to the middle class, still a small percentage of the population, they have yet to reach the bulk of the populace at the lower reaches of the social scale. The current Baath regime has made more of an effort, recently, in this direction, but it has only scratched the surface. Second, even in matters of internal policy the discrepancy between word and deed has been wide. Radical reforms have been introduced only sporadically, often under outside pressure, as in the case of the nationalization measures of 1964. The Baath has been more consistently radical in its stated policies, but has had difficulty in implementing them. Finally, there does not appear to be any obvious and consistent correlation between socioeconomic background and ideology. In fact, several of the reform measures undertaken in Iraq have been proposed and put through by the well-to-do. This was especially true in the early stages of the land reform, whose first architects were Ministers Mohammed Hadid, a rich Mosul industrialist, and Hudaib al-Hajj Hamud, a wealthy southern landowner. In fact, ideology appears to be far more closely related to education and to contact with outside influences.

However, with these reservations in mind, some correlation can be detected between the social backgrounds of the leaders and their outlooks. First, what is important in this context is not so much the economic strata from which the new leaders come, as the environment in which they were born and raised. Real social mobility in Iraq today is measured not so much by social origin (which is very mixed) as by geographic origin—the emergence of more and more men born and raised in provincial, and often very traditional, environments. Many of the current leaders come from families in which neither the father nor the mother had had any secular education, where illiteracy was rife, and where living conditions and standards were rudimentary in the extreme. Only a tiny handful had fathers who had graduated from high school, much less college, spoke a Western language or had traveled. Most important, conservative religious influences were strong. These family influences, rather than economic status, shaped the outlooks of many of the new political leaders. It is this element in their backgrounds which best explains their distrust of foreign influences, in particular their anti-Western postures, as well as their more puritanical outlook.

Second, most of the new regime leaders have not come from the propertied classes and themselves own little property. Nor, as noted earlier, have they been involved to any degree in the private sector. This has certainly affected their attitudes. They can be counted on to support—or at least not to resist—the extension of the state into the private sector; indeed, they have done much to further it. However, it should be noted that this is mainly true of the industrial sector which has never been strong in Iraq, and of large-scale international trade with which the leadership has not been identified. It is far less true of small landed property. Many leaders come from families of small landowners, a group opposed to really radical redistribution of wealth. It was just such families of the northern Tigris and Euphrates who most vigorously and militantly opposed the left wing policies espoused by Kassem.

Ultimately, however, the most important social fact about the new leaders—especially those from lower strata or the provinces—is that they are upwardly mobile. Such men do not usually identify their interests with their past, but with their future expectations—in this case, with their careers in the bureaucracy, the military, and the professions. Most are interested in assured positions within the hierarchy and, while they may give lip service to radical ideology, in practice their actions are more likely to be governed by considerations of job security and advancement. This does not mean that radical ideologies or tendencies do not exist among the newly emerging leaders. Kassem, for example, was genuinely committed to relieving the poor and took steps in this direction. The current Baath regime is sincerely committed to state ownership of the country's resources and has virtually achieved that goal with the nationalization of IPC. It does mean, however, that such ideologies may be in conflict with more fundamental traditional influences as well as with immediate goals in terms of personal and political advancement.

These factors help explain the gap between word and deed in Iraq. However radical a face Iraq may present to the outside world, domestically its revolution has been slow—indeed, almost conservative. The land reform, for example, has been modified many times over but has still left most of Iraq's arable land in the hands of the state rather than the peasant-farmers. The one liberal innovation in social relations—a personal status law passed by Kassem which gave greater rights to women—was emasculated by Abdul Salem Aref, a religiously conservative man of lower class origin. Throughout most of the revolutionary period, leaders have acted in line with their real identification, promoting the military, the bureaucracy, and the educational system, from which their middle-class constituency is drawn. Iraq's revolution is still very middle-class in its origins and its thrust.

Ethnic and Religious Background

The leaders' ethnic and religious backgrounds have had a far more important influence on their politics than have their socioeconomic origins. One of the factors underlying Iraq's instability is the ethnic and sectarian fragmentation of its population. The country is composed of essentially three major groups—the Arab Sunnis, who comprise about 25 percent of the population and inhabit the northwest portion of the country; the Arab Shia, the largest single group and probably a slight majority of the population, who live in the area from Baghdad south; and the Sunni Kurds, who constitute about a fifth of the population of the territory north and east of Baghdad.[37] These three communities have traditionally been separate and insular, often openly hostile to one another. If Iraq is to achieve any stable national identity, some kind of political community must be created among these groups, and each must be given reasonable access to power.

Although the Arab Sunnis are a minority of the population, they have always produced a majority of the leaders. They have constituted over half of all political leaders since 1958 and have held 80 percent of the top posts. The trend has intensified in the current Baath regime, despite the regime's completely secular orientation. Of the current six-member RCC, all are Arab Sunni, although several Shia have reached the top level of party leadership. By contrast the Shia, despite their possible majority in the country, have held only 29 percent of the political posts since the revolution, and only 16 percent of the top posts. The Kurds have also been underrepresented. During the intermittent civil war from 1961 to 1970,

[37] These are the best estimates available. No census has given an ethnic and religious breakdown of the population.

Table 5–10

ETHNIC AND RELIGIOUS BACKGROUND OF LEADERS[a]

Ethnic/Religious Background	Kassem		Baath 1963		Aref		Baath 1968		Total	
	No.	%	No.	%	No.	%	No.	%	No.	%
Arab Sunni	19	55	16	59	47	53	35	59	96	54
Arab Shia	7	20	9	33	29	33	11	19	51	29
Kurd	6	17	2	7	9	10	10	17	22	12
Other	2	6	0	0	1	1	0	0	3	2
Unknown	0	0	0	0	2	2	3	5	5	2
Total	34	100	27	100	88	100	59	100	177	100

[a] See notes to Table 5–1.

their representation in the cabinet dropped to between 7 and 10 percent. After the 1970 agreement with the current Baath government, it rose to a solid 17 percent, but the Kurds have no voice in the all-important RCC and are not likely to acquire such representation.

What accounts for this situation? The dominance of the Arab Sunnis dates from Ottoman times. The Ottoman government, itself composed of Sunnis, gave them preference in appointments to the military, the bureaucracy, and the upper echelons of the educational establishment which prepared young people for such posts. In time they came to dominate these three institutions. While no such discrimination against the Shia and the Kurds has been practiced, at least officially, since the mandate, there is a natural tendency in any society for a dominant ethnic or religious group to perpetuate its power, particularly if it has a disproportionate share of educational and professional advantages. This has certainly been the case with the Arab Sunnis, but it is by no means the whole explanation. The spread of education and other benefits has, by now, extended many of the same opportunities to the Shia and the Kurds. Indeed, by the last decade of the old regime both had made considerable inroads in the leadership. Political factors go much further toward explaining Arab Sunni dominance.

These are essentially two: first, the composition of the Free Officers' movement, which made the revolution and dominated every government up to the 1968 Baath regime; and second, the Arab nationalist orientation of the governments since 1963.

The Free Officers' movement contained no Kurds and very few Arab Shia, largely because the Free Officers were motivated by pan-Arab sentiments and propaganda emanating from Cairo, sentiments which did not attract the Kurds or the bulk of Shia. Free Officers have taken the top posts in all regimes up to 1968, which has meant Arab Sunni domination of the government. It is also worth noting in general that the intrusion of the army into politics has put the Shia at a disadvantage since relatively few Shia have found their way as yet to the top ranks of the military. While this was not true of the Kurds, the intermittent civil war since 1961 has weeded them out of the top ranks of the army and put their top military men at a disadvantage.

The Arab nationalist factor is more important, however. The major support for and leadership of the pan-Arab movement, both pro-Egyptian and Baathist, in Iraq has come from the Arab Sunni population, particularly that portion of it which inhabits the towns and villages along the upper Tigris and Euphrates between Baghdad and Mosul. These Arab Sunnis feel most in common with their coreligionists across the border in Syria and even in Egypt. The domination of the government since 1963 by the Arab nationalists and the Baathists, then, has meant Arab Sunni domination. Conversely, the pan-Arab orientation of these regimes, at least of their public professions, has drawn support from the Arab Sunni population and helped reinforce the presence of the Arab Sunnis in government.

It is important to note, however, that no matter how pro-Arab Iraqi governments have professed to be, inevitably they have had to pull back from any kind of actual confederation or union with other Arab states. No government in Baghdad can ignore the opposition this step would bring from three-quarters of its population. Yet to share real power with either the Kurds or the Shia, particularly in the upper echelons, would not only deprive the Arab Sunnis of their monopoly, but seriously dilute the pan-Arabism which has become part of the official ideology of every Iraqi government.

Where do the Shia and the Kurds stand on Arab nationalism? Both oppose pan-Arab schemes and support policies fostering a limited national identity based on Iraq's present borders. (Many Kurds would go further in demanding autonomy within those borders.) Both have been more prone to side with radical reform parties within Iraq (other than the Baath), precisely because these eschewed pan-Arabism and concentrated on reform at home, particularly programs for the disadvantaged groups which include the majority of the Shia and the Kurds. The Communist party and the now defunct National Democratic party drew considerable support from the Shia, and the Kurdish Democratic party has been strongly influenced by Marxism in the past.

But the two communities in turn react differently to the dominant Arab nationalist ideology. The Shia differ with the Arab Sunnis on religious, not ethnic or linguistic, grounds. During the Sunni Ottoman era the Shia were under suspicion for their orientation toward Shia Iran and were subject to discrimination. Since they had not attended secular government schools, few of them were educated; and since they had been excluded from the army and the bureaucracy, they had no government experience. Both of these deficiencies were partly made up in the first decades after the mandate as newly educated Shia moved into the professions, the bureaucracy, and the cabinet. In the last decade before the revolution, Iraq had no less than four Shia prime ministers.

With the advent of secular nationalism, the Arab Shia can more easily be assimilated into a state in which the dominant orientation is Arabism. Though the pan-Arab movement has not drawn support among the mass of the Shia population, some educated Shia have been among the leaders of the Arab nationalist movements, both Baathist and pro-Egyptian. In general, however, the Shia tend to seek a situation in which they will not be discriminated against in opportunities for professional advancement and participation in government. The present Baathist regime takes the position that all Arabs are equal and that in the face of Arabism religious differences pale. While this does not meet with the approval of traditional Shia elements, it does not cause dissension among educated Shia, provided the regime does not push pan-Arab schemes too far.

The Kurds have always presented a greater problem of assimilation.[38] As Sunnis they were not subject to the same disadvantages as the Shia under the Ottomans; in fact, they were wooed and welcomed into the army and other branches of the establishment. However the creation of the Iraqi state in 1920 with its predominantly Arab establishment, complete with Arab king and government, put the Kurds in an entirely new and disadvantageous position. Ethnic and, above all, linguistic differences have impeded assimilation. However, considerable progress toward assimilation was made under the mandate and after independence. By the last decade of the old regime, Kurds occupied 15 percent of all top-level cabinet posts, as well as key positions in the military command and the bureaucracy. This

[38] For background to the complex Kurdish problem see Dirk Kinnane, *The Kurds and Kurdistan* (London: Oxford University Press, 1964); Lettie Wenner, "Arab-Kurdish Rivalries in Iraq," *Middle East Journal,* Winter and Spring 1963; Israel Naamani, "The Kurdish Drive for Self Determination," *Middle East Journal,* Summer 1966.

trend continued into the Kassem regime. Kurds were welcomed into the government, two Kurds given posts in the cabinet and, most important of all, Kurds were explicitly recognized as "partners" in the first revolutionary constitution.

This situation ended abruptly with the rupture between the Kurds and the central government in 1960. The civil war that followed, which has continued with brief interludes of truce up to the present, broke this tenuous connection between the Kurds and the Iraqi state and reduced Kurdish participation in government. During years when fighting took place there were few Kurds in the cabinet, wholesale defections of Kurds from the army, and some reduction of Kurds in the bureaucracy.

In 1970 the Kurds and the central government came to an agreement which provided for autonomy in domestic affairs in Kurdish territory. A census was to be taken to determine the areas in which the Kurds were a majority, and the Kurdish Democratic party (KDP) was to join the National Front along with the Baath, the Communists and several other groups. The agreement was to take effect in March 1974, by which time it was assumed that the details of the arrangement could be worked out.

The agreement brought a four-year respite in the fighting, but no more. In March 1974, the Kurds made clear their dissatisfaction with the progress achieved in implementing the agreement and resumed fighting in the north. Specifically, they demanded a larger autonomous area than the government was willing to concede (no census had yet been taken), greater autonomy in their area and, above all, some representation on the all-powerful RCC. The Baath refused to acquiesce and immediately announced its own autonomy scheme. Five pro-government Kurds were taken into the cabinet, but not into the RCC. An autonomous Kurdish area was established in the north with legislative and executive councils to deal with domestic Kurdish affairs, but the central government retained substantial veto-power over their actions.[39]

These ethnic and religious differences and imbalances in society are not Iraq's major problem, but they have been a considerable irritant for all regimes. They have delayed social and national integration and, in the case of the Kurds, faced all revolutionary regimes with a festering war that has drained resources and diverted much-needed energies from other problems. Even in peaceful times, these differences provide sources of discontent which can be mobilized and exploited by factions in Baghdad whenever the leadership is divided. In a political situation as unstable as that which exists in Baghdad, this has been a constant danger.

The Political Direction of Iraq's Revolutionary Leaders

Ultimately the most important aspect of Iraq's revolutionary leaders is their political program and their capacity for achieving their goals. There is the crux of Iraq's

[39] During the summer of 1974, fighting between the pro-Barzani Kurds and the central government intensified. It lasted until March 1975, when an agreement between the Iraqi and Iranian governments ended Iran's support for the Barzani movement and with it any hope for a Barzani-led autonomous Kurdistan. Barzani and his following went into exile, along with several hundred thousand Kurds. It is unclear at present writing what the ultimate outcome of these events will be. One thing seems certain, however. Serious military rebellion in the north is over, and this fact enhances the stability of the current Baath regime. It also seems likely that the limited autonomy scheme of the government will be the effective one.

problems. Iraqi society has developed a growing, secularly educated, professional elite with a variety of skills capable of carrying out reforms on a broad scale. However, these reforms have only partially been realized by the leadership. If the revolution is to succeed—if even a modest level of development is to take place—the country must have three things: a consistent sense of direction consonant with Iraqi realities; a measure of political stability; and institutions capable of putting to work the talent that is available. All three have been lacking.

Ideological Disunity. Most glaring since the revolution has been the lack of consistent political direction which, of course, requires some kind of broad consensus on goals and the methods of pursuing them. From the beginning no such consensus has existed. The roots of the difficulty go back to the original coup of 1958. The military men who made the revolution had no ideology and no well-thought-out solutions to Iraq's problems. What they had were vague, unformulated sentiments and tendencies that had not crystallized or been tested at the bar of public criticism. Moreover, differences of opinion among them had not been brought to the fore or ironed out. At best, most of their goals were negative: the removal of the pillars of the old regime—the monarchy, the establishment politicians, the landowners—and a reorientation of Iraq's foreign policy in the direction of neutrality. They had no clear, positive program. What direction the revolution did acquire after the officers were in power was the work of the civilian opposition politicians brought into the first cabinet by Kassem.

While this group had clearer ideas and programs, unfortunately it was no more united than the officers. The result is well known. Within months after the revolution most of these men, military and civilian, were hopelessly divided on all of the critical issues, with disastrous consequences for Iraq. Division spelled the disintegration of the military coalition which had taken power, the withdrawal from the government of the older civilian politicians with whatever experience they might have contributed to the revolution, the concentration of power in the hands of Kassem and, above all, the continual struggle for power among various political factions which has plunged the country into constant political instability. While much of this struggle for power has been personal, real political issues are involved. To understand the twists and turns of Iraqi politics since 1958, one must understand what these issues are and how they have divided the political elite.[40]

Iraqi's political leaders can be divided into five or six different political groupings, each with its own ideology or orientation. Some are well organized political parties, others are amorphous groups. Most overlap somewhat with others in terms of aims and sources of support. It is worth noting that the issues which have most deeply divided them are less those of social or economic reform, although there are some differences on these, than the orientation of Iraq's foreign policy, and who shall hold power and in what manner.

The Left. On the left are the Communists and the remnants of the now defunct National Democratic party. Both played major roles in Kassem's regime from 1958

[40] For background on the Free Officers and the subsequent history of the revolution see Khadduri, *Republican Iraq;* Uriel Dann, *Iraq under Qassim;* George Lenczowski, "Iraq, Seven Years of Revolution," *Current History,* May 1965; Marr, "The Iraqi Revolution," *Orbis,* Fall 1970.

to 1963. The Iraqi Communist party, established in the early 1930s, draws its leadership and some of its following from among intellectuals and students and enjoys support among the members of the trade union movement. Although the Communist party has often been split among several factions, most of these espouse a Marxist line on internal affairs, sometimes softening their stand for tactical reasons. In foreign policy they are pro-Soviet, although Moscow has frequently let them down. In the past, they opposed pan-Arab schemes in favor of reform at home. Recently, under Soviet prodding, they have come to terms with the ruling Baath party. In 1973, they joined the National Front sponsored by the Baath and in 1974 had two members in the cabinet.

The program of the National Democratic party (NDP), which also originated in the 1930s with a group of intellectuals, has been parallel to that of the British Labor party, its chief inspiration. Like the Communist party, the NDP has opposed pan-Arab schemes and favored reform at home. However, its spokesmen have stopped far short of the radical steps advocated by the Communists. In land reform they favored distribution of land among the peasants and the creation of a small landowning class, while the Communists have generally favored collectivization. Although they are moderate socialists, they have had little to say on the issue of state control of industry; significantly, during Hadid's tenure as NDP minister of finance under Kassem, the private sector was not touched. Traditionally, the NDP has been a staunch supporter of democratic freedoms and a parliamentary regime, but this issue split the party after the revolution. Although the party itself has died, its goals still appeal to a broad spectrum among the intelligentsia.

The Arab Nationalists. Confronting the left are the Arab nationalists.[41] These are divided between those wishing to follow the Egyptian model, usually referred to simply as Arab Nationalists, and those committed to the Baath party. Although the two groups cooperated during Kassem's regime to overthrow him, the split between them became evident after 1963 and degenerated into a struggle for power. Both groups regard the issue of Arab nationalism—ill-defined and often unrelated to Iraq's needs—as central, but here similarity ends.

The Arab Nationalists lack, first, any coherent party organization and, second, any firm ideology. They favor Arab unity and pragmatic social reform on the Egyptian model, and in the present political spectrum they are considered moderate. In foreign policy they are pro-Egyptian. This group held sway under the Aref regime from November 1963 to 1968, during which time they put the nationalization laws into effect in an effort to bring Iraq in line with Egypt economically. A few men of this persuasion hold positions in the present cabinet.

The Baath party of Iraq, theoretically a branch of the parent Arab Baath party and founded by Michel Aflaq and Salah al-Din Bitar, emerged in Iraq in the late 1950s. It also espouses Arab unity but subscribes to a more radical ideology, closer to the Marxist model. Indeed, it may now be more radical than the Communist party. Although the Baath party's programs have undergone continual modification, they are still vague. The last party conclave, held in January 1974,

[41] The older Arab nationalist party of pre-revolutionary days, the *Istiqlal* (Independence) party, has now been outflanked by the new pro-Egyptian and Baath groups and has disappeared.

continued to stress Arab unity, complete independence from any foreign influence, and radical social reform. In fact, the party appears to be shifting in a pragmatic direction, as a result of its relative stability and of the economic boom on the horizon. In agriculture it favors the introduction of collective farms on the Soviet model. (By 1971, 29 such farms had been established covering 90,000 *donums* of land.)[42] While theoretically favoring a mixed economy, the Baath had, by 1974, drastically reduced the private sector. In 1968 the Baathist minister of industry stated that the government aimed to make the public sector's industrial output 90 percent of the total,[43] but by 1974 the party had changed its position slightly in favor of the private sector in an effort to stimulate economic growth.

The party's strongest feature is its tight-knit party structure based on a cell system and its long training and indoctrination of recruits. Although the Iraqi party lays claim to being pan-Arab in organization (and has a "national command" that is pan-Arab in composition), it has had very cool relations with the Syrian branch of the party now in power in that country. At the moment it is relatively isolated in the Arab world, although its relations with other Arab states have improved since the October 1973 war. It is flirting with the People's Republic of China, although its strongest ties are with the Soviet Union.

Somewhere between these extremes is a more moderate group, completely unorganized, which, for lack of a better term, may be designated the "Iraq firsters." Their aims, while not clearly articulated, are primarily to set limits to pan-Arabism and concentrate on Iraq first. Internally they advocate a return to civilian rule, more democratic government and a loosening up of state control over the economy. Their position is closest to that of the old regime; hence no one of their persuasion has held power since 1958.

Lastly, following the revolution, various Kurdish parties have emerged and have demanded Kurdish autonomy. The Kurdish Democratic party (KDP), under Mulla Mustafa Barzani's leadership, was the most important of these. In 1974, after the breakdown of the 1970 agreement, a pro-government Kurdish party formed and was taken into the newly established national front. It may now become the dominant Kurdish voice in Iraq.

It is the struggle for power among, and even within, these various groups that has precipitated Iraq's many coups and the succession of four distinct regimes in sixteen years, each representing one or another of the tendencies or ideologies mentioned above, and each claiming to set the revolution back on its proper course.

The Costs of Instability

The second prerequisite for revolutionary reforms—a measure of political stability—was clearly not met until the 1970s. The feature of Iraq's postrevolutionary history that has done most to retard development has been its chronic instability.

The causes of instability have already been mentioned. What is of concern here is its cost to the political elite in terms of achieving political goals. The first of

[42] *Annual Abstract of Statistics, 1971,* p. 129.
[43] Statement by the minister of industry, *Al-Thawrah* (Baghdad), June 12, 1970.

these has been a depletion of the better educated and talented ranks of the elite manifested in the brain drain and in the turnover and low survival rate of top government personnel.

Table 5–11

RATE OF TURNOVER IN CABINETS

Regime	Number	Percentage
Kassem		
Appointed before 1958	3	9
New appointment	31	91
Baath 1963		
Previous appointment	4	14
New appointment	24	86
Aref		
Previous appointment	14	17
New appointment	73	83
Baath 1968		
Previous appointment	13	22
New appointment	46	78

In the cabinets, each change of regime has meant almost a complete turnover. The original revolution of 1958 removed all the old regime ministers except three; in the Baath coup of 1963, only four of the twenty-seven ministers had served before; in the regime of the Aref brothers which followed, some eighty-eight ministers served (itself an indication of high turnover) of whom only fourteen had had previous service; finally, in the 1968 Baath regime about three-quarters of all ministers were completely new, the rest having served mainly in the short-lived Baath regime of 1963. In the sixteen years since the revolution, only twenty-five ministers have been able to survive through two regimes, while only four have lasted through three. None has survived all four.

Similar rates of attrition apply to the bureaucracy and the army. A State Department study in 1965 estimated that two-fifths of the top layers of the civil service had been removed by that time; by now the figure has undoubtedly doubled. The military has suffered even more egregiously from changes in regimes which have meant the continual removal and replacement of their top commands. In 1968 the minister of defense admitted that between 2,000 and 3,000 officers had been retired or otherwise removed.[44] This is an average of 200 to 300 a year. At the same time the Military Academy itself has only graduated about 300 cadets a year—scarcely replacing those who have left. To supplement these numbers, recruits from civilian higher institutions have been given military training and incorporated into the army.

A second cost of instability, closely related to the first, is the loss of experience. Not only has rapid turnover depleted the ranks of the elite, it has made it diffi-

[44] *Al-Hayat* (Beirut), July 24, 1968.

cult, if not impossible, for new members to gain experience in their jobs. Again, the cabinets provide an example. In terms of time spent in office up to 1971, some 36 percent had not survived a year; 13 percent had not survived two; and only 5 percent had survived three. None had survived six years—less than half the span of the revolutionary period. The average time served by ministers had been a little over a year. (The average time in office of ministers in the last decade of the old regime was more than twice this long.)

The current Baath regime has, up to present writing, had a better record of stability in high office. The fifteen-member RCC which came into office in 1969 has now been reduced to six men, but half of these have served over five years in office and half over four. Since these men also occupy key posts in the cabinet and the party hierarchy, there has been considerable continuity in the decision-making process. There has also been less turnover among the ministers. Of the ministers serving in May, 1972, some 29 percent had been in office over three years, 29 percent over two, 15 percent over one, and 21 percent less than a year. More than half of these were still in office at the end of 1974 after an extensive cabinet reshuffle.

While no such figures are available for the bureaucracy, the rapid turnover there suggests that a similar problem must prevail at the upper levels. It is just this experience—at the top as well as at secondary levels—which is needed, regardless of ideology, if reform is to take place. Its loss goes a long way toward explaining why the superior talent and knowledge of the new technocrats have not yet been utilized.

Finally, instability has paralyzed the decision-making process itself. The rapid turnover of personnel, the paramount consideration given to political loyalty in appointments, and the general atmosphere of fear, insecurity, and anxiety that pervades the top levels of the political scene have all severely hampered policy formation. Not only have ministers and upper-level bureaucrats been unable to undertake long-range planning but, for fear of making wrong decisions, they have often failed to make any decision at all. Meanwhile the energies and attention of the top political leaders have been absorbed by the task of maintaining themselves in power, which has left little time for Iraq's real problems. The current Baath regime has begun to reverse this process, but it will take a considerable period of stability, even with the projected increase in revenues, to mend the destabilizing effects of the past decade and a half.

The Weakness of Political Institutions

The new regimes have failed to devise stable political institutions to support their rule and carry out their reforms. The trappings of democracy imported from the West—elections, parliament, political parties—functioned only imperfectly under the old regime. Nevertheless, they helped fill a need and, in time, might have functioned better. Whatever their faults, the abolition of these institutions by the new revolutionary regimes has created a serious void.

Several attempts, so far unsuccessful, have been made to fill the gap. At the beginning of his regime, Kassem promised an election and a national assembly and relied on the old opposition parties, which he included in his cabinet, for public support. When this effort collapsed the parties were abolished and the military rulers were left with a cabinet that functioned both as a legislative and executive agency under Kassem's control; there were no representative bodies of any kind. A second attempt to create representative organs was made by Abdul Salam Aref in 1964. He and his followers introduced the Arab Socialist Union (ASU) on the Egyptian model as a step toward the election of a national assembly. The ASU, a completely contrived entity, had no real roots in the country and soon collapsed, especially after relations between Iraq and Egypt, which had been its real impetus, cooled. Since then, periodic promises have been made by governments to end the "transitional period," to call an election, and to convene some kind of national assembly, but no such event has taken place.

In the meantime a number of professional and occupational associations have proliferated. Some of these antedate the revolution, but most have been established since 1958. They include associations of lawyers, teachers, journalists and writers, the medical profession, and students. In addition there are numerous peasants' associations and trade unions united in grand confederations. Under the Aref and current Baath regimes, some of these associations have functioned, again imperfectly, as surrogates for the old political parties by indicating the trend of public opinion during elections for officers. But professional groupings, which represent only limited interest groups, cannot mobilize public opinion in sufficiently large blocs to affect public policy. Moreover, the Baath regime has placed them under tight control. In short, they cannot be, and have not functioned as, organs of public opinion.

The newest and certainly most significant attempt to fill the void is the Baath party, which is currently in power. Great secrecy surrounds the party's membership and organization, but some tentative statements can be made about it. The party, so far, has successfully achieved a monopoly of power through domination of the RCC, which functions as both executive and legislative and is entirely Baath in composition, the army, and the important cabinet posts. In order to broaden the base of its support, the party announced the establishment of a National Front in 1973, to include the Communists, the KDP, and progressive nationalists. The Communist party and a splinter group of pro-government Kurds have joined. The KDP, led by Mulla Mustafa refused to join before fighting started in 1974. If the front comes into existence as a viable entity, a National Assembly, consisting of representatives of the same groups as those in the Front, is promised. So far, however, the Baath has refused to share real power (which inheres in the RCC and the Regional Command of the party) with others, and it shows no signs of doing so in the near future.

The Baathists have built a relatively cohesive, well-disciplined party with which they expect to maintain their ideological purity, organizational cohesion and revolutionary fervor. The party is the main, if not the sole, organ through which opinion is expressed and policy decisions made. To support this position, a hierarchical organization has been created. A National Command, consisting of Baathists, Iraqi and non-Iraqi, handles inter-Arab Baath affairs, while the Regional Command is the highest organ of the party in Iraq. Members of the Regional Command also staff various RCC bureaus and, since the 1974 cabinet change, key ministerial posts. Below this is a hierarchy of local organizations through which the party communicates with rank-and-file membership. Thus far the party organization is well integrated with the institutions of the state. The party's executive and the RCC have overlapping membership; key party officials maintain control over the military and the bureaucracy through the appointment of Baath members or their supporters to key positions, and in the case of the military, in particular, by an elaborate security system that assigns Baath cadres to all important military officers. If the party manages to maintain its control, it may become more bureaucratized and less clandestine. There is little doubt that it will continue the attempt to associate a variety of progressive groups with it, but it is unlikely to hold any kind of an open election in the near future or to open avenues to real power to any but Baathists.

Whether the party can maintain its dominant status is the question. So far it has been remarkably successful, but its power base is still very narrow. The Communist party, now allied with it in the Front, could well defect in the future, particularly if relations with the Soviet Union deteriorate. The pro-Egyptian Arab nationalists probably have widespread support among the educated classes, and their following might increase if a successful Arab-Israeli solution is negotiated. But both of these groups are largely ineffective since they have no military potential. Far more dangerous was the Kurdish disaffection which now seems to have been neutralized. Most serious of all would be erosion of support in the army, the only element capable of actually forcing the Baath from power. At the moment, the party seems firmly in power.

In the event that the party does not maintain control, there is no political organization on the horizon that seems capable of taking its place. The Communists have much less support than the Baathists; the pro-government Kurds represent a minority; and the pro-Egyptian Arab nationalists are not a party at all. The alternatives would seem to be a renewal of the struggle for power that characterized the early years of the revolution or a return to the more unstructured, personalistic rule of the military and their civilian allies that characterized the Aref regime. It should also be noted that any new political constellation would probably be nationalist in orientation. There is little indication that the leftists have gained much ground since Kassem's day. While these alternatives must be considered, it seems more likely that the Baath will remain the controlling political group for the foreseeable future, but with possible internal changes in leadership.

Finally, the new revolutionary regimes have failed not only to establish popular political organizations, but also to stabilize the executive, which is simultaneously the seat of legislation by decree. Even in form, the executive has undergone four distinct changes. Under Kassem, a three-member Sovereignty Council was designated as the symbol of national power and the final legalizing authority, while Kassem himself, as prime minister and commander-in-chief of the armed forces, governed with the help of a hand-picked cabinet. The Baath changed this in 1963 and briefly introduced several new features. The Sovereignty Council was replaced by a president who was expected to be a figurehead. A Revolutionary Command Council, created and controlled by the Baath party, became the leading policy-making body. Under the Aref regime, the RCC was abolished, and the president became the leading authority, with the power to appoint and remove prime ministers. Under the president, however, the cabinet came to have more authority. With the advent of the Baath in 1968, the ministers have been reduced to department heads, and power has been concentrated in the Baath-controlled RCC. Such changes have not allowed constitutional structure to take root and achieve legitimacy, nor have they provided for the peaceful transfer of power. Moreover, they have thoroughly personalized politics; the ruling group is generally thought of as a tightly knit cabal which might change at any time. The implications of this for policy planning are too obvious to need elaboration.

The Importance of Leadership

The key to future development in Iraq lies in the political sphere, and particularly in the area of political management. This in turn is highly dependent upon the quality of political leadership. So far, the leadership that has emerged since the revolution has been disappointing, although the current Baathist regime may be developing some much-needed skill in this area. Revolutionary leadership has manifestly failed to solve Iraq's traditional problems and has created many new ones. Its failure has been partly due to social, ethnic, and religious divisions in Iraqi society, to a history of political discontinuity, and to the difficulties of instituting radical revolutionary reforms in an essentially conservative Muslim society. But many of the problems Iraq faces today have been brought on by the leaders themselves.

The poor quality of the revolutionary leadership cannot be blamed on Iraq's educational system, which has been training larger and larger numbers of men and women in a variety of fields. Indeed, these increasing numbers of highly qualified people will be a major problem for the future if development does not proceed rapidly enough to satisfy their rising expectations and they are not offered a chance for real political participation. Iraq now has a considerable pool of talented individuals from which to choose its political leaders, but the best of these have not reached the top of the political ladder. One explanation for this has been the domination of politics by middle-rank military officers of lesser education, little exposure to the outside world, and little experience of politics and politicians—men who have been out of touch with political realities inside and outside their country. Since 1968 the Baath has gradually substituted the rule of civilians for that of the military, but this has not improved the regime's contact with the outside world; indeed it has accentuated its isolation. Most Baath politicians have risen to power through clandestine party activity and have had little more exposure to the outside world than the military.

Another explanation for Iraq's leadership problems is the lack of agreement on goals among both civilian and military leaders, which has intensified the struggle for power since 1958. Finally, there has been the loss of certain skills—above all administrative and political skills, and especially the ability and willingness to compromise—that are usually associated with more open political systems. Hence, the leaders have been unable to mobilize the new talent which does exist within Iraqi society.

From the data it is clear that social and economic mobility are increasing in Iraq, and that more and more leaders are coming from the provinces and the lower middle classes. Whether this will affect policy in the future remains to be seen. So far, however, most of the leaders have been solidly middle-class in background, aims, and outlook by the time they have attained power. There is little automatic correlation between lower socioeconomic origin and "radical" ideology; radical ideas are more likely to be related to Western education or to affiliations with parties which originally imported their ideology from the outside. Even more important in shaping the political orientation of leaders has been their ethnic and religious backgrounds. Cabinets, and now the RCC, are still dominated by the Arab Sunni minority, the most staunchly Arab nationalist element in Iraq. As long as this group continues to dominate the scene, Iraq's policies will be more nationalist than leftist, although the Baath party is trying to combine both elements.

While claiming to espouse radical ideologies, the new leadership has introduced radical reforms only spasmodically and often for political, nonideological reasons. Meanwhile, it has consistently allocated funds for measures that benefit the emerging professional and bureaucratic middle classes, although some of these, like the expansion of education, will increase social mobility for all classes. The major focus of Iraqi radicalism has been an increasingly anti-Western foreign policy. This, too, reflects in part the provincial background of the top leaders and their declining contact with the West.

VI. ASPECTS OF THE POLITICAL ELITE IN SYRIA

Gordon H. Torrey

Syria, often acknowledged as the home of Arab nationalism, has long been one of the most politically unstable states in the Middle East. At the same time it has been a leading advocate of political and social change, although its social fabric is basically conservative and overwhelmingly Muslim.

Syria is still a comparatively sparsely inhabited country. It covers 72,000 square miles in area, consisting largely of arid and semi-arid plains, and its population of 6,924,000 is concentrated mainly in the western and northwestern part of the country.[1] The annual rate of population growth is estimated at a high of 3 percent. Interestingly, the urban population is growing less rapidly than that of agricultural areas, a fact that distinguishes Syria from much of the underdeveloped world. Urban areas are growing, however; the population of Damascus grew by 14 percent from 1959 to 1964, that of Aleppo 12 percent. Forty percent of Syria's population is concentrated in the Damascus and Aleppo provinces.

Factors Working against Political Stability

Geographical position, culture, a long history of occupation by foreigners—Egyptians, Assyrians, Persians, Turks, and French—and Syria's relative youth as an independent state (it was established in 1946) all help explain the lack of firmly established political institutions. This lack has been further accentuated by the existence of a great many religious and ethnic cleavages, which have made Syria a fertile field for foreign intrigue, both Arab and non-Arab. These internal and external pressures have inhibited the growth of a stable governmental structure as well as a sense of national identity.

Syria's internal divisions have had a profound influence on its foreign policy. Of paramount importance have been Syria's relationships with Iraq and Egypt. From time immemorial Syria has been the battleground for conflict between the states of the Tigris-Euphrates and Nile basins—that is, in contemporary times, between Egypt and Iraq, regardless of whether they were ruled by monarchs or revolutionaries. While geographic proximity would seem to favor Iraq, Egypt has often prevailed because of its greater political and cultural influence. It does today, even though (or perhaps because) another pan-Arab Baathist regime rules in Baghdad. Latent fear of Turkey has continued, perhaps strengthened by Turkey's membership in NATO and alliance with the United States. Another crucial influence on Syrian attitudes toward the West is the existence of Israel, whose forces defeated the Syrians in 1948 and 1967 and, although less easily, again in 1973. Syrian xenophobia has been heightened in the case of the United States

[1] *Al-Thawrah* (Damascus), November 8, 1970. This article summarizes the results of the 1970 census.

by strong American support of Israel and the presence of the Sixth Fleet in the Mediterranean. The old elite, by and large, was pro-Western, within the general limits of traditional Syrian xenophobia. In fact, this pro-Westernism has been used by the radicals to discredit and unseat the country's traditional elite. It was the radical elements that pushed Syria into a pro-Soviet, anti-Western stance and brought about the equipping of the army with Soviet-bloc weapons and economic assistance. From 1954 to 1970 Syria received over $580 million in arms and about $443 million in economic assistance from Soviet-bloc countries, and was seventh highest recipient of Soviet aid of all underdeveloped countries.[2]

Most Syrians share a common culture, religion, and language, and yet Syria is plagued by a lack of homogeneity. The divisions in Syrian society include differences along religious, ethnic, tribal, and class lines. Sunnis and Shias differ on points of Muslim theology, while both are at odds with the Christian minority, which is itself divided into numerous sects. The religious minorities further include the Alawites, who live in the Latakia area, and the Druze, whose home is in the southwest. Another minority, the Kurds, although Sunni Muslims, are non-Arabs. And then there are the non-Arab Armenians who have their own church and culture.[3]

The *Syrian Statistical Abstract* no longer gives a population breakdown along religious lines. Perhaps this reflects the Baathist regime's desire to deemphasize religion. Nearly 90 percent of the population is Muslim, which can be roughly broken down into 70 percent Sunnis (including 4 percent Kurds), 11 percent Alawites, and about 3 percent Druze. Christians amount to about 7 to 8 percent, Armenians about 2 percent. Roughly 92 percent of the population consists of Arabs.[4] In a society where religion plays an important role in day-to-day life, such a plethora of sects would seem likely to generate almost continual strife. Sectarian cleavages are only heightened by the social demarcations between economic classes, family and clan groupings, urban and rural residents, and the adherents of fiercely warring ideologies.

The extended patrilinear family remains the basic unit of Syrian society and family loyalties far outweigh all others. Furthermore, adherence to other social units is largely based on family ties. Religion remains the next strongest cohesive force. Syrian society is changing, however, and the traditional social and religious barriers are breaking down. This is becoming especially noticeable with regard to family ties; there is now more frequent social intercourse among individuals within professions, industrial concerns, government offices, and business.

While the villages are characterized by homogeneous occupational structures, Syria's towns and cities, like all cities, have a heterogeneous occupational structure and a population increasingly removed from agriculture. Within the urban areas, the characteristics of the traditional Middle Eastern city, with its separate quarters for the various religious sects, are gradually disappearing.

Up to the mid–1960s, the country's political and economic life was dominated

---

[2] Department of State, Bureau of Intelligence and Research, *Communist States and Developing Countries Trade and Aid* (Washington, D.C.: September 22, 1971).

[3] Foreign Area Studies, *Area Handbook for Syria* (Washington, D.C.: Government Printing Office, 1971), pp. 83–84.

[4] Ibid., p. 124.

by a small elite, mostly Sunni, whose members lived in Aleppo and Damascus. Their wealth and position, while ultimately based on the ownership of large estates worked by peasants, came from their domination of finance, industry, and commerce.

The Expansion of Education. One of the most remarkable changes in Syria since independence in 1946 has been the growth of education. In 1943 there were about 46,000 pupils in elementary and secondary schools, and by 1946 the number had grown to 165,000.[5] In 1960 there were 424,000, almost ten times the number enrolled seventeen years before,[6] and by 1968 the number reached 1,156,172.[7] The growth in the number of students has been made possible by the vast expansion of the school system. There were only 249 schools in Syria in 1943; in 1960 there were 3,261 and in 1969 5,827.[8] In addition there are over 38,000 students in universities, 5,600 in normal schools, and 8,498 in technical schools.[9] The number of female university students has risen even more dramatically. From a miniscule 68 in 1946, the number of women in universities rose to 6,212, a ninety-fold increase.[10]

A breakdown of students (undergraduate and graduate) at the two Syrian universities in Damascus and Aleppo according to subjects studied brings out the imbalance between the country's shortage of trained personnel in many fields and the student body's educational goals. In a basically agricultural country there were only 829 students enrolled in the faculties of agriculture at the two schools, and only 621 of these were Syrians.[11] Meanwhile, 14,897 students were majoring in literature, 7,800 in law, and 1,589 in medicine.[12] The total university enrollment was 38,000.[13] One reason for the high number of law students is that a law degree is an entree to a government job.

An interesting facet of education in Syria has been the disparity in educational levels among the various religious sects. Generally the Christians have had a higher level of education than the Muslims, though this disparity has decreased in recent years as the number of schools has grown. The Sunni Muslims, meanwhile, have a general educational level higher than their Shia compatriots. Literacy ranges between 35 and 40 percent at the present time.

The Old Elite. Syria is one of the countries of the Middle East of which almost no sociological studies have been carried out in the last fifteen years.[14] Largely due to Syrian xenophobia, continued political instability, and the emphasis by scholars on political developments, this state of affairs has impeded research on a number

[5] United Arab Republic, Ministry of Planning, Directorate of Statistics, *Statistical Abstract, 1960* (Damascus, 1961), p. 69.

[6] Ibid., p. 68.

[7] Syrian Arab Republic, Office of the Prime Minister, Central Bureau of Statistics, *Statistical Abstract, 1969–1970* (Damascus: Government Printing Press, 1971), tables 176, 178 and 179.

[8] Ibid., table 180.

[9] Ibid., tables 182 and 183.

[10] Ibid., table 186.

[11] Ibid., tables 175 and 178.

[12] Ibid., table 187.

[13] Ibid.

[14] Ibid., p.70.

of basic aspects of Syrian culture. In particular, any analysis of the social forces at work in contemporary Syria largely depends on fragmentary data, information that can be gleaned from political and historical studies, and impressions that can be gained from the heavily censored press and from observers. Equally, studies of Syria's former elite are practically nonexistent. However, certain rough characterizations can be inferred from the composition of the country's parliaments and cabinets from the end of World War I until the Syrian union with Egypt in 1958.

The sparseness of the country's educational facilities was one factor limiting the elite to a very small part of the populace. In the earlier parliaments and well into the 1940s, graduates of Ottoman Turkish educational institutions predominated, and deputies who had received their higher education in France were the second most numerous group. In 1947, graduates of Syrian universities began to predominate, and the number of graduates of Western universities began to decline, while graduates of other Near Eastern universities remained an insignificant, but also declining, group. The general educational level of deputies rose, with the proportion of university graduates increasing from a low of 30 percent in 1932 to 36 percent in 1954. The deputies' knowledge of Western languages grew enormously, from a low of 5 percent in 1919 to 47 percent in 1954. Generally speaking, members of the various Syrian cabinets had a higher level of education and came from the upper elite, often called Syria's "fifty families." [15]

From December 1946 until the union with Egypt in March 1958, the 208 ministerial positions (including the prime ministership) were filled by only about ninety different individuals. During this period, there were twenty-four different cabinets, including three under the Shishakli military dictatorship. Seventeen of these ninety individuals participated in four or more cabinets, and thirteen others had participated at least three times; the record was service in seven different cabinets. Those who held cabinet posts the most often were the old line politicians of the upper elite: the names Ghazzi, Arslan, Asali, Azam, Jabri, Qudsi, Atassi, Barmada, Kayyali, and Buzo appeared time after time.[16] Even during the hectic period after 1955 when more "radical" politicians were elected to parliament and/or became cabinet members, the educational level remained high.

One general characteristic of the old elite was that it had had considerable exposure to Western influence, even though so many of its members had been educated in Turkey. This exposure, however, did not lead to great social innovation or real democracy. Other more basic influences prevailed. Since rural landholders constituted the largest single group of deputies, there was no great push for legislation that would change the social order. As time went on, the gap between the ruling elite and the great mass of the population grew wider, and parliaments simply did not reflect the desires of the Syrian people.[17] Syria's last elected parliament before union with Egypt, that of Shishakli in 1954, had a comparatively high level of education. Interestingly enough, its members were mostly educated in

[15] These statistics were drawn from a study by R. Bayly Winder, "Syrian Deputies and Cabinet Ministers, 1919–1959," *Middle East Journal*, vol. 16, no. 4 (Autumn 1962) and vol. 17, no. 1 (Winter-Spring 1963).

[16] Gordon H. Torrey, *Syrian Politics and the Military* (Columbus: Ohio State University Press, 1964), pp. 405–14.

[17] Kamel S. Abu Jaber, *The Arab Ba'th Socialist Party History, Ideology, and Organization* (Syracuse: Syracuse University Press, 1966), p. 29.

Syria and had had less experience abroad. This would prove to be equally true of the new elite which began to grow after the break from Egypt in 1961.

The New Elite

A lower class group of civil servants, white-collar workers, small merchants, some small farmers, and especially the Syrian military is now taking the place of the old political elite. The laboring class still has not gained political or economic influence, even under the egalitarian Baathist regime. Its plight has been alleviated to some extent by limited social welfare benefits, but these nowhere approximate the welfare benefits available in the more industrialized countries of the West, and it is within this group that Syria's most serious social discontent exists.

According to Baathist theory, the workers and peasants are the foundation of society, and yet the regime has maintained tight control over organized labor. Whatever the theory, the reality is rule by an elite and the control of public organizations as instruments of the state. Labor unions are regarded as vehicles for organized support for the Baathist regime, a means of maintaining labor discipline and increasing production. Government subsidies to the unions are an effective instrument of control. Strikes are forbidden and regarded as treason against the state. Union officers, though not all Baathists, must be approved by the regime. Thus, union leaders are not actually spokesmen for the workers, and any who have "gotten out of line" in the past have been dismissed.

The Role of Intellectuals in Politics. Since March 1963, when a Baathist-inspired military coup toppled the conservative civilian government, Syria has, at least in theory, been governed by a group professing Baathist socialistic ideology.[18] Ultimate control belongs to the army, as it has for many years, but ideology has played a greater role under this regime. The army officers who hold the levers of power dominate the new elite, which has pressed for radical social change. This new elite had no stake in Syria's past, in the institutions and cultural attitudes of the old elite. The Baath's civilian founders, Michel Aflaq and Salah al-Din Bitar, grew up in the era of the French mandate, and their political ideals fused strong Arab nationalism with a commitment to economic equality and social justice. Although the Arab nationalism so prominent in Baathist ideology is often equated with Islam, the Baath party is built on a secular framework. Following its seizure of power in Syria and Iraq in early 1963 the Baath party was torn by a fierce internal struggle over the role of the party on the world scene. The radical faction pushed for alignment with the Marxist doctrine of identity with "oppressed peoples everywhere," and demanded that capitalism be abolished and "socialist systems established in its ruin" all over the world.[19] Friendship with the "socialist camp" was to be consolidated.

The younger, more radical elements advocating this line removed Bitar from his post in the party's command. In 1964 Aflaq was forced to rely on support from the Syrian army in order to remain party leader. He did not succeed for long,

[18] Gordon H. Torrey, "The Ba'th—Ideology and Practice," *Middle East Journal*, vol. 23, no. 4 (Autumn 1969), pp. 445–70.

[19] *Al Baath*, October 28, 1963.

however, and rivalry between the Aflaq-led civilian majority of the party and the military faction led by the extremist Salah Jadid came to a head in late 1965. In February 1966 a coup was carried out by an extremist army-civilian party group, and Aflaq and the orthodox party leadership were denounced and ousted from the party on the charge of having "reactionary mentalities" and rightist connections.[20] Bitar escaped from Syria and has never returned. He later admitted that the military element had seized control of the party, and pointed out that while the party wanted strong military connections, its leaders must not be army men; otherwise, military force and not party ideology would predominate.

Since that time, controversies within the Syrian regime have been largely confined within the military leadership. In fact, Syria's intelligentsia has little influence over political and social matters, except for those of its members who have risen in the Baath party. Position, promotion, and influence depend almost entirely upon party membership, and most intellectuals are antagonistic or apathetic toward the regime. This reaction has led to a general lowering of standards in government and an unwillingness on the part of government officials to take any more responsibility than is absolutely necessary for survival. As a result, the governmental machinery is slow and caught up in red tape. Decisions are made not only on the merits of the case, but also on their correctness in the political sense. Even the most simple procedures are carried out slowly and erratically.[21]

The struggles that are taking place within the regime, meanwhile, are not basically ideological. The pan-Arab aspects of Baathism have been deemphasized in favor of militant socialism. Another strain within the revolution is the fact that the army has come to be dominated by Alawites with some Druze support, and the influence and power of the Sunni Muslim element have greatly diminished.

The Baathist regime has never succeeded in attracting public support. In large part this is due to the Baath's clandestine mentality. Organized along Communist party lines and long a subversive organization before it came to power, the Baath party's structure and activities—membership, officials, organization—remain secret. Despite control of the press, radio, and television, the party has been unable to project an image of real identity with the Syrian people. Its propaganda tends to concentrate on charges against the "imperialists" or Israel. The public has no sense of participation in the governing of the country and, if not alienated, is indifferent or disgusted. This feeling is shared by politically conscious elements, such as students and labor unions. At best the people are neutral toward the regime, mere on-lookers. Even policies that would seem likely to capture the public's imagination—support for the *fedayeen* and other resistance movements, xenophobic agitation against the Western powers, nationalization, and emphasis on economic development—fail to spark any real enthusiasm.

The decline of Sunni Muslim influence in the army has been part of a general trend especially marked in the political realm. The large landowners were mostly Sunnis, and their power has been broken by the seizure of their estates. The political role of the country's religious leaders also has been considerably circumscribed;

[20] Damascus Radio, February 23, 1966.

[21] The number of government employees has grown in a startling manner since the Baath coup in 1963. In 1964 there were 25,317 government employees. By 1969 this had increased by half to 37,473. *Statistical Abstract, 1969–70,* table 216.

some of them have been arrested when their protests against regime policies were considered too strident by the authorities. A number of Baathist leaders are Sunni Muslims, but they are not very religiously oriented, and the secular emphasis of Baathist ideology inclines them to play down their religious origins. Another factor behind the decline of Sunni influence is the fairly large Alawite element of the party's leadership. The Alawites were peasants who worked land largely owned by Sunni landlords.

The Military Elite. The emergence of the new military elite is almost solely attributable to the great expansion of the educational system since Syrian independence. The vast increase in the number of schools has opened up educational opportunities in hundreds of villages and small towns for the sons of the lower classes and even peasants. Of special importance was the opening of secondary schools where students could prepare for entry to the military academy at Homs, itself extensively enlarged following independence, especially after the 1948 Arab-Israeli War. Whereas applicants to the academy had previously been few in number and exclusively middle- or upper-class, in the 1950s and 1960s they could be numbered in the hundreds.[22]

The expansion of the educational system was accompanied by its increased Arabization and the spread of radical ideas among the rural youth. New schools were staffed by teachers of rural origin imbued with strong Arab nationalism and the radical political ideas of the Baath party. Party cells were formed in numerous secondary schools and at the two universities in Aleppo and Damascus. Thus, when students arrived at the military academy they were already politicized. As these students graduated and passed into the army, it became a hotbed of ideological debate.

As time passed and as coups and purges came and went, the character of the officer corps changed considerably. The old "nonpolitical" and generally conservative generation of officers was replaced by a younger generation with strong ideological commitments, almost entirely Syrian educated, and lacking fluency in Western languages and knowledge of the West. More important, it came to have a predominantly rural basis. The existence of a secret Baath party organization within the officer corps into which the new Baathist graduates of the military academy were inducted cut military and civilian members of the Baath party off from one another almost entirely.

The officers of the Syrian army, in effect, became the political elite. Their political opponents were purged, and promotion came to be based on political beliefs and support rather than on professional competence. The military now is regarded primarily as a vehicle for social change equal in importance to its role as a force to oppose the Israelis. This view is held by many younger officers, and the average age of the army leadership is relatively low compared with that of foreign armies. This is an indication of the extent of the generational conflict between

[22] Much of the material for this section is drawn from the author's work *Syrian Politics and the Military,* his article in Sydney N. Fisher, ed., *The Role of the Military in the Middle East* (Columbus: Ohio State University Press, 1963), and the thesis of Michael H. Van Dusen, "Intra- and Inter-Generational Conflict in the Syrian Army," School of Advanced International Studies, The Johns Hopkins University, 1971.

Syria's traditional political and military leadership and the new elite. There is little doubt that the educational level of the new army elite is generally lower than that of previous civilian elites. Homs is only a two-year military academy. The many capable technicians, graduates of the country's universities and recipients of foreign graduate degrees, are not the men who make the major decisions, although they can influence them. They are the nonparty government experts who keep the wheels of government moving despite suspicion of the universities by many military officers.

The basic bonds among members of Syria's military elite are common regional origin and secondary-school ties. The school tie sometimes extends beyond the original region, since many officers of rural origin attended secondary school in large towns. The regional loyalties of the military elite have been demonstrated when individual military men have promoted such local projects as schools, the Latakia port, and other civic improvements.

The Western commitment to civilian control over the military has led some observers to mistakenly assume that the civilian and military components of Syria's political dynamics are separate. In fact, this concept is alien to the Syrian's Islamic heritage. Throughout Arabic history there has been no such division. The Mamluks, who once ruled Syria, were a military dynasty, as were the rulers of numerous Arab kingdoms before them. Only since the penetration of Western ideas into the Arab world have attempts been made to make civilians predominant. (The introduction of parliamentary government during the mandate period was one of those.) Only in Lebanon, with its peculiar religious balance, has the idea of civilian control of the military been maintained, and even there the army has played a definite role.

The army's leadership is already Baathist oriented in various degrees, and a considerable effort has been made to indoctrinate noncommissioned officers and enlisted men with Baathist thinking. A "political department" was established within the army in early 1970, and "political officers" have received indoctrination. Their mission is to guide members of the armed forces ideologically and to instill in them loyalty toward the present regime. It appears that these army political guides will also attempt to improve discipline so that the men will obey their officers without question. If this can be accomplished, the Asad regime will have a praetorian guard to protect it from dissidence inside as well as outside the army.[23]

The Civilian Elite. The civilian Baath party leadership has undergone changes similar to those of the army leadership. It, too, has been ruralized as a result of coups and purges. Among the strongest civilian advocates of the Baath have been school teachers at all levels and members of the medical profession. In fact, there is a certain similarity between the "political" physicians and the army officers, in that most of them regard the political side of their careers as more important than the medical. One reason for the politicization of many members of the medical profession is that, since openings have been available to some extent in the Syrian medical school on the basis of merit, medicine has been one of the few fields in which a great many students from rural areas and small towns can gain higher education. A medical degree has been virtually their only means of upward mobility.

[23] *The Arab World,* March 17, 1972, p. 6.

This is not to say that they have not used their medical knowledge to the people's advantage. Indeed, a considerable number of doctors have put their social beliefs into practice by treating the rural poor.

While information on the backgrounds of the Syrian Baath party civilian leadership is sparse, certain characteristics stand out. The great majority are from small towns and are products of Syrian or other Arab higher education. The holders of Western (mostly French) degrees are a small minority. The medical and legal professions are dominant among civilian leaders, while school teaching ranks third. Prominent examples are the Atassis, Jamal and Nur al-Din, a doctor and a dentist, and Amin al-Hafiz who received degrees from the Syrian University Law School and the Homs Military Academy. None of the leadership has received Soviet-bloc education.[24]

The Brain Drain. As the radicalization of Syria has progressed, large numbers of the middle- and upper-class elite have left the country, most of them for Lebanon. For the most part these were people who had owned property—agricultural estates, or manufacturing concerns—and entrepreneurs whose businesses had been nationalized or who had been frozen out by the regime's economic policies. Many others were people with technical training, many of them Christians who feared the pan-Arab direction of the regime.[25] Still others were political refugees whose basic disagreements with the regime made it impossible for them to live in Syria. The number who fled may have been as high as several hundred thousand.

Syria's radical leaders and military men seemed secretly pleased with this exodus, apparently believing that these people could not be included in the "new society" that the ideologues envisioned. However as time passed, the realization slowly dawned that Syria needed many of its professionals and businessmen and, after the Asad coup, attempts were made to woo them back. An article in a Damascus paper on the emigration of scientists and technicians, especially those who had been trained abroad,[26] acknowledged that these people should have been part of Syria's future leadership, not supplements to the inventory of talent of the more "advanced nations." Seventy percent of Arab scientists who studied in the West did not return home, the article said. The explanations offered, quite realistically, for this startling figure were political instability, stultifying social patterns, and the threat of war in the Arab world, as well as the greater opportunities for individual advancement and innovation in the West. Somewhat off target was the implication that foreign women had lured the emigrants into not returning to Syria.

Considerable blame for the brain drain can be placed on the intellectual climate in Syria's institutions of higher learning where an atmosphere of study and research is lacking, curriculums and facilities are outdated, salaries are low, an antiquated seniority system frustrates the younger faculty, and research funds are almost nonexistent. When offered higher salaries, greater political and social freedom, and better research facilities and opportunities, a significant number of Syria's highly

[24] These "statistics" have been drawn from an informal file compiled by the author over a period of years.

[25] *Area Handbook for Syria,* p. 140.

[26] U.S., Department of Commerce, Joint Publications Research Service, *Translations on Near East,* JPRS no. 52617 (Washington, D.C., March 15, 1971).

educated citizens have preferred not to return to Syria, or to emigrate once again after returning home for a short period.

The Asad Regime. The Asad regime, which is now in power, has encouraged the return from abroad of Syrians with special skills or capital in an attempt to break out of economic stagnation. Asad has also attemped to make his regime more responsive to the desires of the general populace and to encourage participation in government by a more representative political spectrum. Over the past several years he has turned it away from many of the more radical manifestations of Baathism. He has reorganized the Baath party, brought Syria out of its isolation from the other Arab states, especially Egypt, and organized a national front government and a People's Council. While the Baath party was allocated a majority of the council seats, the council included Nasserites, Communists, and representatives of trade unions, professional organizations, and even the *ulema*.

An interesting sidelight on Asad's pragmatic policies, as well as a significant indication of the Baath's failure to gain the approval of the Syrian people, occurred in early March 1972 when elections for local councils were held. The Baathists lost a shocking number of seats. In Damascus only eight of the council's ninety seats were won by Baathists. In one Damascus district a list supported by religious leaders won handily. In Homs, the Muslim Brotherhood-backed list swept the election, and in Syria's second city, Aleppo, the opposition won a majority of the seats. The Baath managed to hang on in Latakia in the Alawite area.[27] The results seemed to indicate either that the Baathists had overestimated their popularity, or that the Asad regime had desired a setback for the party's civilian leaders. Had it seriously desired a victory for the party, of course, the elections could have been rigged. It may be that the free elections demonstrated the Syrian voter's desire for a respite from radicalism and, in effect, gave Asad a vote of confidence for his moderate policies.

The new era under Asad's leadership might be termed "pragmatic Baathism." The original broad ideals of the Baath party continue to be espoused, but their application is more realistic. The national front did not get going until after the local elections when a new cabinet was formed. It included not only Baathists, but Nasserites, Communists, and even followers of Akram Hawrani, a former Baathist leader who had broken with the party some years ago. If this trend continues, it is possible that Syria's intelligentsia will once more have a wider influence on their country's policies. However, unless a freer, more responsible, non-Baathist press is allowed, it is doubtful that this will come about. The army is always waiting in the background.

In a country like Syria where there is a lack of consensus even on basic national goals, instability becomes the norm. Disunity and instability ultimately worked to the advantage of the army, a far more cohesive force than any of the political parties, with their vague goals and internal bickering. Even when the Baath, a political party with better enunciated goals and a better disciplined leadership structure than its rivals, came to power, the army won out in the end. The party, with its elite leadership principle, could neither engender widespread public sup-

[27] *Daily Star* (Beirut), March 12, 1972.

port, nor impress its ideology on the army effectively enough to make the officer corps subordinate its own particular aspirations. And then the party's civilian leaders abdicated their leadership role by their almost continual dissension over theory and tactics. Now, however, the pendulum seems to be swinging back toward the civilians, and with the army leadership's blessing.

VII. THE POLITICAL ELITE AND NATIONAL LEADERSHIP IN ISRAEL

Emanuel Gutmann and Jacob M. Landau

That Israel is a developing state with a Western type of political system is well demonstrated by the nature of its elite. For the purpose of this paper, we have not formulated complex definitions and have therefore ignored the ideological implications of the vast literature on this subject. By political elite we mean those groups that actually exercise, or could exercise, considerable political influence within the political elite—those having power in the system. The national leaders are a more restricted group and include both the occupants of the highest political posts and some other figures who participate directly in policy making without themselves holding formal office.

The Israeli case is striking in that the political elites are entirely party based or affiliated, and most leaders have risen through the ranks of their respective parties. Insofar as economic, religious, military, and other factors play any role in policy making, they generally do so through the political parties or, more precisely, the elites of these parties. This is true also of countergroups within the elite.

This study will examine the composition of selected groups in the political elite using a number of socioeconomic variables, and will assess the trends in the composition of this elite as well as the mechanics of elite circulation. The specific role of the elite in consensus formation within heterogeneous Israeli society will also be examined. This analysis will be preceded by a brief historical description of the political system within which the elite operates.

We shall use a combined behavioral-observational approach, relying heavily on an examination of Israel's "positional elites." Since the focus is on functional political power, symbolic offices, such as state presidency, will not be discussed. Rather, cabinet ministers, their deputies, members of the Knesset (parliament) and other major policy makers and influentials will provide the data for our analysis. We shall also provide biographical notes on a few typical political personalities to illustrate how they became members of the elite.

The Emerging State

On May 14, 1948, the heads of the *Yishuv* (the Jewish community in Palestine) proclaimed the independence of Israel. The Zionist leaders became the rulers of the new state, which proved capable of simultaneously winning a war against the armed forces of five Arab states and of the Palestinian Arabs, creating the machinery of a newly independent state, and absorbing an inflow of immigrants that virtually doubled the country's population in the first three years of independence.

Research for this article was partly financed by a grant from the Levi Eshkol Institute for Economic, Social and Political Research of the Faculty of Social Sciences, the Hebrew University of Jerusalem. The material herein has been updated to April 1974.

Within the rather atypical, colonial, multiethnic and multireligious Palestinian society ruled by the British from 1918 to 1948, the *Yishuv* had constituted a partially autonomous entity, a "state-in-the-making." Its central governing bodies, loosely called the national institutions, were composed of the executive committee of the Zionist organization, which was also known as the Jewish Agency for Palestine, and the Vaad Leumi (the National Council of Palestine Jews). These institutions had been endowed by the British authorities with very limited functions of self-government.[1]

Just after World War I, the tiny Jewish community (in 1922 it numbered about 85,000 in a total population of 750,000) was really a confederation of diverse groups and organizations. There were the ultrareligious indigenous Jews (the *Yishuv yashan,* or "old community"), split into many rival sects, and the *landsmannschaft* (immigrants coming from one country) groups of the Ashkenazi Jews (originally from central and eastern Europe) and the Oriental Jews (from the Mediterranean countries, Asia and North Africa).[2] There were the settlers of the first *aliya* (wave of immigration, approximately 1880 to 1900) who had come primarily from what was then the Russian Empire and Rumania. These settlers founded the earliest agricultural villages, peopled the existing towns and laid the foundations for a middle class. The pioneers of the second *aliya* (1900–1914) came mainly from Russia. Most prominent among them were the socialist founders of the first kibbutzim (collective villages) and *moshavim* (cooperative villages) and the highly motivated urban and agricultural working class; they were divided into a number of ideological groupings. Later came the rather heterogeneous third *aliya* immigrants (1919–1923), also from eastern Europe and again largely socialist pioneers adhering to a variety of movements and parties.[3]

The fourth *aliya* (1924–1932) was made up mainly of people of lower middle-class and proletarian background, chiefly from Poland and other east European countries. These immigrants contributed to the development of the towns and villages. In the 1930s came the fifth *aliya* (1933–1939), the largest until then, predominantly German Jews of middle-class and professional backgrounds, and people from other central and eastern European countries. From the beginning of World War II until independence (1940–1948) the immigrants were, first, refugees from the persecutions of Nazi-occupied Europe and, later, the remnants of the Holocaust.

By the eve of independence, the Jewish population of Palestine was 650,000, out of a total population of almost two million. The national institutions had gradually consolidated their control over the *Yishuv* in spite of evergrowing heterogeneity. Feelings of national solidarity had deepened; the ideological consensus provided by Zionism had been widened by general considerations: the intensifying conflict with the Arabs, the gradual crystallization of an anti-Zionist British policy towards Palestine, and the trauma of the Jews under the Nazis. These factors, along with the political elite's widely recognized role in nation

---

[1] Ben Halpern, *The Idea of the Jewish State* (Cambridge, Mass.: Harvard University Press, 1961).

[2] We include Sephardi Jews among Oriental Jews.

[3] S. N. Eisenstadt, *Israeli Society* (London: Weidenfeld and Nicolson, 1967), part 1; Amos Elon, *The Israelis: Founders and Sons* (London: Weidenfeld and Nicolson, 1971), part 1.

building and in bringing the Zionist aim closer to fulfillment, were the basis of legitimation.[4]

Up to the 1930s, "foreign" policy affecting the *Yishuv* had been made by Jewish movements and organizations based outside Palestine—the World Zionist Organization, the extremely orthodox Agudat Israel, and the dissident New Zionist Organization of the Revisionists. By the end of British rule, the emerging national elite was in effective command of the *Yishuv* and of its policy making. To be sure, new dissident groups, especially the separatist military underground organizations (the Irgun Zvai Leumi, or IZL, and the Freedom Fighters, or Lehi) had threatened the authority of the accepted leadership, but the national leadership had come to an agreement with other groups which until then had remained outside "the organized *Yishuv*." Theirs was "an authority without sovereignty,"[5] presenting a remarkable consensus and unity of action[6] in view of the deep cleavages and wide heterogeneity of the society.[7]

Perhaps the most important factor in this gradual consolidation of political power was the emergence of a dominant political party with resolute and effective leadership. The extreme ideological, religious, *landsmannschaft* or economic fractionalization had continued unabated. However, beginning in the middle 1930s, Mapai (the Palestine Workers' party, set up in 1930 by the fusion of two Zionist labor parties) won a plurality, though never a majority, in various national elections. It was thus able to take over the top positions in the national institutions by means of coalitions. Within the ruling bodies of the Histadrut (the General Federation of Labor), Mapai had an overwhelming majority, which diminished only gradually in the 1950s and 1960s.[8] The party further enhanced its power by its control of the financial resources coming from abroad, which it channeled into the nation-building activities of the *Yishuv*. Mapai and its successor, the reunited (1968) Israel Labor party (ILP), are perhaps the most typical cases of a "dominant party" as characterized by Duverger—that is, a party whose doctrines, ideas, methods, and style are "identified with an epoch." The party's superior status and influence are generally acknowledged, though deplored by some. However, Mapai/ILP outdoes Duverger in certain ways. Its dominance involved both influence *and* strength (not necessarily electoral strength). To a considerable degree

---

[4] M. J. Aronoff, "Party Center and Local Branch Relationships: The Israel Labor Party," in Alan Arian, ed., *The Elections in Israel—1969* (Jerusalem: Academic Press, 1972), p. 150.

[5] Dan Horowitz and Moshe Lissak, "The Origins of the Israeli Political System," in M. Lissak and E. Gutmann, eds., *Political Institutions and Processes in Israel* (New York: Transaction Books, forthcoming), pp. 1–39 and the bibliography cited there. Cf. V. D. Segre, *Israel: A Society in Transition* (London: Oxford University Press, 1971).

[6] S. N. Eisenstadt, "Patterns of Leadership and Social Homogeneity in Israel," *International Social Science Bulletin,* vol. 8, no. 1 (1956), pp. 36–54. See also J. M. Landau, "Israel" in M. Adams, ed., *The Middle East: A Handbook* (London: Anthony Blond, 1971), pp. 213–25.

[7] Inasmuch as Israel's political system is of the type usually called "Western," the broad analytical framework, though perhaps not the wealth of historical detail, of the following is of considerable significance: S. M. Lipset and Stein Rokkan, "Cleavage Structure, Party Systems, and Voter Alignment: An Introduction," in *Party Systems and Voter Alignments* (New York: Free Press, 1967), pp. 1–64. The nation-building elements of an old-new society of immigrants require a different approach, however.

[8] On the complex party system of that time, see Ovadia Shapiro, *Political Parties in a New Society: The Case of Israel* (Ph.D. diss., University of Glasgow, 1971).

the party fashioned the epoch after its own image, rather than the other way around.[9]

The political parties and organizations, then, were the precursors of the state. They had carried out the major governmental functions for the Jewish population, and it was to them that people gave their primary loyalty. Indeed, they may be considered the true creators of the state.[10] By 1948 the political elite had become almost exclusively party related, regardless of initial recruitment patterns or the previous organizational attachments of its members. Those who had started as founders and early leaders of their respective parties, and who had shaped them largely in their own image, had become national leaders and created positions of national power. To use a metaphor attributed to Robert C. Tucker, they were not merely actors in a play, but the playwrights as well.[11]

The Founding Fathers

The thirty-seven signatories of Israel's declaration of independence were all members of the *Moetzet Ha-Am* (National Council), which had been established a few months before in anticipation of independence. They were chosen to serve as members of the *Moetzet Ha-Medina Ha-Zemannit* (Provisional State Council) up to the first general election (1949) and may be thought of as the founding fathers of Israel.[12] About three-quarters of the members of the council had previously been elected either to the executive committee of the Zionist organization or to the Vaad Leumi. The remainder were representatives of groups that had not previously participated actively in the national institutions. Particularly noteworthy was the participation of delegates from the non-Zionist wing of the extreme orthodox Jews (Agudat Israel and their working-class counterpart, Poaley Agudat Israel) as well as leaders from the Revisionist movement.[13] Other than the Arab minority, the only groups of importance not represented on the Provisional State Council were the two dissident military organizations, whose demise had been

---

[9] Maurice Duverger, *Political Parties* (London: Methuen, and New York: Wiley, 1954), pp. 308–9.

[10] Benjamin Akzin, "The Role of Parties in Israeli Democracy," *Journal of Politics,* vol. 17 (1955), pp. 507–45, reprinted in S. N. Eisenstadt, Rivka Bar-Yosef, and Chaim Adler, eds., *Integration and Development in Israel* (Jerusalem: Israel Universities Press, 1970), pp. 9–46. See also Moshe Lissak and Dan Horowitz, *From Yishuv to State: Change and Continuity in the Political Structure of Israel* (in Hebrew) (Jerusalem: Eliezer Kaplan School of Economics and Social Sciences, The Hebrew University, 1972).

[11] See Stanley Hoffmann, "Heroic Leadership: The Case of Modern France," in L. J. Edinger, ed., *Political Leadership in Industrialized Societies* (New York: Wiley and Sons, 1967), p. 109.

[12] For the historical and organizational details, see Zeev Sharef, *Three Days* (London: W. H. Allen, 1962). As is only natural, quite a few prominent leaders of the *Yishuv* of the early *aliyot* (waves of immigration) had not lived to see the day of independence. Dr. Chaim Weizmann, for many years president of the World Zionist Organization, was deeply chagrined to the end of his life that he had not been included among the signatories. Although he owned a house in Palestine, apparently he was not considered a representative of the *Yishuv*. In partial compensation, he was elected, extralegally, president of the Provisional State Council and subsequently became the first president of the state.

[13] A few months after the creation of the state council, three additional members representing these groups were co-opted into the original thirty-seven, so as to give them a more balanced representation.

accompanied by friction with the newly created authorities of the state. Both dissident groups later participated in the first general election and succeeded in gaining representation in the Knesset; one of these, the IZL, became a regular party—Herut—and that party's first-line leadership is still composed almost exclusively of the former top command of IZL.

Most of the founding fathers were in the prime of their lives, having had lengthy and remarkable careers and many years of public service. Thus twenty-seven of the forty members of the Provisional State Council during the last months of its existence were elected to the first Knesset, and most enjoyed long tenures. Ten of them, in fact, were still serving in the Knesset in 1969, four in 1973. One of these four is Golda Meir, the fourth prime minister of Israel.

Of these original thirty-seven founding fathers, not fewer than twenty-nine came from eastern Europe (Russia, including the Baltic countries, and Poland) and six from the rest of Europe. Only one was born in Palestine, and one in the Yemen. Nine emigrated during the second *aliya,* five during the third, seven during the fourth, thirteen during the 1930s, one in 1940, and one in 1947.

Before 1948 the elite was small and most of its members were personally well acquainted. Face-to-face relations, of course, did not necessarily produce amity or cohesion. In fact, personal conflicts often overshadowed political and ideological controversy. Even the intimacy of the elite is gradually disappearing because of its growing size.

The most salient characteristic of members of this group in terms of political culture and style was their dedication to public service for the cause of their choice. It has usually been considered improper political behavior to show one's interest in office and bad taste to declare one's own candidacy. Instead, one has reluctantly obeyed the "call" of the party, of the movement or group, and that call has rarely been refused or revoked. Many members of the elite have been unable to conceive of politics in terms of power and conflict; they have claimed to be motivated only by feelings of duty and burden, even of personal sacrifice.[14] Only very recently has there been a tendency toward a new political style, with candidates seeking office more openly and forcefully.

Only a few members of the elite ever transcend sectional divisions and reach the pinnacle of national leadership. Of these, the most outstanding has been David Ben-Gurion who, as a young labor leader, proclaimed his slogan, "from class to nation." His undisputed charisma made him a heroic civilian leader to whom, more than to any other single political figure, the establishment of the state of Israel should be attributed. Other leaders of that generation enjoyed a "halo effect" not always commensurate with their contribution to nation building. Indeed, at least a few of the thirty-seven signatories of Israel's declaration of independence were little-known personalities who happened to sign because of contingencies of the time. The members of the first Knesset present a much more balanced picture of the political leadership of that heroic period.

---

[14] Elon, *Israelis: Founders and Sons,* p. 304 and passim. For further details about present Israeli elites, particularly economic elites, see Yuval Elizur and Eliahu Salpeter, *Who Rules Israel?* (New York: Harper & Row, 1973).

Party System and the Elite

The establishment of the state considerably altered the functions of the parties in the political system, but their central role was not diminished. On the contrary, they have become more dominant.[15] The parties are no longer colonizing and pioneering associations,[16] nor social movements claiming to totally transform society,[17] but they are still "parties of social integration"[18] and function in spheres far removed from the political.

Israeli parties tend to control, or at least be affiliated with, various economic and commercial enterprises that serve them in many capacities. Among these are banks and financial institutions, housing corporations and other real estate firms, printing presses and a variety of mass communication enterprises, and agricultural production and distribution networks. In view of the party control of the Histadrut and its economic "empire," as well as the close connection between parties and rural settlement organizations (the kibbutz and *moshav* movements, for example), most parties may be thought of as actually being "in business." Although formal lines are usually drawn between the parties and their affiliates, it is more realistic to view the relationship as one of mutual permeation.[19]

Paradoxically, perhaps, this development has been accompanied by a "considerable pragmatization of politics." Almost all parties are paying less and less attention to their ideological activities and instead are becoming increasingly involved in the politics of economic and social interest groups. At the same time, nonpolitical groups try to attach themselves to political parties in order to gain access to the centers of power. The existing parties and their leaders have adapted themselves quite easily to this situation.[20]

There is yet another side to this situation. The government's extremely broad power to control the economy, specifically its power over resource allocation, has contributed substantially to political and administrative centralization. This process has gone further in Israel than in many other countries. It has brought about the undisputed primacy of political considerations, and the preeminence of the political elite over other elites, including economic ones.[21]

Basically, the Israeli party system has shown remarkable stability over the years, much greater than is apparent. Voting behavior on the whole has been rather con-

[15] Amitai Etzioni, "The Decline of Neo-Feudalism: The Case of Israel," in Fred Heady and S. L. Stokes, eds., *Papers in Comparative Public Administration* (Ann Arbor, Mich.: Institute of Public Administration, The University of Michigan, 1962), pp. 229–43. Reprinted in M. Lissak and E. Gutmann, eds., *Political Institutions and Processes in Israel* (Jerusalem: Academon, 1971), pp. 70–87.

[16] Akzin, "Role of Parties in Israeli Democracy," p. 515.

[17] M. H. Bernstein, *The Politics of Israel* (Princeton, N.J.: Princeton University Press, 1957), p. 55; L. J. Fein, *Politics in Israel* (Boston: Little, Brown & Co., 1967), p. 68; Segre, *Society in Transition,* pp. 84–85.

[18] Sigmund Neumann, "Toward a Comparative Study of Political Parties," in S. Neumann, ed., *Modern Political Parties* (Chicago: University of Chicago Press, 1956), pp. 404–5.

[19] Emanuel Gutmann, "Israel," *Journal of Politics,* vol. 25, no. 3 (August 1963), p. 709ff.

[20] M. M. Czudnowski, "Sociocultural Variables and Legislative Recruitment," *Comparative Politics,* vol. 4, no. 4 (1972), pp. 561–87.

[21] M. M. Czudnowski, "Legislative Recruitment under Proportional Representation in Israel: A Model and a Case Study," *Midwest Journal of Political Science,* vol. 14, no. 2 (1970), esp. pp. 240–42. See also Shevah Weis, *Politicians in Israel* (in Hebrew) (Tel-Aviv: Achiasaf, 1973).

servative; the fluctuations in the electoral fortunes of the various parties have not been extensive enough to bring the opposition to power.[22] Political labels, on the other hand, have changed a great deal. No slate of candidates appeared in the 1973 Knesset election under the same label as in the first 1949 election, and a great many party splits and regroupings have taken place. Some of these, such as the founding of Rafi (1965) by a group of dissident Mapai leaders headed by David Ben-Gurion and Moshe Dayan, have had considerable impact on the political scene. There are, however, two stable elements in this seemingly fluid situation.

First, one can easily identify the consistent nuclei of party leaders and their constant elite supporters. These have provided the party system as a whole with remarkable continuity. Second, the key to an understanding of Israel's apparently complex multiparty system is the notion of the "camp" (*mahane,* sometimes translated as "bloc" or "house").[23] The three major camps are usually labeled labor, bourgeois or center/right, and religious.[24] Until recently, political leaders as individuals or in groups have moved from one camp to another only in a few quite notorious cases. On the eve of the December 1973 elections, the first move of a whole group from the labor camp to the center/right occurred. Over the years, there has been a tendency for each camp to consolidate into a big party or a parliamentary bloc of parties. The Alignment (Maarakh) in the labor camp, which combined the Israel Labor party with the Zionist-Marxist Mapam party in 1969, is one example of this; and the Israel Labor party, by far the larger partner in the Alignment, itself constitutes a reunification (1968) of Mapai, the traditional pivot and mainstay of governmental power, with two of its offshoots—Ahdut Ha-Avoda, which had split off in 1944, and Rafi, which did so in 1965.

In the center/right camp the major force is Likkud, formed on the eve of the 1973 elections and combining most parties and groups in this camp. The predominant force within it is Gahal, the parliamentary bloc that was set up in 1965, composed of Herut (usually considered Israel's right-wing party) and the Liberals (who until 1959 went by the name of General Zionists). The other components of Likkud are the Free Center (which had split from Herut in 1966), the State List (which had broken off from the main body of Rafi when the latter reunited with Mapai to form the Israel Labor party in 1968), and the Greater Israel Movement (a group objecting to Israel's withdrawal from the territories under Israeli control since the June 1967 war).

There has been less consolidation in the religious camp since the National Religious party (NRP) was created in the mid–1950s when the two wings of the

---

[22] Emanuel Gutmann, "Some Observations on Politics and Parties in Israel," *India Quarterly* (New Delhi), vol. 17 (1961), pp. 3–29; Herbert Smith, "Analysis of Voting," in Arian, *Elections in Israel—1969,* pp. 63–81.

[23] Amos Perlmutter, *Anatomy of Political Institutionalization: The Case of Israel and Some Comparative Analyses* (Occasional Papers in International Affairs, no. 25, Harvard University, 1970), p. 37ff.

[24] For the sake of simplicity, the labor camp is often called "left" and the nonlabor camp "right," although these terms are apt to mislead. Mapai/ILP is ideologically and institutionally the real center, but the party hangs onto "left" for sentimental reasons and because of competition with parties further left. On the other side, the nonlabor camp resents being called "right," since this term is unpalatable to many Israelis who equate "right" with "Fascist." See also M. Seliger, "Positions and Dispositions in Israeli Politics," *Government and Opposition,* vol. 3, no. 4 (1968), pp. 465–84.

Mizrahi (the Zionist religious movement) reunited. During the elections to the first Knesset, there was a "United Religious Front" of the NRP and the two parties of the extreme orthodox, formally non-Zionist religious movement, Agudat Israel and Poaley Agudat Israel. Since then, all attempts at forming an all-party bloc within the religious camp have failed.

Centrifugal tendencies, however, have usually counteracted the consolidating trends. In the labor camp, as mentioned, Rafi split off from Mapai when the first unification talks with Ahdut Ha-Avoda got under way in 1965. Later, when the Israel Labor party was created by the merger mentioned above, a hard core of Rafi leaders, the State List, split off in order to keep their own flag. When Gahal was formed, the Independent Liberals split off from the Liberal party into which they had combined (under their old name of Progressives) only a few years beforehand with the General Zionists. The Free Center had split off from Herut to pursue more radical foreign policies, but also for reasons of personal incompatibility.

Elite Consensus versus Cleavage

The Israeli party system undoubtedly displays a number of the characteristics of what Sartori has called an extreme multipolar party pluralism without, however, being polarized or having centrifugal drives, as he uses these terms.[25] There exists a political center, namely the government party (Mapai/ILP), which is not just pro-system in Sartori's terminology, but which is to a large measure identified with the system.

Since independence, the overall tendency of the political system has been centripetal in Sartori's sense—that is, the basic consensus and the willingness to collaborate within the prevailing political system have been increasing. This tendency undoubtedly reached its peak with the creation of the Cabinet of National Unity on the eve of the Six-Day War (June 1967) when for the first time Gahal, including its dominant Herut wing which had always been considered the only genuine alternative to the party in power, joined the cabinet. Even after Gahal's withdrawal from the cabinet (1970) over a possible retreat from the Israeli-held territories, its opposition has been moderate. Its more oppositional stance has been reasserted however since the October 1973 war, which polarized attitudes within the Israeli public, and since it (now Likkud) increased its Knesset representation considerably in the December 1973 elections. Allowing for predictable variations, moderation can be claimed for the other extreme opposition groups, and in particular for the small Communist camp,[26] which moderation is reflected in the split (1965) into two parties having widely divergent attitudes toward the Israeli-Arab conflict. While one group (the New Communist List, mainly supported by Arabs) continues in unmitigated opposition to almost all government policies, the other

[25] G. Sartori, "European Political Parties: The Case of Polarized Pluralism," in J. LaPalombara and M. Weiner, eds., *Political Parties and Political Development* (Princeton, N.J.: Princeton University Press, 1966), pp. 137–76.

[26] See M. M. Czudnowski and J. M. Landau, *The Israeli Communist Party and the Elections for the Fifth Knesset, 1961* (Stanford: Hoover Institution on War, Revolution, and Peace, 1965), p. 9ff.

(still called the Israel Communist party) supported the government over the 1967 and the 1973 wars. In the religious camp, however, there is a gradually but unmistakably hardening line in religious affairs in the broader sense, combined with a wider consensus on central national issues such as defense, foreign policy, and the economy.

In spite of minor conflicts, the basic centripetal effect of the major political forces in the country is obvious. However, there is a compensating dialectical development. New extremist or eccentric fringe groups appear on almost all sides and concern themselves with a wide variety of policy issues: foreign and defense matters, social policy, and particularly social injustice and poverty, religious, cultural, or educational problems and, more recently, environmental issues. In the wake of the 1973 war, a number of protest movements, composed mainly of and led by army reservists just released after long terms of service, gained considerable impetus for a short period. The common core of their demands included overall increased democratization, greater grassroots involvement, effective personal accountability of leading politicians and especially of cabinet ministers, and much more rapid advance of young people in politics. However, this activity soon lost its momentum, some of its leading figures being absorbed into the existing parties, others attempting to form new ones, most simply disappearing from the limelight.

Basically, then, the Israeli political system is one of deep-rooted cleavages of ideology and interests, but it has a strong tendency toward accommodation and consensus at the leadership level. There have been "deliberate efforts to counteract the immobilizing and unstabilizing effects of cultural fragmentation" by the political leadership, at least on the central political level; this is what Lijphart has termed "consociational democracy." [27] Of the factors he considers conducive to the maintenance of this model, at least two prevail in Israel. First, there is a continuous external threat to the very existence of the country. Second, no single party has ever had an absolute majority, and parties in the same camp have usually been unwilling to cooperate on the cabinet level, so there has always been a need for cabinet coalitions between camps. This willingness to cooperate has been greater between the ILP and the NRP than of either party with the center/right camp, particularly with Herut, though in recent years the cleavage between Herut and the other parties has been narrowed. The third factor isolated by Lijphart—a relatively low total load on the decision-making apparatus—does not apply to Israel; however, in this instance consociationalism does not suffer for it.

It should be added here that the achievement of intraparty accommodation is at least as important as the interparty consensus, because it is a major factor in overcoming the fissionary tendencies at work within almost all parties. Moreover, it is noteworthy that the "factional elites" tend toward conciliation within their parties, while the second-level party activists and their supporters often support fractionalizing policies.[28]

[27] A. Lijphart, "Consociational Democracy," *World Politics,* vol. 21, no. 2 (1969), pp. 207–225. What we call "camps" are parallel to his "political subcultures," called *Lager* in Austria and *zuilen* in the Netherlands. See also Shapiro, *Political Parties in a New Society,* p. 210ff.

[28] E. Torgovnik, "Election Issues and Interfactional Conflict Resolution," *Political Studies,* vol. 20, no. 1 (March 1972), pp. 79–96. During election campaigns these processes are particularly apt to occur, but they take place at other times, too.

Elite Selection and Circulation

The consociational political system puts a particularly high premium on its elite. The elite has to overcome very considerable social heterogeneity and deep-rooted ideological cleavages in order to create a national consensus.[29] It is therefore interesting to analyze the selection and circulation of Israel's political elite.

Since the early days of Israel's independence there have been two contradictory tendencies: one has been to adjust the composition of the elite to conform to the rapidly changing, increasingly heterogeneous structure of the population at large; the other has been to inhibit any fragmentation of the elite itself, which might undermine the basic national consensus and put an end to the elite's conciliatory and representative role. Israel's future internal stability might depend greatly on whether consensus based on the esprit de corps of the Israeli-born *sabras* will be as conducive to consociationalism as was the Zionist-inspired consensus of the founding fathers.

At the end of the first quarter-century of Israel's existence the original leaders of the founding generation have almost all been replaced by members of the second generation.[30] David Ben-Gurion's career is illustrative. He retired as prime minister in 1963 but still headed a party in the 1965 and 1969 elections, and he finally retired from the Knesset in 1970 with the avowal that henceforth he would deal not with the present, but only with the past and the future. By then, Moshe Sharet and Levi Eshkol, both second *aliya* founding fathers who had been, respectively, the second and third prime ministers, had died. Ben-Gurion himself died in 1973, and Golda Meir of the third *aliya* carried on as fourth prime minister until the spring of 1974.

The transition from first to second generation leaders has been accompanied by special friction arising from the tremendous prestige of the founding fathers and their great power within their parties. The fact that most members created their own leadership positions at a relatively early age accounts for the notorious longevity of Israel's elite.

One commentator has accurately described this transition as one "from a natural to a selected elite."[31] Originality is increasingly useful to leaders, and new and diverse routes of advancement are being followed. There is now, on the one hand, great emphasis on the representation of pressure groups (political, social, economic, and other), whatever the organizational effectiveness of the groups and the type of representation involved,[32] and on the other hand, a high premium on professional and technocratic proficiency and administrative skills. This explains, at least partly, the fairly recent tendency to recruit members to the elite from the top ranks of the vast bureaucracy, and the small but growing number of senior army personnel who, upon retirement, are offered political careers. The vagueness of the distinction between politics and administration furthered this tendency consider-

[29] It is hard to say to what extent this contradicts the findings reported by L. G. Seligman, *Leadership in a New Nation* (New York: Atherton Press, 1964). See, however, Alan Arian, *Ideological Change in Israel* (Cleveland: Case Western Reserve University Press, 1968), chap. 2.

[30] See Fein, *Politics in Israel,* p. 152.

[31] Ibid., p. 156.

[32] Czudnowski, "Sociocultural Variables."

ably, though it is now becoming better defined. As a rule (but with many exceptions), political elite members are now expected to be *bitzuists* ("achievers"), and the old "ideologues" and talkers are spurned. A long, slow party career is now less essential than it once was for access to an elite position. Oriental Jews who reached high office seem to have advanced more rapidly than Ashkenazi Jews.[33] In spite of these trends, it is still true that selection for political positions is generally based less on professional competence than on political acumen and standing within the party. No less important, in many instances, is the step of moving into full-time political office. This is a very wide field in Israel and, more often than not, implies dependence on the support of one's party.

The usual selection process, which permits determination of the composition of the elite from above, is even more oligarchical in Israel than it is elsewhere. The co-optation system, or appointment from above, common to almost all levels of party office and to political office must take party opinion into account, though party opinion does not as a rule determine selection. On occasion, genuine, vigorous competition for political office takes place; but in most cases the actual decision is in the hands of restricted "nomination committees."

It is impossible to go into all the details of party selection patterns for internal offices and of nomination patterns for "outside" positions. However, a few brief examples of how such selections are actually made may illuminate the political process.

The Israel Labor party elects its secretary-general by a vote of the more than six-hundred-member Party Central Committee. In 1972 there was from the start only one candidate for the office, and he had enjoyed almost universal support from the moment the vacancy occurred; but a few other names were mooted. Even so, a special six-member screening committee was appointed by the party bureau which guides everyday party activities. The committee was headed by Yehoshua Rabinowicz, then mayor of Tel-Aviv and reputedly a major figure of the Gush (pronounced goosh), the unofficial and officially nonexistent, national party machine.[34] The committee duly nominated the one serious candidate, who was then unanimously elected. However, in the preceding election (1971) two genuinely competing candidates, one supported by the Gush, presented themselves. Not until the ballots were counted was the issue decided, and then by a very close vote. The Gush man won, but the losing candidate was elected a year later.

Basically the same procedures, *mutatis mutandis,* are followed by many parties for nomination to public office, where names or lists of names are drawn up by the respective nominating committees. Unquestionably, the Israeli electoral system of proportional representation with rigid candidates' lists has been a major factor in making such a procedure virtually unavoidable.[35] The sensitivity to public opinion and responsiveness to group pressures that are necessary in this system and the gradual co-optation of new forces into the elite strata make this basically a demo-

[33] Ibid.

[34] P. Y. Medding, *Mapai in Israel* (Cambridge: Cambridge University Press, 1972), p. 136ff.

[35] Abraham Brichta, "The Social and Political Characteristics of Members of the Seventh Knesset," in Arian, *Elections in Israel—1969,* pp. 112–17.

cratically mellowed version of oligarchy, modified by the gradual broadening of the representative structure of the parties.[36]

In any political system one of the key problems is *quis custodiet ipsos custodes,* but the Israeli system invites the further question, who nominates the nominators? To this there is no single answer. It can be said that in all parties the very top leadership exercises remarkable control over the nominating processes and thereby determines the intake into the elite. This process is perhaps more noticeable in Israel than elsewhere.

Occasionally there occur genuine democratic breakthroughs in the intraparty decision-making and nominating process, even though they involve party activists rather than the membership at large. Thus, in 1965 the central committee of Mapam, itself an elite organ, surprised almost everybody by rejecting the candidate slate for the approaching Knesset election as it was tabled by the nominating committee. Instead, the party's central committee altered quite drastically the order of appearance of some of the top candidates. In particular it removed the cabinet ministers-designate to "unsafe" places in the list, thus deciding that they should not represent the party in the Knesset.

More recently (1972), when the parliamentary group of the ILP had to nominate its candidate for the speaker of the Knesset, the usual decision by fiat was replaced by an open contest by ballot which resulted in a very narrow victory for the favorite of the party leadership. An even more striking example occurred in April 1974, following Golda Meir's resignation, when the ILP central committee decided by a close vote to nominate Itzhak Rabin over Shimon Peres as the party's candidate for prime minister.

The intraparty selection procedures constitute just one element in the much wider organization. Any generalization creating an impression of uniformity in the modus operandi of elites within their respective parties would be misleading. What can be asserted is that most parties have, in varying degrees, a formal democratic structure of the usual pyramid shape from which they all diverge in practice. As in other countries, all Israeli parties have informal decision-making bodies parallel to their formal organs. The Gush is one such interparty force. When its meetings are reported in the press, fact and fancy tend to intermingle. One of the reputed founders of the Gush was Shraga Netzer, who was the "grey eminence" of the party during the 1940s and 1950s. Although he had no formal authority in such matters, he tackled all internal party operations in order to release top party leaders for politics on the national level. Only later, during the 1960s, did Netzer become a member of the bureau and of major nomination committees.

At the top, the most famous single informal institution is Golda Meir's "kitchen cabinet," which often met literally in her kitchen on Saturday nights before the regular Sunday morning cabinet meetings. To the kitchen cabinet the inner core of the ILP ministers were summoned, together with a few other confidants, for deliberations on top policy and political strategy. It is characteristic that a secretary-general-designate of the ILP, who could not himself be counted among the

[36] We cannot deal at length here with the endless controversy concerning Michel's theorems. See, however, J. D. May, "Democracy, Organization, Michels," *American Political Science Review,* vol. 59 (1965), pp. 417–29; and P. Y. Medding, "A Framework for the Analysis of Power in Political Parties," *Political Studies,* vol. 18, no. 1 (1970), pp. 1–17.

top leadership, has made acceptance of that office conditional upon his having access to these meetings.

Attempts to institutionalize such informal arrangements have been quite common. Thus, Mapai ministers within the cabinet formed a sort of inner cabinet, the so-called *Sareynu* ("our ministers"); when other leaders of the party were invited, they were called *Havereynu* ("our members" or "our friends").[37]

There is an irreconcilable contradiction between the tendency of representative bodies to broaden membership and the fact that actual decision making in these enlarged bodies becomes impossible and so invites private consultation and the formation of cliques. To overcome this, informal bodies are given formal standing with responsibility and accountability, but the co-optation process, of course, makes for a very select membership.

The political elite of Israel, then, is composed of politically active figures who are members of the top bodies of major parties. Obviously it would be wrong to include among the elite all delegates to party conferences and members of the numerous central committees, but by and large it is from these that the elites are recruited. Even so, valid generalizations are not possible; not only are differences between parties substantial, but parties constantly change their organizational structure and the formal and informal functions of the various governing bodies and their powers. For example, at times the incumbent secretary-general of the Israel Labor party was the "strong man" of the party (such as Pinhas Sapir) or "strong woman" (Golda Meir); at other times a man of the second echelon or lower exercised most power. Similarly, the top party bureau of the Mapai/ILP had for many years very few members, all of the first rank. With the reunification of the Israel Labor party and the need for suitable representation of the constituent parts and groups, the bureau had to grow considerably. At the same time, the Mapai ministers were not offered seats in order to reduce the number somewhat. Consequently, the bureau lost in stature and authority.[38]

The Cabinet System

Israel's governmental system, habitually classified as cabinet government, has always been based on multiparty coalitions determined by relative party strength in the Knesset.

Knesset. Next to the cabinet, the Knesset is the most prestigious government organ, despite the considerable disparity in the actual power these two bodies wield. There is nothing unusual in the familiar argument about the "weakness" of the Knesset, but in Israel it would be imprecise to speak of the "decline" or "weakening" of parliament, for the simple reason that the Knesset has always been more prestigious than powerful (although there have been some signs, in the early 1970s, of increased independence of the Knesset vis-à-vis the cabinet).

[37] Fein, *Politics in Israel,* p. 180. For detail, see Michael Brecher, *The Foreign Policy System of Israel* (London: Oxford University Press, and New Haven: Yale University Press, 1972), p. 430ff and passim.

[38] Shevah Weis, "The Composition of the Israel Labor Party Bureau" (in Hebrew), *Medina U-Mimshal* (Jerusalem), vol. 1, no. 2 (1971), pp. 124–28.

In view of this power relationship, the intense personal competition for seats in the Knesset is remarkable. The top political elite of Israel sits (or has sat) in the Knesset with the exception of a limited number of leaders who have preferred not to become members. In other words, the sum of the individuals making up the Knesset is much more powerful than the institution itself.

Given Israel's electoral system with its long, rigid candidates' lists (usually 120 names, their order determined by the nomination committees of the parties), the respective place of candidates on the lists is generally the best indicator of a politician's rank in his party. This place will not only decide almost definitively where a candidate will become a member of the Knesset (MK) or not; it reflects, at least for the so-called "safe" seats, the power or popularity of the candidate within the party. Indeed, one way to differentiate between national leaders and sectoral or group representatives is to analyze those who got onto the candidates' list in their own right, and those for whom a place on the list reflects merely the bargaining power of their real or alleged group.[39]

Within the Knesset, offices and positions can be ranked in a way that gives some indication of the political status of Knesset members. One can hardly speak of any typical parliamentary career pattern. In Britain, politicians make their careers in parliament, often entering while quite young and with little political experience. By contrast, in Israel, with few exceptions, politicians enter the Knesset only after considerable previous career building. It is former party service and political experience outside the Knesset that lead to senior positions in the Knesset and cabinet.

Highest in rank in the Knesset is the speaker, who also serves as acting president of the state and ranks third in the official ceremonial, after the president and the prime minister.[40] His political role, however, is not commensurate with this status. The deputy speakers, whose number is not legally stipulated but determined by party power relations in each Knesset, are another highly prestigious group.

There are nine standing committees, with chairmanships allocated to coalition and opposition parties alike according to their respective size in the Knesset rather than to seniority. Although the chairmen cannot compare in power and prestige with their American counterparts, they constitute a select group within the Knesset, and many retain their positions for several Knesset terms.

The most hotly contested committee assignments are to the Foreign Affairs and Defense Committee and to the Finance Committee. The former is the more prestigious though its impact on policy is rather limited. It alone in the Knesset is given secret and classified information. The latter, however, is certainly the Knesset's most powerful committee with its considerable power over the formation and implementation of economic policy.[41]

Cabinet. Undoubtedly, major policy is made in the cabinet, the center of political power. This has come about largely because cabinet members are, on the whole, the top political leaders of the coalition parties. Their standing in the party and

---

[39] Hanan Kristal, "The Nomination of Israel Labor Party Candidates for the Seventh Knesset" (in Hebrew) (M.A. thesis, The Hebrew University of Jerusalem, 1971).

[40] A. Zidon, *Knesset* (New York: Herzl Press, 1967), p. 60.

[41] Ibid., pp. 208, 212 and passim.

membership in the cabinet serve to enlarge their power base. Only in one party (Mapam) have its two founding fathers (Meir Yaari and Yaaqov Hazan) consistently abstained from cabinet office, and sent others to serve in their place.

Over the years the cabinet has grown from twelve to more than twenty members in order to accommodate all party and personal exigencies. During the Government of National Unity, there were actually twenty-four members. The cabinet is based on the principle of collective responsibility, with formal equality of all members. In fact, in spite of the coalition of parties necessary to form a government, Israel is close to a "prime ministerial" system,[42] although the prime minister's power to appoint ministers is not as absolute as that of his British counterpart. Among cabinet members, some are more equal than others; all ILP members are not necessarily among the more important ministers. With the exception of those few who served as ministers without portfolio, cabinet members have doubled as collective chief policy makers and as heads of their respective ministries; they are also national party leaders. The major party represented in the coalition (Mapai/ILP) has so far always held the majority of seats in the cabinet. This fact has usually ensured effective decision making. However, one result of the mergers which created the ILP was that the inner nucleus of the "old" Mapai lost its majority.

The office of deputy minister, which does not entitle its bearer to cabinet membership, is the least institutionalized of all governmental offices. Most ministers do not have and do not want deputies. When deputy ministers are appointed, it is often in order to solve the problems of coalition formation and placate the small parties over the distribution of offices, or to meet the no less delicate problem of demands for personal advancement. This has so far been one of the highest offices achieved by Arab politicians.

Nor does the usual Israeli parliamentary career resemble the British model with its gradual advancement from back bench to front bench. Instead, the phenomenon of the "parachutist," a nonparliamentarian appointed from outside to a cabinet post, is becoming less infrequent. However, most of those few who have been deputy ministers have advanced toward full cabinet rank.

Histadrut. For many reasons the Histadrut holds a very special position in Israel's political structure.[43] Its members and their families number over 70 percent of the total population of the country, and for that reason alone some critics have called it "a state within a state." It may have been so before independence, when the Histadrut was one of the major nation-building organizations, but it has since handed over to Israel's government many of its general service functions and powers. It has remained, however, the main repository of Israel's special brand of

[42] R. H. S. Crossman, "Introduction" to Walter Bagehot, *The English Constitution* (London: Fontana Library, 1963), p. 51.

[43] The political role of the Histadrut has not yet been adequately studied. See, however, N. Safran, *The United States and Israel* (Cambridge, Mass.: Harvard University Press, 1963), pp. 127–46; W. Preuss, *The Labour Movement in Israel* (Jerusalem: R. Mass, 1965). Idem, "Die Arbeiterbewegung Israels," in J. M. Landau, ed., *Israel,* 2d ed. (Nuremberg: Glock and Lutz, 1970), pp. 203–34; I. Avrech and D. Giladi, eds., *Labor and Society in Israel* (Tel-Aviv: Department of Labor Studies, Tel-Aviv University, and Department of Higher Education, Histadrut, 1973).

socialism or welfare statism. At the same time, it has enormous economic power, with approximately 20 percent of the economy affiliated with it in one way or another. In addition, it enjoys a complete or nearly complete monopoly in several crucial branches of the economy. This economic power, together with its role as trade union, could enable it to paralyze the economic life of the country overnight. One must bear in mind, however, that the Histadrut is far from a monolithic institution and that its central bodies find it increasingly difficult to impose their will on particularistic interests and groups within it. Although it is not equal in power and prestige to the formal governmental structure, it does come second. The Histadrut is not a counterforce to regular government, mainly because the same political parties, and in particular the ILP, control both. Many of the founding fathers of Israeli politics started their public careers in the service of the Histadrut; the first was Ben-Gurion, who was its first secretary-general for fifteen years. Since independence, there has been an interchange of personnel between these two wings of the labor movement: all secretaries-general have sat in the Knesset, and the two most powerful (Pinhas Lavon and Itzhak Ben-Aharon) were cabinet ministers before their secretaryships. There is also a noteworthy interchange between the Histadrut's top Vaada Merakezzet (Central Committee) and the Knesset, while some have held membership in both simultaneously. This central committee is a powerful body, and its members must be counted among the country's elite.

Local Government. As in so many other countries, local government in Israel is in an unenviable position. Perpetual financial straits hamper its activities, and potentially first-rate politicians are increasingly reluctant to make their career at the local level. Municipal politics is now only rarely a steppingstone to national prominence. The late Abba Hushi, who renounced a national role to become the dynamic mayor of Haifa for seventeen years, is an unusual case. Nevertheless, on the municipal councils of Israel's large- and medium-sized cities are found people of local and, in a few cases, national stature. This is even more true for the mayors of these cities. The larger the city, the greater the mayor's role in national politics.

Socio-demographic Analysis of the Elite

Component Groups. For the purpose of our analysis, the cabinet, the Knesset, the Histadrut's Vaada Merakezzet, and the mayors of the large municipalities will be taken as constituting the components of Israel's political elite. Some members of these bodies are the top political leaders of the state; only rarely does one achieve this rank without first serving an apprenticeship somewhere within the elite. Membership in these groups is as follows:[44]

—Knesset members in all of Israel's eight legislatures. They number 374: 354 Jews and 20 Arabs.[45]

[44] The following figures are chiefly based on our own calculations, in which we were helped by our assistants, Ora Arokh, Abraham Fattal, Hanan Kristal, Ron Linenberg, and Yacov Levy.

[45] The Druzes are included among the Arabs in this study. For the distinction between Druzes and Arabs, see J. M. Landau, "Jewish-Christian-Moslem Relations in the State of Irsael: Problems and Perspectives," *Perspectives in Jewish Learning,* vol. 3 (Chicago, 1967), pp. 1–8.

—Seventy cabinet members, or ministers, drawn primarily from the Knesset. (In Israel, only the prime minister must be a member of the Knesset.)

—Twenty-three deputy ministers, all of them MKs.

—MKs holding central positions in the legislature on the nomination of their parliamentary groups. We have selected all members in the eight legislatures who have served as (1) chairmen (forty) of the Knesset's nine standing committees, (2) members (sixty-eight) of the Knesset's Foreign Affairs and Defense Committee, and (3) members (seventy-six) of the Knesset's Finance Committee.

—Eighty-four mayors of Israeli towns that in 1972 had at least 30,000 inhabitants. There are twenty of these towns, including the Arab town of Nazareth.

—Forty-one people who have served on the Histadrut's Vaada Merakezzet.

Israel's political elite, then, is made up of several hundred people. The 374 MKs, the dozen or so cabinet ministers who were not MKs, the eighty-four mayors and the forty-one members of the Histadrut's Vaada Merakezzet add up to about five hundred (although the actual total over the years is rather less than this, since some mayors and members of the Vaada Merakezzet have also been MKs at one time or another). An analysis of the most salient characteristics of this elite and their correlation with the characteristics of Israel's population in general leads to a number of conclusions.

Variables within the Knesset. First, Israel's parliamentarians are quite a heterogeneous group.[46] This heterogeneity will be analyzed by looking at the number of terms the MKs have served, their age, residence, profession, public service, date of immigration to Palestine/Israel, country of birth, and education.

(1) *Length of service* (see Table 7–1). As of April 1974, eighty-two MKs, or between a quarter and a fifth of the total, had served five terms or more (out of the eight possible) and another sixty-seven, or between a fifth and a sixth, have served either three or four terms. Two hundred twenty-six MKs served only one or two terms. That only twenty-four have served seven or eight terms is due partly, of course, to mortality. The turnover is considerable, although a core of veterans has maintained itself in the Knesset for a long period.[47]

(2) *Age* (see Table 7–2). Not surprisingly, a majority of MKs first entered the Knesset when they were between the ages of thirty-five and sixty-four. In Israel, one is considered too young for important political office before the age of thirty-five. In all eight Knessets, only twenty-three MKs were less than thirty-five years old at the time of their first entry. This does not reflect the effective age level in every Knesset, since about two-thirds of all MKs served more than one term. Thus, in the seventh and again in the eighth Knesset there were only ten

[46] For our purposes, it was simpler to tabulate the available data by Knesset. We have considered those MKs who served for a part of the Knesset's full term as having served for the full term. Unless otherwise stated, the data below are based on official statistics (whenever available) and on the information supplied by the MKs themselves to various *Who's Who* volumes, and refer to their entry into the Knesset. See also Zidon, *Knesset,* and Benjamin Akzin, "The Knesset," *International Social Science Bulletin,* vol. 13, no. 4 (1961), pp. 567–82.

[47] For the first six legislatures, Czudnowski has found a median legislative tenure of six years for the Jewish MKs. See his "Legislative Recruitment."

Table 7–1

LENGTH OF SERVICE IN THE KNESSET, BY PARTY

Number of Terms	Mapai (including Rafi)		Ahdut Ha-Avoda		Mapam		National Religious Party		Agudat Israel		Poaley Agudat Israel		Herut		Progres-sive/ Indepen-dent Liberal		General Zionist/ Liberal		Commu-nist		Other	
	No.	%	No.	%	No.	%	No.	%	No.	%	No.	%	No.	%	No.	%	No.	%	No.	%	No.	%
1	56	36	5	31	13	41	15	44	2	29	—	—	16	36	4	29	14	35	2	25	13	72
2	38	24	2	13	9	28	5	15	1	14	1	25	12	27	2	14	11	28	—	—	4	22
3	18	11	—	—	3	9	—	—	—	—	—	—	5	11	2	14	8	20	1	13	1	6
4	10	6	5	31	1	3	5	15	—	—	2	50	2	5	2	14	2	5	—	—	—	—
5	23	15	—	—	4	12	1	3	2	29	—	—	1	2	2	14	2	5	1	13	—	—
6	9	6	1	6	—	—	4	12	—	—	—	—	4	9	2	14	—	—	2	25	—	—
7	2	1	3	19	2	6	2	6	2	29	—	—	1	2	—	—	3	8	—	—	—	—
8	1	1	—	—	—	—	2	6	—	—	1	25	3	7	—	—	—	—	2	25	—	—
Total	157	100	16	100	32	99	34	101	7	101	4	100	44	99	14	99	40	10[illegible]	8	101	8	100

Note: For reasons of statistical consistency, MKs are counted here by their original party affiliation. MKs belonging to small parties are included in the "others" column.

MKs under forty (as compared to twenty-two in the first) but thirty-four over sixty (as compared to nineteen in the first).[48]

(3) *Residence.* No geographic location is represented in the Knesset directly since the whole state is considered as one constituency. The MKs are overwhelmingly urban—almost 200 come from the Tel-Aviv area, about fifty live or have lived in Jerusalem, and some twenty-five live in the Haifa area. As many as sixty-five live in kibbutzim, ten in *moshavim,* and the rest in various towns and villages. (This is true mainly for Arab MKs, only some of whom live in Nazareth and Haifa.) The trend toward the predominance of Tel-Aviv—more than half of the seats in all legislatures were held by MKs living in its metropolitan area—continued in the seventh and eighth Knessets. This preponderant urban representation is not remarkable since Israel's Jewish population is about 80 percent urban. What is striking is the large proportion of kibbutz members in the Knesset where they account for between a fifth and a sixth of the total. Thus in the seventh Knesset almost one-sixth of the total membership was from kibbutzim.[49] At the time of the elections to the seventh Knesset, the kibbutz population was only 3.4 percent of Israel's total population,[50] and that means this group has five times the representation it would have if representation were based on population ratio. This disparity emphasized the disproportionate place of kibbutz members in Israel's political elite, and it also indicates that the labor parties have among their leadership dedicated kibbutz members, many of whom belong to the political elite.

(4) *Profession.* The 374 MKs represent a large number of occupations. Of these, the more important numerically are 92 *asqanim* (plural of *asqan*) or professional politicians, 55 lawyers, 42 farmers, 33 educators, 29 company managers, 28 journalists, and 26 officials. Each of the other occupational groups rated 8 MKs or fewer. While lawyers, educators, and journalists are well represented in elected assemblies in other countries, as are representatives of the managerial and clerical professions, the relatively large number of farmers in the Knesset is remarkable. The explanation for this is the presence of representatives from kibbutzim and *moshavim;* actually, there must have been more than 42 of these, but presumably they had other declared occupations and so were counted in other categories. What is perhaps more significant is the high number of *asqanim,* who make up almost a quarter of the overall Knesset membership. For the most part they were party officials and will be discussed in the occupational breakdown of the party parliamentary groups.

(5) *Public service.* In addition to the above breakdown of the occupations engaged in by members immediately before entering the Knesset, the MKs' background of public service has been studied. Quite a few MKs had had experience in more than one area. At least ninety had had some military experience—in Israel's Defense Forces, the Hagana and Palmach, IZL, Lehi, the British, or other armies. At least eighty-three were active in Zionist affairs abroad, and forty-two had participated in Zionist congresses. At least forty-nine were active in the Hista-

[48] These are Brichta's calculations referring to the 113 Jewish MKs in the seventh Knesset. See his "Social and Political Characteristics," p. 127.

[49] Ibid., table 2.

[50] Cf. Central Bureau of Statistics, *Statistical Abstract of Israel 1970* (Jerusalem: Government Press, 1970), table B/9, pp. 32–33.

Table 7–2

AGE OF ELITE MEMBERS ON FIRST ASSUMING POSITION

Age on First Assuming Position	Members of the Knesset		Cabinet Ministers		Deputy Ministers		Chairmen of Knesset Committees		Foreign Affairs and Defense Committee		Finance Committee		Mayors	
	No.	%	No.	%	No.	%	No.	%	No.	%	No.	%	No.	%
24–29	8	2	—	—	—	—	—	—	—	—	—	—	—	—
30–34	15	4	—	—	—	—	—	—	—	—	—	—	4	5
35–39	57	15	—	—	5	21	1	2	2	3	7	9	7	8
40–44	71	19	6	9	5	21	3	8	8	12	11	15	14	17
45–49	70	19	10	14	4	18	6	15	10	15	14	18	17	20
50–54	65	17	16	23	6	26	9	23	11	16	22	29	19	23
55–59	39	10	17	24	2	9	7	17	18	27	11	15	12	14
60–64	33	9	16	23	1	5	7	17	8	12	9	12	7	8
65–69	10	3	4	6	—	—	5	13	9	13	2	3	4	5
70–74	2	1	—	—	—	—	1	2	2	3	—	—	—	—
75–	—	—	1	1	—	—	—	—	—	—	—	—	—	—
Unknown	4	1	—	—	—	—	1	2	—	—	—	—	—	—
Total	374	100	70	100	23	100	40	99	68	101	76	101	84	100

drut, thirty-eight in some type of Jewish agency work, and forty-five in local government. These figures, although not surprising, are significant in pointing out some of the main avenues of access to the political elite in Israel.

(6) *Time of immigration to Palestine* (see Table 7–3). Only sixty-seven Jewish and twenty Arab MKs (all the Arab ones) were born in Palestine. Except for four whose immigration dates are not available, all others came to Palestine or Israel between 1904 and 1959. Thirty immigrated between 1904 and 1914. Most came during the large immigration waves of the 1920s and 1930s. As we have already pointed out, the composition and characteristics of the core of the political elite were formed to a great extent in the prestate days, largely in the first quarter of the twentieth century. This is gradually changing, since age and date of immigration tend to be correlated. While in the first Knesset 38.4 percent of all MKs had immigrated to Palestine between 1904 and 1923, in the seventh Knesset the same group was down to 8.3 percent. Even the percentage of those who had immigrated between 1924 and 1932 was down from 25 percent in the first Knesset to 17.5 percent in the seventh. This phenomenon will have a part in shaping the elite of the future.

(7) *Country of birth* (see Table 7–4). Since 1948 many of the immigrants have come from Afro-Asian lands, and this has changed the profile of the Jewish population in Israel. It is now about half Ashkenazi and half of Oriental background. However, this has affected the composition of the Knesset only slightly. A breakdown of the MKs by country of birth gives the following figures: Palestine/Israel, 87; Asia [51] and Africa,[52] 37; Europe, the Americas, and South Africa, 250.

Asian and African Jews in Israel are underrepresented in the Knesset, although there are 11 MKs from Iraq, 6 from Yemen, 8 from Morocco, 3 each from Tunisia and Syria, 2 each from Egypt and Libya, and 1 each from Iran and Turkey. What is no less noteworthy is that the MKs from Poland (96) and Russia (86) form just under half of all the MKs and almost two-thirds of the 287 MKs born out of Palestine/Israel. Several of these were born in Poland or Russia, then emigrated to the United States, Argentina and other countries, and came from there to Palestine/Israel; but these exceptions are few. Moreover, the total number of MKs born in eastern Europe is actually larger if one includes those from Rumania (11), Latvia (7), Hungary (6), Bulgaria (4), and Lithuania (4). Altogether, there are 215 MKs from eastern Europe, or 78 percent, almost four-fifths of the 287 MKs born outside of Palestine/Israel. In recent years this overrepresentation of east Europeans in the Knesset has decreased. In the seventh Knesset, MKs from Poland and Russia made up only 48 percent of the total membership,[53] as compared with 70 percent in the first. Of the 40 new members of the eighth Knesset there were still 12 born in Poland (10) and Russia (2), as against 7 born in Afro-Asian countries (4 in Morocco and 3 in Iraq) and 19 born in Palestine/Israel (of whom only two have parents from Oriental countries and two were Arabs). The ratio of MKs born in Afro-Asian countries (excluding Palestine/Israel) has increased from 3.3 percent in the first Knesset to ten percent in the eighth. However, this was far from being representative of the community breakdown of

[51] Excluding Palestine/Israel.
[52] Excluding the Republic of South Africa.
[53] Based on Brichta, "Social and Political Characteristics," table 3.

Table 7–3

YEAR OF IMMIGRATION OF ELITE MEMBERS INTO PALESTINE/ISRAEL

Year of Immigration	Members of the Knesset		Cabinet Ministers		Deputy Ministers		Chairmen of Knesset Committees		Foreign Affairs and Defense Committee		Finance Committee		Histadrut's Central Committee		Mayors	
	No.	%	No.	%	No.	%	No.	%	No.	%	No.	%	No.	%	No.	%
1904–1914	30	8	5	7	2	9	3	8	6	9	6	8	—	—	4	5
1918–1923	36	10	7	10	—	—	5	12	8	12	8	11	5	12	9	11
1924–1932	71	19	29	41	5	21	16	40	28	41	24	32	13	32	23	27
1933–1939	85	23	14	20	4	17	5	13	11	16	14	18	10	24	22	26
1940–1947	27	7	4	6	3	13	4	10	5	7	5	7	4	10	3	4
1948–1952	27	7	1	1	2	9	2	5	1	2	6	8	4	10	10	12
1953–	7	2	2	3	—	—	—	—	—	—	1	1	—	—	—	—
Born in Palestine/ Israel	87	23	8	12	7	30	5	12	9	13	12	16	5	12	13	16
Unknown	4	1	—	—	—	—	—	—	—	—	—	—	—	—	—	—
Total	374	100	70	100	23	99	40	100	68	100	76	101	41	100	84	101

Table 7–4

COUNTRY OF BIRTH OF ELITE MEMBERS

Country of Birth	Members of the Knesset		Cabinet Ministers		Deputy Ministers		Chairmen of Knesset Committees		Foreign Affairs and Defense Committee		Finance Committee		Histadrut's Central Committee		Mayors	
	No.	%	No.	%	No.	%	No.	%	No.	%	No.	%	No.	%	No.	%
Palestine/Israel	87	24	8	11	1	30	4	10	8	12	12	16	5	12	13	16
Eastern Europe	215	58	48	69	13	57	30	75	50	74	55	72	27	66	53	63
Western Europe	29	8	8	11	2	9	4	10	7	10	5	7	3	7	7	8
Africa and Asia (excluding Palestine and Israel)	37	10	4	6	1	4	2	5	3	4	4	5	6	15	8	10
North and South America, South Africa	6	1	2	3	—	—	—	—	—	—	—	—	—	—	3	4
Total	374	101	70	100	23	100	40	100	68	100	76	100	41	100	84	101

the Jewish population.[54] Israel's political parties are well aware of these facts. They have become a public issue in Israeli politics, and the parties are striving to increase the representation of Afro-Asian Jews.

(8) *Formal education* (see Table 7–5). This is not easy to determine since not all MKs have provided specific data.[55] Even so, the overall number (218) of those with some university education is impressive. Of these, about fifty have degrees in law, and an additional twenty have doctorates of law; over a dozen hold other Ph.D.'s. Zionists in Palestine between the two world wars (particularly in the kibbutzim) tended to look down on higher education. Now, however, specialization and expertise seem to be highly valued by the parliamentary elite. There is no significant differential with respect to higher education over the period of all eight legislatures. The fact that the level of education has varied only slightly from one Knesset to another may be attributed partly to the fact that the same MKs have been reelected over and over. It should be emphasized that, in recently elected legislatures, there has been a clear increase in the number of members whose higher education is complete.

Cabinets and Knesset Committees. Let us now compare the above data for the whole of the Knesset membership with the data (see Tables 7–2 through 7–5) for five smaller groups: seventy cabinet ministers, twenty-three deputy ministers, forty chairmen of all the Knesset's standing committees, sixty-eight members of the Foreign Affairs and Defense Committee, and seventy-six members of the Finance Committee. Of these, only the first group includes some who are not MKs; however, most cabinet ministers have been MKs at one time or another.

Not surprisingly, the age of ministers on first assuming cabinet posts was generally higher than that of MKs (none under forty). All had records of public service, in most cases dating to pre-independence days. Lately there has been a growing tendency for parties to appoint ministers with considerable administrative experience in the higher echelons of the bureaucracy or the army.

Eight of the cabinet ministers were born in Palestine; of the rest, all but seven had come before the outbreak of World War II, and all but three in the pre-independence times. Those born in eastern Europe are a proportionately stronger contingent in the cabinet than in the Knesset as a whole; forty-eight out of seventy (69 percent). Their relative significance is still more striking when one remembers that they number forty-eight of the sixty-two born outside of Palestine. Only four cabinet ministers have been born in Afro-Asian countries (excluding Palestine/Israel). Although the Oriental Jewish element is partly represented among the eight ministers born in Palestine, the percentage is much lower than in the Knesset (6 percent as opposed to 10 percent). In Israel's first cabinet (1949–1950), out of twelve ministers eight were born in Russia and Poland, none in Afro-Asian countries, and one in Palestine. In the cabinet of early 1974, out of twenty-two ministers, eleven were born in Russia and Poland, two in Afro-Asian countries (Iraq and Tunisia) and four in Palestine. Proportionately, the figures for these three groups of countries have not altered much despite the changes in the com-

[54] Details in the *Statistical Abstract of Israel 1970,* table B/1, p. 23 and table B/19, p. 49.
[55] In addition, some MKs have indicated both a religious and a university education.

Table 7–5

EDUCATION OF ELITE MEMBERS

Level of Education Reached	Members of the Knesset		Cabinet Ministers		Deputy Ministers		Chairmen of Knesset Committees		Foreign Affairs and Defense Committee		Finance Committee		Mayors	
	No.	%	No.	%	No.	%	No.	%	No.	%	No.	%	No.	%
Elementary	12	3	3	4	1	4	—	—	—	—	4	5	—	—
Secondary (high school)	72	19	7	10	3	13	4	10	8	12	16	21	18	21
Vocational	9	2	—	—	—	—	—	—	—	—	—	—	—	—
Agricultural	3	1	1	1	2	9	—	—	1	2	2	3	1	1
Religious	33	9	6	9	4	17	3	8	6	9	9	12	18	21
Teachers' college	14	4	2	3	—	—	—	—	—	—	—	—	—	—
University	218	58	47	67	11	48	33	83	52	77	42	55	41	49
Unknown	13	4	4	6	2	9	—	—	1	1	3	4	6	7
Total	374	100	70	100	23	100	40	101	68	101	76	100	84	99

position of Israel's population and even in that of the Knesset. The proportion of those with a university education is higher in the cabinet than in the Knesset.

The deputy ministers as a group are younger than the ministers on first assuming office. Thirteen out of the total twenty-three were born in eastern Europe, seven were born in Palestine (30 percent of the total, as compared with 11 percent of the ministers). Perhaps this is the best indication of the gradual increase in the share of the Palestinian-born in the policy-making elite.

Two features stand out in a comparison of the three select groups of chairmen of the nine standing Knesset committees, and of the MKs in the Foreign Affairs and Defense Committee and in the Finance Committee with Knesset membership as a whole. One is the higher ratio of university-educated members of these three groups; the other is the even heavier proportion of those born in eastern Europe (between 72 percent and 75 percent of all the members of these three groups in all eight legislatures).

The mayors of Israel's cities and larger towns, as a group, show many of the same traits: Most (63 percent) were born in eastern Europe, and about half of the total have at least a partial university education. This holds true of the origin of members in the Histadrut's Vaada Merakezzet as well, although data about their formal education are not available.

Common to all members of the elite groups we have discussed is that the largest single group immigrated to Palestine between 1924 and 1932 (the fourth *aliya*). The only exception is the group of deputy ministers, of whom more are Palestine-born than fourth *aliya* immigrants. In each case the largest group resides in the Tel-Aviv area, again, with the exception of the deputy ministers of whom only 35 percent reside in the Tel-Aviv area, and another 35 percent in kibbutzim.

Political Parties. So far we have dealt with politicians of all parties as a group, but it is worth examining them by party, according to several of the variables we have already used. To do this, we will revert to the Knesset and briefly examine its membership according to the party affiliation of the MKs, using the following variables: length of service in the Knesset, ratio of *asqanim* to those having other sources of livelihood, and ethnic composition.

The small, doctrinaire parties, mainly the Communists and, to a lesser degree, the ultra-orthodox Agudat Israel parties, have a pattern of nominating the same MKs time after time, even up to eight terms (see Table 7–1). The size of the parliamentary group has a bearing on this. However, to a considerable extent, this also applies to larger ideological parties as well, such as the National Religious party and Herut. Mapai/ILP is at the other end of the scale, with two MKs serving in seven legislatures, one (Golda Meir) in all eight, and twelve (8 percent) between six and eight terms. This size factor is apparent also from a division by parties of all MKs who have served to date for four terms at most, and those who have served to date for five or more terms (see Table 7–6). All parties except the Communists and Agudat Israel share the tendency of renewing their membership not later than after the fourth term of their respective MKs.

Asqanim, professional politicians, prevail mostly in the labor parties in the following order: Ahdut Ha-Avoda, Mapam, Communists, and Mapai (see Table 7–7). These parties have a high ratio, among the MKs representing them, of party officials whose sole or primary source of livelihood when they entered the Knesset was their party. This is consistent with these parties' view that theirs is "a whole way of life" and, with the exception of the Communists, they were in office and therefore had the power to distribute jobs. Consequently, if and when these MKs left the Knesset, it would be the party that would once more be expected to take care of their material future. At the other end of the scale are the General Zionists/Liberals and Herut, a large number of whom had nonparty livelihoods upon entering the Knesset. This is at least partly explained by the fact that these are right-of-center parties and many of their MKs were professionals or businessmen not financially dependent on the party. Between these two extremes are the religious parties with their MKs evenly divided between *asqanim* and others.

There are marked differences among the various parliamentary groups in their ethnic composition (see Table 7–8). The Jewish-Arab division is relatively easy to describe. Only Mapai/ILP, Mapam and the Communists have had Arab MKs affiliated with them (in the case of Mapai/ILP) or in their own ranks (in the case of the other two parties).[56] This results from the fact that only these three parties have invested considerable, fairly constant effort in recruiting Arab support, while other political parties have seriously sought Israeli Arab support only on the eve of elections.[57] There is no doubt that the recruitment of Arabs into Israel's political elite as expressed in Knesset membership has been achieved by the three above-mentioned parties.

The breakdown between Ashkenazi and Oriental Jews within the various parliamentary groups is somewhat more complex. While there have been several short-lived parliamentary groups of Oriental Jews, all other small groups in the Knesset have had exclusively Ashkenazi members. The larger ones have always included one or two MKs from Oriental Jewish communities. Herut usually included more, and Mapai/ILP always did. Just as in the case of the Arab MKs, the relatively few Oriental Jews who were recruited into the political elite were usually placed in the Knesset to attract votes.[58] When the composition of the recent Knessets is compared to that of the first, the increase in the number of Arab and Oriental Jewish MKs is obvious. It is an indication of both the increased political participation of these communities and of the intention of the predominantly Ashkenazi leadership of the political parties to increase the representation of other groups within the state's political elite.

Some Concluding Remarks

Israel's political elite has features both common to, and different from, those of other Middle Eastern states. While a full-scale comparative analysis of these elites

[56] Further details in J. M. Landau, *The Arabs in Israel: A Political Study,* 2d impression (London: Oxford University Press, 1970), chap. 4.

[57] Ibid., chaps. 5 and 6. Idem, "Les Arabes israéliens et les élections à la Quatrième Knesset," *International Review of Social History,* vol. 7, no. 1 (1962), pp. 1–32; Abner Cohen, *Arab Border-villages in Israel* (Manchester: Manchester University Press, 1965); Subhi Abu Ghosh, "The Election Campaign in the Arab Sector," in Arian, *Elections in Israel,* pp. 239–52; and J. M. Landau, "The Arab Vote," ibid., pp. 253–63.

[58] Moshe Lissak, "Continuity and Change in the Voting Patterns of Oriental Jews," in Arian, *Elections in Israel,* pp. 264–77.

Table 7–6

CUMULATIVE LENGTH OF SERVICE IN THE KNESSET, BY PARTY
(percentages)

Number of Terms	Mapai (including Rafi)	Ahdut Ha-Avoda	Mapam	National Religious Party	Agudat Israel	Poaley Agudat Israel	Herut	Progressive/ Independent Liberal	General Zionist/ Liberal	Communist	Other
One to four terms	78	75	81	70	43	80	75	71	88	38	100
Five to eight terms	22	25	19	30	57	20	25	29	12	62	—

Note: See footnote to Table 7–1.

Table 7–7

SOURCE OF LIVELIHOOD OF MKs BEFORE ENTERING THE KNESSET, BY PARTY

Occupation	Mapai (including Rafi)		Ahdut Ha-Avoda		Mapam		National Religious Party		Agudat Israel		Poaley Agudat Israel		Herut		Progressive/ Independent Liberal		General Zionist/ Liberal		Communist		Other	
	No.	%	No.	%	No.	%	No.	%	No.	%	No.	%	No.	%	No.	%	No.	%	No.	%	No.	%
Asqanim	99	63	15	94	25	78	20	59	4	57	2	50	16	36	7	50	7	18	6	75	4	22
Other occupations	58	37	1	6	7	22	14	41	3	43	2	50	28	64	7	50	33	82	2	25	14	78
Total	157	100	16	100	32	100	34	100	7	100	4	100	44	100	14	100	40	100	8	100	18	100

Note: See footnote to Table 7–1.

would be premature, a brief examination of the relevant differences may add insight into the nature of Israel's political elite.

Unlike many states in the area, Israel has maintained essentially its pre-independence elite. This is particularly true of the political leadership as expressed in the cabinet and other top elected groups. The average age of Israel's political elite is considerably higher than that of its immediate neighbors, and the political experience of its members is in general rather longer.

A second difference is the role of the military in the political elite. After independence had been achieved in Syria, Egypt, Iraq, and the Sudan, and to a lesser degree in Jordan and Turkey, the armed forces intervened in politics.[59] Indeed, in some cases they superseded the existing positional elite. In others, they crashed into it and allied themselves with other forces new to the political elite. In other Middle Eastern states, the officer class, in uniform or mufti, generally has the final say in major policy making.[60] In Israel the situation is quite different.[61] Although military experts are frequently consulted on defense and related matters, they are not regarded either by themselves or by others as part of Israel's political elite. The official policy of keeping politics out of the armed forces and the armed forces out of politics has with rare exceptions been adhered to. Retired top military officers, including chiefs of staff and generals—Moshe Dayan, Ezer Weizmann, Haim Bar-Lev, Itzhak Rabin, Aharon Yariv, and Ariel Sharon, for example—have been co-opted into the political elite and appointed to cabinet posts or other key positions.[62] Their military experience and success were at least as important as their political background, probably more so. However, their appointments resulted from decisions made by the political parties (Mapai/ILP, Gahal); the political futures of these men rest solely on their connection with the party and the public as a whole, not on ties with the military. Neither army personnel in service nor retired officers active in politics on a civilian basis act as a political pressure group in Israel.

A third distinction of Israel is the role that institutionalized religion plays within the state's political elite. In Israel, as in Lebanon and elsewhere, religion is taken seriously by many, although some oppose its impact on public life.[63] The relationship between state and religion in Israel, however, is radically different from that found in Iran, Iraq and Egypt.[64] In these countries the religious establishment often intervenes in politics with varying degrees of success, performing somewhat the function of a counterelite. In Israel, the religious establishment is part of the

[59] See S. Finer, *Man on Horseback* (London: Pall Mall, 1962).

[60] For a recent study of this situation, see J. C. Hurewitz, *Middle East Politics: The Military Dimension* (New York: Praeger, 1969). For an earlier one, see P. J. Vatikiotis, *The Egyptian Army in Politics: Pattern for New Nations?* (Bloomington: Indiana University Press, 1961). For the background, consult George Lenczowski, *The Middle East in World Affairs*, 3d ed. (Ithaca, N.Y.: Cornell University Press, 1962).

[61] The fullest treatment of the Israeli case, in this context, is by Amos Perlmutter, *Military and Politics in Israel: Nation-Building and Role Expansion* (London: Frank Cass, 1969).

[62] This carried some dissatisfaction among second-rank political leaders who felt they had been passed over. Recently, some apprehension has been voiced over the growing number of ranking officers entering politics.

[63] See details in Emanuel Gutmann, "Religion in Israeli Politics," in J. M. Landau, ed., *Man, State and Society in the Contemporary Middle East* (New York: Praeger, 1972), pp. 122–34.

[64] See Morroe Berger's enlightening *Islam in Egypt Today* (Cambridge: Cambridge University Press, 1970).

Table 7–8

MEMBERS OF THE KNESSET, BY ETHNIC COMMUNITY, KNESSET, AND PARTY

Knesset	Community	Mapai (including Rafi)		Ahdut Ha-Avoda		Mapam		National Religious Party		Agudat Israel		Poaley Agudat Israel		Herut		Progressive/ Independent Liberal		General Zionist/ Liberal		Communist	
		No.	%	No.	%	No.	%	No.	%	No.	%	No.	%	No.	%	No.	%	No.	%	No.	%
1st	Ashkenazi Jews	48	86	5	100	12	92	12	100	2	100	2	100	12	86	5	100	9	100	3	75
	Oriental Jews	6	11	—	—	1	8	—	—	—	—	—	—	2	14	—	—	—	—	—	—
	Arabs	2	4	—	—	—	—	—	—	—	—	—	—	—	—	—	—	—	—	1	25
2d	Ashkenazi Jews	43	78	4	100	8	89	10	100	5	100	2	100	9	90	6	100	18	95	4	67
	Oriental Jews	7	12	—	—	—	—	—	—	—	—	—	—	1	10	—	—	1	5	—	—
	Arabs	5	10	—	—	1	11	—	—	—	—	—	—	—	—	—	—	—	—	2	33
3d	Ashkenazi Jews	44	81	8	89	9	82	9	90	5	100	3	100	13	87	5	100	13	100	4	67
	Oriental Jews	5	9	1	11	1	9	1	10	—	—	—	—	2	13	—	—	—	—	—	—
	Arabs	5	9	—	—	1	9	—	—	—	—	—	—	—	—	—	—	—	—	2	33
4th	Ashkenazi Jews	40	75	7	87	8	80	10	91	5	100	3	100	16	89	6	100	7	77	3	75
	Oriental Jews	8	15	1	13	1	10	1	9	—	—	—	—	2	11	—	—	2	22	—	—
	Arabs	5	9	—	—	1	10	—	—	—	—	—	—	—	—	—	—	—	—	1	25
5th	Ashkenazi Jews	40	77	7	77	9	81	11	85	5	100	2	100	15	83	5	100	11	91	4	67
	Oriental Jews	8	15	1	11	1	10	2	15	—	—	—	—	3	17	—	—	1	8	—	—
	Arabs	4	8	1	11	1	10	—	—	—	—	—	—	—	—	—	—	—	—	2	33

Table 7–8 (continued)

Knesset	Community	Mapai (including Rafi)		Adhut Ha-Avoda		Mapam		National Religious Party		Agudat Israel		Poaley Agudat Israel		Herut		Progressive/ Independent Liberal		General Zionist/ Liberal		Communist	
		No.	%	No.	%	No.	%	No.	%	No.	%	No.	%	No.	%	No.	%	No.	%	No.	%
6th	Ashkenazi Jews	42	68	5	71	7	78	9	81	5	100	2	100	12	80	6	86	10	100	2	50
	Oriental Jews	16	26	2	29	1	11	2	18	—	—	—	—	3	20	1	14	—	—	—	—
	Arabs	4	6	—	—	1	11	—	—	—	—	—	—	—	—	—	—	—	—	2	50
7th	Ashkenazi Jews	37	73	5	83	5	83	12	86	4	100	1	100	12	73	3	75	10	83	2	50
	Oriental Jews	10	18	1	17	—	—	2	14	—	—	—	—	4	27	1	25	2	17	—	—
	Arabs	4	8	—	—	1	17	—	—	—	—	—	—	—	—	—	—	—	—	2	50
8th	Ashkenazi Jews	28	72	6	75	6	86	8	80	3	100	2	100	17	77	4	100	13	87	2	50
	Oriental Jews	8	20	2	25	—	—	2	20	—	—	—	—	5	23	—	—	2	13	—	—
	Arabs	3	8	—	—	1	14	—	—	—	—	—	—	—	—	—	—	—	—	2	50

Note: See footnote to Table 7–5. The "other" category is left out.

political system but not part of the political elite in spite of the political activity of the religious parties. Rulings and proclamations of the chief rabbis and other established rabbinical authorities are heeded by orthodox Jews, but attempts to dictate political moves to the NRP leadership have often been rejected—as in March 1974 when the NRP joined the government coalition in spite of an adverse injunction by the Supreme Rabbinical Council. The rabbinate can hardly be considered part of the political elite. Indeed, the orthodox Jews who are part of this elite, particularly the NRP leaders, have joined it via the religious parties and rely on the political backing of their parties for support rather than on the Jewish orthodox establishment. Not infrequently the religious establishment vehemently disapproves of the policies of the cabinet ministers representing religious parties.

Most of what has just been said also applies to the non-Jewish communities in Israel. The Muslims in Israel, like Sunni Muslims elsewhere, have never had a hierarchical clergy. The Druzes have, but their sages have meddled little in Israeli politics, partly because they regard local community affairs as their main concern. They cannot be considered part of Israel's political elite. The Druze MK, Jabr Muaddi, entered the Knesset through his connections with Mapai; that is, via a political party. Nor can the religious leaders of the Christian communities be considered part of the elite. What political influence is exercised, for instance, by the head of the Greek Catholic community in Israel is related to personal standing, his ties with the Vatican, and the economic activity of the community.

The several hundred men and women who are the subject of our analysis are mostly Jews; the few Arabs among them have been co-opted.[65] They form a fairly homogeneous group, despite obvious variations in age, residence, profession, experience, education, date of immigration to Palestine/Israel, and country of birth. This elite is a formally elected one, whether elected to positions within the parties or Histadrut hierarchy, or to government office: the Knesset, the cabinet and the municipalities. This is true despite the very considerable role that co-optation plays in the selective process. The top bureaucracy (sometimes called "technical elite")[66] has not been included in the political elite discussed in this article. All civil servants in Israel are appointed; although they participate in public policy making, they have no independent political power base and may not legally participate in domestic politics.

Of course, elite members differ on many political questions, but they often cooperate on the basis of a broad consensus on the major national issues facing Israel. The top leadership, in particular, shows a considerable degree of cohesion and generally succeeds in functioning together effectively; indeed, past experience and a shared outlook ensure intimacy among the leaders. The political elite in Israel has shown until recently considerable stability, due to the limited admission of new members. However, it also demonstrates flexibility, which has enabled it to survive several crises almost unharmed.

---

[65] Cf. J. M. Landau, "A Note on the Leadership of the Israeli Arabs," *Il Politico* (Pavia), vol. 27, no. 3 (Sept. 1962), pp. 625–32. Reprinted in J. M. Landau, *Middle Eastern Themes: Papers in History and Politics* (London: Frank Cass, 1973), pp. 189–97.

[66] Brecher, *Foreign Policy System of Israel,* esp. chaps. 17 and 18.

Appendix: Profiles of Some Elite Members

The following sixteen profile sketches of members of the Israeli political elite do not present proportionally, nor do they reflect accurately, all the variables discussed in this article. Rather, they provide an indication of various types of elite members (not necessarily the most outstanding), and illustrate their political careers in different elite roles and institutions.

David Ben-Gurion, statesman and prime minister, was born in Russia in 1886 and immigrated to Palestine in 1906. His first year in Palestine he spent working on the land at Sejera. In 1907 he presided over the foundation meeting of Poaley Zion party, and from 1910 edited its newspaper. By the outbreak of World War I he was one of the leaders of the *Yishuv*. In 1915 he was deported from Palestine by the Ottoman authorities, and went to the United States where he was active in Zionist affairs. In 1918 he volunteered for the Jewish Legion to serve with the British armed forces. He was one of the founders of the Ahdut Ha-Avoda party in 1919, and a year later of the Histadrut, whose first secretary-general he was from 1921 to 1935. In 1929 he was among the founders of Mapai. During the 1920s and 1930s he participated in *Yishuv* and World Zionist affairs, becoming in 1933 a member of the political department of the Zionist Organization. From 1935 to 1948 Ben-Gurion was chairman of the Executive of the Jewish Agency in Palestine, and served in the Vaad Leumi. In these capacities he led Zionist action for the establishment of Israel. After Israeli independence he became prime minister and minister of defense, first of the Provisional Government and then of the elected governments, and he held these positions until 1963 except for a brief period in 1954–1955. He was also a member of the first seven Knessets until his final retirement from politics in 1970. In 1965 he left Mapai at the head of the Rafi group, and did not rejoin the party when Rafi reunited with Mapai to form the ILP. He died in 1973.

Shraga Netzer, party organizer, was born in 1898 in Russia where he graduated from high school and became active in the outlawed Zionist movement. In 1925 he went to Palestine, and from then until his retirement he worked in the sanitation department of the Tel-Aviv municipality. The first ten years he was a sanitation worker, the next fifteen inspector of the night shift, and finally deputy director. In 1927 he became a member of the Tel-Aviv Workers' Council of the Histadrut, and has been active in the Histadrut in many other capacities such as Ha-Mashbir Ha-Merkazi (the wholesale cooperative) and mutual aid funds. He was also a member of the Histadrut's highest tribunal. He held many Mapai/ILP positions, was a delegate to a number of Zionist congresses, and was elected to the *Yishuv's* Assembly of Delegates as well as to the Tel-Aviv municipal council. During and after the 1940s he was regarded as the head of the Gush, Mapai's party machine. From 1956 he was a member of the secretariat of Mapai and later also of the party bureau. His wife, Dvora, has also been active in the party, and was a member of the first through the sixth Knessets.

Emma Talmi (Levin), kibbutz member and MK, was born in Poland in 1905 and reached Palestine in 1924. Since her youth she had been active in the radical Zionist-socialist youth movement Ha-Shomer Ha-Tzair and she traveled widely through eastern Europe for it. She is a founding member of the kibbutz Mishmar Ha-Emeq and has been active in Mapam's leading organs as well as those of its kibbutz movement of which she edits the quarterly journal. She has participated in women's labor organizations. She was a member of the third through the fifth Knessets, and was a deputy speaker of the Knesset for one term.

Israel Yeshayahu, speaker of the Knesset, was born in Sana, Yemen, in 1910 and immigrated to Palestine in 1920. He graduated from a yeshiva and later pursued secular studies. For many years he worked as a weaver. From 1934 to 1936 he was the secretary of the Yemenite Workers' Club, and from 1936 to 1948 director of the department for Yemenite Jews in the Histadrut. He has represented Yemenite Jews in various party organs. In those years, he was a member of Mapai's central committee, a delegate in the Assembly of Delegates, an alternate delegate in the Executive Committee of the World Zionist Organization, a deputy member in the Histadrut's Executive Committee, and a member of the Tel-Aviv local Committee of Mapai. He became a member of the executive of the Association of Yemenite Jews in Israel, a delegate to the twentieth and twenty-first Zionist Congresses, and a deputy member of the Vaad Leumi. From 1948 to 1951 he was an employee of the Knesset, serving as secretary of its constitutional committee. He was active in "Operation Magic Carpet," which brought to Israel the greater part of Yemen's Jewry. He entered the first Knesset in 1951, and has remained a member ever since. From 1955 to 1967 he was one of the deputy speakers in the Knesset. Since the mid–1950s he has been a member of Mapai's secretariat, and since the early 1960s a member of its bureau as well. From 1967 to 1970 he was minister of posts, and from 1971 to 1972 secretary-general of the ILP. He was elected speaker of the Knesset in 1972 and reelected in 1974.

Zalman Susayeff, industrialist and deputy minister, was born in Riga, Latvia, in 1911. He graduated from Riga University and arrived in Palestine in 1935. He served as president of the Association of Importers and Wholesale Merchants in Israel from 1949 to 1950. In the years 1950–1952 he was chairman of the Tel-Aviv Chamber of Commerce. An MK during the second and third Knessets for the General Zionists' party, from 1953 to 1955 he was deputy minister of commerce and industry. Until 1969 he was president of the Manufacturers' Association. He was active in public organizations, has served on the Advisory Board of the Bank of Israel, and headed the public committee of the Government Security Loans.

Sayf al-Din al-Zuabi, deputy speaker of the Knesset and mayor, a Muslim Arab, was born in Palestine in 1913. A figure well known in Nazareth, he ran for the Knesset in 1949 at the head of an all-Arab slate supported by Mapai and was elected. He served in the first, second, sixth, seventh and eighth Knessets. Since 1959 he has more than once served as mayor of Nazareth. In 1972 he was elected deputy speaker of the Knesset, the first Israeli Arab to fill this post.

Natan Almoslino, member of the Vaada Merakezzet, was born in 1913 in Bulgaria where he finished high school and attended university. He belonged to the executive organs of the Ha-Shomer Ha-Tzair youth movement and He-Halutz, the Zionist pioneer movement for immigration. He came to Palestine in 1936, where he spent three years in a kibbutz and later served in the British army.

Between 1941 and 1947 he was secretary of the Histadrut-affiliated Ha-Poel sports organization in Rehovot, and director of the labor exchange there. From 1948 to 1955 he was secretary-general of the central labor exchange bureau, and from 1955 to 1959 he headed the building workers' department in the Histadrut. He was a member of the secretariat of the Ahdut Ha-Avoda party from its inception, represented it in the Rehovot Workers' Council, and during the period 1959–1964 was the party's full-time organizational secretary. From 1964 he has been a member of the Vaada Merakezzet, first for Ahdut Ha-Avoda and then for the ILP, as well as a member of the party's highest central organs. He is also the chairman of Amal, the Histadrut-affiliated technical high school system. His wife, Iraq-born Shoshana Arbeli-Almoslino, for many years also active in the Histadrut, has been an MK since the sixth Knesset and is chairman of its Labor Committee.

Eliezer Goelman, party organizer, was born in Poland in 1914 and immigrated to Palestine in 1933. A yeshiva graduate, he was active as an instructor and organizer in the orthodox youth movement, Bnei Aqiva, and was a founder of the Religious Workers' Youth Movement. Since 1952 he has been a full-time party official—first, secretary of the Ha-Poel Ha-Mizrahi Labor Organization, later a salaried member of the NRP and one of its secretaries. He has also been the party's treasurer.

Moshe Dayan, general and minister, was born in Deganya, Palestine in 1915. He joined the Hagana in 1929, and eight years later was a member of Charles Orde Wingate's "night squads." Since 1939 he was an instructor in various military schools of the Hagana, and was arrested by the British and jailed in the Acre prison. In 1941 he was wounded and lost his left eye in commando action in Syria for the British. In spite of this he continued to fill various positions in the Hagana. During Israel's war of independence, he fought successfully on various fronts. After playing key military roles, he served as Israel's chief of staff during the years 1953 to 1958, which included the Sinai campaign of 1956. He studied law at Tel-Aviv University and political science at the Hebrew University of Jerusalem. Since 1959 he has held a series of offices in Mapai, including positions on its secretariat and bureau. He served as MK for this party in the fourth through the eighth Knessets. From 1959 to 1964, he was minister of agriculture, until he left the cabinet because of the intraparty friction in Mapai. From 1965 to 1967 he was a member of the Knesset's Foreign Affairs and Defense Committee. He was one of the founders of Rafi and joined the ILP upon its foundation in 1968. On the eve of the Six-Day War in 1967 he entered the cabinet as minister of defense, a post he held until 1974.

Gideon Hausner, lawyer and MK, was born in Poland in 1915 and came to Palestine in 1927. He studied humanities at the Hebrew University of Jerusalem and was chairman of its student union. His legal training was in the law classes of the Palestine government. Before independence he was active in a movement of youth pioneers and served in the Hagana, mainly as lecturer and legal consultant. During Israel's war of independence he was first a military prosecutor, then president of a military court. Until 1960, and again after leaving government service, he was in private legal practice and was a member of the central bodies of the bar association. He has been a central figure of the Progressive party (later the

Independent Liberals' party) from its early days, representing its professional circles, and became chairman of its Jerusalem branch and member of its highest national organs. In 1960 he was appointed attorney general, a post he occupied until 1963. In that capacity he led the prosecution in the Eichmann trial. He became a member of the sixth Knesset, serving also in the seventh and eighth, and was chairman of the party's parliamentary group. In March 1974, he became a cabinet minister. He has also represented the party on the Executive Committee of the World Zionist Organization.

Rabbi Menahem Porush, MK, was born in Jerusalem in 1916—a seventh-generation Palestinian and son of one of the leaders of the most orthodox wing of the *Yishuv yashan.* A yeshiva graduate, he edited several Hebrew newspapers for many years and headed a private publishing house and printing press for religious books. He also has other business interests. In his party, Agudat Israel, he has held a series of positions, succeeding his father in some cases. He is a member of the Agudat Israel national center in Jerusalem as well as of its world executive council. In the party he represents the Jerusalem branch. He had held the position of political secretary of the party for a number of years. He was one of the founders of Agudat Israel's separate school system and is a supporter of many of its other educational activities. He is involved in the work of the party's construction and building societies. He represented the party in the fourth through the eighth Knessets, and was a deputy mayor of Jerusalem from 1959 to 1974.

Haim Landau, MK and minister, was born in Poland in 1916 and immigrated to Palestine in 1935. He is a graduate of the Haifa Institute of Technology (HIT) and was a civil engineer until 1942. At the age of seventeen he had been a staff officer in the Beytar (the youth organization of the Revisionist movement) in the Cracow district. He was a member of the National Students' Association and chairman of the HIT nationalist students. In 1940 he commanded the Beytar "base" in Haifa. Five years later he was nominated deputy chief of staff and, later that year, chief of staff of the Irgun Zvai Leumi. He has been an MK for Herut from the first Knesset through the eighth and has served on several of its key committees. In 1970 he served briefly as minister of development in the Cabinet of National Unity. He is a member of the policy-making bodies of Herut, and also of Gahal and Likkud.

Tawfiq Tubi, MK, a Greek Orthodox Arab from Haifa, was born in 1922. Tubi received his education at a British missionary school in Jerusalem, then at the American University in Beirut. A labor inspector during the later years of the British mandate in Palestine, he participated in strikes and workers' demonstrations. In 1949 he was one of the founders of the Israel Communist party and subsequently one of its leaders, representing it in the first through the eighth Knessets. When the party split in 1965, he led the New Communist List. Tubi has represented Israeli Communists in many international gatherings.

Shaul Ben-Simhon, member of the Vaada Merakezzet, was born in Morocco in 1931 and immigrated to Israel in 1948, settling first in Jerusalem. He started his political activity in the local branch of Mapai's Junior Guard while working in various capacities in the Jerusalem Workers' Council. He was also, for a time, secretary of the Jerusalem branch of the North African Immigrants' Association.

During the period 1955–1957 he studied at Beit Berl, Mapai's training center for party cadres. He moved to Ashdod, the new port town in central Israel, when he was elected secretary of its Workers' Council, a position he held until 1961 when he was sent to Senegal as a delegate of the Histadrut. In 1964 he was elected secretary of the Ashdod branch of Mapai and in 1965 returned to the town's Workers' Council. He joined Rafi upon its split from Mapai, was a member of its central institutions and represented it on the Vaada Merakezzet of the Histadrut, continuing in this post when Rafi became part of the ILP. In 1974 he was elected to head the Histadrut's manpower department.

Zvi Aldurati, mayor and administrator, was born in Israel in 1934 to Oriental Jewish parents. He reached officer's rank in the Israel Defense Forces and took a B.A. degree in political science at the University of Haifa. For three years he was secretary, then for thirteen years chairman (mayor) of the local council of Migdal Ha-Emeq, a new immigrants' town. He served on the executive committee of the Local Authorities' Union and on the managing board of its bank, as well as that of the leading Histadrut industrial concern, Koor. He is a member of the Israel Labor party's central committee and of its secretariat. Since 1972 he has been general manager and later chairman of the board of Amidar, a national housing corporation. In 1974 he returned to be chairman of the Migdal Ha-Emeq local council.

Zevulun Hammer, youth leader and MK, was born in Haifa in 1936 to parents who had come to Palestine from Poland. In his youth he was an instructor in the orthodox youth movement, Bnei Aqiva. Later (1958–1966) he was organizer of the Junior Guard in the NRP and then spokesman for the younger generation of the party. Since 1966 he has been member of the party secretariat and many other central party bodies. He took a B.A. in bible studies and literature at Bar-Ilan University in Ramat-Gan. He has been a member of the seventh and eighth Knessets.

VIII. POLITICAL ELITE OF LEBANON

Iliya F. Harik

Elites are, by definition, the few who enjoy sufficient political power to stand out from the rest of society. The top political elite of Lebanon to be considered here are the members of parliament, the cabinet ministers, and the presidents of the republic. Like political leaders elsewhere, those occupying formal decision-making positions in Lebanon are influenced by other elite groups in society in a variety of ways and in varying degrees. However, since no study has yet been made of what those influences are, they cannot be considered in this essay. Emphasis will be put here on social characteristics of the elite, the recruitment process, the staying power of its members, and their ability to determine their own succession.

Because the representative system of Lebanon and its political history are unique in the Middle East, there is a tendency to deal with it as a *sui generis* case. This should not, however, be an excuse to deal with Lebanese politics as a phenomenon defying comparative treatment, and comparisons will occasionally be made between Lebanon and other political systems.

An important theme commonly discussed in many elite studies is the strong tendency of political elites to monopolize power and select their successors.[1] Another theme is the tendency of traditional elites to flourish under a representative system. As summed up by one scholar, the "effect of democracy is to disperse power among a plurality of more traditional elites." [2] Here we will attempt to provide conclusions relative to these themes with measured rather than impressionistic evidence.

Background of the Elite

Patricians and Plebeians. It is not possible to determine social status precisely in a changing society such as Lebanon's, which is characterized by a growing bourgeoisie and disturbed scales of social worth. We shall use two criteria of social status: formal title and occupation. This is especially appropriate in the case of Lebanon since an aristocracy is still socially, though not officially, recognized.

Lebanon's aristocrats are descendants of the feudal nobility, which disintegrated in the middle of the nineteenth century. Contrary to general impressions, the aristocracy is a negligible minority among the top political elite of Lebanon today. The

---

[1] See Frederick W. Frey, *The Turkish Political Elite* (Cambridge, Mass.: The M.I.T. Press, 1965), pp. 22–23. The classic reference to the oligarchic tendency among elite is Robert Michels, *Political Parties: A Sociological Study of the Oligarchical Tendencies of Modern Democracy* (Glencoe, Ill.: The Free Press, 1958). As for the Lebanese case, Michael C. Hudson describes it as oligarchic; see *The Precarious Republic: Political Modernization in Lebanon* (New York: Random House, 1968).

[2] See Samuel P. Huntington, *Political Order in Changing Societies* (New Haven: Yale University Press, 1968), pp. 443–61. Quote taken from page 445.

average number of aristocrats in the last three parliaments has been ten, out of a ninety-nine–member chamber.[3] Only three of these titled members are prominent leaders in parliament.[4] Not only are aristocrats few in number, but in some cases their social origin is overshadowed by professional identity.

Members of the aristocracy have occupied few top offices since the beginning of the Lebanese Republic in 1926, and the role they have played in the cabinet is not any more distinguished than their role in parliament. Between the achievement of independence in 1943 and 1969, 139 men have served as ministers for 389 terms, an average of less than three terms per minister. Fifteen aristocrats have served as ministers a total of 46 times; they account for 12 percent of all the ministerial terms served. More than half of these appointments were held by Amir Majid Arslan, a perennial though not very powerful deputy. Of the eleven presidents of the Lebanese Republic only three were descendants of aristocratic families (Habib al-Saad, Bisharah al-Khouri and Fuad Shihab).

Descendants of the feudal aristocracy are neither dominant nor numerous in Lebanese political life. Their decline started more than a century ago, and most of them have now disappeared from the political arena.[5] Rhetoric, inadequate knowledge of social history,[6] and poor political terminology have resulted in the use of the inappropriate term "feudalist" in reference to the political elite of Lebanon. Any man who has been in the public eye long enough and has control over other less prominent members of the elite is often referred to as a feudalist. Long political tenure and patronage are considered relics of feudalism inconsistent with democracy. Use of the term "feudal" is sometimes defended on the grounds that it refers to traditional outlook and political control rather than to the historical phenomenon of feudalism.

What has perhaps added to the confusion is the indiscriminate use of the aristocratic title of *shaykh* in current political and social parlance. It is often used in a complimentary way when addressing a revered person and particularly in reference to village headmen *(mukhtars)* or descendants of village headmen who acquired the title without the honor. Not more than twenty deputies in the present chamber would qualify as notables because of local tradition or religious title.

---

[3] This essay was completed in September 1971 and does not take into account the ninth parliament elected in the spring of 1972. Suffice it here to say that the results of the 1972 elections confirm most generalizations noted here.

[4] These are *shaykhs*: Kamal Jumblat, Kamil al-Asad, and Sabri Hamadah.

[5] For the disintegration of the feudal aristocracy see Iliya F. Harik, *Politics and Change in a Traditional Society: Lebanon 1911–1945* (Princeton, N.J.: Princeton University Press, 1968).

[6] One example is Arnold Hottinger's "Zu'ama in Historical Perspective," in Leonard Binder, ed., *Politics in Lebanon* (New York: Wiley, 1966), pp. 85–105. Hottinger mistakenly gives the impression that the feudal aristocracy dominates the political scene and also makes several specific errors. He lists five deputies as belonging to the "great feudal families," but only one of them is a descendant of the feudal aristocracy. The other four he mentions, Boulos, Franjieh, Mu'awwad, Duwaihi (p. 87) are commoners. An established historian writes incorrectly that deputy Maurice Zuwain belongs to a feudal family. See Nicola A. Ziadeh, "The Lebanese Elections, 1960," *Middle East Journal,* vol. 14, no. 4 (August 1960), p. 375. A Lebanese author who compiled a volume on the elections and deputies of 1968 gives the title of *shaykh* to eight deputies, only two of which can be correctly called "shaykh," then misses four deputies who are entitled to the honor. See Jean Ma'luf, *Khafaya wa Arqam* (Beirut: Matba'at al Matni, n.d.), pp. 34–35.

Occupational Background. Members of the Lebanese elite are distinguished more by occupation than by social origin. The most striking feature of the Lebanese political elite since independence is their rapidly changing occupational characteristics. The number of people involved with agriculture has declined rapidly while businessmen and professionals have increased sharply since 1943 (Table 8–1). The figures presented in Table 8–1 are based on biographical abstracts available in parliament or in the press, which do not always reveal much about the complexities of occupational classifications. A careful examination of the ninety-nine deputies of the parliament elected in 1968 shows that a large number of deputies have more than one occupation, and multiple coding was necessary to determine their occupational status.[7]

To facilitate analysis of occupations it is necessary to separate basic occupation from other activities. A basic occupation is a person's primary economic pursuit. It is not always easy to separate a basic from a secondary occupation; a person who inherits agricultural land but has at the same time a law practice may be said to hold two basic occupations. In such cases, the one he lists in his biographical account will be considered the basic occupation. We are interested mainly in the real number of occupations represented in the chamber, and this cannot be obtained from basic listings only.

[7] A variety of sources were used and checked against one another. In most cases informants were also consulted and contributed additional information and corrected published sources. The written sources are the biographical abstracts of all deputies and candidates published by *An-Nahar* and *Al-Jaridah,* Beirut dailies. *An-Nahar* research institute and publishing house also provided biographical abstracts of the 1964 deputies in Malaf an-Nahar, *al-Hayat al-Niyabiyah fi Lubnan* (no. 3): *al-Nuwwab bil-Ihsa'* (Beirut: Dar an-Nahar, 1968). The last source is *Who's Who in Lebanon, 1970–1971.*

Table 8–1

DISTRIBUTION OF DEPUTIES IN SEVEN LEBANESE PARLIAMENTS, BY OCCUPATION
(as percentage of all deputies)

	Parliament							
Occupation	1943	1947	1951	1953	1957	1960	1964	1968[a]
Landlords	46.5	48.2	42.5	40.9	33.3	23.0	23.2	10
Lawyers	33.9	27.3	25.0	34.1	36.3	29.0	27.3	44
Businessmen	10.2	10.9	12.5	6.8	11.1	14.0	17.2	17
Professionals	10.2	12.7	20.0	18.2	19.0	34.0	32.3	28
Total[b]	100.0	100.0	100.0	100.0	99.7	100.0	100.0	99

[a] Updated by the author of this chapter.
[b] Figures may not add due to rounding; also there were discrepancies due to lack of occupational data in some cases (5 out of 250 men) and the inclusion of replacements for deputies who died or resigned.
Source: Michael Hudson, "The Electoral Process and Political Development in Lebanon," *Middle East Journal,* vol. 20 (Spring 1966), p. 178. It is not clear whether Hudson includes under the category of lawyers all those with a law degree or only practicing attorneys. Another source, for instance, shows that the 1960 parliament had 32.32 percent lawyers and magistrates. See Mary-Ann Gebara, "The Social Background of the Lebanese Parliamentary Elite (1960–1964)" (M.A. thesis, American University of Beirut, 1964), p. 65.

Compound computation of occupations is a method which determines the number of economic pursuits followed by each individual at the same or at different times. The compound aggregate shows all the occupations represented and is, of course, greater than the total number of deputies. Percentages can then be determined on the basis of the occupational aggregate rather than on the total number of deputies. This also makes it possible to determine an occupational diversity index.

Multiple Occupations in the Eighth Parliament. Occupational distribution in the eighth parliament (1968) shows the continuing decline in agricultural occupations (Table 8–2). Compound computation shows, however, that the decline is not as sharp as it appears to be in the basic occupations listing (Table 8–3). Individuals in agricultural occupations cannot be classified simply as landlords since some of them are small farmers or entrepreneurs. The landlords are the heirs of large estates[8]—about ten deputies who include Bashir al-Uthman, Kamil al-Asad, al-Zayn brothers, Kamal Jumblat, Raymond Eddé—whereas the small farmers are individuals who own modest amounts of land as an additional source of income. Three examples are Dr. Bakhus Hakim, Qiblan Isa al-Khouri and Mohammed Fatfat. The first two are professionals, and the latter was originally an agricultural worker who, after serving as a gendarme, bought a plot of land and listed himself as farmer. A third category that should be distinguished here is that of the entrepreneurs—usually urban professionals who have acquired extensive areas of agricultural land as a business enterprise (for example, Abdullah al-Yafi, Yusuf Salim and Kamil Shamoun).

[8] Some, who are often considered landlords, hold small plots of land such as Bahij al-Qaddur, a descendant of the erstwhile landholding family of Akkar region. On the other hand, Joseph Skaf of Zahli could be considered either a landlord or an entrepreneur, since the large estates he inherited had been acquired by his father who was an urban businessman, not a descendant from the landed families.

Table 8–2

DISTRIBUTION OF BASIC AND SECONDARY OCCUPATIONS, 1968 PARLIAMENT

		Secondary Occupations				
Basic Occupations		Landowners	Lawyers and judges	Businessmen	Professionals	**Total Secondary Occupations**
Landowners	10	—	—	1	1	2
Lawyers and judges	44	12	—	9	14	35
Businessmen	17	1	—	12[a]	1	14
Professionals	28	5	—	6	4[b]	15
Total	99	18	0	28	20	66

[a] Businessmen who added new business lines to their enterprise.
[b] Professionals who entered into new professional enterprises.

Table 8–3

DISTRIBUTION OF OCCUPATIONS HELD, BASIC AND SECONDARY

	As a Basic Occupation	As a Secondary Occupation	Total	Percentage of Total
Landowning	10	18	28	17
Legal professions	44	—	44	27
Business	17	28	45	27
Other professions	28	20	48	29
Total	99	66	165	100

Those who have training in law and are using their legal skills as lawyers, judges, or officials, form a very large group (44 percent in the eighth parliament). However, in terms of compound computation of occupations, there are as many in business as in the legal profession (Table 8–2 and Figure 8–2), a fact which would have been concealed if we had accepted basic occupational listings only. Those in the legal professions show the greatest occupational mobility (Table 8–2, Figure 8–2), extending their activities to occupations such as business, journalism, or government service. The association between the legal profession and landholding is not strong; fewer than one-fourth of the lawyers are also landowners (Table 8–2).

Business occupies second position after the legal profession in the ranking of occupational distribution (Table 8–3). Not all businessmen, however, have extensive enterprises.[9] Businessmen usually expand their activities within the field of business rather than moving to other careers, whereas lawyers and professionals go beyond their professions to business enterprises (Table 8–2). A businessman may enlarge his activity from trade to finance, or from contracting to industry, or from finance into real estate, but he is not likely to venture into journalism, government employment, or teaching.

The professions such as engineering, medicine, or journalism come first in strength of representation in the chamber (Table 8–3); professional and business pursuits are most commonly sought by deputies from other professions (Figure 8–1). Representatives of the professions, on the other hand, show occupational mobility in two different directions: toward other professional pursuits such as teaching and government service, or into business, usually contracting and management of business firms (Table 8–2).

[9] For instance, Sayd Akl of al-Batrun had a very small enterprise not sufficient for his livelihood and depended on his wealthy uncle and then his wife's income. Similarly, Suleiman Franjieh, now President of the Republic, started out as an employee in the waterworks company of Tripoli and then established a small business office. He is known to be of modest means and a professional politician, not an economically active individual. For some reason there is considerable confusion among writers over his occupation and the *An-Nahar* compendium, *Al-Hayat al-Niyabiyah* (no. 3), lists him as a landowner, Hottinger, in "Zu'ama in Historical Perspective," mistakenly as a feudalist. In contrast, Pierre Farawn, Yusuf Salim, Andre Taburian and Munir Abu-Fadil are among those who have extensive enterprises and are very wealthy.

The increase in the number of professionals and businessmen among the Lebanese political elite is indicative of the change in the national economy. Industry, commerce, banking, and insurance contributed half the gross national product in the 1960s, whereas agriculture contributed only 12 percent. Thus, Huntington's observation that representative systems in developing countries favor the political ascendancy of landlords may hold true only where the national economy and education are not changing rapidly. In Lebanon most villagers are so exposed to

Figure 8-1

OCCUPATIONAL DISTRIBUTION OF BASIC AND SECONDARY OCCUPATIONS

Figure 8-2

OCCUPATIONS WHOSE HOLDERS TEND TO ACQUIRE SECONDARY OCCUPATIONS

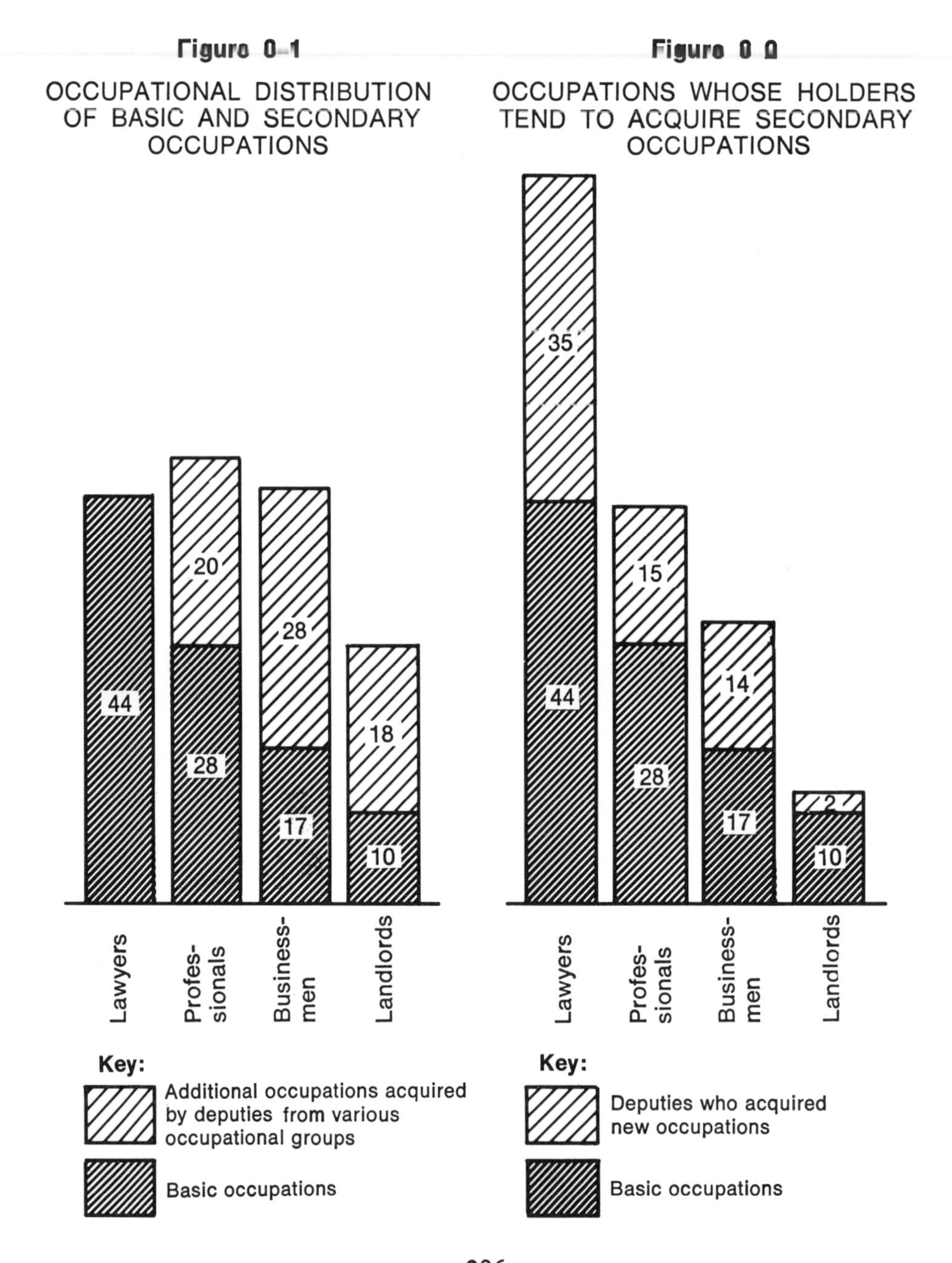

modernizing influences that urban-rural divisions do not reflect fundamental differences as in less developed countries.

The changing occupational composition of the Lebanese parliament since 1943 suggests that access to the highest political positions in the country is wide open. As the occupational diversity index of 1.65 (based on data in Table 8–3) indicates, the elite is economically very active and occupationally mobile. And while the political elite of Lebanon does not belong to a high social caste, it does come from high status occupations such as law, medicine, engineering and business.

The preponderance of high status occupations and the high level of education among the political elite sets them apart from the general population. In the 1968 parliament, 70 percent of the deputies were holders of a university degree obtained in Lebanon or in Europe, and 15 percent of these had Ph.D. degrees. It is a common finding that in most contemporary systems a political elite has a higher educational level than the people they represent. An elite also tends to be more advanced in age than the average citizen. In Lebanon the mean age of deputies for the last two chambers was fifty years at the time of elections, whereas half the population was under twenty.[10] This figure compares favorably with the average age of United States senators and British M.P.s.[11]

To summarize: the Lebanese political leader today is an educated person of middle or upper income, economically very active as a businessman, lawyer, or professional. The competitive political game of parliamentary government has not enhanced the political fortunes of the declining patrician families. Instead, it has advanced the position of those distinguished in terms of their skills. The change from a preponderantly landowning elite to a business and professional elite shows that in at least one respect the top political elite have failed to perpetuate their own kind.

The Cabinet Member

As in most parliamentary representative systems, Lebanon's political elite rises primarily through elections to parliament or through co-optation into the cabinet. The usual practice has been for ministers to be recruited from the parliament; from independence to 1971, thirty-two cabinets have been formed from members of parliament, while members of eleven cabinets were recruited elsewhere among public figures in business, the professions, or diplomacy.[12] Most nonparliamentary cabinets were caretaker governments during transitional periods.

The president of the republic, as the chief executive and most powerful officer of state, selects a prime minister and influences the composition of the cabinet. The tradition has been for the prime minister-designate to negotiate with leaders in parliament and with the president on a set of acceptable names. The president and the prime minister have the major responsibility in selecting favored candidates;

[10] Institute de Formation en Vue de Développement, *Le Liban Face à Son Développement* (Beirut: Imprimerie Catholique, 1963), p. 210.

[11] See Michael Hudson, "The Electoral Process and Political Development in Lebanon," *Middle East Journal*, vol. 20 (Spring 1966), and J. F. S. Ross, *Parliamentary Representation* (New Haven: Yale University Press, 1949), p. 33.

[12] A very small number of cabinets had mixed membership of deputies and nondeputies.

but in order to satisfy the numerous deputies in a fragmented parliamentary leadership, cabinets are often reshuffled after one year to give other deputies the chance to occupy coveted executive posts.[13]

A cabinet post is a strong political resource and offers its holder visibility and patronage, plus moral endorsement by the highest authority in the state. Once a person becomes a minister, he increases his chances for political survival and for the expansion of his influence.

We have examined the careers of cabinet ministers from the start of the Mandate in 1922 to 1969 to determine their staying power in politics. This examination is complicated by the fact that in Lebanon a relative may replace a political leader when he dies or retires. Should this "hereditary" phenomenon occur frequently, the turnover rate of deputies and ministers would be a deceptive indicator of change in the ranks of the political elite. To avoid this, the family was taken as the unit of analysis, and it is the staying power of the family rather than the individual that is analyzed.[14] The term "family" in Lebanon refers to holders of the same surname, who are also believed to be descendants of the same ancestor, like the Saltonstalls of Massachusetts or the Byrds of Virginia. What is implied is not strong kinship solidarity, but rather family ties of varying degrees of strength.

When political careers from various families whose members occupied a ministerial post were analyzed, it emerged that ministers have a weak political survival ability and that most of those who survived had a political base independent of the ministerial post they occupied. Figures show that during the French Mandate (1922–1943) individuals from 45 families occupied cabinet posts at various times but members of 12 families only survived in parliament to the 1960s.[15] Similarly, since independence in 1943, individuals from 109 families have occupied cabinet posts. Of these families, 31 have never had a member in parliament, and 65 failed to survive politically to the parliament of 1968.

Further analysis shows that the staying power of ministers originally recruited from parliament is much greater than that of those who came to cabinet post without previous parliamentary experience. All but two ministers who survived during both the Mandate and Independence periods were recruited after they had been elected to parliament at least once. Thus a ministerial post without an independent political base (a parliamentary seat) does not necessarily lead to a secure political career. A cabinet post is, however, a valuable asset and may be considered a reward to deputies for their ability to survive the fierce competition for office. In the present chamber, for instance, there are twelve perennial deputies, eleven of whom have occupied ministerial office at least once. Those who survived in parliament for only two decades were less favored; only half of them were given ministerial posts.

---

[13] Useful treatment of Lebanese cabinets may be found in Elie Salem, "Cabinet Politics in Lebanon," *Middle East Journal,* vol. 21, no. 4 (Autumn 1967), pp. 488–502; and Malcolm Kerr, "Political Decision Making in a Confessional Democracy," in Binder, *Politics in Lebanon,* pp. 192–203.

[14] Political careers in Lebanon are primarily parliamentary careers since cabinets change practically every year and a minister is not often recalled unless he becomes a deputy. This is perhaps because the majority of cabinets, as we have seen above, are recruited among deputies.

[15] It should be mentioned, however, that during the French Mandate, elections were not free but subject to a considerable degree of interference and outright co-optation.

Contrary to popular belief, cabinet ministers have enjoyed no monopoly over the cabinet system, but rather have shown relatively little staying power in politics. Those who have shown a greater staying power made their political capital on their own, and not as a result of a cabinet post. The large number of individuals from different families who have occupied ministerial posts and the high rate of turnover in personnel show clearly that access to executive power has been quite open and that a cabinet post does not lead to a secure political career. These findings also underline the pluralistic nature of the system which, by sharing executive powers with as many political forces as possible, maintains national unity and blunts the opposition. Except in critical times, political opposition in parliament tends to be mild; hardly ever do deputies burn their bridges to the executive branch.

Turnover and Recruitment in Parliament

Like ministers of state, most members of parliament are constantly threatened and unseated by challengers. The average turnover rate for the eight parliaments since independence has been 42 percent.[16] This is higher than in some Western democracies and therefore calls for an explanation. Before 1964, the electoral laws were changed several times, altering the number of deputies from one election to the next, and thereby affecting the turnover rate. The rate of 42 percent change in the personnel of the chambers since 1943 does not necessarily reflect a normal turnover rate. The highest turnover rates occurred in the chambers of 1943, 1951, and 1960, each of which was enlarged by an average of twenty-three new seats over preceding chambers. Similarly, the smallest number of newly elected deputies occurred in the elections of 1953 when the size of the parliament was sharply reduced.

A more reliable indicator of normal turnover rate among the parliamentary elite may be established on the basis of change in parliaments elected after 1960, when the number of deputies was stabilized at ninety-nine. The change in parliamentary personnel for the seventh and eighth parliaments (1964 and 1968), including members with previous but interrupted parliamentary experience, is 44.5 percent. The high turnover tendency is thus confirmed, regardless of the changing size of parliament. New members not previously elected constitute 28 percent, a figure comparable to the House of Commons in Great Britain where the turnover rate was 29 percent for the seven parliaments elected between the two world wars.[17] In the United States Congress, on the other hand, the rate of change of parliamentary elite is much lower, amounting to less than 15 percent for both the Senate and the House of Representatives.[18] The high turnover rate among deputies has become a trend in Lebanese politics.

The rate of change in the Lebanese parliament is higher than it is often thought

[16] Based on Hudson, "Electoral Process," p. 176; average turnover rate was calculated by the author of this chapter.

[17] Ross, *Parliamentary Representation,* p. 107.

[18] Lewis A. Froman, *The Congressional Process: Strategies, Rules and Procedures* (Boston: Little, Brown and Company, 1967), p. 170; also Donald R. Matthews, *U.S. Senators and Their World* (Chapel Hill: University of North Carolina Press, 1960), p. 240. Incumbents reelected in the 1968 chamber in Lebanon make 65, since 10 deputies either died or did not present themselves for reelection.

to be. The erroneous impression may be created by the fact that those few members of parliament who are often reelected are prominent and well known by the public. This gives the impression of a stable oligarchy entrenched in the chamber.[19] In fact, a career in the Lebanese parliament is quite insecure, and even among the dozen prominent members all but two have lost their seats at least once. There is a tendency for old-timers to drop out gradually. Dates of first entry of deputies in the chamber elected in 1968 were as follows:

Date	*Number of Deputies*
Pre–1943	5
1943–1950	7
1950–1960	24
1960–1964	35
1968	28
Total	99

The average experience of a member of the 1968 parliament was 11.44 years, a service of about three terms only. This is comparable to the House of Commons where tenure is estimated at fifteen years,[20] or at least three terms.

The Hereditary Phenomenon. It is quite possible to argue that the figures on elite change belie the facts, since deputies are often elected to fill seats vacated by kinsmen. A look at the new members of the last two parliaments shows that eight deputies, or 29 percent of the newly elected members, occupied seats vacated by relatives.[21] Half of those, however, ran against other relatives, which indicates that succession is not without struggle and is often contested by both relatives and strangers. Later we shall discuss the importance of kinship ties in recruitment of parliamentary elite. Here it is sufficient to point out that seven of the eight parliamentary heirs in the elections to the 1964 chamber came from south Lebanon where entrenched families have succeeded in restricting access to parliament.

Historical evidence shows that deputies whose families have retained seats are a small proportion of the parliamentary elite. From 1922 to 1943, deputies from 103 different families occupied parliamentary seats. Of these, 80 failed to contribute deputies to the 1968 chamber. Among the 23 remaining families of the pre-independence period, who have contributed twenty-four deputies to the 1968 parliament, many are confined to specific regions and particular groups. For instance, seven belong to the aristocracy, four to the landed Shiite families of the south and the Biqaa, and four are still the same persons. Three of these[22] do not have apparent successors.

The political casualty rate among families is similar for the post-independence period. The deputies of the 1940s and 1950s belong to 136 different families, of which 85 have demonstrated no staying power and are not represented in the

[19] See for instance Hudson, "Electoral Process," pp. 176–77.

[20] Ross, *Parliamentary Representation,* p. 107.

[21] Two deputies succeeded their fathers in recent by-elections and a third succeeded a relative. These will not be taken into account here because the discussion is based on deputies elected in 1968.

[22] These are Yusuf Salim, Abdullah al-Yafi, and Majid Arslan.

present chamber. This means that for every family which returned members to the parliament of 1968 nearly two (1.6) failed to do so.

In short, the turnover rate of Lebanese deputies and cabinet ministers is high and does not warrant the charge of oligarchy. The phenomenon of succession by relatives and political traditions in the family affects only one-third of the elite, so it does not invalidate findings on elite turnover.

Political Recruitment. Deputies are elected by universal adult suffrage for four-year terms; they in turn elect a president for the republic who appoints a prime minister. The president and the prime minister choose the cabinet members in consultation with members of parliament.

A seat in parliament is clearly the basis for higher political positions in Lebanon. This gives the member of parliament in Lebanon more power than his counterpart elsewhere. Besides their legislative role, members of parliament become an electoral college once every six years to elect a president, share in the privilege of occupying executive posts in the cabinet, and enjoy special relations with provincial officials in their districts. Despite these privileges, however, many Lebanese deputies bemoan their weak legislative role and feel ineffective in checking the authority of the president and the cabinet. This feeling is not uncommon among legislators in other parliamentary systems, notably the British. In Lebanon the top political elite are inbred since most presidents and ministers come from the chamber itself.

It is sometimes said that the real power is held by figures behind the parliamentary facade: religious and military leaders and foreign diplomats. The relationship between these elements and holders of political office is thought to be of a clandestine nature, so it is difficult to prove or disprove this theory. It is a highly emotional political debate and is not, therefore, a fruitful direction for scholarship. Whether or not these "powers behind the scenes" are all-powerful, they do have a legitimate role in politics by virtue of their public character. Religious and military leaders have business with the government pertaining to their organizations and, as important public figures, they maintain contact with the civil authorities. Under conditions of national crisis and division among the top political leaders, religious and military leaders assume greater political importance, but not enough to seriously threaten the civilian leaders.

The civil war of 1958 and its repercussions clearly demonstrated these tendencies. The increase in the role of the military under Presidents Fuad Shihab and Charles Hilu and the disturbing interference of the Deuxième Bureau, the military intelligence department, in politics generated a wave of public resentment and protest in the chamber of deputies. This antimilitary climate enabled President Suleiman Franjieh in 1970 to curtain the military and purge the Deuxième Bureau practically overnight. Civilian leadership is clearly still supreme.

Foreign embassies in Lebanon play a political role as salesmen for their countries; in times of crisis, such as 1958, ambassadors of the great powers become quite influential. A small number of embassies such as those of the United States, France, Great Britain and Egypt are particularly deferred to because of the importance, both locally and internationally, of the countries they represent. After the Arab-Israeli war of 1967 the Russian ambassador emerged as a member of this club. Deputies also take these diplomats into account, especially during presidential elections. Deputies need to know the reactions of influential foreign powers in the region regarding presidential candidates, because it would be unthinkable for a president to be elected if he were objectionable to these powers.

To recapitulate, the top political elite of Lebanon are those who occupy legislative office in the chamber of deputies, cabinet ministers, and the president. All other segments of the political elite who interact with these figures are subordinate to those in the power hierarchy. With this in mind, we may now underline these factors which determine the recruitment channels through which political leaders ascend.

Political Parties. In the last parliamentary elections, political parties raised thirty-three deputies to the chamber, or one-third of all members. This appears to be a very limited accomplishment until it is realized that thirty-three is the highest number of successful candidates that political parties in Lebanon have ever produced, and it took all seven of the existing parties to do it. Only two of the seven, the Kataib and the Armenian nationalist party, the Tashnaq, have a following disciplined enough so that the party leadership determines the nomination of candidates whose victory depends on the party following rather than their local strength. In a recent interview with deputies and candidates conducted by the prominent daily, *An-Nahar,*[23] the deputies who most frequently indicated that their future candidacy depended on the decision of the party were members of the Kataib. The rest of the parties are more like coalitions of leaders in various constituencies bound to one figure prominent in national politics such as Shamoun, Eddé, Jumblat, and the like. About half the thirty-three partisan deputies in parliament were elected on their own strength with only minor help from the party to which they belonged.

The fact that two-thirds of the members of parliament are independent deputies without allegiance to any political party often raises doubts about the validity of the democratic process in Lebanon. Most intellectuals, including deputies, are familiar with Western democracies whose parliaments are organized on the basis of political parties. This has created an inferiority complex among the top political elite themselves, who feel that without political parties their democracy is deficient. Statements to this effect in the newspapers, in journals, and in *An-Nahar* interviews have been made at one time or another by most Lebanese statesmen, including the current president and prime minister. It is therefore curious that these deputies, and many unsuccessful candidates, run again and again as independents rather than as party members. Some admit candidly that most voters are not party members and want an independent to represent them. The dilemma and hypocrisy in which deputies are caught was unwittingly exposed in the response of an independent deputy and former minister who sharply criticized the Lebanese parliament for being based on strong regional leaders instead of on political party lines. When asked if he planned to run again in the coming elections, he responded affirmatively and proceeded to compliment the strong regional leaders with whom he was collaborating. "A deputy who started his political career," he said, "by

[23] See pages 214-15.

establishing strong ties with leaders [*zuaama*] in his district and with voters is not free to resign his duties and abandon his friends half way on the path."

The political party complex is an artificial issue generated by a chameleon intellectual community able to reproduce the forms of other systems without understanding their country's political reality. The existing system of independent deputies does have some important advantages when viewed in terms of realization of democratic ideals as well as of feasibility for Lebanese conditions. These should be considered seriously along with criticisms of the system and suggestions for change.

When running as an independent, a deputy must rely primarily on local resources and cultivate enduring relations with his constituents. This emphasizes the local orientation of deputies and leads to an arrangement whereby contact between a representative and the voters is stronger than in nationally oriented party systems. This is, of course, very demanding for candidates, and it is therefore not surprising that they should desire or hope for a party system where the party organization assumes a major part of the campaigning burden.

The localism of the Lebanese deputy is particularly suited to developing countries in which one usually finds overbearing national leadership making policy free from public pressures. Such governments often emphasize national projects and invest in urban centers, but in Lebanon the local orientation of deputies has influenced the government to render essential developmental services to the provinces. Even the smallest and most remote of villages play their hands during election periods, bargaining with candidates for their share of such essentials as schools, communication facilities like roads and telephones, water, electricity, and similar services. The fact that half the deputies interviewed by *An-Nahar* placed special emphasis on services they had rendered or planned to render for their constituents clearly indicates the importance which a deputy attaches to his district. Deputies, especially those from the provinces, are always reminded of their districts' needs by letters and cables, 74 percent of which come from villages [24] requesting such services as electricity, water, telephones, schools, and roads.

Another advantage of the no-party system lies in what is often considered the worst evil of Lebanese parliaments: the fragmentation of political leadership. Contrary to this view, fragmentation has increased the power of the individual deputy and may actually have improved his ability to serve his constituents. The large number of independent deputies compels the executive to take each one of them into account in the bargaining process. In response to an *An-Nahar* interview, one candidate stated outright that in return for supporting the president in forming a cabinet freely, he and his colleague on the district ticket received what they had been trying to attain for a long time—the building of two schools and a road in their district. Furthermore, the government's need to maintain consensus and receive support from a majority of deputies results in a system that works to the advantage of constituents. Parliamentary support for the executive is achieved by the reshuffling of cabinets, which occurs almost annually, to accommodate deputies awaiting their turn to enjoy the fruits of executive office. This practice has given

---

[24] An-Nahar, *Al-Hayat al-Niyabiyah fi Lubnan* (no. 2): *al-Tashri' bil-Khara'it* (Beirut: Dar an-Nahar, 1968), p. 18.

more power to individual deputies and has prevented the emergence of a radical opposition group in parliament bent on destroying the system.

It is often pointed out that such a fragmented system leads to political instability. However, most of the serious political crises in Lebanon have not resulted from the fragmentation of political leadership in parliament but from other causes. Lebanon is able to withstand much diversity in its legislative body because of the strong leadership provided by the presidency. The presidency is the reference point around which everything in Lebanese politics revolves.

A system of this kind has its own shortcomings. A great deal of energy and time are wasted in politicking to maintain the balance in the system. Deputies often appear petty in their struggles to secure benefits for their constituents, and political calculations often interfere with sound policy.

A Constituency-Bound System. That members of parliament show greater concern for their constituencies than for national issues can be inferred from an opinion survey of seventy deputies conducted by the research institute of *An-Nahar* newspaper and publishing house in Beirut. Responses to three questions designed to indicate a deputy's orientation on national and local matters were coded.[25] (The responses of only sixty-six deputies were relevant to this topic.)[26] More than half the respondents show strong local orientation (Table 8–4) compared to only one-third who are more nationally oriented. The deputies from Beirut make up exactly one-half the nationally oriented group of twenty-two. Even the attitude of Beirut deputies is not without a local orientation. One respondent commented that the concerns of the voter in Beirut are entirely different from those in the provinces. Unlike his counterpart in the provinces, the Beirut voter is not concerned with the need for electricity, roads, and so on. He may be interested in free education or free medical care, which are national in nature and could not be requested for the city of Beirut alone. A Beirut deputy can, in fact, be considered constituency-oriented, because when he advocates national programs of popular interest he is really appealing for local approval.

[25] The following questions were asked: (a) What was your program? (b) What were your accomplishments? (c) In what did you succeed or fail? Points which referred to national matters and those which referred to local affairs in the respondents' statement were counted, and the scores determined the position of the deputy on the attitude scale.

[26] Three deputies who were elected in by-elections responded to the survey but were not included here, because they lacked the time and experience to make significant statements.

Table 8–4

LOCAL VERSUS NATIONAL ORIENTATION OF DEPUTIES, 1968 PARLIAMENT[a]

	High		Medium		Low	
	Number	Percent	Number	Percent	Number	Percent
Constituency orientation	36	54	15	23	15	23
National orientation	22	33	30	46	14	21

[a] With a total of 66 members.

Another indicator of the strong ties of deputies with their constituencies is the fact that almost all were born in the constituencies which they represent. Only eleven of the ninety-nine deputies [27] in parliament were not born in the constituency they represent, and many of these belong to a national political party, the Kataib, whose loyal members support the party candidate regardless of his birthplace. (One consequence of parliamentary localism in Lebanon is the even distribution of strong parliamentary leaders over all the regions. This distribution gives the provinces strong representation in the national government.)

It is a common complaint among Lebanese leaders that their parliamentary duties are too demanding and often unbearable. One irate deputy exclaimed that a deputy "won't have a chance of being reelected unless he works as a broker between the voters and the real authorities." [28] He must attend to problems ranging from skirmishes with the law to differences between brothers over inheritance. Social duties are another factor a deputy has to keep in mind if he wants reelection. He should be present at religious feasts, weddings, funerals, and other social occasions.

Personal Organization. The fact that deputies are sensitive to their local bases is indicative of the weak forces emanating from national organizations such as political parties. The absence of national political party organizations compels a candidate to build his own personal organization and, therefore, to rely on his kinsmen and friends for political support. Kinship ties are crucial to a candidate in that they provide therewith a personal organization to run a successful election. Of course, the status of the family, its wealth, numbers, and local ties are important, but the main factor is the personal organization. A personal organization consists of relatives and friends of the family who extend their services and funds to finance and run the candidate's campaign. Deputies make no secret of their family connections. A group of forty-four deputies out of the seventy surveyed by *An-Nahar* mentioned their relatives as the people who helped them most in the campaign. (It is interesting to note that twenty-two of them paid special tribute to their wives for their help and understanding.)

This election procedure is also responsible for creating and maintaining client groups. When a candidate wins an election, his future in politics depends to a large extent on his ability to strengthen his personal machine and his ties with constituents. If he attains an executive post, he acquires additional political capital and augments his local resources by patronage, starting with members of his electoral machine, who may be given influential jobs in the government and thus generate further patronage and services to the constituents.

Importance of Heredity. The fact that nearly one-third of the members of parliament are succeeded by their relatives is directly related to this constituency-oriented system. Since a deputy's strength is based on his personal organization of relatives

[27] Two of these are naturalized, refugee Armenians who were born abroad. Two others, Adnan Hakim and Maurice al-Jumayyil, were born abroad also, but their parents belonged to the constituencies in which they ran, and they have lived most of their lives in these constituencies.

[28] *An-Nahar* interview, June and July 1971.

and friends, his political capital, like his property, is subject to the law of inheritance by his sons, brothers, and other relatives in the organization. As members of the electoral machine, the heirs enjoy an advantage over outside contenders by virtue of an established clientele that is likely to transfer loyalty to the heir of their leader. In view of this continuity, it may be predicted that the hereditary phenomenon among some members of the Lebanese elite is not likely to fade away in the near future but rather may increase. The growth of national political parties is very slow and therefore not likely to replace the personal electoral machine very soon, a fact underlined by an examination of the contenders against the deputies in the election of 1968 showing that they are more local in orientation and background.

There are serious limitations which keep this hereditary tendency in check. Among these considerations are a division among the possible candidates in the personal organization leading to dispersion and waste of resources, lack of a suitable heir in the personal organization, and finally, the volatile political situation itself. Any of these factors may help contain the tendency among the parliamentary elite to determine their own succession.

The Electoral Ticket. Two other factors contributing in a major way to the making of the Lebanese political elite are the forming of the right ticket and favors from "higher up." All but one of the Lebanese constituencies are multiple candidate districts with from two to eight representatives. It is, therefore, of great importance in an electoral contest for candidates to pool their resources. In the 1968 elections only one candidate not running on a slate won a seat in parliament, despite the fact that such lone contenders ran in the elections in practically every district. Slates in Lebanese elections (usually referred to as lists) become like party tickets in U.S. elections where the question of straight party as opposed to split voting is significant. The tendency to vote for the whole ticket is fairly strong. In the 1968 elections, for instance, fourteen slates out of twenty-five were elected *in toto*. The importance of these slates is such that a major part of the campaign is spent in the delicate task of forming the slates.

This process of ticket forming reveals the leadership stratification in Lebanon. Not every member of the Lebanese parliament is of equal weight. Members of parliament may be classified as "bloc" leaders,[29] followers, and independents. A bloc leader is a deputy whose electoral strength dominates or extends beyond his own constituency because of a sizeable political inheritance like that of Kamil al-Asad, or as a result of attaining national status, like that of Kamil Shamoun. Bloc leaders are sometimes strong enough to select for their slates weak candidates whose loyalty is assured. Usually a bloc leader brings from two to nine followers with him to parliament. Such men are Rashid Karami of Tripoli, Kamil al-Asad of Marjiyun, Shamoun and Jumblat of al-Shuf, Skaf of Zahli, and others. Thus the Lebanese parliament is really a constellation of several small groups of deputies, a fact which makes bargaining on the floor arduous and lengthy.

Official Endorsement by the Presidency. Elections cannot be discussed without taking into account the great political force of the presidency. Experts in electoral

[29] The term as used in Lebanon refers to a leader of a group of deputies.

affairs, including former president Shamoun, estimate that the presidency has the power to sway one-third of the electorate. Since independence, there has not been any president who has not used his influence to affect the outcome of elections, some through legitimate means and others going beyond them. The president together with his cabinet can influence the planning of electoral slates, use his powers of patronage, and inspire local brokers eager to please the authorities. Power is like a magnet—the politically ambitious are attracted to it.

In conclusion, several factors seem to carry equal weight in the making of the Lebanese elite: family traditions in politics, political parties, personal ability to cooperate with other leaders in the district, and presidential favor in the elections. Elite status is the outcome of a combination of several of these factors, as well as of the skill of the candidate in using them. This is clearly understood by deputies in their assessment of their own political resources as expressed in the *An-Nahar* survey. Most deputies stressed their personal role as leader—personal contacts and services rendered to voters. Some deputies, such as Rashid Karami, Kamal Jumblat, and Kamil Shamoun, have exhibited considerable political skill and increased their initial political capital several times over.

This assessment of political recruitment and elite position in Lebanon has not considered the religious communalism that is often a prominent part of studies or discussions of Lebanese affairs. Political attitudes of most Lebanese are still affected by their religious background, although the importance of this is often exaggerated. Sectarianism in Lebanon actually has been beaten by a process of political routinization. Lebanon has been constitutionally divided into religious communities, each of which is entitled by law to a fixed number of deputies relative to the size of its population. In effect, the electoral law limits political competition to individuals from the same religious sect and precludes competition between candidates from different religious communities. As a consequence, the voter's religious attitude has been deactivated, since he is deprived of a religious option in casting his vote.[30] In view of this, it is surprising that so many Lebanese intellectuals are still agitated about the issue.

The "Counter-Elite"

The contenders for top leadership position in the political life of Lebanon, parliamentary candidates who lose their bids for office, are similar to those they have challenged. The average contender is not a party member and is constituency-oriented with strong local connections; he competes with the incumbents for positions on the tickets of prominent leaders, seeks presidential favors, and on the whole is less politically articulate than the winner. This may come as a disappointment to those who have hoped that what seems like the vicious circle of Lebanese politics and the crass realism of politicians will be replaced by constitutional means.

This picture of contenders for political leadership in Lebanon emerges from an analysis of the background of 117 candidates who ran unsuccessfully in the elec-

[30] For a detailed account of this view, see my article, "The Ethnic Revolution and Political Integration in the Middle East," *International Journal of Middle East Studies,* vol. 3, no. 3 (1972).

tions of 1968 and from an analysis of an *An-Nahar* survey which included candidates obtaining the highest number of votes next to the winner.

Analysis of the contenders' background shows that more of them are independents than is the case with the actual winners of parliamentary seats in 1968. Only 14 percent of the 117 candidates belonged to political parties compared with 33 percent among the present deputies in parliament. If our earlier generalizations regarding deputies' relations to parties are true, then we may expect the contenders to be more local in orientation, more bound to family status and relations, and more dependent on a combination of local forces. Their localism is confirmed by the fact that only 3.5 percent of the contenders were not born in the constituency in which they ran for elections compared with 11 percent of the present members of parliament.

The orientation index shows that the orientations of the contenders, like those of the deputies, are more local than national (Table 8–5). Considerably more contenders (39 percent) betray a lack of interest in national issues, and fewer among them show a strong attitude on either local or national issues. It is thus obvious that the degree of indifference to issues among the contenders is higher than it is among deputies.

Table 8–5

ATTITUDES OF DEPUTIES AND CONTENDERS

(percentages)

	Deputies		Contenders	
Orientation	High	Low	High	Low
Local	54	23	33	21
National	33	21	27	39

Note: Percentages do not add to 100 because those who fell between categories were omitted in order to highlight the difference in attitude between deputies and their opponents.

Occupational distribution of the 117 candidates shows no marked difference from the previous parliaments of the 1960s and manifests almost the same order of frequency. Professionals come first, followed by lawyers, landowners, and businessmen.[31] A large proportion of the contenders are men of declining political fortunes who had belonged to the elite but could not keep their political standing. Thus a group of 54, about half the total, were former deputies, 17 of whom held cabinet posts at one time or another.

The contenders for political leadership are less articulate and less willing to discuss their political views and programs than are the deputies. For instance, fifty-eight out of ninety-nine contenders whose opinions were solicited responded to the *An-Nahar* survey, compared with 70 percent of the members of parliament.

[31] The candidates' occupation is based on the listed biographical abstracts reported in the Beirut daily, *Al-Jaridah,* in March and April of 1968. They are thus comparable to Hudson's results in that they are based on one listed occupation rather than on all the occupations and economic pursuits followed by the individual. Time limitations did not permit researching the occupational status of candidates further as was done with deputies.

The number of those who had a compelling reason for not responding, such as absence or sickness, was about equal in the two groups, 10 percent. This leaves 31 percent of the contenders who did not reply, compared to 20 percent of the deputies. Failure to respond to an opinion survey intended for publication by the leading newspaper in the country does not reflect well on the political skills of the contenders. Those challengers who did respond were brief, and showed a marked reticence in discussing their political ideas and programs; some did not seem to have any. The majority failed to answer specific questions about their views regarding the constitutional system of Lebanon *(al-nizam)* or to offer assessments of the policy implementation record of the system. Also, most missed the opportunity to make political suggestions regarding the system and its performance when asked if they had any to offer. Except for a few cases which will be discussed separately, none of these inarticulate respondents were anti-system or had radical opinions that might jeopardize their positions. On the contrary, they tended to be on the conservative side and to take the existing political order for granted. Most of them, however, showed an admirable civic attitude when asked their opinion of their successful opponents: thirteen praised the opponent, nineteen refused to pass judgment, fifteen made polite and intelligent criticism of the opponent's program, and eight were scathing and personal in their attacks.

The reluctance of contenders to speak out is not the result of a withdrawal from politics subsequent to defeat, for only one contender stated outright that he was not running for office again.[32] Joseph Nasr of *An-Nahar,* who designed and conducted the survey, thought that some candidates were reluctant to respond to the interviews in order not to limit by public statement their maneuverability in the 1972 elections. This may be so, but it suggests that those contenders were as cautious and practical as the deputies they wished to replace.

A much greater disparity in the extent to which they expressed well-thought-out ideas and views appeared in the contenders' responses compared with those of the deputies. While the majority are very inarticulate, a handful among the contenders are outspoken and revolutionary. The latter few are well educated (mostly professionals) and have elaborate positions on all the questions raised. Four of those surveyed are revolutionaries in that they wish to replace the Lebanese political and economic systems with Arab nationalism and socialist doctrine. Three of them come from Tripoli and one from Beirut, and although they did not fare well at the polls, they should be interesting to watch in the future.

Conclusion

Those who become involved in politics and acquire power in any society gain social deference and disrespect at the same time, and this is as true in Lebanon as anywhere else. The common man sees politics as an unpleasant, a suspect, and certainly an opportunistic activity, and abuse of politicians is a sign of sophistication and a reflection of political frustration. Abuse of political leaders by intellectuals, on the other hand, is coupled with a sense of righteous indignation and superior knowledge. Modesty, therefore, may well be forced on the political elite in a

[32] Two deputies in contrast stated that they were not running for office again.

country where neither law nor cultural norms inhibit the public from displaying their gifts of self-expression. It may also be that Lebanon's political elite has a great deal to be modest about, having displayed no remarkable qualities of efficiency, imagination, or social zeal. The genius of the Lebanese elite has been confined to their pragmatism in attending to the problems of creating and maintaining a political order in a turbulent environment. They may also be credited for not obstructing a spirited citizenry from improving its socioeconomic standards, and for creating the conditions necessary for progress: peace and order, schools, roads, telephones, and a post office of sorts.

As a matter of fact, the Lebanese elite are anxious to maintain favorable conditions for business and economic prosperity not only to generate political support but also because they are successful business and professional men. Although their occupational characteristics have changed since 1943, they still belong to the high status occupations and stand out from the rest of society in terms of wealth and skills. There are no peasants or workers in their ranks to shield them against the charge of being a minority that is consistently recruited from the economically and educationally advanced segment of the population. If this is what is meant by the ruling class concept, then the Lebanese elite do come from a ruling class rather than from the mass population. The bridges between them and the people, as observed in this study, lie in their awareness of the need to attend to their constituents as the *sine qua non* for political survival. The localism of the elite, their feeling of being brokers, and the fact that they are treated as such may be the main nexus between this ranking elite and the mass of the population. But how responsive the Lebanese political elite are to the electorate cannot be precisely assessed before a study is made of how deputies reach political decisions.

The Lebanese elite are the main gate-keepers to their exclusive club, according to all indicators of recruitment examined in this study. Presidential favor, the prominent leaders' role in making up electoral tickets, hereditary political capital, and political party leadership determine who will be admitted into the circle. In other words, aspirants to membership in the elite group may not join unless they approach through the right channel—that is, through those who are already there. There is no contradiction here with the observation of a high rate of elite turnover in Lebanon and the insecurity of political tenure, for the elite are the source of both admission of new elements and defeat of their colleagues. Without doubt, the source of novelty in the chamber of deputies is the division and differences among the elite themselves. The Lebanese parliament, which is the principal center of political leadership, consists of numerous competing groups each seeking to maximize its political power over the others by replacing them with its own allies. Competition will perhaps also be the source of future innovation and the initiation of outsiders into the club. For the hallmark of the Lebanese elite is their sense of pragmatism; should labor forces or even ideological radicals organize themselves and demonstrate vote-getting ability, the present elite would be vying to sponsor their admission into the charmed circle.

GENERAL INDEX

Agudat Israel party, 165, 166, 170, 188, 198
Ahdut Ha-Avoda party (Israel), 169, 188, 195, 197
Alawites (Syria), 152, 156, 157, 160
Aliyot (Israel), 164, 167, 172, 188
Angora Reform (Turkey), 49
Arab nationalism, 110, 138, 139, 142, 143, 147, 155, 219
Arab Socialist Union (ASU)
  Egypt, 91 n, 92, 93, 95, 97, 100, 101, 103, 105, 106;
  Iraq, 146
Armenians, 152, 212
Asqanim (Israel), 181, 188, 189
Ashkenazi Jews, 164, 173, 183, 189

Baath party
  Iraq, 9, 13, 109, 112, 114 n, 122, 126, 127, 130, 131, 134, 135, 137–49 passim;
  Syria, 155, 157, 158, 160
Baghdad Pact, 110, 111, 112
Bitzuists (Israel), 173
"Brain drain"
  Iraq, 123, 124, 144;
  Syria, 159
Bureaucracy
  Egypt, 98, 100, 101, 105;
  Iran, 26;
  Iraq, 131, 144;
  Israel, 172, 194;
  Turkey, 61

Cabinet of National Unity (Israel), 170, 198
Cabinet system
  Israel, 175–78, 186–88;
  Lebanon, 207–09
Camps (Israel), 165, 166, 169, 170, 171, 198
Capitalism, 2, 3, 5
Christian minorities
  Israel, 194;
  Syria, 152, 153, 159
Class theory, 1–4
Clientelism, 12;
  Egypt, 86, 87–106;
  Turkey, 66.
  See also Dawrah, Dufaa, Familism, Personalism, *Shilla*
Committee of Union and Progress (Turkey), 65
Communist party
  Iraq, 139, 141, 142, 146, 147;
  Israel, 170, 171, 188, 189, 198;
  Syria, 160
Consociational democracy, 171, 172
Constitution. *See* individual countries
Co-optation, 15, 175, 191, 194, 207, 208.
  See also Elite recruitment
Courage culture (Turkey), 68, 69

Dawrah (Iran), 18–19, 96 n
Democracy, 2, 3, 4, 5, 50, 71, 72, 171, 201, 212
Democratic party (Turkey), 50, 51, 52, 53, 58, 78, 79
Deuxième Bureau (Lebanon), 211
Druze, 152, 156, 178 n, 194
Dufaa (Egypt), 12, 93, 97–99, 101

Egalitarianism, 2, 66
Egypt, 10, 11, 12, 83–107;
  National Assembly, 90, 94;
  People's Assembly, 91 n, 92, 95;
  political parties, 94, 104;
  union with Syria, 154
Elite education
  Egypt, 97–99;
  Iran, 27, 36–38;
  Iraq, 113–25, 148;
  Israel, 186, 187;
  Syria, 153, 154, 157, 159;
  Turkey, 56–61, 63
Elite ethnic background
  Iraq, 137–40, 149;
  Israel, 189, 192, 193
Elite occupation
  Iraq, 125–33;
  Israel, 181–83;
  Lebanon, 203–07;
  Syria, 155–59;
  Turkey, 56–59
Elite recruitment, 10–15;
  Egypt, 91, 92, 93–105;
  Iran, 18, 23, 32, 33, 35, 37, 38;
  Israel, 172–75, 189, 194;
  Lebanon, 211–217.
  See also Co-optation
Elite religious background, 14;
  Iraq, 137–40, 149
  Syria, 152
Elite social background
  Iraq, 133–37;
  Israel, 178–89;
  Lebanon, 201, 202;
  Syria, 155–59;
  Turkey, 54–64
Elite theory, 6–15, 21, 109, 163, 201
Electoral system
  Israel, 173–77;
  Lebanon, 209–19;
  Turkey, 76–82
Emigration. *See* "Brain drain"
Engineers' Syndicate (Egypt), 104

Familism, 12;
  Egypt, 93–97;
  Iran, 32–36;
  Lebanon, 201, 202, 208–11, 215, 216;
  Syria, 152, 154;
  Turkey, 45, 66

Fassi notables, 89
Feudalism (Lebanon), 201–02
France
and Lebanon, 208;
and Syria, 154, 155, 159;
and Turkey, 71
Free Center party (Israel), 169, 170
Freedom Fighters (Israel), 165, 181
Free Officers movement
Egypt, 94, 99;
Iraq, 111, 138, 141 n

Gahal (Israel), 169, 170, 191, 198
General Zionist party, 169, 170, 189
Government of National Unity (Israel), 177
Grand National Assembly (Turkey), 10, 50, 53, 54, 56, 62, 69
Great Britain
and Iraq, 110, 111;
and Israel, 164, 176, 177, 181, 198;
and Lebanon, 209, 211
Greater Israel movement, 169
Gush (Israel), 173, 174, 195 n

Hagana, 181, 197
Hashemite monarchy (Iraq), 110
Herut party (Israel), 167, 169, 170, 171, 188, 189, 198
Hizb al-Watani (Egypt), 104
Histadrut (Israel), 14, 165, 168, 177, 178, 181, 188, 194–97, 199

Ideology
Iraq, 140–43, 149;
Israel, 168;
Syria, 155–57;
Turkey, 69, 70
Imams, 44, 45
Independent Liberal party (Israel), 170
Individualism
Egypt, 83;
Turkey, 67, 68, 70
Ingroup-outgroup orientation (Turkey), 65--67, 82
Intelligentsia
Iran, 36, 37, 39;
Iraq, 112;
Lebanon, 219;
Syria, 155, 156;
Turkey, 44
Iran, 9–10, 17–40;
bureaucratic elite, 26;
modernization, 28–32;
parliament (Majlis), 18, 22, 26, 28, 32, 36;
political parties, 9, 17–40;
Iranian party, 36;
Iran Novin party, 36;
Security Organization, 24 n, 25
Iraq, 12, 109–49;
academic elite, 128–29, 130;
civil service, 129;
constitution, 140;
civil war, 137, 138, 140;
higher education, 116–19, 127, 129;
National Assembly, 146;
parliament, 110, 112, 130;
political parties
Istiqlal, 142 n;
Kurdish Democratic, 139ff, 143, 146, 147;
National Democratic, 139, 141, 142;
National Front, 142, 146
Iraq Petroleum Company (IPC), 123, 132, 133
Irgun Zvai Leumi (IZL), 165, 167, 181, 198
Islam, 11, 49, 65, 85, 90, 151, 152, 155, 158
Israel, 14, 15, 163–99;
Arab minority, 166, 170, 177, 181, 189, 194;
Ashkenazi Jews, 164, 173, 183, 189;
declaration of independence, 166;
elections, 169–70, 173–76;
founding fathers, 14, 166, 167, 172, 178;
governing bodies
Finance Committee, 176, 179, 186, 188;
Foreign Affairs and Defense Committee, 176, 179, 186, 188, 197;
Histadrut, 14, 165, 168, 177, 178, 181, 188, 194–97, 199;
Knesset, 14, 163, 167, 170, 172, 174, 175, 176, 178, 179, 181, 183, 186, 188, 189, 194;
Provisional State Council *(Moetzet Ha-Medina Ha-Zemannit),* 166;
Vaada Merakezzet, 178, 188, 197, 198, 199;
Vaad Leumi, 164, 166, 195, 196
immigration, 164, 167, 172, 183, 184, 188, 196
local government, 178, 179, 188;
nation building, 163–67, 177;
October 1973 war, 170, 171;
Oriental Jews, 15, 164, 173, 183, 186, 189;
orthodox Jews, 166, 194;
political blocs, 165, 166, 169, 170, 171, 198;
religious influence, 191, 194;
Yishuv, 163–65, 195, 196
Israeli political parties and alignments
Agudat Israel, 165, 166, 170, 188, 198;
Ahdut Ha-Avoda, 169, 188, 195, 197;
Free Center, 169, 170;
Gahal, 169, 170, 191, 198;
General Zionist, 169, 170, 189;
Herut, 167, 169, 170, 171, 188, 189, 198;
Independent Liberal, 170;
Irgun Zvai Leumi (IZL), 165, 167, 181, 198;
Israel Communist, 171;
Israel Labor (ILP), 165, 169, 171, 173, 174, 175, 177, 178, 195, 197, 199;
Liberals, 169, 170, 189;
Likkud, 169, 198;
Mapai/ILP, 169 n, 170, 175, 177, 188, 189, 191, 195;
Mapai (Palestine Workers), 165, 169, 175, 177, 188, 194–199;
Mapam, 169, 174, 177, 188, 189, 196;
Mizrahi (Zionist Religious movement), 170;

National Religious (NRP), 169, 170, 171, 188, 194, 197, 199;
New Communist List, 170, 198;
Poaley Agudat Israel, 166, 170;
Poaley Zion, 195;
Progressive, 170, 197–98;
Rafi, 169, 170, 195, 197, 199;
State List, 169, 170;
United Religious Front, 170;
Istiqlal party (Iraq), 142 n

Jewish Agency for Palestine, 164, 195
Jewish community in Palestine. *See Yishuv*
Justice party (Turkey), 51, 52, 53, 55, 59, 78, 79, 81

Kanun-e Taraqqi (Iran), 19
Kataib party (Lebanon), 212, 215
Kemalists, 43, 49, 50, 54, 56, 58, 59, 61, 70, 73
Kibbutzim, 164, 168, 181, 186, 188, 196
Kurdish Democratic party. *See* Iraq
Kurds, 127, 137–40

Landowners
Iran, 26;
Iraq, 129, 136;
Lebanon, 204;
Syria, 154, 156, 159
Landsmannschaft (Israel), 164, 165
Lebanon, 13, 14, 201–19;
civil war, 211;
constitution, 219;
parliament, 202–07, 209–17;
political parties, 212, 215;
religious communalism, 14, 217
Legal profession, 129, 205
Lehi (Israel), 165, 181
Liberal party (Turkey), 58
Liberal Republican party (Turkey), 58, 66
Likkud (Israel), 169, 198
Linkage figures (Iran), 27
Localism
Lebanon, 213, 218, 220;
Turkey, 59

Maarakh (Israel), 169
Mahane. See Israeli political blocs and alignments
Mahdawi trials (Iraq), 126
Majlis (Iran), 18, 22, 26, 28, 32, 36
Mamluks, 84, 85 n, 87, 88, 158
Mapai, 165, 169, 175, 177, 188, 194–99
Mapai/ILP (Israel), 169 n, 170, 175, 177, 188, 189, 191, 195
Mapam party (Israel), 169, 174, 177, 188, 189, 196
Marxism, 2, 70, 139, 141, 142, 169
Methodology, 1–15, 22, 42, 163
Middle class
Iran, 36, 37;
Iraq, 111, 112, 133, 134, 137
Military influences and institutions
Egypt, 105;
Iran, 25, 26;
Iraq, 112, 116, 117, 118, 119, 122, 125, 127, 129, 132, 138, 140, 141, 144;
Israel, 172, 181, 191;
Lebanon, 211;
Syria, 155–58, 159, 160;
Turkey, 44, 47, 53, 55, 61
Misr al-Fatat (Egypt), 104
Mizrahi (Israel), 170
Modernization. *See* Iran, Turkey
Modir-e Koll (Iran), 28
Moetzet Ha-Am (Israel), 166
Moshavim (Israel), 164, 168, 181
Mosul rebellion (Iraq), 112
Moukhabarat (Egypt), 99 n
Muslim Brotherhood (Syria), 160
Muslims. *See* Alawites, Islam, Shia Muslims, Sufi, Sunni Muslims, *Ulama, Ulema*

Nasserism, 87, 93, 160
National Assembly. *See* Egypt, Iraq
National Council of Palestine Jews, 164, 166, 195, 196
National Democratic party (Iraq), 139, 141, 142
National Front (Iraq), 142, 146
Nationalization of private firms (Iraq), 132, 133
National Religious party (NRP) (Israel), 169, 170, 171, 188, 194, 197, 199
National Salvation party (Turkey), 53, 56, 78, 79
National Unity Committee (Turkey), 55
National Union (Egypt), 104
Nation party (Turkey), 78
New Communist List (Israel), 170, 198
New Iran group, 18–19
New Turkey party, 51, 78
New Zionist Organization, 165

October 1973 war, 170, 171
Oil revenues, 31, 123, 135
Operation Magic Carpet, 196
Oriental Jews, 15, 164, 173, 183, 186, 189
Orthodox Jews, 166, 194
Ottoman Empire, 43–50, 61, 74, 84, 85, 87, 110, 111, 138, 139, 154, 195

Palestine, 167, 183, 186, 195
Palestine Workers party. *See* Mapai
Pan-Arabism, 11, 138, 139, 156, 159
Parliament. *See* individual countries
Patriarchalism, 17
Patrimonialism, 9, 17, 21, 22, 31, 32
Patronage. *See* Clientelism
People's Council (Syria), 160
People's party (Turkey), 50–53, 55, 56, 58, 61, 78, 79, 80, 81, 82
Personalism, 9, 19–22, 37, 215.
See also Familism

Pluralism, 4, 44, 170
Poaley Agudat Israel, 166, 170
Poaley Zion party, 195
Political culture
  Egypt, 83–90;
  Iran, 17–21;
  Israel, 167;
  Lebanon, 219, 220;
  Syria, 151–53;
  Turkey, 46–48, 64–72
Political parties. *See* individual countries
Politicians, 130, 181, 188, 189
Pressure groups (Israel), 172
Professional syndicates and associations
  Egypt, 105;
  Iraq, 146;
  Syria, 160
Progressive Republican party (Turkey), 58, 66
Progressives (Israel), 170, 197–98

Rafi (Israel), 169, 170, 195, 197, 199
Reliance party (Turkey), 52, 53, 78
Religion. *See* Alawites, Druze, Islam, Religious leaders, Shia Muslims, Sufi brotherhoods, Sunni Muslims, individual countries
Religious leaders, 85–86, 156, 160, 194, 211. *See also Imams,* Supreme Rabbinical Council, *Ulama, Ulema*
Republican Peasant Nation party (Turkey), 51, 78
Republican People's party (Turkey). *See* People's party
Revisionists (Israel), 165, 166, 198
Revolution, 2, 69.
  See also individual countries, White Revolution, Young Turk revolution
Revolutionary Command Council
  Egypt, 91;
  Iraq, 12, 109, 113, 114 n, 122, 126, 129, 133, 137, 140, 146
Royal Military Academy (Iraq), 116, 117, 118, 119, 127, 129, 144

Shah of Iran, 9, 18, 19, 20, 22, 24, 25, 27, 30, 39
Shaykhs, 85–86, 202
Shia Muslims, 137–39, 152, 153
Shilla, 12, 93, 96, 98–104
Six-Day War (1967), 170, 171, 197, 211
Socialism, 2, 155, 156, 178, 219
Social mobility, 3, 133–37, 149, 158, 205
Sovereignty Council (Iraq), 147
State List (Israel), 169, 170
Sufi brotherhoods, 85, 101, 105
Sunni Muslims, 137–39, 152, 153, 156, 194
Supreme Rabbinical Council, 194
Syria, 12, 151–61;
  labor unions, 155, 156, 160;
  medical profession, 158;
  military coups, 155, 156;
  religious groups, 152–53;
  union with Egypt, 154;
  xenophobia, 151, 153

Tashnaq party (Lebanon), 212
Technocrats
  Iran, 26, 37, 39;
  Iraq, 129, 130, 131, 145;
  Israel, 194
Turkey, 10, 41–82;
  constitution, 51, 54;
  governing bodies, 49, 50, 59;
  Grand National Assembly, 10, 50, 53, 54, 56, 62, 69;
  military coup (1960), 50, 55, 65;
  modernization, 45, 46, 50, 59–61, 70, 82;
  Ottoman institutions, 44;
  religious institutions, 47–48, 59;
  revolution (Kemalist), 48, 50, 61, 70, 73;
  village government, 75–76;
  Young Turk revolution, 65
Turkish political parties
  Justice, 51, 52, 53, 55, 59, 78, 79, 81;
  Labor, 78, 79, 80;
  Liberal, 58;
  Liberal Republican, 58, 66;
  Nation, 78;
  National Salvation, 53, 56, 78, 79;
  National Unity Committee, 55;
  New Turkey, 51, 78;
  People's, 50–53, 55, 56, 58, 61, 78, 79, 80, 81, 82;
  Progressive Republican, 58, 66
  Reliance, 52, 53, 78;
  Republican Peasant Nation, 51, 78;
  Republican People's. *See* People's;
  Turkish Labor, 78, 79, 80;
  Unity, 78, 79

Ulama (Egypt), 85, 86, 87
Ulema (Turkey), 45, 46, 160
Union of Soviet Socialist Republics
  and Iraq, 112, 143, 147;
  and Syria, 152
United Religious Front (Israel), 170
Unity party (Turkey), 78, 79

Vaada Merakezzet. *See* Israel

White Revolution (Iran), 9, 30, 31
World Zionist Organization, 165, 166 n, 195, 196, 198

Yemen, 167, 196
Yishuv (Israel), 163–65, 195, 196
Young Turk revolution, 65

Zionism, 164–67, 169, 172, 181, 195
Zionist Religious movement, 170
Zuaama, 89, 213

INDEX OF NAMES

Aalam family, 34
Abadan, Nermin (cited), 65
Abaza, Wagih, 94
Abidine, Ali Zein, 96
Abu-Fadil, Munir, 205 n
Adl family, 33 n, 34
Adl, Yahya, 25
Adl-e Tabatabai family, 33
Afkhami family, 33 n, 34
Afshar family, 33
Akbar family, 33 n, 34
Ali, Mohammed, 85 n, 86, 88
Akl, Sayd, 205 n
Alam, Amir Asadollah, 24, 25, 34 n
Alam family, 33, 34
Aldurati, Zvi, 199
Almoslino, Natan, 196
Amer, Abdul Hakim, 91, 94, 95, 99, 106
Ameri family, 33
Amini family, 34, 35
Amir-Ebrahimi family, 33
Amirshahi family, 33
Ansari, Hushang, 24, 25
Arbeli-Almoslino, Shoshana, 197
Ardalan family, 33, 34
Aref, Abdul Salam, 111, 114, 124, 133, 134, 137, 146, 147
Arjomand family, 33
Arslan, Amir Majid, 202, 210 n
Arslan family, 154
Asad, Hafez, 158
Asad, Kamil al-, 202 n, 204, 216
Asadi family, 33
Ashiry, Hashem al-, 96
Ashtiyani family, 34
Atassi family, 154
Atassi, Jamal, 159
Atassi, Nur al-Din, 159
Ataturk. *See* Kemal, Mustafa
Aflaq, Michel, 142, 155, 156
Ayadi, Abdol Karim, 24, 25, 27
Aydemir, Talat, 55
Azam family, 154

Baghdadi, Abdul Latif, 91, 95
Baghdadi, Mohammed, 94
Baharlu family, 33
Bakhtiyari family, 33 n, 34
Bakr, Ahmad Hasan al-, 126, 129, 134
Bar-Lev, Haim, 191
Barmada family, 154
Barzani, Mulla Mustafa, 140, 143, 146
Bayar, Celal, 50
Bayat family, 34, 35
Ben-Aharon, Itzhak, 178
Ben-Gurion, David, 167, 169, 172, 178, 195
Ben-Simhon, Shaul, 198
Bitar, Salah al-Din, 142, 155
Borolossy family, 94
Bottomore, T.B. (cited), 5, 6
Boulos family, 202 n
Busheiri family, 33, 34
Buzo family, 154

Daftari family, 34
Dahl, Robert (cited), 4
Davison, Roderic H. (cited), 43, 48 n
Dayan, Moshe, 169, 191, 197
Demirel, Suleiman, 52, 55
Dessouki, Salah, 94
Diba family, 33, 34
Diba-Valatabar-Shahmir family, 35
Dowlatshahi family, 33 n, 34, 35
Dowleh, Ezzat al-, 33 n
Duverger, Maurice (cited), 165, 166 n
Duwaihi family, 202 n

Ebrahimi family, 33, 34
Ecevit, Bulent, 53, 56, 80
Eddé, Raymond, 204, 212
Ellis, Howard (cited), 123
Emami family, 33, 34, 35
Emami-Khoy family, 34
Emami, Seyyid Hassan, 24 n
Eqbal family, 33 n, 34
Eqbal, Manuchehr, 24, 25, 27
Erim, Nihat, 52
Esfandiari family, 33–35
Eshraqi family, 33

Faik, Mohammed, 96
Faisal I, 110
Faisal II, 110
Farahat, Morsi, 96
Farawn, Pierre, 205 n
Fardust, Hossein, 24
Farmanfarmaian family, 33–35
Farouk I, 99
Fatfat, Mohammed, 204
Fawzi, Mahmoud, 92
Fawzi, Mohammed, 96
Firuz-Farmanfarmaian family, 35
Fotuhi family, 33
Franjieh family, 202 n
Franjieh, Suleiman, 205 n, 211

Gallal, Sayed, 89, 90
Ghaidan, Saadoun, 126
Ghazi family, 33
Ghazzi family, 154
Goelman, Eliezer, 197
Gökalp, Ziya (cited), 68
Gomaa, Shaarawi, 92, 95, 96, 101

Hadid, Mohammed, 133, 135, 142
Hafiz, Amin al-, 159
Haidar, General (Mohammed), 94

Hakim, Adnan, 215 n
Hakim, Bakhus, 204
Hakimi family, 34
Haj Seyyid Javadi family, 33
Hamadah, Sabri, 202 n
Hammer, Zevulun, 199
Hamud, Hudaib al-Hajj, 135
Harati family, 33
Harris, George (cited), 67
Hashim, Jawad, 123
Hassanein family, 94
Hassanein, Magdi, 102
Hatem, Abdul Qader, 103
Hausner, Gideon, 197
Hawrani, Akram, 160
Hazan, Yaaqov, 177
Hedayat family, 34
Heikal, Mohammed Hassanein, 102
Hilu, Charles, 211
Holt, P.M. (cited), 88
Hoveyda, Amir Abbas, 24, 28, 33
Hudson, Michael (cited), 203
Hughes, H. Stuart (cited), 4
Huntington, Samuel (cited), 206
Hushi, Abba, 178
Hussein, Saddam, 126, 129, 134
Hyland, Michael P. (cited), 66

Ilah, Amir Abdul, 110
Inönü, Ismet, 50, 51, 52, 55, 62
Irmak, Sadi, 54
Ismail, Hafez, 103

Jabri family, 154
Jadid, Salah, 156
Jahanbani family, 33 n, 34
Jomeh, Emam, 24 n
Jamayyil, Maurice al-, 215 n
Jumblat, Kamal, 202 n, 204, 212, 216, 217

Kalantari family, 33
Kalifa, Hassan Mahmoud, 90
Karami, Rashid, 216, 217
Karpat, Kemal H. (cited), 70 n, 71 n
Kasemi family, 33
Kashefi family, 33
Kassem, Abdul Karim, 111, 114, 122, 124, 126, 127, 133, 134, 136, 140, 146
Kayyali family, 154
Kazeruni family, 33
Kemal, Mustafa (Ataturk), 48, 49, 50, 54, 58, 59
Khajeh-Nuri family, 34, 35
Khalatbari family, 34, 35
Khalil, Mustafa, 102
Khatami, Mohammed, 24, 25
Khouri, Bisharah al-, 202
Khouri, Qiblan Isa al-, 204
Khozemeh Alam family, 33

Landau, Haim, 198
Lasswell, Harold (cited), 4
Lavon, Pinhas, 178
Legg, Keith (cited), 89
Lemarchand, René (cited), 83 n, 89
Levy, Avigdor (cited), 45
Lijphart, Arend (cited), 171

Mahdavi family, 33, 34
Mahmud II, Sultan, 44
Mansur family, 34
Mardin, Serif (cited), 43, 66, 67
Marei family, 94
Marei, Sayed, 92, 96, 97, 102
Marx, Karl (cited), 1, 2
Masud family, 33
Mehmet VI, Sultan-Caliph Vahdeddin, 49
Meir, Golda, 167, 172, 174, 175, 188
Melen, Ferit, 52
Menderes, Adnan, 50
Michels, Robert (cited), 1, 2, 174 n, 201 n
Minbashian-Pahlbod family, 35
Mohieddin, Khaled, 94
Mohieddin, Zakaria, 91, 106
Moinian, Nosratollah, 24
Mokri family, 33
Molk, Shirkhan Eyn al-, 33 n
Moore, Clement Henry (cited), 11
Mosca, Gaetano (cited), 1–5
Monscf family, 33
Muaddi, Jabr, 194
Mu'awwad family, 202 n
Muharrem, Ahmed, 96
Musaddeq, Mohammed, 25

Nasser, Gamal Abdul, 11, 12, 84, 86, 88, 91–96, 98, 102, 103, 104, 106, 107, 111, 127
Nasr, Joseph, 219
Netzer, Dvora, 195
Netzer, Shraga, 174, 195
Nikpay family, 33

Okasha, Sarwat, 103
Okyar, Fethi, 58
Okyar, Makbule, 58
Osman, Osman A., 96
Ozbudun, Ergun, 77 n, 79

Pahlavi, (Princess) Ashraf, 24
Pahlavi family, 25, 33–35
Pahlavi, (Empress) Farah Diba, 24, 25, 31
Pahlavi, Mohammed Reza Shah, 9, 18, 19, 20, 22, 24, 25, 27, 30, 39
Pahlavi, Reza Shah the Great, 9, 35
Panahi family, 33, 34
Pareto, Vilfredo (cited), 1–5
Peres, Shimon, 174
Pirnia family, 33, 34
Porush, Rabbi Menahem, 198

Qaddur, Bahij al-, 204 n
Qajar, Fath Ali Shah, 35
Qajar, Naser al-Din Shah, 33 n
Qajar dynasty, 9, 35

Qaragozlu family, 33, 34, 35
Qashqai family, 34, 35
Qavam family, 34
Qudsi family, 154

Rabin, Itzhak, 174, 191
Rabinowicz, Yehoshua, 173
Radwan, Fathi, 104 n
Razmara, Ali, 33
Riad, Mahmoud, 96
Riesman, David (cited), 4
Roos, Leslie L. (cited), 75 n
Rustow, Dankwart (cited), 5, 47, 66

Saad, Habib al-, 202
Sabeti, Parviz, 24 n
Sabry, Ali, 90, 91, 92, 94, 95, 96, 101, 106
Sadat, Anwar as-, 91, 92, 93, 95, 96, 98, 103, 106, 107
Sadri family, 33, 34
Saffari family, 33, 34
Said, Hilmy, 96
Said, Nuri al-, 110, 111, 112, 128
Salim, Yusuf, 204, 205 n, 210 n
Samii family, 33, 34
Sang family, 33
Sapir, Pinhas, 175
Sarfarraz family, 33
Sartori, G. (cited), 170
Scott, James C. (cited), 83 n, 88, 106
Shadman family, 33
Shamoun, Kamil, 204, 212, 216, 217
Sharaf, Sami, 91, 92, 95, 96, 101, 102, 106
Sharet, Moshe, 172
Sharif-Emami, Jaafar, 24
Sharon, Ariel, 191
Shihab, Fuad, 202, 211
Shishakli, Adib al-, 154
Sidky, Aziz, 92, 102
Skaf, Joseph, 204 n, 216
Sunay, Cevdet, 52
Susayeff, Zalman, 196
Szyliowicz, Joseph S. (cited), 67

Tabatabai family, 33
Taburian, Andre, 205 n
Taleb, Naji, 127
Talmi, Emma (Levin), 195, 196
Tarraf family, 94
Tarraf, Nur al-Din, 104 n
Tubi, Tawfiq, 198
Tucker, Robert C. (cited), 166

Uthman, Bashir al-, 204

Vakili family, 33, 34
Venizelos, Eleutherios, 49
Vusuq family, 33, 34

Wafia, Abu, 95
Wahba, Magdi, 103
Weber, Max (cited), 17
Weizmann, Chaim, 166 n
Weizman, Ezer, 191
Wingate, Charles Orde, 197

Yaari, Meir, 177
Yafi, Abdullah al-, 204, 210 n
Yalman, Osman Nur (cited), 66 n
Yar Afshar family, 33
Yariv, Aharon, 191
Yeshayahu, Israel, 196

Zahedi, Ardeshir, 24, 25
Zahedi, Fazlollah, 25, 33
Zand family, 34, 35
Zanganeh family, 34
Zayed, Saad, 96
Zayn family, 204
Zayyat family, 94
Zolfaqari family, 34
Zuabi, Sayf al-Din al-, 196